A Pictorial History of the

AMERICAN THEATRE

by Daniel Blum

1900-1956

GREENBERG : PUBLISHER   New York

ACKNOWLEDGEMENTS: I wish to thank the following for pictures and for assistance: Torben Prestholdt, John Willis, May Davenport Seymour, John D. Seymour, Tom Salisbury, Whitford Kane, Joseph Cameron Cross, Maynard Morris, Earle Forbes, the Messrs. Shubert, Vandamm Studio, the Museum of the City of New York, the New York Public Library, the New York Post and especially D. Jay Culver and Florence Culver of Culver Service whose collection is represented by many pictures in this book.

TO

MY MOTHER AND **FATHER**

WHO LIVE IN MY HEART

FOREWORD

There has been no book up to now which will be as valuable to actors in years to come and theatre lovers as this pictorial history of the American stage by Daniel Blum. Here is a permanent record of all the great plays and players of our time.

The camera as it has been used by many masters of the photographic art has an ability which is almost uncanny in capturing mood and interpretation as well as likeness. Only the camera was able to capture the grace of Ethel Barrymore in "Captain Jinks of the Horse Marines," the charm of Maude Adams in "Peter Pan" and the sheer beauty of John Barrymore's "Hamlet." The camera has provided Mr. Blum with more than a complete and moving history of our stage. It is also a history of acting, its growth and its development which should be an invaluable aid to young performers and students of the theatre.

Very often I am asked by young people interested in the theatre as a career, to explain my life in the theatre in terms which would help them on their careers. It is impossible to do so. All you can say is "I interpreted the role in this or that fashion because this way or that is the way I felt." But this collection of pictures — and I am very happy that I am so well represented — makes it easy. The camera understands and can adequately explain how things were done and very often why. I wish that when I had been young that there had been such a picture book. I might have had an easier time understanding when I was told, "You should have seen her. She was an actress!"

Helen Hayes —

MRS. LESLIE CARTER IN "ZAZA"

1900

As the bells rang in the new year of 1900, the theatre was in a healthy state. The star system was flourishing. The player was the thing, not the play. Over four hundred 'Dramatic' companies and stock companies were touring the United States. Over forty 'Opera and Extravaganza' companies were in existence, vaudeville was popular and so was burlesque. There were eighteen minstrel companies trouping the land. In New York City there were over forty legitimate theatres, six top vaudeville houses and several theatres catering to Hebrew trade. At the turn of the Century, New York attractions were varied. William Gillette was having his greatest success with "Sherlock Holmes;" Julia Marlowe was delighting audiences with a Civil War play, "Barbara Frietchie;" "Ben Hur," adapted from Lew Wallace's popular book, was a record-breaking attraction; Anna Held was winning new admirers with "Papa's Wife;" at the Old Herald Square, Primrose and Dockstader, popular minstrels of the day, were holding forth; and at the Weber and Fields' Music Hall, Joe Weber and Lew Fields, with their company which included Lillian Russell, David Warfield, Peter F. Dailey and Frankie Bailey of the beautiful legs, were successful with their musical, "Whirl-i-gig." These Weber and Fields musical extravaganzas, as they were called, burlesqued the important plays of the year and were very

SARAH BERNHARDT in
"L'AIGLON"

BENOIT COQUELIN
as "CYRANO DE BERGERAC"

HENRIETTA CROSMAN
in "MISTRESS NELL"

THE FLORODORA SEXTETTE

popular. Later in the year, when they produced "Fiddle-dee-dee," DeWolf Hopper and Fay Templeton joined the company.

Richard Mansfield, one of the great actors of his day, was having a season of repertoire with his well-known success, "Beau Brummell," "Cyrano de Bergerac," "The Devil's Disciple," "Dr. Jekyll and Mr. Hyde," "The First Violin" and "Arms and the Man." His company included Beatrice Cameron, his wife, and a juvenile named William Courtenay.

At the Casino, Alice Nielsen and her Comic Opera Company, which included Joseph Cawthorn, May Boley, Eugene Cowles and Richie Ling, presented Victor Herbert's "The Singing Girl." Maxine Elliott and Nat C. Goodwin, who were husband and wife at this time, were playing in "When We Were Twenty-One." Henry Woodruff, an upcoming juvenile, was in their company, and so was Frank Gilmore, who was later to become the president of Actors' Equity. Other attractions available to playgoers were Mrs. Leslie Carter in a return engagement of her great success, "Zaza;" May Irwin in "Sister Mary;" Frank Daniels in "The Ameer;" and James T. Powers in "San Toy."

Gus and Max Rogers, popular comedians, used their names in the title of their offering which they called "a vaudeville farce," and each year had a different locale. In January it was "The Rogers Brothers in Wall Street" with Louise Gunning, Ada

HELENA MODJESKA in "TWELFTH NIGHT"

JAMES O'NEILL in "MONTE CRISTO"

WILLIAM GILLETTE as "SHERLOCK HOLMES"

7

WILLIAM FAVERSHAM, GUY STANDING, MARGARET ANGLIN in
"BROTHER OFFICERS"

MARIE CAHILL

MRS. FISKE

JAMES A. HERNE

MAY IRWIN

DELLA FOX

WILTON LACKAYE

Lewis and Georgia Caine in the cast, and in September, it was "The Rogers Brothers in Central Park" with Della Fox, who started the fad of the spit curl in the middle of the forehead.

"Three Little Lambs" had no stars, but the company included three who later achieved stardom: Marie Cahill, Raymond Hitchcock and Adele Ritchie.

On the road, Viola Allen was playing one of her most famous roles, Glory Quayle in "The Christian," for a second season. At the end of the year, she opened "In the Palace of the King" with Robert T. Haines and William Norris in her support. Maude Adams was trouping in "The Little Minister." Later in the year she appeared in "L'Aiglon." Mrs. Fiske was appearing in "Becky Sharp," and her leading man was Maurice Barrymore, the father of Lionel, Ethel and John. Other stars on the road included: Helena Modjeska playing "Macbeth," "Twelfth Night" and "Much Ado About Nothing;" Julia Arthur in "More Than Queen;" Herbert Kelcey and Effie Shannon in "The Moth and the Flame;" Stuart Robson in "Oliver Goldsmith" with Henry E. Dixey and Florence Rockwell; Chauncey Olcott in "A Romance of Athlone;" Wilton Lackaye in "Children of the Ghetto;" Francis Wilson in a revival of "Erminie" with Pauline Hall; Sol Smith Russell in "A Poor Relation;" Denman Thompson in "The Old Homestead;" Robert B. Mantell in "The Dagger and

JULIA MARLOWE in
"BARBARA FRIETCHIE"

WILLIAM FARNUM and WILLIAM S. HART in
"BEN HUR"

JAMES K. HACKETT and BERTHA GALLAND in
"THE PRIDE OF JENNICO"

MAURICE BARRYMORE

ANNA HELD

JOSEPH HAWORTH, ALICE FISCHER, EDMUND D. LYONS in
"QUO VADIS"

the Cross" and Rose Melville in "Sis Hopkins."

There were seven companies of "Uncle Tom's Cabin" touring. Other popular plays of the time trouping the country were "Way Down East," "The Three Musketeers," "In Old Kentucky," "Shenandoah," "Sporting Life," "Peck's Bad Boy," "Pudd'nhead Wilson" and "The Great Ruby."

Out on the West Coast, Nance O'Neil, prior to leaving for a successful Australian tour, was trouping in repertoire, two of her popular roles being "Magda" and "Camille."

On April 9th, New Yorkers saw an unusual event when two productions, with different adaptations, of the famous novel, "Quo Vadis," opened on the same night. The dramatization of Stanislaus Stange with Arthur Forrest, Maude Fealy, Alice Fischer, Edmund D. Lyons and Joseph Haworth was the more popular and ran 96 performances as against the other adaptation of Jeannette L. Gilder which played 36 times.

An event that caused considerable talk was the arrest and acquittal of Olga Nethersole and her company for appearing in what the law termed an indecent play, namely "Sapho."

"Florodora," which featured the famous Florodora Sextette singing "Tell Me, Pretty Maiden," had Edna Wallace Hopper, Cyril Scott and Mabel Barrison in the cast. It opened in Novem-

STUART ROBSON

NANCE O'NEIL

FRANK DANIELS

SOL SMITH RUSSELL

JOHN DREW and IDA CONQUEST in
"RICHARD CARVEL"

ELEANOR ROBSON and VINCENT SERRANO in
"ARIZONA"

ESTELLE MORTIMER, NAT C. GOODWIN, MAXINE ELLIOTT in
"WHEN WE WERE TWENTY-ONE"

9

ALICE NIELSEN in
"THE SINGING GIRL"

PRIMROSE & DOCKSTADER'S

ROSE MELVILLE as
"SIS HOPKINS"

JULIA ARTHUR in
"MORE THAN QUEEN"

E. H. SOTHERN as
"HAMLET"

ANNIE RUSSELL in
"A ROYAL FAMILY"

CHAUNCEY OLCOTT in
"A ROMANCE of ATHLONE"

10 ROBERT T. HAINES and VIOLA ALLEN in
"IN THE PALACE OF THE KING"

WILLIAM H. CRANE in "DAVID HARUM"

MARY MANNERING and ROBERT DROUET
"JANICE MEREDITH"

JOE WEBER and LEW FIELDS

DAVID WARFIELD, FAY TEMPLETON, DE WOLF HOPPER in
"FIDDLE-DEE-DEE"

PETER F. DAILY and LILLIAN RUSSELL in
"WHIRL-I-GIG"

MAUDE ADAMS and EDWIN STEVENS in
"L'AIGLON"

ber, 1900, and ran into January, 1902, with 505 performances to its credit. It has since been revived several times.

Other popular plays of the year were "Brother Officers" with William Faversham, Margaret Anglin and Mrs. Thomas Whiffen; "The Pride of Jennico" starring James K. Hackett and with Bertha Galland; Annie Russell supported by Charles Richman, Lawrence D'Orsay and Orrin Johnson in "A Royal Family;" John Drew in "Richard Carvel;" William H. Crane in "David Harum;" Henrietta Crosman in "Mistress Nell;" a revival of "Monte Cristo" starring James O'Neill, the father of playwright Eugene O'Neill; Mary Mannering making her debut as a star in "Janice Meredith," and "Arizona" with Eleanor Robson, Vincent Serrano and Theodore Roberts.

James A. Herne, a successful playwright and actor, produced and acted in his own play, "Sag Harbor," with his daughters Julie and Chrystal Herne in a cast that included Lionel Barrymore and William Hodge.

In September E. H. Sothern made his first appearance in New York as "Hamlet." Virginia Harned, who was his wife then, played Ophelia.

Late November Sarah Bernhardt and Benoit Constant Coquelin appeared in "L'Aiglon," "Cyrano de Bergerac," "La Tosca" and "La Dame Aux Camelias" in repertoire.

The leading producers of the period were Charles Frohman, David Belasco, Klaw and Erlanger, Daniel Frohman, Liebler and Company, Weber and Fields, William A. Brady, George Lederer, Nixon and Zimmerman, and Jacob Litt.

OLGA NETHERSOLE and HAMILTON REVELLE in
"SAPHO"

DENMAN THOMPSON and COMPANY in "THE OLD HOMESTEAD"

12   RICHARD MANSFIELD as PRINCE KARL, CYRANO DE BERGERAC and
BEAU BRUMMELL

WILLIAM COURTLEIGH, ARTHUR HOOPS, VIRGINIA HARNED in
"ALICE OF OLD VINCENNES"

MACLYN ARBUCKLE, BLANCHE BATES, FRANCIS CARLYLE, EDWARD ABELES in
"UNDER TWO FLAGS"

1901 January saw Ada Rehan, a popular star since 1879 when she made her debut under Augustin Daly's management, appearing in "Sweet Nell of Old Drury."

Julia Marlowe, with Bruce McRae as her leading man, was having success with "When Knighthood Was in Flower," a dramatization of a popular novel.

E. S. Willard, an English actor with a great following since his American debut in 1890 with "The Middleman," was appearing in repertoire with "The Professor's Love Story," "David Garrick," "Martin Chuzzlewit," "Tom Pinch" and "The Middleman" which was his most popular play.

Charles Hawtrey and Robert Lorraine, two other English actors, were making their first American appearance. Hawtrey was in "A Message From Mars," and Lorraine was in "To Have and To Hold" with a cast that included Isabel Irving, Holbrook Blinn and Cecil B. de Mille, who later became one of filmland's top directors.

Amelia Bingham, a popular actress of the preceding decade, achieved her life's ambition by becoming an actress-manager and a star when she presented herself in Clyde Fitch's "The Climbers." Her company was a good one and included Robert Edeson, Clara Bloodgood, Frank Worthing, Madge Carr Cook, Annie Irish, Minnie Dupree and Ferdinand Gottschalk.

Another actress to gain stardom in 1901 was twenty-one year old Ethel Barrymore, and her vehicle, also by Clyde Fitch, was called "Captain Jinks of the Horse Marines." One of the critics said, "Miss Barrymore is rather young and inexperienced to be starred, but she is clever and has a charming personality

MARIE DRESSLER

JAMES K. HACKETT

CISSIE LOFTUS, E. H. SOTHERN in
"IF I WERE KING"

GUY STANDING, LIONEL BARRYMORE, JOHN DREW in
"THE SECOND IN COMMAND"

MACLYN ARBUCKLE, AUBREY BOUCICAULT, VINCENT SERRANO, NAT C. GOODWIN, MAXINE ELLIOTT in
"THE MERCHANT OF VENICE"

ANNIE IRISH, FRANK WORTHING, ROBERT EDESON, AMELIA BINGHAM, JOHN FLOOD in
"THE CLIMBERS"

JOSEPHINE LOVETT, ANDREW MACK in
"TOM MOORE"

ADA REHAN

and a refinement of manner that is often wanting on the stage."

Others making their debuts as stars were David Warfield, Virginia Harned, William Faversham and Bertha Galland. Warfield, who had been a dialect comedian at Weber and Fields' Music Hall, appeared in "The Auctioneer," one of the great successes of his career, and it was the beginning of a long and profitable association with David Belasco.

Virginia Harned was a universal favorite with the Lyceum stock company, and in 1895 had an overwhelming success playing the title role in "Trilby," but it was not until late in 1901 that she became a star in "Alice of Old Vincennes." Her leading man was William Courtleigh, often confused with William Courtenay another leading man of the period who later married Miss Harned. Cecil B. De Mille also appeared in this play.

Daniel Frohman took Bertha Galland, who had been James K. Hackett's leading lady the season before, and starred her in "The Forest Lovers." Both the star and the play received adverse criticism, and one writer suggested that Miss Galland costume herself differently as "her scant attire as a page in the fourth act, showing her generously rounded figure, hardly lent itself to the poetic drama."

William Faversham, a leading man with the Empire Stock Company since 1893, chose "A Royal Rival" for his first stellar effort. Julie Opp, who later

FANNY A. PITT, SIDNEY COWELL, ETHEL BARRYMORE, H. REEVES SMITH in
"CAPTAIN JINKS OF THE HORSE MARINES"

became his wife, and Edwin Stevens and Jessie Busley were in his cast. The play was an adaptation of "Don Caesar de Bazan," and another version of this play, "Don Caesar's Return," starring James K. Hackett, was running simultaneously.

From California came a young actress named Blanche Bates who was also destined for fame. She scored in the role of Cigarette in "Under Two Flags."

In April Charles Frohman revived Sardou's "Diplomacy" which had first been presented in New York in 1878. The cast included Margaret Anglin, William Faversham, Jessie Millward, Charles Richman, Mrs. Thomas Whiffen and Margaret Dale.

Among the established stars, Richard Mansfield was appearing in Booth Tarkington's "Beaucaire;" William Collier was in the Augustus Thomas comedy, "On the Quiet;" Lulu Glaser was in "The Prima Donna;" the Rogers Brothers were "In Washington;" Mrs. Leslie Carter was in "Du Barry;" Edna May, who had made such a hit a few years earlier in "The Belle of New York," was playing in "The Girl from Up There" with two promising young actors, Fred Stone and David Montgomery, in the cast; John Drew was in "The Second in Command" with his nephew Lionel Barrymore and Hassard Short, who became famous as a director of musicals, in the cast; Anna Held was in "The Little Duchess;" Mrs. Fiske was in "The Unwelcome Mrs. Hatch;" and Henry Miller

MRS. THOMAS WHIFFEN, ETHEL HORNICK, MARGARET ANGLIN, JESSIE MILLWARD, WILLIAM FAVERSHAM,
CHARLES RICHMAN in "DIPLOMACY"

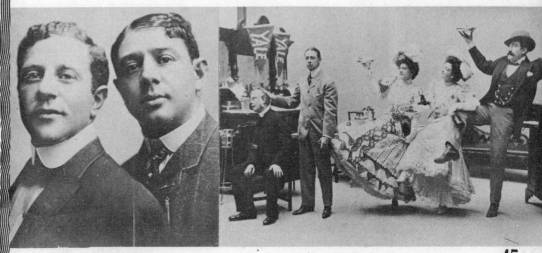

THE ROGERS BROTHERS

WILLIAM COLLIER and his company in
"ON THE QUIET"

KYRLE BELLEW, ELEANOR ROBSON in
"A GENTLEMAN OF FRANCE"

DAVID WARFIELD, MARIE BATES in
"THE AUCTIONEER"

JULIE OPP, WILLIAM FAVERSHAM in
"A ROYAL RIVAL"

CECIL B. DE MILLE

THE FOUR COHANS: GEORGE M., HELEN, JOSEPHINE and
JERRY J.

ANDREW MACK

HAMILTON REVELLE, MRS. LESLIE CARTER in
"DU BARRY"

SYDNEY BROUGH, MAUDE ADAMS in
"QUALITY STREET"

EDDIE FOY, FRANCIS WILSON
in "THE STROLLERS"

DAN DALY, EDNA MAY in
"THE GIRL FROM UP THERE"

MAY ROBSON, JAMES T. POWERS
in "THE MESSENGER BOY"

LOTTA FAUST

was in "D'Arcy of the Guards" with Florence Rockwell, a California favorite, as his leading lady.

Andrew Mack and Chauncey Olcott, two popular Irish tenors, appeared each year in plays with music. This year Mack was in "Tom Moore" while Olcott's vehicle was "Garrett O'Magh."

George M. Cohan with his parents, Jerry J. and Helen, and his sister, Josephine, had been playing in vaudeville as The Four Cohans. This year, they appeared in New York and on the road in "The Governor's Son," a musical farce which he had written himself. Ethel Levey, who became the first Mrs. George M. Cohan, and Georgie White were in the cast.

Nat C. Goodwin and Maxine Elliott were playing in an elaborate production of "The Merchant of Venice." The critics thought Mr. Goodwin's Shylock was dignified and forceful, but their opinions of Miss Elliott's Portia were conflicting.

Kyrle Bellew cut a romantic figure in "A Gentleman of France."

ELSIE FERGUSON

ELSIE DE WOLFE, FRANK MILLS (in auto)
in "THE WAY OF THE WORLD"

CHAUNCEY OLCOTT and HIS COMPANY in
"GARRETT O'MAGH"

17

CHARLES HAWTREY, HENRY STEPHENSON
in "A MESSAGE FROM MARS"

GRACE GEORGE, RALPH STUART
in "UNDER SOUTHERN SKIES"

PAULINE CHASE (extreme left) in
"THE LIBERTY BELLES"

BERTHA GALLAND

JULIA MARLOWE

Eleanor Robson was his leading lady and Edgar Selwyn, who later became a producer, and Charlotte Walker also supported him.

Maude Adams was making her initial appearance in James M. Barrie's "Quality Street." Her leading man was Sydney Brough, imported from England.

Elsie de Wolfe, who became Lady Mendl and a favorite with the International Set, was starring in "The Way of the World."

Weber and Fields were still burlesquing the current plays in "Hoity Toity." Lillian Russell, Fay Templeton and DeWolf Hopper were still present, while Sam Bernard and Bessie Clayton were newcomers to the company.

Other musicals running were "The Sleeping Beauty and the Beast" with Joseph Cawthorn; Marie Dressler in "The King's Carnival;" James T. Powers and May Robson in "The Messenger Boy;" Francis Wilson in "The Strollers" with Eddie Foy and Irene Bentley; and a frothy musical called "The Liberty Belles" in which Pauline Chase made a big hit and became known as "The Pink Pajama Girl," while two other girls who played small parts became famous later as Elsie Ferguson and Lotta Faust.

E. H. Sothern had been on the stage nearly twenty years, but he scored his first big hit with "If I Were King." His leading lady was Cecilia Loftus, known as Cissie to friends and admirers, and until now her career had been devoted mostly to vaudeville, giving imitations of her fellow artists.

"Under Southern Skies" was a praiseworthy production of William A. Brady, and in the leading role was Grace George, a young actress who became his wife.

It is interesting to note that at this time New York had more legitimate theatres than any other city in the world. Paris had 24, London had 39 and New York 41.

HENRY MILLER

MR. WILLARD in
"TOM PINCH"

E. S. WILLARD

MR. WILLARD in
"THE PROFESSOR'S LOVE STORY"

ROBERT LORAINE

CHORUS of "THE SHOW GIRL"

MRS. PATRICK CAMPBELL

CHARLES RICHMAN, WM. COURTENAY, MARGARET ANGLIN, MARGARET DALE in "THE IMPORTANCE OF BEING EARNEST"

HENRIETTA CROSMAN
as ROSALIND

HENRY WOODRUFF
as ORLANDO

1902

One of the hits of 1902 was "As You Like It" with Henrietta Crosman as Rosalind and Henry Woodruff as Orlando. Produced by Miss Crosman's husband, Maurice Campbell, it ran in New York for sixty consecutive performances, a record held until 1950 when Katharine Hepburn broke it by playing the Shakespearean comedy 145 times.

In January, Mrs. Patrick Campbell, a popular English actress and a brilliant wit, made her first appearance in New York, offering a repertoire that included "The Second Mrs. Tanqueray," "Magda," "The Happy Hypocrite" and "Pelleas and Melisande." George Arliss was in her company, also making his American debut.

Early in the year, Otis Skinner was starring in a revival of "Francesca da Rimini;" Amelia Bingham was in "A Modern Magdalen;" Kyrle Bellew gave a special performance of Sheridan's "School For Scandal" with Marie Wainwright as Lady Teazle; in "Her Lord and Master," which starred Effie Shannon and Herbert Kelcey, Douglas Fairbanks was making his initial stage appearance; Robert Edeson was being starred for the first time in the Augustus Thomas play, "Soldiers of Fortune;" William A. Brady starred his wife, Grace George, in a revival of Sardou's "Frou Frou;" and Charles Frohman revived Oscar Wilde's "The Importance of Being Earnest" with Margaret Anglin, Charles Richman, William Courtenay, Margaret Dale and Mrs. Thomas Whiffen.

Two of David Belasco's stars were appearing in their successes of the previous year. Mrs. Leslie Carter was again seen as the royal courtesan in "Du Barry," and David Warfield continued to draw laughs and tears with the sentimental comedy hit, "The Auctioneer."

Among the musicals in favor were Francis Wilson supported by Christie MacDonald and Adele Ritchie in "The Toreador;"

THOS. W. ROSS, ROBERT EDESON,
GRETCHEN LYONS in
"SOLDIERS OF FORTUNE"

AMELIA BINGHAM

GRACE GEORGE

OTIS SKINNER, MARCIA
VAN DRESSLER in
"FRANCESCA DA RIMINI"

JULIA DEAN

WM. BLACK, ALBERT HART, CAROLINE PERKINS, EDDIE FOY, IRENE BENTLEY, DAVID LYTHGOE, MARIE CAHILL, JUNIE McCREE, MARGUERITE CLARK, EVELYN NESBIT, DAVID BENNETT, in "THE WILD ROSE"

EVELYN NESBIT

MARIE WAINWRIGHT

MRS. LESLIE CARTER as "DUBARRY"

Frank Daniels in "Miss Simplicity;" Raymond Hitchcock in "King Dodo;" Frank Moulan in "The Sultan of Sulu;" "A Chinese Honeymoon" starring Thomas Q. Seabrooke; and "The Show Girl" with Paula Edwardes.

A musical comedy, "The Wild Rose," opened in May with an imposing cast which included Eddie Foy, Marie Cahill, Irene Bentley, Marguerite Clark, Evelyn Florence and Elsie Ferguson. Marie Cahill introduced a song, "Nancy Brown," written by Clifton Crawford, a musical comedy actor who was appearing in "Foxy Grandpa" with Joseph Hart and Carrie De Mar. Miss Cahill made the song and herself famous and her first starring vehicle in 1903 was named after the song. Another song she made famous was "Under the Bamboo Tree" which she sang in "Sally in Our Alley." Evelyn Florence became Evelyn Nesbit who married Harry K. Thaw and became involved in the Thaw-Stanford White murder case.

Lulu Glaser was singing in "Dolly Varden," one of the hits of her career. Blanche Ring, a young singer from Boston, the daughter of actor James F. Ring, was stopping a musical, "The Defender," every night with her spirited rendition of "In The Good Old Summer Time," a song hit which was written by George "Honey

MABELLE GILMAN

FRANCIS WILSON

ELSIE LESLIE

FRANK MOULAN AND CHORUS in "THE SULTAN OF SULU"

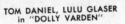
TOM DANIEL, LULU GLASER
in "DOLLY VARDEN"

JOSEPH JEFFERSON

EMILY STEVENS

Boy" Evans and Ben Shields. Two of Blanche's sisters, Frances and Julie Ring, and a brother, Cyril, also had careers in the theatre. Pauline Frederick, another young lady from Boston, also made her first New York appearance in the chorus of "The Roger Brothers in Harvard."

Playing to full houses at Weber and Fields Music Hall was "Twirly Whirly" with such old standbys as Lew Fields, Joe Weber, Lillian Russell, Fay Templeton, Peter F. Dailey and Bessie Clayton, while newcomers to the company were William Collier and Mabel Barrison. Lillian Russell introduced her hit song, "Come Down, My Evening Star," in this show.

Edna Wallace Hopper was starring in "The Silver Slipper." Opening at the same time was "Old Limerick Town" starring Chauncey Olcott with Blanche Sweet who was a child actress at this time and who later became a noted film star. Mabelle Gilman was appearing in a comic opera, "The Mocking Bird." In 1907, she married William E. Cory, a Pittsburgh steel millionaire, and retired from the stage. "The Billionaire," a musical with Jerome Sykes, May Robson, Sallie Fisher, introduced lovely Marie Doro to New York audiences.

Later in the year, English actress Edith Wynne Matthison made her American

MARIE DORO

MARY MANNERING

BLANCHE RING

THOMAS Q. SEABROOKE and CHORUS
in "A CHINESE HONEYMOON"

PAULINE FREDERICK

EDNA WALLACE HOPPER

BLANCHE SWEET

21

MRS. LILY LANGTRY

NAT C. GOODWIN, F. OWEN BAXTER, JULIA DEAN, FRED TIDEN, NEIL O'BRIEN, MAXINE ELLIOTT, J. CARRINGTON YATES in "THE ALTAR OF FRIENDSHIP"

debut in the Fifteenth Century morality play "Everyman." Mrs. Fiske, who earlier apeared in revivals of "Tess of the D'Urbervilles," "Divorcons" and "A Doll's House," was playing under the management of her husband, Harrison Grey Fiske, in "Mary of Magdala" with Tyrone Power, Henry Woodruff, Rose Eytinge and Mrs. Fiske's niece, Emily Stevens. Blanche Bates was having great success with "The Darling of the Gods," a play produced and written by David Belasco with John Luther Long.

"The Altar of Friendship," produced by Nat C. Goodwin and starring Maxine Elliott and himself, served as the metropolitan debut of Julia Dean, a young actress and namesake of her famous aunt, who had been winning admirers on the West Coast the two previous years.

John Drew opened his regular fall season at the Empire Theatre in "The Mummy and the Humming Bird" supported by Margaret Dale, Lionel Barrymore and Guy Standing. Ethel Barrymore, newly risen to stardom, was appearing in "A Country Mouse" preceded by "Carrots," a one-act play.

In October, Annie Irish and her husband, J. E. Dodson, made their debut as stars in "An American Invasion." Mary Mannering was in "The Stubbornness of Geraldine;" James K. Hackett and Charlotte Walker were playing in "The Crisis;" Viola Allen was in Hall Caine's dramatization of his own novel, "The Eternal

BESSIE CLAYTON
in "TWIRLY WHIRLY"

RAYMOND HITCHCOCK
in "KING DODO"

ROBERT DROUET, CLARA BLOODGOOD
in "THE GIRL WITH THE GREEN EYES"

FREDERIC DeBELLEVILLE, VIOLA ALLEN
in "THE ETERNAL CITY"

EDITH WYNNE MATTHISON
in "EVERYMAN"

22

BLANCHE BATES, GEORGE ARLISS, ROBERT T. HAINES
in "THE DARLING OF THE GODS"

ELEONORA DUSE

City;" Richard Mansfield was playing Brutus in "Julius Caesar;" Clara Bloodgood was in "The Girl With The Green Eyes," written especially for her by Clyde Fitch.

Eleonora Duse, famous Italian actress, who had made her American debut in 1893 as "Camille," arrived in New York in November and appeared in three plays all written by her great friend, Gabriele D'Annunzio, namely, "La Gioconda," "La Citta Morta" and "Francesca Da Rimini." Signora Duse spoke little English and her American performances were all given in Italian.

As the year neared the end, Mrs. Lily Langtry, famous English beauty who was known as the "Jersey Lily" because she was born on the Isle of Jersey, opened in "The Cross-Ways," a play she had written with J. Hartley Manners who became a well-known playwright and married Laurette Taylor.

On the road, Joseph Jefferson, now in his sixty-eighth year as an actor, was toddling about the country in his famous successes, "Rip Van Winkle" and "The Cricket on the Hearth." Elsie Leslie, who had won fame in the title role of "Little Lord Fauntleroy" in 1888, was playing Viola Allen's role in "The Christian" with E. J. Morgan as her co-star. In California, James Neill and Edyth Chapman, great favorites in the West, were playing in "The Red Knight."

J. E. DODSON, ANNIE IRISH
in "THE AMERICAN INVASION"

ETHEL BARRYMORE, BRUCE McRAE
in "CARROTS"

CHAUNCEY OLCOTT in
"OLD LIMERICK TOWN"

JAMES NEILL, EDYTH CHAPMAN
in "THE RED KNIGHT"

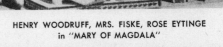

HENRY WOODRUFF, MRS. FISKE, ROSE EYTINGE
in "MARY OF MAGDALA"

23

LILLIAN RUSSELL

DAVID C. MONTGOMERY
and FRED STONE

"THE WIZARD OF OZ"

FRITZI SCHEFF in
"BABETTE"

EDDIE FOY in
"MR. BLUEBEARD"

1903 Over twenty-five percent of the productions playing in New York and on the road in 1903 were musicals. It is interesting to note that many of them were being billed as musical comedies. They had been labeled an extravaganza, a spectacular fantasy, a burlesque revue, a musical farce, a comic opera, a musical extravaganza or a vaudeville farce. The comic opera too was beginning to be known more widely as an operetta.

Among the musicals presented were several with special appeal for children: "The Wizard of Oz" was adapted by L. Frank Baum from his book of the same title. He also wrote the lyrics. Fred Stone and David Montgomery performed as the team of Montgomery and Stone from 1894 until Montgomery's death in 1917. This was their first starring vehicle and their leading lady was Anna Laughlin, mother of Lucy Monroe. "Babes In Toyland" had William Norris, Mabel Barrison and Bessie Wynn in the cast and one of Victor Herbert's most tuneful scores. "Mr. Pickwick" was based on Charles Dickens' book and had De Wolf Hopper in the title role. The cast included Digby Bell, Louise Gunning and little Marguerite Clark. "Mr. Bluebeard," the attraction that was playing in the Iroquois Theatre at the time of its fire, had Eddie Foy in the title role.

Other musicals of the year were: "The Prince of Pilsen" with Arthur Donaldson; "Nancy Brown" with Marie Cahill starring for the first time; Williams and Walker, a popular colored team, playing "In Dahomey;" the Four Cohans with Ethel Levey in "Running For Office" "The Runaways" with Fay Templeton; "Peggy From Paris" with Georgia Caine; Francis Wilson in a revival of "Erminie" with Marguerite Sylva in the title role;

MARIE CAHILL in
"NANCY BROWN"

LOUISE GUNNING, DE WOLF HOPPER, MARGUERITE
CLARK in "MR. PICKWICK"

PAULA EDWARDES in
"WINSOME WINNIE"

"BABES IN TOYLAND"

PAULINE CHASE   MARGUERITE SYLVA   GUS ROGERS   JULIA SANDERSON   MAX ROGERS   MABEL BARRISON   PHOEBE DAVIES

HENRY IRVING in
"DANTE"

ANNA BUCKLEY, MACLYN ARBUCKLE, EARLE BROWNE
in "THE COUNTY CHAIRMAN"

HENRY IRVING

ARNOLD DALY, HERBERT STANDING,
LOUISE CLOSSER HALE in "CANDIDA"

EDGAR SELWYN, TYRONE POWER
in "ULYSSES"

"The Girl From Kay's" with Sam Bernard, Hattie Williams and two beautiful girls and future stars, Marie Doro and Elsie Ferguson, in lesser roles; Frank Daniels in "The Office Boy;" Grace Van Studdiford in "Red Feather;" "Babette," a comic opera which brought Fritzi Scheff, who had been singing sixteen leading roles with the Metropolitan Opera Company while still in her teens, to the Broadway stage for the first time; Paula Edwardes bowing as a star in "Winsome Winnie" with Julia Sanderson in a minor role; Anna Held in "Mam'selle Napoleon;" Irene Bentley in "The Girl From Dixie" and the perennial "Roger Brothers in London."

Weber and Fields were in "Whoop-Dee-Doo" and Lillian Russell was still their main attraction while Louis Mann and Carter De Haven were new to the Music Hall clients.

"The Little Princess," an adaptation by Frances Hodgson Burnett from her own book, "Sara Crewes," was especially produced for children and gave only matinee performances. Millie James, daughter of Louis James, a star of the 'Nineties, played the lead and the cast included Pauline Chase, Mabel Taliaferro, Edith Storey and May Davenport Seymour, the niece of Fanny Davenport, famous actress of yesteryear. Edith Storey became a star of the silent films with the

"WAY DOWN EAST"

JOE WEBER, LEW FIELDS, LOUIS MANN
in "WHOOP-DEE-DOO"

BESSIE WYNN   ANNA LAUGHLIN   DIGBY BELL   IRENE BENTLEY   HASSARD SHORT   GEORGIA CAINE   MAY DAVENPORT SEYMOUR

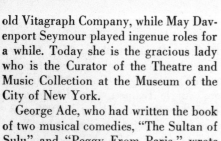

EDGAR SELWYN, G. H. HUNTER, MAUDE ADAMS, HENRY AINLEY in
"PRETTY SISTER OF JOSÉ"

MAURICE WILKINSON, FRED LEWIS, VIRGINIA
KLEIN, MARY SHAW in "GHOSTS"

old Vitagraph Company, while May Davenport Seymour played ingenue roles for a while. Today she is the gracious lady who is the Curator of the Theatre and Music Collection at the Museum of the City of New York.

George Ade, who had written the book of two musical comedies, "The Sultan of Sulu" and "Peggy From Paris," wrote "The County Chairman," a straight comedy that proved one of the year's hits and made a star of Maclyn Arbuckle.

Annie Russell was playing in "Mice and Men" with John Mason. Bertha Galland was starring in "Dorothy Vernon of Haddon Hall" with May Robson playing Queen Elizabeth. Amelia Bingham produced and starred in "The Frisky Mrs. Johnson" while Blanche Walsh reaped applause in a dramatized version of Tolstoy's "Resurrection." Mary Shaw was in a revival of "Ghosts." Charles Hawtrey was in "The Man From Blankley's," Elsie de Wolfe and Charles Cherry were in "Cynthia," Grace George and Robert Loraine played in "Pretty Peggy," Mrs. Langtry was in "Mrs. Deering's Divorce," Cecil Spooner, a famous stock company star, was in "My Lady Peggy Goes To Town" and Henry Woodruff was in a revival of "Ben Hur." Thomas W. Ross was in "Checkers," Richard Mansfield played in "Old Heidelberg," Ethel Barrymore's

EDWIN ARDEN, ELEANOR ROBSON in
"MERELY MARY ANN"

BRUCE McRAE, ETHEL BARRYMORE in
"COUSIN KATE"

GERTRUDE ELLIOTT, J. FORBES-ROBERTSON in
"THE LIGHT THAT FAILED"

"THE PRINCE OF PILSEN"

MRS. LANGTRY in
"MRS. DEERING'S DIVORCE"

27

GEORGE WALKER, ADAH OVERTON WALKER,
BERT WILLIAMS in "IN DAHOMEY"

HENRY WOODRUFF, STELLA WEAVER in
"BEN HUR"

KYRLE BELLEW, E. M. HOLLAND in
"RAFFLES"

WILLIAM GILLETTE in
"THE ADMIRABLE CRICHTON"

FRANCIS WILSON in
"ERMINIE"

ELSIE De WOLFE in
"CYNTHIA"

THOMAS W. ROSS in
"CHECKERS"

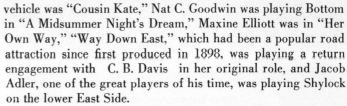

vehicle was "Cousin Kate," Nat C. Goodwin was playing Bottom in "A Midsummer Night's Dream," Maxine Elliott was in "Her Own Way," "Way Down East," which had been a popular road attraction since first produced in 1898, was playing a return engagement with C. B. Davis in her original role, and Jacob Adler, one of the great players of his time, was playing Shylock on the lower East Side.

Augustus Thomas' new play, "The Earl of Pawtucket," was written for Lawrence D'Orsay and he scored his biggest hit and became a star.

Mrs. Fiske made her first appearance in "Hedda Gabler." Maude Adams, after a year's rest because of ill health, returned in another of Frances Hodgson Burnett's plays, "The Pretty Sister of Jose" with Henry Ainley, handsome matinee idol from London. William Gillette was appearing in James M. Barrie's "The Admirable Crichton." Marie Tempest, one of England's brightest stars who had made her American debut in 1890, was playing in "The Marriage of Kitty." Doris Keane made her New York debut in a small role in a comedy, "The Whitewashing of Julia." George Bernard Shaw's "Candida" was having its first professional production with Dorothy Donnelly in the title role and Arnold Daly as Marchbanks. Tyrone Power was in "Ulysses" with Rose Coghlan, an illustrious veteran. Joseph Santley, at the

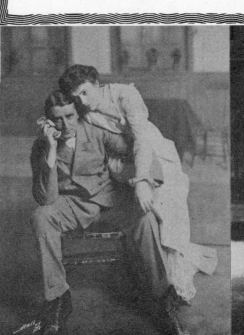

28 WILTON LACKAYE, AMELIA BINGHAM, W. L. ABINGTON in
"THE FRISKY MRS. JOHNSON"

CHARLES CHERRY. ELSIE De WOLFE in
"CYNTHIA"

CHARLES HAWTREY in
"THE MAN FROM BLANKLEY'S"

NEST ELTON, LAWRENCE D'ORSAY in
"THE EARL OF PAWTUCKET"

INA BROOKS, BLANCHE WALSH in
"RESURRECTION"

FRANK GOLDSMITH, ORRIN JOHNSON, MRS. GILBERT,
ANNIE RUSSELL in "MICE AND MEN"

age of twelve, was heading a company trouping in "From Rags to Riches" and "Billy the Kid." May Vokes was beginning a career of comic maids in "A Fool and His Money."

Henrietta Crosman, fresh from her triumph as Rosalind, scored heavily again in "Sweet Kitty Bellairs." Two young people in the cast were Shelley Hull and Jane Cowl, making her first appearance on any stage.

Eleanor Robson, who earlier in the year had played Juliet to Kyrle Bellew's Romeo, was in "Merely Mary Ann," a comedy by Israel Zangwill which served her for several seasons. Edwin Arden, Laura Hope Crews and Julia Dean were in the cast. Kyrle Bellew was creating a role that became world famous, "Raffles," the Amateur Cracksman.

On December 28, 1903, John Barrymore made his first appearance on the New York stage in Clyde Fitch's "Glad Of It."

Henry Irving, distinguished English actor, played in "Dante" for two weeks then "The Bells ," "Waterloo," "Louis XI" and "The Merchant of Venice" in repertoire. Another of his countrymen, J. Forbes-Robertson was playing in "The Light That Failed" with his wife, Gertrude Elliott.

The year ended on a grim note on December 30th when 602 lives were lost in the Iroquois Theatre fire in Chicago. The asbestos curtains in all our theatres today are a visual reminder.

MILLIE JAMES in
"THE LITTLE PRINCESS"

ANNA HELD in
"MLLE. NAPOLEON"

JOSEPH SANTLEY in
"RAGS TO RICHES"

CECIL SPOONER in
"MY LADY PEGGY GOES TO TOWN"

SAM BERNARD, HATTIE WILLIAMS in
"THE GIRL FROM KAY'S"

ROBERT LORAINE, GRACE GEORGE in
"PRETTY PEGGY"

JERRY J. COHAN, JOSEPHINE COHAN, GEORGE M. COHAN,
HELEN F. COHAN in "RUNNING FOR OFFICE"

FAY TEMPLETON in
"THE RUNAWAYS"

BERTHA GALLAND, FRANK LOSEE, MAY ROBSON, WILLIAM LEWERS,
GEORGE LESOIR in "DOROTHY VERNON OF HADDON HALL"

HENRIETTA CROSMAN in
"SWEET KITTY BELLAIRS"

MARIE TEMPEST

KYRLE BELLEW, ELEANOR ROBSON in
"ROMEO AND JULIET"

MAXINE ELLIOTT

MRS. FISKE

GRACE VAN STUDDIFORD

JACOB ADLER as
"SHYLOCK"

MAY VOKES

ROSE COGHLAN

VIOLA ALLEN as
VIOLA

E. H. SOTHERN as
ROMEO

JULIA MARLOWE as
VIOLA

J. FORBES-ROBERTSON as
HAMLET

1904 Shakespeare was the favorite playwright of the year. Ada Rehan included in her repertoire "The Taming of the Shrew" and "The Merchant of Venice" and was playing Katharine and Portia to Otis Skinner's Petruchio and Shylock. Viola Allen had great success as Viola in "Twelfth Night" and later in the year she received acclaim for her revival of "The Winter's Tale." Her father, C. Leslie Allen, was in the cast.

Charles Frohman presented E. H. Sothern and Julia Marlowe in their first joint appearance with Shakespearean repertoire of "Romeo and Juliet," "Much Ado About Nothing" and "Hamlet." Mr. Frohman also presented Ben Greet's company in "Twelfth Night" with Mr. Greet playing Malvolio and Edith Wynne Matthison as Viola. Robert B. Mantell's repertoire also included two of the Bard's plays: "Othello" and "Richard III." His leading lady and current wife was Marie Booth Russell. A production of "Much Ado About Nothing" boasted Jessie Millward, Florence Rockwell, William Morris, Theodore Roberts and Wallace Eddinger in its cast. Johnston Forbes-Robertson made his first New York appearance as "Hamlet." His wife, Gertrude Elliott, was Ophelia.

Among revivals there were two of "Camille." Virginia Harned with William Courtenay as her Armand revived "Camille" on the same night as Margaret Anglin and Henry Miller. There was an outstanding revival of that famous old melodrama, "The Two Orphans," star-studded with Kyrle Bellew, Grace George, Margaret Illington, James O'Neill, Annie Irish, E. M. Holland, Elita Proctor Otis and veteran Clara Morris, who had been one of

EDITH WYNNE MATTHISON as
VIOLA

ROBERT B. MANTELL as
RICHARD III

MARIE BOOTH RUSSELL as
DESDEMONA

ADA REHAN as
KATHERINE

OTIS SKINNER as
SHYLOCK

GERTRUDE ELLIOTT as
OPHELIA

JULIA MARLOWE and E. H. SOTHERN in
"ROMEO AND JULIET"

C. LESLIE ALLEN, JAMES YOUNG, VIOLA ALLEN, BOYD PUTMAN,
FRANK VERNON in "THE WINTER'S TALE"

DUSTIN FARNUM in
"THE VIRGINIAN"

Augustin Daly's most illustrious stars and who was making her farewell stage appearance. While on the subject of farewells, Mrs. G. H. Gilbert, who supported many great stars through the years, was starring for the first time in a play written especially for her by Clyde Fitch. Called "Granny," and with Marie Doro as the ingenue, it was to have been her farewell to the stage, but following her New York engagement, Mrs. Gilbert's tour ended abruptly, four days after opening in Chicago, when she died suddenly on December 2, 1904, at the age of 83.

Amelia Bingham was in "Olympe" with Henry Woodruff, Dorothy Russell and Gilbert Heron in her supporting cast. Dorothy Russell was Lillian's daughter, and Gilbert Heron was Henry Miller's son who later made a name for himself as producer Gilbert Miller.

David Warfield was appearing in another great success, "The Music Master." It served him for several seasons, and he revived it in 1916. Minnie Dupree was his leading lady and Jane Cowl had a small role in the original production.

Wilton Lackaye had a hit with Channing Pollock's "The Pit." His cast included Douglas Fairbanks and Hale Hamilton.

Minnie Maddern Fiske was appearing at the Manhattan Theatre, which had been acquired by her husband and manager, Harrison Grey Fiske, in "Leah Kleschna," and revivals of "Hedda Gabler" and "Becky Sharp."

John Drew's vehicle was "The Duke of Killicrankie,' while his niece, Ethel Barrymore, was in "Sunday," a play of little consequence, but a line, "That's all there is, there isn't any more," spoken in it by Miss Barrymore, is still remembered. Maude Adams revived "The Little Minister."

MAUDE ADAMS in
"THE LITTLE MINISTER"

William Collier was appearing in "The Dictator," a farce by Richard Harding Davis, with Lucile Watson, Thomas Meighan and John Barrymore in the cast. Wright Lorimer, an actor from the West, starred and made his New York debut in his own play, "The Shepherd King." It served him for three seasons. Two of the outstanding matinee idols were James K. Hackett, who produced and starred in "The Crown Prince," and William Faversham, who was in "Letty" with his wife, Julie Opp, and Carlotta Nillson.

"Mrs. Wiggs of the Cabbage Patch" was one of the comedy hits. Madge Carr Cook, the mother of Eleanor Robson, played the title role with Mabel Taliaferro, William Hodge, Helen Lowell and Thurston Hall in the cast.

Denman Thompson, who made his first appearance in New York with "The Old Homestead" in 1887 and continued to play it at frequent intervals until his death April 14, 1911, was back in town with his old stand-by.

Nance O'Neil, who was making her first appearance in New York as "Magda" and "Hedda Gabler," also played in "The Fires of St. John" and "Judith of Bethulia" with Lowell Sherman making his metropolitan debut in the latter cast.

Madame Gabrielle Rejane, famous French actress who had not appeared in America since 1895, returned for a short season of repertoire. Charles Wyndham, over from England, was playing with Mary Moore in a revival of "David Garrick," a play they first acted for New York audiences in 1889.

"The College Widow," a George Ade comedy, had a long run with Dorothy Tennant and Frederick Truesdell in the leads. Mr. Ade also wrote the book for a

DAVID WARFIELD in
"THE MUSIC MASTER"

MADGE CARR COOK AND THE CHILDREN in
"MRS WIGGS OF THE CABBAGE PATCH"

33

MAY IRWIN in
"MRS. BLACK IS BACK"

DENMAN THOMPSON in
"THE OLD HOMESTEAD"

VIRGINIA EARLE in
"SERGEANT KITTY"

De WOLFE HOPPER in
"WANG"

DOUGLAS FAIRBANKS (left center) in
"THE PIT"

popular musical, "The Sho-gun," which was running with Charles Evans, Christie MacDonald and Georgia Caine.

Other events included: Ibsen's "Rosmersholm," having its first American production with William Morris and Florence Kahn; Clara Bloodgood in Clyde Fitch's "The Coronet of the Duchess;" Mrs. Patrick Campbell's appearance in Sardou's "The Sorceress;" May Irwin cutting capers in "Mrs. Black Is Back;" Chauncey Olcott delighting the customers with his Irish ballads in "Terence;" Dustin Farnum causing the matinee girls' hearts to skip a beat in "The Virginian" and Louis Mann appearing in "The Second Fiddle."

In the musical comedy field, Virginia Earle was starring in "Sergeant Kitty;" Richard Carle wrote the book and starred in "The Tenderfoot;" Raymond Hitchcock with Flora Zabelle, his wife, was in "The Yankee Consul;" "Piff! Paff! Pouff!!!" was a big hit with Eddie Foy, Alice Fischer and John Hyams; Sam S. Shubert revived "Wang," a popular musical of the 'nineties, with De Wolf Hopper, and one of the chorus boys was Mack Sennett who became famous for his film comedies. Edna May continued to win admirers with "The School Girl;" Lulu Glaser was attractive in "A Madcap Princess;" while "Woodland," an operetta with the novelty of having all its characters birds, repeated its Boston success in New York.

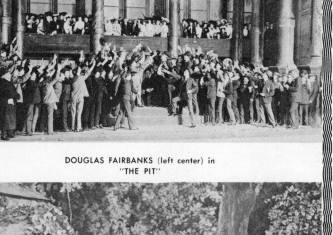

ROLAND CUNNINGHAM, M. W. WHITNEY, JR., FRITZI
SCHEFF in "THE TWO ROSES"

CHRISTIE MacDONALD

ELITA PROCTOR O'

MINNIE DUPREE

LUCILE WATSON

MRS. G. H. GILBERT

ANNIE IRISH

GABRIELLE REJANE

CLARA BLOODGO

JULIAN ELTINGE in
"MR. WIX OF WICKHAM"

LEW DOCKSTADER in
"HIS MINSTREL SHOW"

NANCE O'NEIL in
"JUDITH OF BETHULIA"

GEORGE M. COHAN in
"LITTLE JOHNNY JONES"

Julian Eltinge, most famous of all the female impersonators of his day, made his first professional stage appearance in "Mr. Wix of Wickham."

Primrose and Dockstader's Minstrel men split up and Lew Dockstader's Minstrels appeared. Weber and Fields had split too, and Joe Weber, with Florenz Ziegfield, Jr., presented "Higgledy-Piggledy" with Anna Held and Marie Dressler. Lew Fields produced and starred in a Victor Herbert musical, "It Happened in Nordland," with Marie Cahill, May Robson, Bessie Clayton and Pauline Frederick. Lillian Russell, who had been with Weber and Fields, was playing in "Lady Teazle," a musical version of Sheridan's "The School For Scandal." Charles B. Dillingham, was presenting Fritzi Scheff in a musical version of Goldsmith's "She Stoops to Conquer," called "The Two Roses."

George M. Cohan had his first starring engagement in "Little Johnny Jones." In the cast, besides his mother and father, were Ethel Levey and Donald Brian. His sister, Josephine, had married Fred Niblo and was with him in "The Roger Brothers in Paris."

Mme. Schumann-Heink, famous grand opera star, made her only Broadway appearance in "Love's Lottery," a comic opera which was not a success.

In the vaudeville field, James J. Corbett, world's heavyweight boxing champion, was telling amusing stories of his experiences.

FREDERICK TRUESDELL (center)
in "THE COLLEGE WIDOW"

JOSEPHINE
COHAN

FLORENCE
ROCKWELL

MARIE CAHILL, LEW FIELDS in
"IT HAPPENED IN NORDLAND"

DOROTHY
TENNANT

CLARA MORRIS in
"THE TWO ORPHANS"

MADGE CARR
COOK

E. M. HOLLAND

FREDERICK
TRUESDELL

ALICE
FISCHER

JOHN MASON, MRS. FISKE in
"LEAH KLESCHNA"

GEORGE ARLISS, MRS. FISKE in
"HEDDA GABLER"

WILLIAM FAVERSHAM, CARLOTTA NILLSON
in "LETTY"

MAY BUCKLEY, WRIGHT LORIMER
in "THE SHEPHERD KING"

EDNA MAY, GEORGE GROSSMITH
in "THE SCHOOL GIRL"

OLIVE NORTH, HANS ROBERTS
in "WOODLAND"

ETHEL BARRYMORE in
"SUNDAY"

36 GRACE GEORGE, MARGARET ILLINGTON
"in "THE TWO ORPHANS"

MRS. G. H. GILBERT, MARIE DORO
in "GRANNY"

MME. SCHUMANN-HEINK in
"LOVE'S LOTTERY"

WILLIAM COLLIER, NANETTE COMSTOCK, THOMAS McGRATH, GEORGE NASH,
JOHN BARRYMORE in "THE DICTATOR"

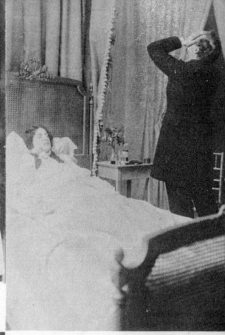

MARY MOORE, CHARLES WYNDHAM in
"DAVID GARRICK"

HENRY MILLER, MARGARET
ANGLIN in "CAMILLE"

RAYMOND HITCHCOCK in
"THE YANKEE CONSUL"

MRS. PATRICK CAMPBELL in
"THE SORCERESS"

JOHN DREW in
"THE DUKE OF KILLICRANKIE"

LILLIAN RUSSELL in
"LADY TEAZLE"

ETHEL LEVEY in
"LITTLE JOHNNY JONES"

LOUIS MANN in
"THE SECOND FIDDLE"

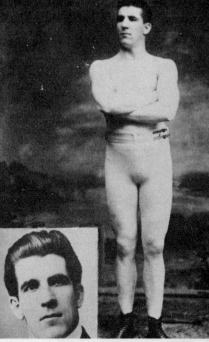

JAMES K. HACKETT

ANNA HELD and CHORUS in
"HIGGLEDY PIGGLEDY"

JAMES J. CORBETT in
VAUDEVILLE

37

MAUDE ADAMS
AND SCENES FROM "PETER PAN"

CHRYSTAL HERNE, DODSON MITCHELL, ARNOLD DALY in
"JOHN BULL'S OTHER ISLAND"

LOIS F. CLARK, FAY DAVIS, RICHARD BENNETT, EDWARD ABELES,
LOUIS MASSEN, ROBERT LORAINE in "MAN AND SUPERMAN"

RICHARD MANSFIELD in
"MISANTHROPE"

BERTHA KALICH in
"MONNA VANNA"

1905 This might well be called George Bernard Shaw year. Four of his plays were produced for the first time in New York and several others were revived. Arnold Daly, who had introduced "Candida" and "The Man of Destiny" to American audiences, now gave New Yorkers their first look at "You Never Can Tell," "John Bull's Other Island" and "Mrs. Warren's Profession." His production of "You Never Can Tell" ran 129 performances early in the year and Mr. Daly put it on again in the fall with Shaw's "Candida," "The Man of Destiny," "John Bull's Other Island" and "Mrs. Warren's Profession" in repertoire. This latter production caused the arrest of Arnold Daly and his leading lady, Mary Shaw, charged with appearing in an immoral play. Brought to trial, they were promptly acquitted.

"Man and Superman" was the other Shaw play presented for the first time by Charles Dillingham with Robert Loraine making the hit of his career as John Tanner. Clara Bloodgood, Richard Bennett and Edward Abeles were in the cast.

Maude Adams' revival of "The Little Minister" ran well into 1905, and in February she added a one-act play, "Op o' Me Thumb," as a curtain raiser. On November 6th she opened at the Empire in Barrie's "Peter Pan," her most famous role. It served her several seasons and she revived it in 1915. Ethel Barrymore was also appearing in a Barrie play, "Alice-Sit-by-the-Fire," with Bruce McRae, Mary Nash, May Davenport Seymour and brother John in her cast.

The biggest hit and the longest run of the year was "The Lion and the Mouse" which opened in the fall and ran in New

MARY SHAW

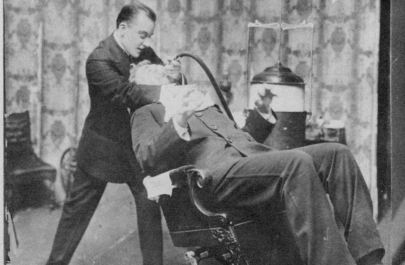

ARNOLD DALY, GEORGE FARREN in
"YOU NEVER CAN TELL"

ARNOLD DALY as
MARCHBANKS in "CANDIDA"

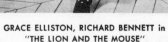

York for two years, achieving 686 performances. Grace Elliston, Edmund Breese and Richard Bennett had the leads in the original production. "The Squaw Man," starring William Faversham supported by William S. Hart and George Fawcett, and "The Girl of the Golden West," starring Blanche Bates with Robert Hilliard and Frank Keenan, were also great hits.

Mrs. Leslie Carter was appearing in "Adrea," a new play by David Belasco and John Luther Long. In the fall she did revivals of "Zaza" and "Du Barry." It was her last appearance under David Belasco's management. The split followed her marriage to William Louis Payne, a young actor. Belasco never forgave her.

Holbrook Blinn, who had been away from the New York stage since 1901 making a name for himself in London, returned in the leading role of Napoleon in a light opera, "The Duchess of Dantzic."

Bertha Kalich, an idol of the Yiddish theatre, made her English-speaking debut on Broadway in Sardou's "Fedora," followed later by Maeterlinck's "Monna Vanna."

Interesting revivals were "Rip Van Winkle" with Thomas Jefferson playing his father's famous role; "She Stoops to Conquer" with Kyrle Bellew, Eleanor Robson, Sidney Drew, Isabel Irving, Louis James and Olive Wyndham; and "Trilby" with

MRS. LESLIE CARTER in "ADREA"

WILLIAM FAVERSHAM, MABEL MORRISON, EVELYN WRIGHT in "THE SQUAW MAN"

FRITZI SCHEFF in "MLLE. MODISTE"

Virginia Harned who created the title role in 1895. Wilton Lackaye, Burr McIntosh and Leo Ditrichstein from that earlier production played their same roles. Later Miss Harned appeared with William Courtenay in "La Belle Marseillaise," a minor drama.

Richard Mansfield was appearing in a repertoire of his favorite plays and presenting for the first time, Moliere's "Misanthrope." E. H. Sothern and Julia Marlowe were presenting Shakespearean repertoire and so was Robert B. Mantell. Olga Nethersole was appearing in a new play, "The Labyrinth," and two old ones, "Sapho" and "Carmen," with Hamilton Revelle still her leading man. Marie Doro was gaining in popularity in "Friquet," while Mary Mannering and James K. Hackett, husband and wife at this time, were co-starring in "The Walls of Jericho."

"Buster Brown," a comedy depicting one of the well-known characters of the 'funny papers,' as the comics were called then, was popular with Master Gabriel playing Buster.

Chauncey Olcott's vehicle was "Edmund Burke." In the cast were listed Charlotte, Edith, Lottie and Gladys Smith. Gladys Smith became Mary Pickford of film fame; Charlotte was her mother, Lottie, her sister and Edith was brother Jack.

Other stars and their plays were Robert Edeson in "Strong-

VIRGINIA HARNED in "TRILBY"

WILTON LACKAYE as SVENGALI in "TRILBY"

SCENE FROM "MLLE. MODISTE"

"ROGER BROTHERS IN IRELAND"

VALLI VALLI in "VERONIQUE"

THE PLUNGING HORSES in "THE RAIDERS"
HIPPODROME EXTRAVAGANZA

SIDNEY DREW

MARGARET DALE, JOHN DREW in "De LANCEY"

GRACE GEORGE, BEN WEBSTER in "THE MARRIAGE OF WILLIAM ASHE"

MARIE DORO, W. J. FERGUSON in "FRIQUET"

BESSIE CLAYTON

WM. COURTENAY, FAY DAVIS, LOUIS PAYNE, MARGARET ILLINGTON in "MRS. LEFFINGWELL'S BOOTS"

JOHN BUNNY, RAYMOND HITCHCOCK in "EASY DAWSON"

KATIE BARRY, ADELE RITCHIE, JEFFERSON DeANGEL "FANTANA"

MARIE CAHILL

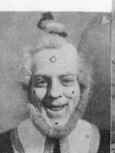

LIONEL BARRYMORE

BLANCHE WALSH in "THE WOMAN IN THE CASE"

heart," Maxine Elliott with Charles Cherry in "Her Great Match," John Drew in "De Lancey," Margaret Anglin in "Zira," Henry E. Dixey in "The Man on the Box," Grace George in "The Marriage of William Ashe," Margaret Illington in "Mrs. Leffingwell's Boots," Francis Wilson with May Robson in "Cousin Billy," Blanche Walsh in "The Woman in the Case" and Cyril Scott in "The Prince Chap."

On April 12th, the New York Hippodrome opened its doors for the first time. Its attractions were large scale extravaganzas which employed the use of a swimming pool. Matinees were given daily and these elaborate spectacles were usually in two parts with specialty numbers between. The first part was "A Yankee Circus on Mars," a musical extravaganza in two scenes featuring Bessie McCoy and Marceline, a famous clown who was popular in London. The second part was "The Raiders," a war drama in two tableaux which featured the Plunging Horses.

Fritzi Scheff who had played earlier in the year in "Boccaccio," opened on Christmas night in "Mlle. Modiste," which proved to be the greatest triumph of her theatrical career. She made Victor Herbert's song, "Kiss Me Again," famous and played the Victor Herbert operetta through 1906 and 1907 and revived it in 1913 and 1929.

Edna May in "The Catch of the Season" turned out to be her

COURT OF THE GOLDEN FOUNTAIN in "A SOCIETY CIRCUS"
HIPPODROME EXTRAVAGANZA

LULU GLASER in
"MISS DOLLY DOLLARS"

KITTY GORDON in
"VERONIQUE"

RICHARD CARLE, MAY BOLEY in
"THE MAYOR OF TOKIO"

CYRIL SCOTT, EDITH SPEARE in
"THE PRINCE CHAP"

MARY MANNERING, JAMES K. HACKETT in
"THE WALLS OF JERICHO"

MARCELINE

MAXINE ELLIOTT, CHARLES CHERRY in
"HER GREAT MATCH"

PERCITA WEST, ROBERT EDESON (Left) in
"STRONGHEART"

WILLIAM COURTENAY, VIRGINIA HARNED in
"LA BELLE MARSEILLAISE"

BLANCHE RING

last appearance on the American stage. She went to England, was London's pet for a few years, then married millionaire Oscar Lewisohn and retired.

James McIntyre and Thomas K. Heath, two clever blackface comedians who worked together as a team for over half a century, were delighting their admirers in "The Ham Tree," a musical vaudeville which served them off and on for over sixteen years. A young juggler named W. C. Fields was in their cast for two of those years.

Among the other musicals were "Fantana" with Jefferson De Angelis, Adele Ritchie, Julia Sanderson and Douglas Fairbanks; Frank Daniels in "Sergeant Brue" with Blanche Ring and Sallie Fisher; Sam Bernard in "That Rollicking Girl" with Hattie Williams, Edna Goodrich and Eugene O'Brien; Raymond Hitchcock in "Easy Dawson" with Flora Zabelle and John Bunny who became famous as an early silent film comedian; Lulu Glaser in "Miss Dolly Dollars" with Ralph Herz, her husband, and Carter De Havén; Max and Gus Rogers in "The Roger Brothers in Ireland;" Marie Cahill in "Moonshine;" Eddie Foy in "The Earl and the Girl;" De Wolf Hopper in "Happyland" with Marguerite Clark; Richard Carle in "The Mayor of Tokio;" and "Veronique" which introduced two English beauties, Kitty Gordon and Valli Valli, to American audiences.

MARGUERITE CLARK in
"HAPPYLAND"

MARGARET ANGLIN

HENRY E. DIXEY

43

BEATRICE AGNEW, ETHEL BARRYMORE, BRUCE McRAE, JOHN BARRYMORE in
"ALICE SIT-BY-THE-FIRE"

W. C. FIELDS in
"THE HAM TREE"

JAMES McINTYRE and THOMAS K. HEATH in
"THE HAM TREE"

MAUDE ADAM
"OP-O'-ME-TH"

OLGA NETHERSOLE in
"CARMEN"

SAM BERNARD in
"THE ROLLICKING GIRL"

MASTER GABRIEL in
"BUSTER BROWN"

FRANCIS WILSO
"COUSIN BILL"

44

EDNA MAY in
"THE CATCH OF THE SEASON"

CHAUNCEY OLCOTT with MARY, LOTTIE and JACK PICKFORD in
"EDMUND BURKE"

FAY TEMPLETON

VICTOR MOORE, DONALD BRIAN, FAY TEMPLETON in
"FORTY-FIVE MINUTES FROM BROADWAY"

VICTOR MOORE

CLARA LIPMAN, LOUIS MANN in
"JULIE BONBON"

1906 The first night of the New Year saw three openings, all of them were successful. They were George M. Cohan's "Forty-five Minutes From Broadway" with Fay Templeton, Victor Moore and Donald Brian; "Julie Bonbon" a comedy written by Clara Lipman who also starred in it with Louis Mann, her husband; and "Twiddle-Twaddle" a musical revue starring Joe Weber and Marie Dressler and with Trixie Friganza and Aubrey Boucicault.

The next week an adaptation of G. B. Shaw's novel "Cashel Byron's Profession" was produced by Henry B. Harris with James J. Corbett, heavyweight champion, playing the prize fighter and Margaret Wycherly in the cast. Shaw's "Arms and the Man," which had first been seen by New Yorkers in 1894 with Richard Mansfield and Beatrice Cameron and was the first Shaw play ever presented in America, was revived with Arnold Daly and Chrystal Herne.

"Charley's Aunt," which had been written by Brandon Thomas, an obscure London actor, and which had its original American presentation in 1893, was revived with Etienne Girardot playing the role he created originally.

Rose Stahl, who had been playing the two previous years in a one-act vaudeville sketch, "The Chorus Lady," was appearing in a four act version of it written especially for her by James Forbes. It was her greatest success and she played it until 1911.

Margaret Anglin and Henry Miller were together again in "The Great Divide." It was a smash hit and so was "The Man of the Hour" which starred George Fawcett. Frances Starr was coming into prominence under David Belasco's guiding hand in "The Rose of the Rancho" which he had written for her.

Edward Abeles was debuting as a star in a comedy, "Brewster's Millions," and Carlotta Nillson made the hit of her career in "The Three of Us." Mr. Abeles was supported by Mary Ryan

JOHN DREW, MARGARET ILLINGTON in
"HIS HOUSE IN ORDER"

JOE WEBER, MARIE DRESSLER in
"TWIDDLE-TWADDLE"

ELLIS JEFFREYS, FRANK WORTHING in
"THE FASCINATING MR. VANDERVELDT"

MARGARET WYCHERLY, JAMES J. CORBETT, KATE LESTER in
"CASHEL BYRON'S PROFESSION"

HENRY MILLER, HENRY B. WALTHALL, MARGARET ANGLIN in
"THE GREAT DIVIDE"

45

MME. NAZIMOVA

GEORGE FAWCETT

while Miss Nillson's leading man was Henry Kolker. Henry Woodruff also reached stardom in a popular play, "Brown of Harvard." Laura Hope Crews, his leading lady, was later replaced by Willette Kershaw.

H. B. Irving, son of Henry Irving, was over from England with Dorothea Baird, his wife, making their first American stage appearance in repertory.

J. Forbes-Robertson and Gertrude Elliott were appearing in the first New York production of Shaw's "Caesar and Cleopatra" for a run of 49 performances. Viola Allen was appearing in the rarely produced Shakespeare play, "Cymbeline."

Other stars and their attractions were John Drew with Margaret Illington in "His House in Order," Grace George in "Clothes," Eleanor Robson with H. B. Warner in "Nurse Marjorie," Mrs. Fiske with John Mason and George Arliss in "The New York Idea," Otis Skinner in "The Duel," William Gillette with Marie Doro in "Clarice," Ellis Jeffreys and Frank Worthing in "The Fascinating Mr. VanderVeldt" Dorothy Donnelly with Julia Dean in "The Little Gray Lady," Francis Wilson in "The Mountain Climbers," William H. Crane in "The Price of Money," Jessie Millward with Richard Bennett and Doris Keane in "The

HENRY WOODRUFF in
"BROWN OF HARVARD"

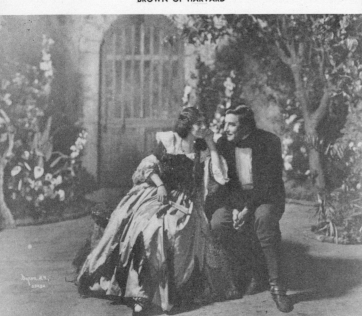

FRANCES STARR, CHARLES RICHMAN in
"THE ROSE OF THE RANCHO"

EDWARD ABELES in
"BREWSTER'S MILLIONS"

MINNIE DUPREE in
"THE ROAD TO YESTERDAY"

HERBERT KELCEY   EFFIE SHANNON

Hypocrites," Minnie Dupree in "The Road to Yesterday," William Farnum with Adelaide Keim in "The Prince of India," Chauncey Olcott in "Eileen Asthore," Effie Shannon and Herbert Kelcey in "The Daughters of Men" and William Collier in "Caught in the Rain." None of these plays were particularly outstanding but they served as vehicles for the stars.

Nat C. Goodwin was appearing with his new wife, Edna Goodrich, in a farce, "The Genius" while Lillian Russell was starring in her first play without music, "Barbara's Millions." Raymond Hitchcock was appearing in "The Gallop," a farce without music.

The fall saw two productions of "The Kreutzer Sonata" on the boards. One starred Blanche Walsh, the other Bertha Kalich.

In 1905, Paul Orleneff came over from Moscow and with his company inaugurated the first Russian theatre on the lower East Side. Mme. Nasimoff was the leading actress of the Orleneff company and she created a sensation. Henry Miller brought her uptown. On November 13, 1906, with her name slightly altered, Alla Nazimova made her debut on the English-speaking stage in "Hedda Gabler" and soon she had joined the ranks of the truly great actresses of the American theatre.

Among the musical comedy stars, Elsie Janis, who as Little

ROSE STAHL in
"THE CHORUS LADY"

VIOLA ALLEN in
"CYMBELINE"   CARLOTTA NILLSON in
"THE THREE OF US"   WILLIAM ELLIOTT, ETIENNE GIRARDOT,
FRANK HOLLINS in "CHARLEY'S AUNT"

WILLETTE KERSHAW   DORIS KEANE   JACK HENDERSON   MARY RYAN   HENRY MILLER   LAURA HOPE CREWS   CLARA LIPMAN

AUBREY BOUCICAULT   GERTRUDE ELLIOTT as CLEOPATRA   "CAESAR AND CLEOPATRA"   J. FORBES-ROBERTSON as CAESAR   OTIS SKINNER in "THE DUEL"

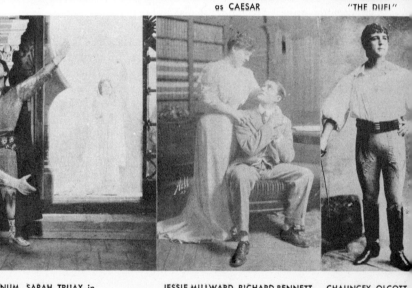

NAT C. GOODWIN in "THE GENIUS"   HATTIE WILLIAMS, TOM WISE in "THE LITTLE CHERUB"   WILLIAM FARNUM, SARAH TRUAX in "THE PRINCE OF INDIA"   JESSIE MILLWARD, RICHARD BENNETT in "THE HYPOCRITES"   CHAUNCEY OLCOTT "EILEEN ASTHORE"

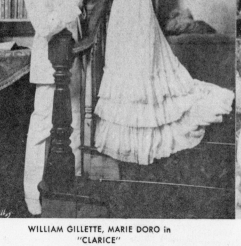

48 H. B. IRVING   WILLIAM COLLIER, NANETTE COMSTOCK in "CAUGHT IN THE RAIN"   WILLIAM GILLETTE, MARIE DORO in "CLARICE"   GRACE GEORGE, ROBERT T. HAINES in "CLOTHES"   BLANCHE WALSH in "THE KREUTZER SONATA"

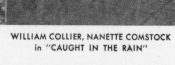
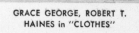

MIRIAM NESBITT   CHRYSTAL HERNE   GEORGE M. COHAN   MARGARET WYCHERLY   DONALD BRIAN   ADELAIDE KEIM   ADELE RITCHIE

ANNA HELD in
"THE PARISIAN MODEL"

MONTGOMERY and STONE in
"THE RED MILL"

MARIE CAHILL, WILLIAM COURTLEIGH in
"MARRYING MARY"

JULIA SANDERSON, RICHARD GOLDEN in
"THE TOURISTS"

VALESKA SURATT, JACK GARDNER, IRENE BENTLEY,
VAN RENNSSELAER WHEELER, CHRISTIE Mac DONALD, IGNACIO
MARTINETTI, RICHARD F. CARROLL in "THE BELLE OF MAYFAIR"

SAM BERNARD, GEORGIA CAINE in
"THE RICH MR. HOGGENHEIMER"

ELSIE JANIS in
"THE VANDERBILT CUP"

LINA ABARBANELL in
"THE STUDENT KING"

Elsie had become famous in vaudeville for her imitations of the theatre's great, was starring at the age of sixteen for the first time on Broadway in "The Vanderbilt Cup." George M. Cohan wrote and composed "George Washington, Jr." for himself, Adele Ritchie had a good engagement in "The Social Whirl" and Blanche Ring was winning new admirers in "His Honor the Mayor." Other musicals popular at this time were "The Little Cherub" with Hattie Williams and Tom Wise, "The Tourists" with Julia Sanderson, Grace LaRue, Jack Henderson and Vera Michelena, "Marrying Mary" starring Marie Cahill, "About Town" with Lew Fields, Edna Wallace Hopper, Lawrence Grossmith, Louise Dresser, George Beban, Jack Norworth, Mae Murray and Vernon Castle part of the impressive cast, Richard Carle assisted by Bessie McCoy and Adele Rowland in "The Spring Chicken," Sam Bernard in "The Rich Mr. Hoggenheimer," James T. Powers in "The Blue Moon," Anna Held in "The Parisian Model," "The Belle of Mayfair" with Irene Bentley, Christie MacDonald, Valeska Suratt and Bessie Clayton, and Lina Abarbanell making her debut in light opera in "The Student King."

MABEL TALIAFERRO, MALCOLM WILLIAMS in
"POLLY OF THE CIRCUS"

1907 The most famous of all the attractions produced in 1907 was "The Merry Widow." It opened October 21st at the New Amsterdam Theatre and ran 416 performances. There were many touring companies of the Lehar operetta in America, and it played in all the capitols of the world. It is still revived nearly every year. In the original production, Ethel Jackson played the title role of Sonia while Donald Brian as Prince Danilo made the hit of his career. During the New York run, Sonia was also played by Lois Ewell, Lina Abarbanell, Rosemary Glosz, Georgia Caine and Ruby Dale.

Among the outstanding dramatic plays were: "The Witching Hour," the Augustus Thomas play about telepathy with John Mason; "Salomy Jane," Paul Armstrong's play based on a Bret Harte story which starred Eleanor Robson supported by H. B. Warner and Holbrook Blinn; "The Thief" with Kyrle Bellew and Margaret Illington; "The Warrens of Virginia," a play written by William C. de Mille and with his brother Cecil in the cast which included Charlotte Walker, Frank Keenan, Emma Dunn, Ralph Kellard and little Gladys Smith, using the name Mary Pickford on playbills for the first time.

50

DONALD BRIAN and ETHEL JACKSON in
"THE MERRY WIDOW"

MARGARET ILLINGTON, KYRLE BELLEW in
"THE THIEF"

JOHN DREW, BILLIE BURKE in
"MY WIFE"

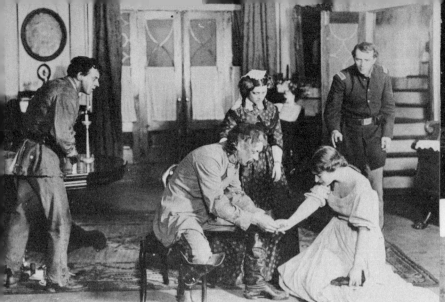

CECIL B. DeMILLE, FRANK KEENAN, EMMA DUNN, CHARLOTTE WALKER, CHARLES WALDRON in
"THE WARRENS OF VIRGINIA"

RICHARD STORY, CHARLOTTE WALKER,
MARY PICKFORD in
"THE WARRENS OF VIRGINIA"

ROBERT WARWICK, VIRGINIA HARNED in
"ANNA KARENINA"

PAULINE FREDERICK, FRANCIS WILSON in
"WHEN KNIGHTS WERE BOLD"

WALTER HAMPDEN, ALLA NAZIMOVA in
"THE MASTER BUILDER"

JAMES SEELEY, H. B. WARNER, ELEANOR ROBSON, RALPH DELMORE,
HOLBROOK BLINN, EARLE BROWN in "SALOMY JANE"

Mabel Taliaferro was having her greatest success with "Polly of the Circus." Her sister, Edith Taliaferro, played the role in one of the road companies, and so did Ida St. Leon who was in the original cast.

Billie Burke, who had made her music hall debut at the age of fifteen in England, made her first professional appearance in her native land as John Drew's leading lady in "My Wife."

"The Round Up" was one of the comedy hits of the year. It made a star of Maclyn Arbuckle and man and wife of the romantic leads, Julia Dean and Orme Caldara.

Arnold Daly temporarily forsook Shaw for Rida Johnson Young's comedy, "The Boys of Company B." In his cast were Frances Ring, Howard Estabrook, Mack Sennett and Florence Nash making her New York debut. Later John Barrymore played his first major role when he replaced Mr. Daly. Meanwhile sister Ethel had a short session in John Galsworthy's "The Silver Box." Grace George with Robert T. Haines and Frank Worthing appeared in "Divorcons." Francis Wilson was occupied with Pauline Frederick in a farce, "When Knights Were Bold." Virginia Harned was starring in "Anna Karenina," a drama based on Tolstoi's novel, with Robert Warwick and Elliott Dexter. Dustin Farnum was in "The Ranger," and his leading lady was

JOHN MASON, GEORGE NASH in
"THE WITCHING HOUR"

MACLYN ARBUCKLE, JULIA DEAN in
"THE ROUND UP"

ELEANOR ROBSON as
"SALOMY JANE"

H. B. WARNER, ELEANOR ROBSON in
"SALOMY JANE"

51

ORME CALDARA ERMETE NOVELLI FRANCES RING JOHN BARRYMORE MARY BOLAND FRANK WORTHING JOE E. HOWARD

GRACE LARUE

FRANCES RING, ARNOLD DALY, MORGAN COMAN, FLORENCE NASH in
"THE BOYS OF COMPANY B"

JACK STOREY, MAY ROBSON in
"THE REJUVENATION OF AUNT MARY"

JULIA MARLOWE, E. H. SOTHERN in
"JOHN THE BAPTIST"

ALLA NAZIMOVA in
"COMTESSE COQUETTE"

DAVID WARFIELD in
"A GRAND ARMY MAN"

MARIE DORO, C. AUBREY SMITH in
"THE MORALS OF MARCUS"

BEN GREET

JEFFERSON DE ANGELIS, BLANCHE
RING, ALEXANDER CARR in
"THE GAY WHITE WAY"

Mary Boland who had caused favorable comment in her first New York appearance when she took over the feminine lead opposite Robert Edeson later in the run of "Strongheart" the year before. Edeson, meanwhile, had relinquished that part to Edgar Selwyn and was appearing in "Classmates."

May Robson was starring for the first time in "The Rejuvenation of Aunt Mary," a comedy which served her for many seasons before the films claimed her. Marie Doro, a fragile lovely beauty, reached stardom this year under Charles Frohman's guiding hand. Her vehicle was "The Morals of Marcus."

David Warfield, who had built up a large following with "The Auctioneer" and "The Music Master," had a moderate success with "A Grand Army Man."

Clara Bloodgood was playing the last role of her short but brilliant career in Clyde Fitch's "The Truth." The play opened in January and was not a success, but in the fall she decided to take it on tour. While in Baltimore, she shot herself in a hotel room just before an evening performance. The motives for her suicide were never clearly established.

Ellen Terry, beloved English actress who had celebrated her fiftieth anniversary on the stage the year before, was appearing in "The Good Hope" and in the first American presentation of Shaw's "Captain Brassbound's Conversion." Her

AUDE FULTON   FLORA ZABELLE   FRANK DANIELS   CARRIE DE MAR   EDDIE FOY   EMMA CARUS   JULIA DEAN

JAMES CAREW, ELLEN TERRY in
"CAPTAIN BRASSBOUND'S CONVERSION"

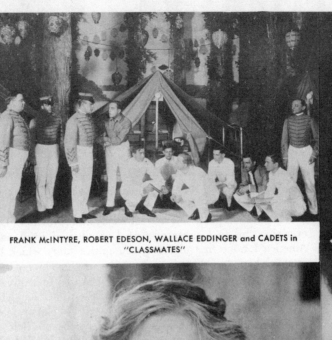

FRANK McINTYRE, ROBERT EDESON, WALLACE EDDINGER and CADETS in
"CLASSMATES"

ELLEN TERRY

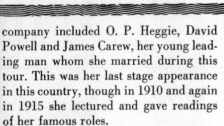

CLARA BLOODGOOD

EDGAR SELWYN in   ETHEL BARRYMORE in
"STRONGHEART"   "THE SILVER BOX"

company included O. P. Heggie, David Powell and James Carew, her young leading man whom she married during this tour. This was her last stage appearance in this country, though in 1910 and again in 1915 she lectured and gave readings of her famous roles.

Mme. Nazimova was appearing in Ibsen's "A Doll's House" and "The Master Builder" in English for the first time. New Yorkers also saw her in "Comtesse Coquette" and "The Comet."

Julia Marlowe and E. H. Sothern had added "John the Baptist," "Jeanne D'Arc" and "The Sunken Bell" to their Shakespearean repertoire, while Robert B. Mantell was playing in "Richelieu" as well as six of the Bard's classics. Ben Greet was over from England also giving a series of Shakespearean plays as well as "Everyman." His company included Sybil Thorndike, Fritz Leiber and Sydney Greenstreet.

Sam S. and Lee Shubert had imported Ermete Novelli, famous Italian actor, and he made his first New York appearance in a series of plays which included "Hamlet," "King Lear," "Othello" and "Oedipus Rex."

Richard Mansfield was playing an engagement in "Peer Gynt" which he later added to his repertoire. His role of Baron Chevrial in "A Parisian Romance" was the last he ever played on the New Amsterdam Theatre stage March 23, 1907.

DUSTIN FARNUM, MARY BOLAND in
"THE RANGER"

FREDERICK BOND, ADELE RITCHIE, LOUIS
HARRISON in "FASCINATING FLORA"

ADELAIDE NOWAK, RICHARD MANSFIELD in
"PEER GYNT"

HARRY LAUDER

MABEL HITE, JOHN SLAVIN in
"A KNIGHT FOR A DAY"

LEW FIELDS, CONNIE EDISS in
"THE GIRL BEHIND THE COUNTER"

FANNIE WARD

LOUIS MANN, LOTTA FAUST in
"THE WHITE HEN"

He died August 30, 1907, in his summer home in New London, Conn.

Harry Lauder, who was a great music hall favorite in London ever since his first appearance in December of 1900, came to America for the first of many triumphant tours which helped establish his international reputation.

On July 8th, Florenz Ziegfeld, Jr., who had been presenting his wife, Anna Held, in musicals, produced the "Ziegfeld Follies of 1907," and it was the first of a series of elaborate revues that gained him theatrical immortality as the glorifier of the American girl. In the cast were Harry Watson, Jr., Mlle. Dazie, Emma Carus, Grace LaRue and Helen Broderick.

Other musical attractions included: Louis Mann in "The White Hen" with Lotta Faust and Louise Gunning; Frank Daniels in "The Tatooed Man;" "The Land of Nod" with Mabel Barrison, Joseph E. Howard and Carrie De Mar; Eddie Foy in "The Orchid" with Trixie Friganza, Maude Fulton and Irene Franklin, upcomers in the cast; Adele Ritchie in "Fascinating Flora;" "The Time, The Place and The Girl" which was a bigger hit in Chicago than New York with Cecil Lean and Florence Holbrook in the leads; "A Yankee Tourist" with Raymond Hitchcock, Flora Zabelle and Wallace Beery of film fame in the cast; "The Dairymaids" with Julia Sanderson; Gus and Max Rogers had their last engagement together in "The Roger Brothers in Panama;" Lew Fields in "The Girl Behind the Counter" with Connie Ediss, Lotta Faust, Louise Dresser and Vernon Castle; "The Gay White Way" with Jefferson De Angelis, Blanche Ring and Alexander Carr; Elsie Janis, still the youngest star on Broadway, was in "The Hoyden;" and "Miss Hook of Holland" with Christie MacDonald, Tom Wise and Bertram Wallis.

JULIA SANDERSON, GEORGE GREGORY in
"THE DAIRYMAIDS

CHRISTIE MAC DONALD, BERTRAM WALLIS in
"MISS HOOK OF HOLLAND"

CECIL LEAN, GEORGIE DREW MENDUM, TOM CAMERON, FLORENCE HOLBROOK in
"THE TIME, THE PLACE AND THE GIRL"

ELSIE JANIS, ARTHUR STANFORD in
"THE HOYDEN"

MAUDE ADAMS in
"THE JESTER"

E. PEYTON CARTER, RICHARD BENNETT, MAUDE ADAMS, FRED TYLER, DAVID TORRENCE in
"WHAT EVERY WOMAN KNOWS"

BLANCHE BATES in
"THE FIGHTING HOPE"

MRS. FISKE in
"SALVATION NELL"

1908 With the great success of "The Merry Widow," it was inevitable that it would be burlesqued. On January 2, 1908, "The Merry Widow Burlesque" opened a successful run. Lulu Glaser played the widow and Joe Weber, Peter F. Dailey, Charles J. Ross, Bessie Clayton and Albert Hart were prominent in the cast.

A week later Maude Adams opened at the Empire in "The Jester," a poetic drama that was not popular. Just before Christmas, however, she returned to the Empire with a new comedy by James Barrie, "What Every Woman Knows," and scored one of her greatest hits. Her leading man was Richard Bennett.

Mary Boland became John Drew's leading lady in Somerset Maugham's "Jack Straw" while his former vis-a-vis, Billie Burke, became a star in "Love Watches," her second Broadway role. Ethel Barrymore was also appearing in a Somerset Maugham comedy, "Lady Frederick." William Gillette with Constance Collier, Pauline Frederick and Arthur Byron in his company was appearing in Henri Bernstein's play, "Samson." Among the other Charles Frohman stars, Otis Skinner reaped much praise with "The Honor of the Family;" William H. Crane pleased the customers in a George Ade comedy, "Father and the Boys;" May Irwin was playing in George Ade's one-actor, "Mrs. Peckam's Carouse," as a curtain raiser for Frohman's production of "The Mollusc;" William Collier was in a farce he wrote with J. Hartley Manners called "The Patriot" with his son, William Collier, Jr., billed as "Buster" Collier, making his acting debut; Edward Sheldon, having just graduated from Harvard, was having, at twenty-two, his first play, "Salvation Nell," produced. Mrs. Fiske played the title role and Holbrook Blinn was her leading man.

JOE WEBER, LULU GLASER in
"THE MERRY WIDOW BURLESQUE"

JOHN DREW, MARY BOLAND in
"JACK STRAW"

WALTER HAMPDEN, ARTHUR LEWIS, TYRONE POWER in
"THE SERVANT IN THE HOUSE"

BILLIE BURKE, W. H. CROMPTON in
"LOVE WATCHES"

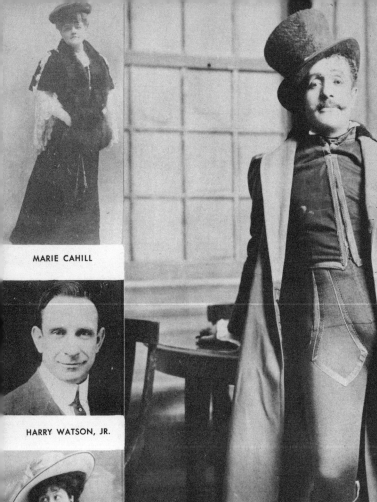

MARIE CAHILL

HARRY WATSON, JR.

LOTTA FAUST

OTIS SKINNER in "THE HONOR OF THE FAMILY"

DOROTHY DORR, EDWIN STEVENS,
PAUL McALLISTER in "THE DEVIL"

"THE HONOR OF THE FAMILY"

Charles Rann Kennedy's play, "The Servant in the House," with Walter Hampden, Edith Wynne Matthison and Tyrone Power was causing much comment. Blanche Bates had a hit in "The Fighting Hope" while James K. Hackett revived one of his earlier successes, "The Prisoner of Zenda."

Olga Nethersole returned for another season of repertoire which included "Adrienne Lecouvreur," "Carmen," "Sapho," "Magda," "Camille" and "The Second Mrs. Tanqueray." Mrs. Patrick Campbell gave nine performances of Sophocles' tragedy, "Electra."

William Hodge reached star status and had the hit of his career in "The Man From Home" by Booth Tarkington and Harry Leon Wilson. It served him for five years. "The Traveling Salesman" by James Forbes was another comedy hit and it established Frank McIntyre as a star.

An amusing event was the arrival of two productions of Ferenc Molnar's play, "The Devil," on the night of August 18th. Harrison Grey Fiske and Henry W. Savage both claimed they had the rights, so they both produced the play. The Fiske production had George Arliss in the title role and it ran for 175 performances. Edwin Stevens played the lead in the Savage version which lasted for 87 performances, and in the cast was Theodosia de Cappet who later became Theda Bara, the famous screen vamp.

WILLIAM HODGE in "THE MAN FROM HOME"
IDA VERNON (seated), OLIVE WYNDHAM, HASSARD SHORT (extreme right)

HAMILTON REVELLE, GEORGE ARLISS, GRACE ELLISTON in "THE DEVIL"

"MISS INNOCENCE"

Lillian Russell turned her attention to drama and achieved a great personal success with "Wildfire." In her cast were Thurston Hall and a youngster named Ernest Truex. Irving Cummings was another young actor in her support who gained fame as a silent screen star and later as a film director. William A. Brady was having great success with "A Gentleman From Mississippi," and it helped the prestige of both Thomas A. Wise and Douglas Fairbanks. "Paid In Full," a drama with Tully Marshall, Oza Waldrop and Lillian Albertson, was also a hit. E. H. Sothern appeared in a series of plays including a revival of one of his father's great successes, "Our American Cousin."

Edgar Selwyn, who was establishing himself firmly as a leading man, wrote and acted in "Pierre of the Plains" with Elsie Ferguson, but it was only moderately successful. Other moderate successes were: Louis Mann in "The Man Who Stood Still," Henry E. Dixey in an Edith Ellis comedy, "Mary Jane's Pa," Wilton Lackaye in "The Battle," and a Clyde Fitch comedy, "Girls," starring Charles Cherry.

In the musical comedy field, William Kolb and Max Dill, who had been called the Weber and Fields of the West Coast, tried their luck on Broadway in "Lonesome Town." Maude Lambert and Georgia O'Ramey were in the cast. An operetta called "A Waltz Dream" opened with Edward Johnson in the lead. This same

ANNA HELD in "MISS INNOCENCE"

GEORGE W. MONROE

VERNON CASTLE

FRANK McINTYRE

ERNEST TRUEX, LILLIAN RUSSELL, FRANK SHERIDAN in "WILDFIRE"

MLLE. DAZIE

57

RICHARD CARLE

ADELINE GENEE in "THE SOUL KISS"

LILLIAN ALBERTSON, TULLY MARSHALL in "PAID IN FULL"

MARGARET DALE, WILLIAM H. CRANE in "FATHER AND THE BOYS"

LINA ABARBANE

ROBERT EDESON

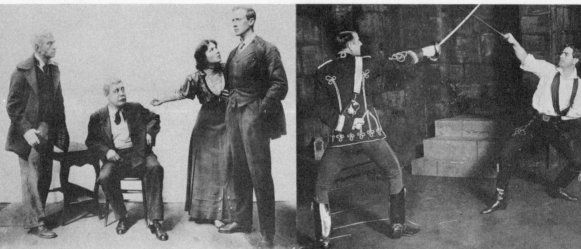

E. M. HOLLAND, WILTON LACKAYE, JOSEPHINE VICTOR, H. B. WARNER in "THE BATTLE"

ARTHUR HOOPS, JAMES K. HACKETT in "THE PRISONER OF ZENDA"

EDGAR SELWYN

CONSTANCE COLLIER

MABEL BARRISON   HOLBROOK BLINN   MAY IRWIN   IRVING CUMMINGS   TRIXIE FRIGANZA   RICHARD BENNETT   BUSTER COLLIER   JOHN BUNNY

WILLIAM GILLETTE, CONSTANCE COLLIER in "SAMSON"

58 GERTRUDE COGHLAN

Mr. Johnson went on to greater fame as a star and the head of the Metropolitan Opera Company. Adeline Genee, a dainty Danish dancer, made her first New York appearance and scored in "The Soul Kiss." Her support included Ralph C. Herz, Florence Holbrook and Cecil Lean. Williams and Walker were starring in "Bandanna Land;" Edna Wallace Hopper was in the Cohan musical, "Fifty Miles From Boston;" Sam Bernard aided by Ethel Levey, Ada Lewis and Zelda Sears had success with "Nearly A Hero;" George M. Cohan and His Royal Family, as he billed them, were reunited in "The Yankee Prince;" "Three Twins" with Clifton Crawford and Bessie McCoy as the Yama Yama Girl was a big hit; Ziegfeld produced "Miss Innocence" with Anna Held, and his second revue, "Ziegfeld Follies of 1908," with Lucy Weston, Barney Bernard, Nora Bayes, Grace LaRue, Mlle. Dazie, Jack Norworth, Harry Watson, Jr., Mae Murray, Florence Walton, Rosie Green and Gertrude Vanderbilt in the cast; the Shuberts with Lew Fields had a hit in "The Mimic World" with Lotta Faust, Charles King, Vernon Castle, Roy Atwell and George W. Monroe; Cohan and Harris Minstrels

ACK NORWORTH | GERTRUDE COGHLIN, FRANK McINTYRE in "THE TRAVELING SALESMAN" | GLADYS HANSON, E. H. SOTHERN in "OUR AMERICAN COUSIN" | EDGAR SELWYN, ELSIE FERGUSON in "PIERRE OF THE PLAINS" | MARY MANNERING

MARGARET DALE

NORA BAYES

JAMES BLAKELEY, GERTIE MILLAR, LIONEL MACKINDER in "THE GIRLS OF GOTTENBURG" | HENRY E. DIXEY, GRETCHEN HARTMAN in "MARY JANE'S PA" | EDWARD JOHNSON, SOPHIE BRANDT in "THE WALTZ DREAM"

MAE MURRAY | RALPH C. HERZ | TYRONE POWER | OLIVE WYNDHAM | JOSEPH CAWTHORN | OZA WALDROP | EDWIN STEVENS | BILLIE BURKE

BESSIE McCOY

with George Evans, Eddie Leonard and Julian Eltinge in the cast was a quick failure and proved that this type of entertainment was on the wane; Hattie Williams in a musical, "Fluffy Ruffles," was supported by John Bunny and Violet Heming, making her New York debut; Master Gabriel with Joseph Cawthorn and Billy B. Van was in "Little Nemo," another musical based on a comic strip character; "The Girls of Gottenburg" featured Gertie Millar, an English favorite; Marie Cahill was in "The Boys and Betty;" Fritzi Scheff was appearing in "The Prima Donna," a comic opera by Victor Herbert and Henry Blossom; Eddie Foy was in "Mr. Hamlet of Broadway;" Richard Carle was in "Mary's Lamb;" Mabel Barrison starred in "The Blue Mouse;" "Sporting Days" was the spectacular musical production at the Hippodrome; in "The American Idea" cast were Trixie Friganza and George Beban; Louise Gunning was in "Marcelle," and "The Queen of the Moulin Rouge" had an interesting cast with Carter De Haven, Flora Parker, Patricia Collinge and Francis X. Bushman, who became an early screen idol.

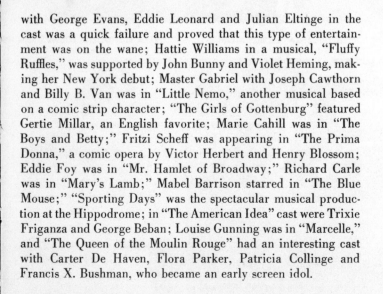

LOLA MAY, TOM WISE, DOUGLAS FAIRBANKS in "THE GENTLEMAN FROM MISSISSIPPI"

CLIFTON CRAWFORD

ELIZABETH BRICE, FRANKLYN ROBERTS, NEVA AYMAR, ETHEL LEVEY, SAM BERNARD, BURRELL BARBARETTI, DAISY GREENE, SAMUEL EDWARDS, ZELDA SEARS in "NEARLY A HERO"

GRACE LA RUE, NORA BAYES, LUCY WESTON, ANNABELLE WHITFORD in "ZIEGFELD FOLLIES OF 1908"

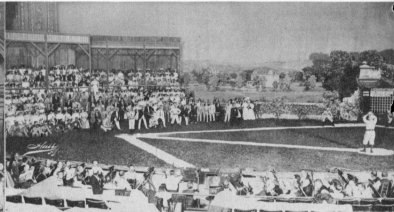

GEORGE M. COHAN AND CHORUS in "THE YANKEE PRINCE"

BASEBALL GAME in "SPORTING DAYS" AT HIPPODROME

HARRY CORSON CLARK, LOTTA FAUST in "THE MIMIC WORLD"

MABEL BARRISON, HARRY CONOR in "THE BLUE MOUSE"

TRIXIE FRIGANZA, GEORGE BEBAN in "THE AMERICAN IDEA"

FRANK RUSHWORTH, LOUISE GUNNING "MARCELLE"

FRITZI SCHEFF

RUTH MAYCLIFFE, ZELDA SEARS, LAURA NELSON HALL, CHARLES CHERRY in "GIRLS"

GERTRUDE VANDERBILT

HELEN WARE, EDMUND BREESE in
"THE THIRD DEGREE"

ELEANOR ROBSON in
"THE DAWN OF TOMORROW"

JOSEPH KILGOUR, FRANCES STARR in
"THE EASIEST WAY"

J. FORBES-ROBERTSON, HAIDEE WRIGHT in
"THE PASSING OF THE THIRD FLOOR BACK"

MARY RYAN, JOHN BARRYMORE in
"THE FORTUNE HUNTER"

MARGUERITE CLARK in
"THE BEAUTY SPOT"

LOTTA FAUST in
"THE MIDNIGHT SONS"

1909 Eugene Walter's "The Easiest Way" was the first play of note to arrive in 1909. It opened January 19th and with its heroine, Frances Starr, won acclaim and served Miss Starr for two years. She revived it in 1921.

The next week Eleanor Robson arrived in "The Dawn of To-morrow" and also met with success. This was Miss Robson's final appearance on the professional stage. In 1910 she married August Belmont, millionaire banker, and retired at the height of her career. In recent years she has been active in the affairs of the Metropolitan Opera Guild.

Other popular plays of the year were: "The Third Degree" with Helen Ware, Edmund Breese and Wallace Eddinger, "The Climax," "The Fortune Hunter" with John Barrymore scoring his first hit, "The Passing of the Third Floor Back" with J. Forbes-Robertson, "Seven Days," "Is Matrimony A Failure?" with Jane Cowl playing her first important role; "Arsene Lupin" with William Courtenay and Doris Keane; and "The City" with Tully Marshall and Mary Nash.

The biggest hits in the musical comedy field were "The Chocolate Soldier," "The Dollar Princess" with Donald Brian, "The Midnight Sons" with Lotta Faust, "The Beauty Spot" with Jefferson De Angelis and Marguerite Clark and "Havana" with James T. Powers.

Among the stars, Nance O'Neil, ably supported by Julia Dean and Leo Ditrichstein, had great success under David Belasco's management with "The Lily;" Robert Hilliard was in the hit of his career. "A Fool There Was;" Margaret Anglin had suc-

61

VIOLA ALLEN in
"THE WHITE SISTER"

LILLIAN RUSSELL, FREDERICK TRUESDELL in
"THE WIDOW'S MIGHT"

LAURETTE TAYLOR, GEORGE FAWCETT in
"THE GREAT JOHN GANTON"

DUSTIN FARNUM in
"CAMEO KIRBY"

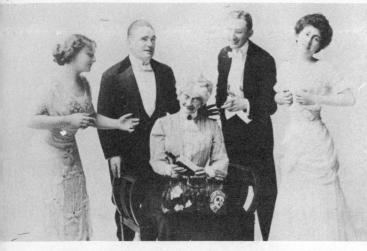

FLORENCE REED, HERBERT CORTHELL, LUCILLE LA VERNE, ALAN POLLOCK,
GEORGIA O'RAMEY in "SEVEN DAYS"

cess with "The Awakening of Helena Richie;" Viola Allen was supported by James O'Neill and William Farnum in "The White Sister;" John Drew still had Mary Boland as his leading lady in "Inconsistant George;" Guy Bates Post in "The Bridge;" Fannie Ward in "The New Lady Bantock;" Kyrle Bellew with Gladys Hanson and Eugene O'Brien was in "The Builder of Bridges;" Cyril Scott made the hit of his life in "The Lottery Man;" Grace George was in "A Woman's Way;" George Fawcett with Laurette Taylor scored in "The Great John Ganton."

Other stars and their vehicles were Henrietta Crosman in "Sham," Olga Nethersole in "The Writing on the Wall," Bertha Galland in "The Return of Eve," William Collier in a revival of "The Man from Mexico," Maxine Elliott in "The Chaperon," Sidney Drew in "Billy," Walker Whiteside in "The Melting Pot," Lillian Russell in "The Widow's Might," Mabel Taliaferro billed as Nell for a time in "Springtime," Constance Collier in "Israel," Mildred Holland in "A Royal Divorce," William Faversham and Julie Opp in "Herod," Marie Tempest in "Penelope," Dustin Farnum in "Cameo Kirby," Mrs. Leslie Carter in "Kassa," Francis Wilson in "The Bachelor's Baby," Robert Edeson in "The

WILLIAM COURTENAY, DORIS KEANE, SIDNEY HERBERT in
"ARSENE LUPIN"

ELSA MAXWELL

GUY BATES POST

SALLIE FISHER

CHRYSTAL HERNE, GRANT STEWART, WALKER WHITESIDE,
HENRY BERGMAN in "THE MELTING POT"

EVA TANGUAY

W. J. FERGUSON, LOUISE MACKINTOSH, JANE COWL,
FRANK WORTHING in "IS MATRIMONY A FAILURE?"

CYRIL SCOTT

BERTHA GALLAND in
"THE RETURN OF EVE"

CHRISTINE NORMAN, CONSTANCE COLLIER in
"ISRAEL"

VALLI VALLI, DONALD BRIAN in
"THE DOLLAR PRINCESS"

WILLIAM FAVERSHAM in
"HEROD"

Noble Spaniard" with Ann Murdock in a small role, and Marie Doro in "The Richest Girl" with Elsa Maxwell, famous international party giver, in a minor part.

Robert B. Mantell was having a successful season in repertory of plays that included Shakespeare's "King John" which had not been seen in New York since the early 'Seventies when Junius Brutus Booth, Jr., played it.

Elsie Ferguson was on her way to stardom in "Such A Little Queen." "Going Some" was a comedy hit and so were "The Girl From Rector's" and "The House Next Door" with J. E. Dodson and an upcoming young actress, Fania Marinoff. Another young actress, Ethel Clayton, who became a silent film star, was appearing in "His Name on the Door."

On November 6th, the New Theatre opened its doors. It was the nearest approach this country has come to a national theatre, having been built at great cost by thirty wealthy men. The enterprise was under the direction of Winthrop Ames and the Messrs. Shubert, and the opening bill of the repertory was "Antony and Cleopatra" starring E. H. Sothern and Julia Marlowe. Other plays of interest produced in repertory at the New Theatre were

WILLIAM LEWERS, LEONA WATSON, ALBERT BRUNING, EFFINGHAM PINTO in
"THE CLIMAX"

ELSIE JANIS

MILDRED HOLLAND

GLADYS HANSON, KYRLE BELLEW, EUGENE O'BRIEN in
"THE BUILDER OF BRIDGES"

ANN MURDOCK

JULIA DEAN, NANCE O'NEIL in
"THE LILY"

FANIA MARINOFF

FREDERICK ESMELTON, FRANK WORTHING, EVELYN
CARRINGTON, GRACE GEORGE, CHARLES STANLEY in
"A WOMAN'S WAY"

ETHEL CLAYTON

63

KATHARINE KAELRED, ROBERT HILLIARD in
"A FOOL THERE WAS"

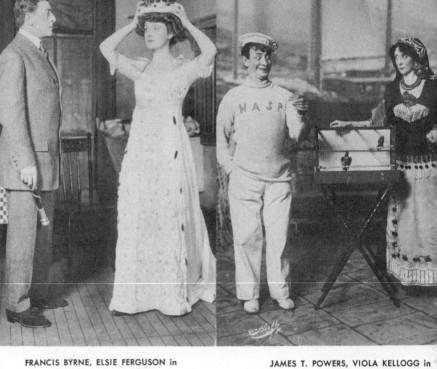

FRANCIS BYRNE, ELSIE FERGUSON in
"SUCH A LITTLE QUEEN"

JAMES T. POWERS, VIOLA KELLOGG in
"HAVANA"

"THE CHOCOLATE SOLDIER"

KITTY GORDON, SAM BERNARD in
"THE GIRL AND THE WIZARD"

JOHN FINDLAY, RAYMOND HACKETT, MARGARET
ANGLIN in "THE AWAKENING OF HELENA RICHIE"

CYRIL SCOTT, LOUISE GALLOWAY, JANET BEECHER, HELEN LOWELL,
MARY MAYO in "THE PRINCE CHAP"

"THE GIRL FROM RECTORS"

"A STUBBORN CINDERELLA"

64 HERBERT CORTHELL, WILLIAM HARRIGAN, MURIEL STARR, LAWRENCE
WHEAT, OZA WALDROP, WALTER JONES in "GOING SOME"

LOUISE DRESSER in
"THE CANDY SHOP"

ROBERT HOMANS, OSWALD YORKE, GUY BATES POST,
PEDRO DE CORDOBA in "THE NIGGER"

HELEN HAYES in
"OLD DUTCH"

JOHN BARRYMORE in
"A STUBBORN CINDERELLA"

FLORA ZABELLE, RAYMOND HITCHCOCK in
"THE MAN WHO OWNS BROADWAY"

ROBERT B. MANTELL as
"KING JOHN"

LEW FIELDS in "OLD DUTCH"
HELEN HAYES (left, sitting)

THOMAS FINDLAY, FANIA MARINOFF in
"THE HOUSE NEXT DOOR"

OLGA NETHERSOLE, WILLIAM MORRIS, ROBERT T. HAINES in
"THE WRITING ON THE WALL"

HARRY KELLY in
"ZIEGFELD FOLLIES OF 1909"

JANE MARBURY, SIDNEY DREW, MRS. STUART ROBSON
MME. NEVENDORFF in "BILLY"

Edward Sheldon's "The Nigger" with Annie Russell and Guy Bates Post, John Galsworthy's "Strife," and "The School for Scandal" with Grace George, Rose Coghlan, Louis Calvert, E. M. Holland, Matheson Lang and Olive Wyndham.

Among the other musicals of the year were "Kitty Grey" with Julia Sanderson; Elsie Janis in "The Fair Co-ed;" "A Stubborn Cinderella" with Sallie Fisher and John Barrymore doing a song and dance in the one and only musical of his career; "The Candy Shop" with Maude Fulton, William Rock and Louise Dresser; Sam Bernard with Kitty Gordon in "The Girl and the Wizard;" Raymond Hitchcock in "The Man Who Owns Broadway;" Frank Daniels in "The Belle of Brittany;" Marie Dressler in "A Boy and a Girl;" Adeline Genee in "The Silver Star" and Lew Fields in "Old Dutch" with a little girl billed as Helen Hayes Brown making her Broadway bow.

"The Ziegfeld Follies of 1909" had an imposing array of talent with Nora Bayes, Harry Kelly, Billie Reeves, Sophie Tucker, Gertrude Vanderbilt, Bessie Clayton, Jack Norworth, Lillian Lorraine, Mae Murray and, shortly after the opening, Eva Tanguay, who had been a vaudeville favorite, was added to the cast.

B. HUNTER, JULIA MARLOWE, E. H. SOTHERN, JESSIE BUSLEY in
"ANTONY AND CLEOPATRA"

MAUDE FULTON, WILLIAM ROCK in
"THE CANDY SHOP"

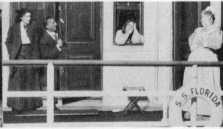

65

ALLA NAZIMOVA

JOHN DREW, MARY
BOLAND in "SMITH"

LAWRENCE REA, CHRISTIE
MacDONALD in "THE SPRING MAID"

WILLETTE KERSHAW, FORREST
WINANT in "THE COUNTRY BOY"

LEO DITRICHSTEIN, JANET
BEECHER in "THE CONCERT"

FRANK MONROE, EARLE BROWNE, ALMA SEDLEY, H. B. WARNER,
LAURETTE TAYLOR in "ALIAS JIMMY VALENTINE"

LEO DITRICHSTEIN

FRANCES RING, HALE HAMILTON (left) in
"GET-RICH-QUICK WALLINGFORD"

H. B. WARNER

EMMA DUNN

1910 Judging from the length of its run, "Get-Rich-Quick Wallingford" was the greatest success of 1910. It opened in September and ran through the following year piling up 424 performances. Cohan and Harris, the producers, also sent several companies on tour, and it was a popular play with the stock companies. Hale Hamilton, Frances Ring, Edward Ellis, Fay Wallace and Grant Mitchell were in the original New York company. Among the other big hits of the year were "Alias Jimmy Valentine" with H. B. Warner and Laurette Taylor, "Madame X" with Dorothy Donnelly, "Baby Mine" with Marguerite Clark and Ernest Glendinning, "The Country Boy" with Willette Kershaw and Forrest Winant, "Mother" with Emma Dunn, "Rebecca of Sunnybrook Farm" with Edith Taliaferro and Ralph Kellard, "The Concert" with Leo Ditrichstein, "The Gamblers" with Jane Cowl, and "Pomander Walk."

The musical hits were "Madame Sherry" starring Lina Abarbanell, "Naughty Marietta" with Emma Trentini, "Alma, Where Do You Live?" with Kitty Gordon, "The Spring Maid" starring Christie MacDonald, "The Arcadians" with Frank Moulan and Julia Sanderson and "The Old Town" starring Montgomery and Stone. In the cast were Allene Crater, whom Fred Stone had married in 1906, and a young Brooklyn girl named Peggy Wood making her Broadway debut.

Among the stars and their plays were Otis Skinner in "Your Humble Servant," William Collier in "A Lucky Star," Blanche Bates was "Nobody's

EDITH STOREY, ERNEST TRUEX, ARCHIE BOYD, EDITH
TALIAFERRO in "REBECCA OF SUNNYBROOK FARM"

EDITH TALIAFERRO

WILLIAM ELLIOTT, DOROTHY DONNELLY, ROBERT P. GIBBS,
ROBERT DROUET, L. ROGERS LYTTON in "MADAME X"

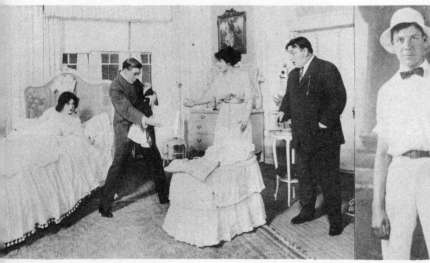

MARGUERITE CLARK, ERNEST GLENDINNING, IVY TROUTMAN,
WALTER JONES in "BABY MINE"

ERNEST GLENDINNING

JANE COWL, CHARLES STEVENSON, GEORGE NASH in
"THE GAMBLERS"

LINA ABARBANELL, JACK GARDNER, FRANCES DEMAREST, CARL MARTENS,
ELIZABETH MURRAY, IGNACIO MARTINETTI in "MADAME SHERRY"

68

SARAH BERNHARDT

PHYLLIS YOUNG, WILLIAM COLLIER, WALLACE WORSLEY, PAULA MARR,
KATHARINE MULKINS in "A LUCKY STAR"

ETHEL BARRYMORE in
"MID-CHANNEL"

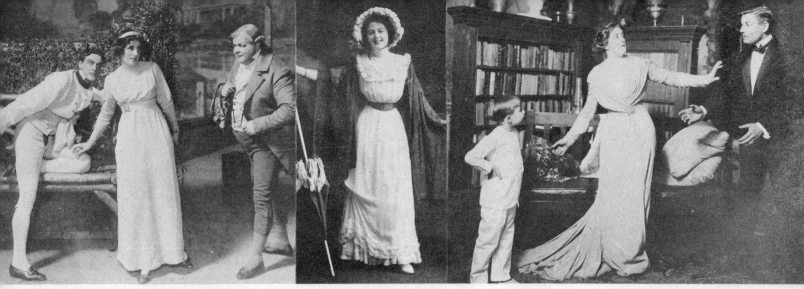

RVILLE HARROLD, EMMA
INI in "NAUGHTY MARIETTA"

BLANCHE BATES, BRUCE McREA in
"NOBODY'S WIDOW"

RUTH SHEPLEY, DOUGLAS
FAIRBANKS in "THE CUB"

MONTGOMERY & STONE in
"THE OLD TOWN"

OLGA NETHERSOLE, EDWARD MACKAY in
"MARY MAGDALENE"

Widow," Maxine Elliott in "The Inferior Sex,"
Billie Burke in "Mrs. Dot," Ethel Barrymore
in "Mid-Channel," Mary Mannering in "A
Man's World," Mabel Barrison in "Lulu's Hus-
band," Charles Cherry in "The Spitfire," Louis
Mann in "The Cheater," Clara Lipman in "The
Marriage of a Star," John Drew in "Smith,"
Douglas Fairbanks in "The Cub," Kyrle Bellew
in "The Scandal," Marie Doro in "Electricity,"
May Irwin in "Getting a Polish," Mrs. Leslie
Carter in "Two Women," Wallace Eddinger in
"The Aviator," Olga Nethersole in "Mary Mag-
dalene" and Mrs. Patrick Campbell in "The
Foolish Virgin." None of these plays were par-
ticularly outstanding but served as vehicles for
the stars. William Gillette was playing in a
series of revivals of his own plays: "Sherlock
Holmes," "The Private Secretary," "Secret
Service," "Too Much Johnson" and "Held By
The Enemy."

Sarah Bernhardt was on one of her many
farewell tours. Lou Tellegen was her leading
man and it was his first appearance in America.
Sothern and Marlowe were giving Shakespeare's plays in repertoire. Nazimova was
appearing in the first New York production of
Ibsen's "Little Eyolf." Maude Adams was playing "As You Like It" at the Greek Theatre in
Berkeley, Calif. The New Theatre's outstanding production was Maeterlinck's "The Blue-
bird" with Margaret Wycherly, Louise Closser

LINA ABARBANELL as
"MADAME SHERRY"

BASIL HALLAM, FRED KERR, BILLIE BURKE, KATE
MEEK in "MRS. DOT"

WALTER PERCIVAL, HELEN HAYES
in "THE SUMMER WIDOWERS"

IRENE FRANKLIN, PAUL NICHOLSON, JACK HENDERSON, CHARLES JUDELS,
VERNON CASTLE, LEW FIELDS in "THE SUMMER WIDOWERS"

ROBERT WARWICK, MRS. LESLIE CARTER, BRANDON HURST in "TWO WOMEN"

MABEL BARRISON in "LULU'S HUSBAND"

MAY IRWIN

KYRLE BELLEW in "THE SCANDAL"

PAULINE CHASE in "OUR MISS GIBBS"

CHAUNCEY OLCOTT in "RAGGED ROBIN"

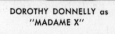

G. P. HUNTLEY, ELSIE FERGUSON, MARIE TEMPEST in "CASTE"

DOROTHY DONNELLY as "MADAME X"

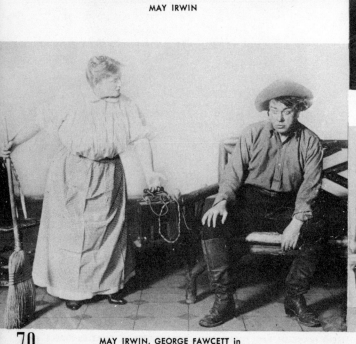

MAY IRWIN, GEORGE FAWCETT in "GETTING A POLISH"

"THE BLUE BIRD"

BLANCHE RING in
"THE YANKEE GIRL"

EDDIE FOY in
"UP AND DOWN BROADWAY"

ADELINE GENEE, SHERER BEKEFI in
"THE BACHELOR BELLES"

CLARA LIPMAN

WILIAM ELLIOTT

JANE COWL

HALE HAMILTON

FLORENCE ROCKWELL,
WILTON LACKAYE in
"JIM THE PENMAN"

EDITH WYNNE MATTHISON,
HENRY KOLKER in
"THE WINTER'S TALE"

MARIE DRESSLER and
THE GORMAN BROTHERS in
"TILLIE'S NIGHTMARE"

MARIE CAHILL

Hale, Irene Browne and Gladys Hulette. Among their repertory this year were "Twelfth Night" with Annie Russell, Louis Calvert and Matheson Lang; "The Winter's Tale" with Edith Wynne Matthison, Henry Kolker and Rose Coghlan; and "A Son of the People" with John Mason and George Fawcett.

Among the interesting revivals were Mrs. Fiske with Holbrook Blinn in "Pillars of Society," Marie Tempest and Elsie Ferguson in "Caste," Wilton Lackaye, John Mason, Marguerite Clark and Florence Roberts in "Jim, the Penman" and "Diplomacy" with Charles Richman, Chrystal Herne and Milton Sills.

The musicals and their stars on the boards included "The Jolly Bachelors" with Nora Bayes and Jack Norworth, Blanche Ring in "The Yankee Girl," "Madame Troubadour" with Grace LaRue, Marie Dressler in "Tillie's Nightmare," "The Mikado" with Fritzi Scheff, Andrew Mack, Jefferson DeAngelis, Christie MacDonald and Christine Nielson, Lew Fields in "The Summer Widowers" with little Helen Hayes, "The Ziegfeld Follies of 1910" with Lillian Lorraine, Bert Williams and Fannie Brice, Eddie Foy in "Up and Down Broadway," Pauline Chase in "Our Miss Gibbs," Sam Bernard in "He Came From Milwaukee," "The Girl in the Train" with Vera Michelena, Marie Cahill in "Judy Forgot," "The Girl in the Taxi" with Carter De Haven, Adeline Genee in "The Bachelor Belles" and Lulu Glaser in "The Girl and the Kaiser."

MARIE CAHILL, ARTHUR STANFORD in
"JUDY FORGOT"

71

JULIA MARLOWE as
ROSALIND

WILLIAM PRUETTE, JOSEPHINE JACOBY, JEFFERSON DeANGELIS, CHRISTIE MacDONALD,
CHRISTINE NIELSON, ARTHUR CUNNINGHAM in "THE MIKADO"

MAUDE ADAMS as
ROSALIND

CHARLES CHERRY, RUTH MAYCLIFFE in
"THE SPITFIRE"

"ZIEGFELD FOLLIES OF 1910"

FRED BOND, CARTER DE HAVEN in
"THE GIRL IN THE TAXI"

IDA CONQUEST, ROBERT T. HAINES, NAZIMOVA,
BRANDON TYNAN in "LITTLE EYOLF"

JACK NORWORTH

FANNIE BRICE

LOUIS MANN, MATHILDE COTTRELLY, EMILY ANN
WELLMAN in "THE CHEATER"

WALLACE EDDINGER in
"THE AVIATOR"

WILLIAM GILLETTE in
"SECRET SERVICE," "HELD BY THE ENEMY," "SHERLOCK HOLMES"

LULU GLASER, THOMAS RICHARDS in
"THE GIRL AND THE KAISER"

MRS. FISKE

HAZEL DAWN in
"THE PINK LADY"

LILA RHODES, GEORGE M. COHAN in
"THE LITTLE MILLIONAIRE"

MAUDE ADAMS in
"CHANTECLER"

CHARLES RICHMAN, JULIA DEAN in
"BOUGHT AND PAID FOR"

ANN MURDOCK in
"EXCUSE ME"

JULIA DEAN in
"BOUGHT AND PAID FOR"

1911

The star system was still an important factor in 1911, but of the ten plays (including musicals) achieving the longest run of the year in New York, less than half had players with star billing. The ten, with their number of performances, were: "Bought and Paid For" (431), "Bunty Pulls the Strings" (391), "The Pink Lady" (312), "Disraeli" (280), "The Woman" (247), "The Garden of Allah" (241), "The Quaker Girl" (240), "The Return of Peter Grimm" (231), "The Little Millionaire" (192), "Kismet" (184). George Arliss starred in "Disraeli," David Warfield was the star of "The Return of Peter Grimm," Otis Skinner starred in "Kismet" while George M. Cohan's name was above the title of "The Little Millionaire." "The Garden of Allah" cast included Mary Mannering, a great star, and Lewis Waller, a romantic English star, but evidently Liebler and Co., the producers, thought the play was more important for they were not given star billing. "The Deep Purple," "Excuse Me" and "Over Night" were the only other plays that ran over 150 performances and none of them boasted a star. Many of these plays had players who later achieved stardom and fame. Julia Dean, Frank Craven and Charles Richman were in "Bought and Paid For." Hazel Dawn skyrocketed to fame from "The Pink Lady." Mary Nash in "The Woman," Ina Claire and Olga Petrova in "The Quaker Girl," Ann Murdock in "Excuse Me," Margaret Lawrence in "Over Night," Richard Bennett and Catherine Calvert in "The Deep Purple" all became stars of various magnitude.

NAZIMOVA, FRANK GILMORE in
"THE MARIONETTES"

WILLIAM FAVERSHAM in
"THE FAUN"

MOLLY PEARSON, EDMUND BERESFORD in
"BUNTY PULLS THE STRINGS"

GEORGE ARLISS in
"DISRAELI"

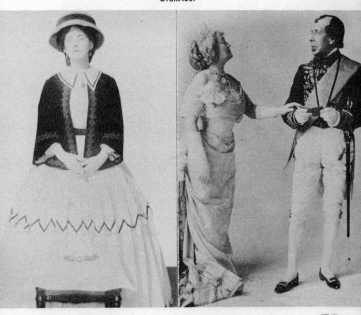

MOLLY PEARSON in
"BUNTY PULLS THE STRINGS"

MARGUERITE ST. JOHN, GEORGE
ARLISS in "DISRAELI"

Other stars and their plays in 1911 were: Rose Stahl in "Maggie Pepper," Mrs. Fiske in "Mrs. Bumpstead-Leigh" and a revival of "Becky Sharp," Edgar Selwyn in "The Arab," William Faversham in "The Faun," Maude Adams in "Chantecler," Holbrook Blinn in "The Boss," Henry Miller in "The Havoc," Constance Collier and Tyrone Power in "Thais," John Mason in "As A Man Thinks," Henrietta Crosman in "The Real Thing," John Drew in "A Single Man," Margaret Anglin in "Green Stockings," Billie Burke in "The Runaway," Nazimova in "The Marionettes," Elsie Ferguson in "The First Lady in the Land," William H. Crane in "The Senator Keeps House," Margaret Illington in "Kindling," Helen Ware in "The Price," Frank McIntyre with Willette Kershaw in "Snobs," Viola Allen in "The Lady of Coventry," William Collier in "Take My Advice" and Chauncey Olcott in "Barry of Ballymore."

Ethel Barrymore appeared in a revival of Pinero's "Trelawney of the Wells" with Constance Collier, Lawrence D'Orsay and Eugene O'Brien in her cast. Later she revived "Alice-Sit-By-The-Fire" and as a curtain raiser used "The Twelve Pound Look," a one-act Barrie play which proved popular for her later in vaudeville. Charles Cherry was starring in "Seven Sisters," though Laurette Taylor, his leading lady, received most of the acclaim. "Everywoman," a morality play, was widely discussed. Laura Nelson Hall in the title role was supported by Patricia Collinge, Wilda Bennett and Frederic de Belleville.

75

HAROLD VOSBURGH, MARY NASH in
"THE WOMAN"

BILLIE BURKE in
"THE RUNAWAY"

ELSIE JANIS in
"THE SLIM PRINCESS"

ALICE JOHN, CARLOTTA DOTY, EVA McDONALD, LAURETTE TAYLOR, GLADYS SMIT
VIRGINIA HAMILTON, ORILLA MARS, CHARLES CHERRY in "SEVEN SISTERS"

KITTY GORDON in
"THE ENCHANTRESS"

ADA DWYER, EMMETT CORRIGAN, WILLIAM A. NORTON, RICHARD BENNETT,
CATHERINE CALVERT in "THE DEEP PURPLE"

MARGARET LAWRENCE, HERBERT A.
YOST in "OVER NIGHT"

WILLIAM H. CRANE, EVA FLOWER in
"THE SENATOR KEEPS HOUSE"

"EXCUSE ME" with ANN MURDOCK (third from right)

An all star revival of "The Lights O' London" blazed with Holbrook Blinn, Doris Keane, Douglas Fairbanks, Marguerite Clark, William Courtenay, Tom Wise, Charles Richman, Leonore Harris, Jeffreys Lewis, Lawrence D'Orsay and Thomas Q. Seabrooke. "Ben Hur" was also revived with Richard Buhler in the title role. And an "H.M.S. Pinafore" revival had an impressive cast with Marie Cahill, De Wolf Hopper, Henry E. Dixey, Louise Gunning, Alice Brady, George Macfarlane and Eugene Cowles.

Douglas Fairbanks later appeared in "A Gentleman of Leisure" with George Fawcett and Ruth Shepley. Richard Bennett was steadily gaining in stature as an actor in "Passers-By." In "The Great Name" with Henry Kolker was a young actress, just getting started, named Ruth Chatterton. "The Million" was a popular comedy with Taylor Holmes, Irene Fenwick and Eugene O'Brien. Ibsen's "The Lady From The Sea" was presented in New York for the first time with Hedwig Reicher playing the title role.

George Beban, a dialect comedian in musicals since Weber and Fields Music Hall days, was appearing in "The Sign of the Rose." It did not go as a four act play but later he had great success with it as a one-act vaudeville skit and also as a motion picture.

The Irish Players made their first New York appearance in November. The company included Sara Allgood, Cathleen Nesbitt, J. M. Kerrigan, Una O'Connor and Arthur Sinclair. Among the plays presented were Shaw's "The Shewing of Blanko Posnet," St. John Ervine's "Mixed Marriage," and J. M. Synge's "The Shadow of the Glen," "The Well of the Saints," "Riders to the Sea" and "The Playboy of the Western World." During the opening of the latter play there was

DAVID WARFIELD in
"THE RETURN OF PETER GRIMM"

OTIS SKINNER in
"KISMET"

JANET DUNBAR, THOMAS MEIGHAN, DAVID WARFIELD, JOHN SAINPOLIS in
"THE RETURN OF PETER GRIMM"

quite a disturbance in the gallery when partisan Irishmen showed their objections to certain lines by throwing potatoes and booing.

Madame Simone, well-known French actress, was making her first American appearance in a revival of "The Thief," while Sarah Bernhardt and her company were trouping in repertoire. Shakespeare was well represented with three repertory companies headed by E. H. Sothern and Julia Marlowe, Robert B. Mantell and John E. Kellerd. Mr. Kellerd included "Oedipus Rex" in his repertory and his company included Lillian Kingsbury, Aubrey Boucicault and Viola Fortescue. Fritz Leiber and Genevieve Hamper were newcomers to Mr. Mantell's company. The New Theatre productions included "Vanity Fair" with Marie Tempest, Louis Calvert, Rose Coghlan, Gail Kane, Olive Wyndham and Stewart Baird; "The Piper" with Edith Wynne Matthison, Frank Gilmore, Thais Lawton and Olive Oliver; and "The Arrow Maker" with Miss Matthison, E. M. Holland and Reginald Barlow. This was the last season of this organization. Winthrop Ames and the Shuberts resigned and in October, renamed the Century Theatre, it opened with "The Garden of Allah."

The "Ziegfeld Follies of 1911" had a talented cast including Bessie McCoy, Bert Williams, the Dolly Sisters, Leon Errol, Fannie (she was spelling it Fanny at this time) Brice, Harry Watson, Jr., Lillian Lorraine, George White and Vera Maxwell.

Gaby Deslys, famous French musical comedy actress, made her American debut at the Winter Garden under the Shubert's management in "The Revue of Revues" on September 27th. Two months later at the same house she appeared in "Vera Violetta." The cast had many un-

EDGAR SELWYN in
"THE ARAB"

AMELIA BARELON, RITA JOLIVET, OTIS SKINNER in
"KISMET"

ETHEL BARRYMORE, CHARLES DALTON in
"THE TWELVE POUND LOOK"

EUGENE O'BRIEN, ETHEL BARRYMORE, LAWRENCE D'ORSAY in
"TRELAWNEY OF THE WELLS"

MARY MANNERING

FRANKLYN HURLEIGH, MARY MANNERING, LEWIS WALLER in
"THE GARDEN OF ALLAH"

77

OLIVE OLIVER · INA CLAIRE · JOHN MASON · LEONORE HARRIS · WILLIAM H. CRANE · RITA JOLIVET · PERCY HASWELL

MAE WEST · RAYMOND HITCHCOCK · MARIE TEMPEST · CHARLES CHERRY

LAURA NELSON HALL AND COMPANY in
"EVERYWOMAN"

TYRONE POWER, CONSTANCE COLLIER in
"THAIS"

CLIFTON CRAWFORD, OLGA PETROVA, INA CLAIRE in
"THE QUAKER GIRL"

HARRISON HUNTER, HELEN WARE in
"THE PRICE"

WILLETTE KERSHAW, FRANK McINTYRE
"SNOBS"

IVY HERZOG, RICHARD BENNETT in
"PASSERS-BY"

ARTHUR ALBRO, MARGUERITE SYLVA in
"GYPSY LOVE"

FLORINE ARNOLD, MRS. FISKE in
"MRS. BUMPSTEAD-LEIGH"

EMILY STEVENS, HOLBROOK BLINN
"THE BOSS"

MARGUERITE CLARK

EUGENE COWLES

ALICE BRADY

LOUISE GUNNING

CATHERINE CALVERT

JOSEPH SANTLEY

PATRICIA COLLINGE

WILLIAM FARNUM, MARY MILES MINTER, DUSTIN FARNUM in
"THE LITTLEST REBEL"

ELIZABETH FIRTH, DONALD BRIAN, JULIA
SANDERSON in "THE SIREN"

ROSE STAHL, FREDERICK TRUESDELL in
"MAGGIE PEPPER"

MARGARET ANGLIN, H. REEVES
SMITH in "GREEN STOCKINGS"

ELSIE FERGUSON, ORME CALDARA in
"THE FIRST LADY IN THE LAND"

GERTRUDE BRYAN in
"LITTLE BOY BLUE"

RALPH HERZ in
"DOCTOR DE LUXE"

GRACE VAN STUDDIFORD,
GEORGE LEON MOORE in
"PARADISE OF MAHOMET"

ROBERT WARWICK in
"THE BALKAN PRINCESS"

GEORGE MacFARLANE, MARIE CAHILL in
"H.M.S. PINAFORE"

SHELDON LEWIS, HEDWIG REICHER in
"THE LADY FROM THE SEA"

knowns who became famous as Al Jolson, Mae West, Belle Baker, Frank Tinney, Barney Bernard, Jose Collins, Stella Mayhew and Melville Ellis. A one-act water ballet called "Undine" and featuring Annette Kellerman was also part of the show.

Musicals were: Elsie Janis in "The Slim Princess;" "Marriage a la Carte" with Emmy Wehlen; Grace Van Studdiford in "The Paradise of Mahomet;" Lew Fields in "The Hen-Pecks;" Louise Gunning with Robert Warwick in "The Balkan Princess;" Richard Carle in "Jumping Jupiter" with Edna Wallace Hopper, Ina Claire, Jeanne Eagels and Natalie Alt; "La Belle Paree" with Kitty Gordon, Al Jolson, Stella Mayhew, Mitzi Hajos, Barney Bernard, Mlle. Dazie and Dorothy Jardon; Nora Bayes and Jack Norworth in "Little Miss Fix-It;" Ralph Herz in "Dr. De Luxe;" Mabel Hite in "A Certain Party;" Valeska Suratt in "The Red Rose;" John Hyams and Leila McIntyre in "The Girl of My Dreams;" Donald Brian with Julia Sanderson in "The Siren;" Julian Eltinge in "The Fascinating Widow;" "The Kiss Waltz" with Flora Zabelle, Robert Warwick, Elsa Ryan, Adele Rowland and Eva Davenport; "The Never Homes" with George W. Monroe, Joseph Santley and Helen Hayes; Fritzi Scheff in "The Duchess;" "Gypsy Love" with Marguerite Sylva; Kitty Gordon in "The Enchantress;" Raymond Hitchcock in "The Red Widow;" "Little Boy Blue" with Gertrude Bryan, Otis Harlan and Maude Odell; Grace LaRue in "Betsy;" and "The Wedding Trip" with Dorothy Jardon, Edward Martindel and Fritzi Von Busing.

79

HARRY TANSEY, HENRY KOLKER, RUTH
CHATTERTON in "THE GREAT NAME"

AS THE BRIDE

JULIAN ELTINGE in
"THE FASCINATING WIDOW"

AS THE BATHING GIRL

LILLIAN LEE, LEW FIELDS, GERTRUDE QUINLAN, VERNON CASTLE,
ETHEL JOHNSON, LAURENCE WHEAT, EDITH FROST, STEPHEN
MALEY, BLOSSOM SEELEY in "THE HEN-PECKS"

RUTH SHEPLEY, DOUGLAS FAIRBANKS in
"A GENTLEMAN OF LEISURE"

MABEL HITE in
"A CERTAIN PARTY"

ROBERT WARWICK and CHORUS in
"THE KISS WALTZ"

BERNARD GRANVILLE, ALEXANDER CARR, SOPHIE
TUCKER in "LOUISIANA LOU"

HEDWIG
REICHER

THAIS
LAWTON

LEILA McINTYRE in
"THE GIRL OF MY DREAMS"

FRANK
GILMORE

JANE
OAKE

MARGARET ILLINGTON, BYRON BEASLEY in
"KINDLING"

MARY MILES MINTER in
"THE LITTLEST REBEL"

J. M. KERRIGAN, EILEEN O'DOHERTY, U. WRIGHT, KATHLEEN
DRAGO, J. A. ROURKE, SYDNEY J. MORGAN, SARA
ALLGOOD in "RIDERS TO THE SEA"

ANNETTE KELLERMAN

NORA BAYES, JACK NORWORTH in
"LITTLE MISS FIX-IT"

VALESKA SURATT

ROBERT B. MANTELL as
HAMLET

DWARD MARTINDEL, DOROTHY JARDON in
"THE WEDDING TRIP"

BABY SEAWILLA, MARY SHERIDAN, GEORGE BEBAN in
"THE SIGN OF THE ROSE"

RICHARD
CARLE

FANNIE
BRICE

KITTY GORDON, HAL FORDE and COMPANY in
"THE ENCHANTRESS"

ROSE
COGHLAN

LAWRENCE
D'ORSAY

GABY DESLYS

BESSIE McCOY and the DAFFYDIL GIRLS in
"ZIEGFELD FOLLIES OF 1911"

LEON
ERROL

THE DOLLY
SISTERS

CECIL KERN, RICHARD BUHLER, LILLIAN LAWRENCE,
ALICE HAYNES, ROSE BRANDER in
Revival of "BEN HUR"

LAURETTE TAYLOR as PEG

Top—Scene from "PEG O' MY HEART"
Center—LAURETTE TAYLOR in "BIRD OF PARADISE"
Bottom—MISS TAYLOR, LEWIS STONE

MARY BARTON, ARNOLD LUCY in
"FANNY'S FIRST PLAY"

GLADYS HULETTE, MARIE PAVEY, ALICE BRADY, BEVERLY WEST in
"LITTLE WOMEN"

WARBURTON GAMBLE, AURIOL LEE in
"MILESTONES"

1912 The year 1912 saw Laurette Taylor and Jane Cowl win stardom. Early in the year Miss Taylor had quite a success in "The Bird of Paradise" with Guy Bates Post and Lewis S. Stone, but near the end of the year she opened in "Peg O' My Heart," a mild little comedy by J. Hartley Manners, her husband. She had the longest run (603 performances) of her career with it, and she revived it in 1921. Mary Turner in "Within the Law" was one of Jane Cowl's great roles and the play was a smash hit, running 541 performances. Many companies of these plays trouped the land.

The other long run plays of the year were G. B. Shaw's "Fanny's First Play," "Milestones," "A Butterfly on the Wheel" with Madge Titheradge, "Officer 666" with Wallace Eddinger and Vivian Martin, "Little Women" with Alice Brady, "The Argyle Case" starring Robert Hilliard, the Drury Lane success "The Whip" with John Halliday and Leonore Harris, and "Years of Discretion" with Effie Shannon, Herbert Kelcey, Lyn Harding and Bruce McRae.

The long run musicals were "Oh! Oh! Delphine" starring Frank McIntyre, "The Lady of the Slipper" co-starring Montgomery and Stone with Elsie Janis, "The Rose Maid," and "A Winsome Widow" with the Dolly Sisters, Frank Tinney, Mae West, Kathleen Clifford, Leon Errol, Charles King, Emmy Wehlen and Elizabeth Brice.

Among the interesting events was the dramatization of "Oliver Twist" with Nat C. Goodwin, Marie Doro, Constance Collier, Lyn Harding and Olive Wyndham; the Max Reinhardt production of "Sumurun," a pantomime in nine tableaux with the com-

ROBERT HILLIARD in
"THE ARGYLE CASE"

JANE COWL in
"WITHIN THE LAW"

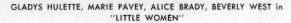

IAN MARTIN, PERCY AMES, CAMILLA CRUME, WALLACE EDDINGER,
RUTH MAYCLIFFE in "OFFICER 666"

MADGE TITHERADGE,
CHARLES QUARTERMAINE in
"A BUTTERFLY ON THE WHEEL"

Scene from "WITHIN THE LAW"
JANE COWL and ORME CALDARA at left

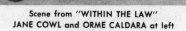

NAT C. GOODWIN
as FAGIN

CONSTANCE COLLIER, LYN HARDING, NAT C. GOODWIN, CHARLES ROGERS,
PERCIVAL VIVIAN, MARIE DORO in "OLIVER TWIST"

MARIE DORO
as OLIVER TWIST

EFFIE SHANNON, LYN HARDING, BRUCE McREA, HERBERT KELCEY in
"YEARS OF DISCRETION"

EFFIE SHANNON

OSWALD YORKE, DORIS KEANE, JOHN BARRYMORE in
"THE AFFAIRS OF ANATOL"

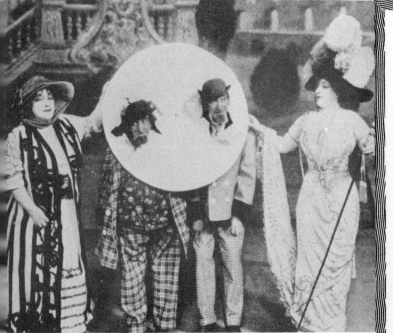

FAY TEMPLETON, WEBER AND FIELDS, LILLIAN RUSSELL in
"HOKEY-POKEY"

plete company from the Deutsches Theatre, Berlin; a production of Strindberg's "The Father" with Warner Oland and Rosalind Ivan; "The Affairs of Anatol" by Arthur Schnitzler with John Barrymore, Doris Keane, Marguerite Clark and Gail Kane; "The Yellow Jacket," a Chinese play, with Juliette Day, George Relph, Antoinette Walker, Schuyler Ladd, Grace Valentine, Reginald Barlow and Chamberlain Brown who later became an actor's agent; a dramatized version of Grimm's "Snow White and the Seven Dwarfs" which starred Marguerite Clark and was played for 72 matinee performances only; John E. Kellerd broke Edwin Booth's record of playing "Hamlet" two more than Booth's one hundred performance record; "Hindle Wakes" with Emilie Polini and Roland Young; "Stop Thief," a Cohan and Harris farce, with Richard Bennett, Mary Ryan, Vivian Martin and Frank Bacon; Winthrop Ames' production of John Galsworthy's "The Pigeon" with Pamela Gaythorne; and David Belasco's production of "The Governor's Lady" with Gladys Hanson, Emmett Corrigan, Emma Dunn, Milton Sills and Stuart Walker.

Mme. Simone, over from France, was appearing in "The Return to Jerusalem" with Arnold Daly, "The Lady of Dreams" with Margaret Wycherly and Julian L'Estrange, and "Frou-Frou." Lewis Waller, over from England, appeared in "Monsieur Beaucaire," "The Explorer," "Discovering America" and "Henry V."

MYRTLE TANNEHILL, GEORGE M. COHAN
in "BROADWAY JONES"

Scenes from "THE WHIP"

MARGUERITE CLARK in
"SNOW WHITE AND THE SEVEN DWARFS"

"THE GOVERNOR'S LADY"
with EMMA DUNN and GLADYS HANSON

WILLIAM FAVERSHAM, KENNETH HUNTER
in "JULIUS CAESAR"

FRANK McINTRYE, FRANK DOANE in
"OH! OH! DELPHINE!"

HARRY GILFOIL, BLANCHE RING in
"THE WALL STREET GIRL"

DAVID MONTGOMERY, ELSIE JANIS, FRED STONE
in "THE LADY OF THE SLIPPER"

Weber and Fields reunited for "Hokey-Pokey," a musical potpourri with Lillian Russell, William Collier, Fay Templeton, Bessie Clayton, Frankie Bailey, Ada Lewis and George Beban, all alumni of their old Music Hall days.

The revivals included "45 Minutes from Broadway" with George M. Cohan and Sallie Fisher; all star productions of Gilbert and Sullivan's "Patience" with Marie Doro, De Wolf Hopper, Cyril Scott, Christine Nielson, Alice Brady and Eugene Cowles and "H.M.S. Pinafore," "The Mikado" and "The Pirates of Penzance;" "Man and Superman" with Robert Loraine; "Julius Caesar" with William Faversham, Frank Keenan, Tyrone Power and Julie Opp; Maude Adams in "Peter Pan;" and Annie Russell and her Old English Company in "She Stoops to Conquer," "The Rivals" and "Much Ado About Nothing" in repertory.

The stars and the plays they were in included James K. Hackett in "The Grain of Dust;" Tully Marshall in "The Talker" with Pauline Lord making her first Broadway appearance; Louis Mann in "Elevating a Husband;" Gertrude Elliott in "White Magic;" Charlotte Walker in "The Trail of the Lonesome Pine" with William S. Hart; Ethel Barrymore in Barrie's "A Slice of Life" with John Barrymore and Hattie Williams, preceded by a revival of "Cousin Kate" with Miss Barrymore and Mrs. Thomas Whiffen; Mrs. Fiske in "Lady Patricia" and later "The High Road;" Henry Kolker in

TULLY MARSHALL

LILLIAN LORRAINE

WALLACE EDDINGER

ANNIE RUSSELL

CHARLES KING, ELIZABETH BRICE, EMMY WEHLEN, HARRY CONOR,
IDA ADAMS, CHARLES J. ROSS, KATHLEEN CLIFFORD in
"A WINSOME WIDOW"

85

CHARLOTTE WALKER, BERTON CHURCHILL, WILLIAM S. HART,
WILLARD ROBERTSON in "THE TRAIL OF THE LONESOME PINE"

VIOLA ALLEN, BASIL GILL in
"THE DAUGHTER OF HEAVEN"

JAMES K. HACKETT, FRANK BURBECK in
"THE GRAIN OF DUST"

LULU GLASER in
"MISS DUDELSACK"

ANN SWINBURNE,
GEORGE L. MOORE in
"THE COUNT OF LUXEMBOURG"

ROLAND YOUNG, EMELIE POLINI, ALICE O'DEA, JAMES C. TYLER
HERBERT LOMAS in "HINDLE WAKES"

NAZIMOVA in
"BELLA DONNA"

CHARLES BRYANT, NAZIMOVA in
"BELLA DONNA"

MME. SIMONE, JULIAN L'ESTRANGE in
"THE LADY OF DREAMS"

MARY BOLAND, JOHN DREW i
"THE PERPLEXED HUSBAND"

"The Greyhound;" Walker Whiteside with Florence Reed in "The Typhoon;" Charles Hawtrey in "Dear Old Charlie;" William Courtenay in "Ready Money;" John Drew with Mary Boland in "The Perplexed Husband;" Billie Burke in "The 'Mind-the-Paint' Girl;" John Mason with Martha Hedman in "The Attack;" George M. Cohan in "Broadway Jones;" Sothern and Marlowe in Shakespearean repertory; Frances Starr in "The Case of Becky;" Viola Allen in "The Daughter of Heaven;" Douglas Fairbanks in "Hawthorne of the U.S.A.;" Nazimova in "Bella Donna;" William Collier in "Never Say Die;" John Emerson in "The Conspiracy."

The musicals and their stars were Eddie Foy in "Over the River;" "The Rose of Panama" with Chapine, Forrest Huff and Fay Bainter; Marie Cahill in "The Opera Ball;" "Whirl of Society" with Al Jolson, Jose Collins, Barney Bernard, Stella Mayhew, Blossom Seeley, Lawrence D'Orsay and Kathleen Clifford; Blanche Ring in "The Wall Street Girl;" James T. Powers in "Two

BERNARD GRANVILLE, JOSIE SADLER, HARRY WATSON, JR., CHARLES JUDELS,
LILLIAN LORRAINE, GRACE DuBOISE, LEON ERROL
in "ZIEGFELD FOLLIES OF 1912"

JULIETTE DAY, GEORGE RELPH and COMPANY in "THE YELLOW JACKET"

LOUIS MANN, EMILY ANN WELLMAN in "ELEVATING A HUSBAND"

JOHN E. KELLERD as "HAMLET"

ROY ATWELL, AUDREY MAPLE, EMMA TRENTINI, KATHERINE STEWART, RUBY NORTON, CRAIG CAMPBELL in "THE FIREFLY"

EMMA TRENTINI in "THE FIREFLY"

CHAPINE, FORREST HUFF in "THE ROSE OF PANAMA"

AULINE LORD, TULLY MARSHALL in "THE TALKER"

SHELLEY HULL, MRS. FISKE in "LADY PATRICIA"

PAMELA GAYTHORNE, RUSS WHYTAL, SIDNEY VALENTINE in "THE PIGEON"

ETHEL and JOHN BARRYMORE in "A SLICE OF LIFE"

FRANK BACON, RUTH CHESTER, WILLIAM BOYD, VIVIAN MARTIN, H. C. BRADLEY, RICHARD BENNETT, MARY RYAN, PERCY AMES, LOUISE WOODS in "STOP THIEF"

Little Brides;" "The Passing Show of 1912" with Willie and Eugene Howard, Trixie Friganza, Charlotte Greenwood, Adelaide and Hughes, Anna Wheaton, Harry Fox and Jobyna Howland; "Hanky Panky" with Florence Moore, William Montgomery and Max Rogers; Richard Carle in "The Girl from Montmarte;" "The Merry Countess" with the Dolly Sisters, Jose Collins and Martin Brown; "The Count of Luxembourg" with Ann Swinburne and Frank Moulan; "Ziegfeld Follies of 1912" with Bert Williams, Leon Errol, Lillian Lorraine, Bernard Granville and Ray Samuels who later became known as the Blue Streak of vaudeville; Gertrude Hoffmann in "Broadway to Paris" with Louise Dresser, Maurice, Florence Walton and Irene Bordoni in her first Broadway appearance; Emma Trentini in "The Firefly;" and Sam Bernard with Adele Ritchie in "All For The Ladies."

MARTHA HEDMAN

STAFFORD PEMBERTON

GLADYS HANSON

HENRY KOLKER

ELIZABETH BRICE

IRENE BORDONI

ROBERT LORAINE

BILLIE BURKE in
"THE 'MIND-THE-PAINT' GIRL"

DOUGLAS
FAIRBANKS

PAULINE
LORD

FLORENCE FISHER, WALKER WHITESIDE, FLORENCE
REED in "THE TYPHOON"

HENRY KOLKER, ELITA PROCTOR OTIS, DOUGLAS J.
WOOD in "THE GREYHOUND"

FLORENCE NASH in
"WITHIN THE LAW"

LINA ABARBANELL,
ROBERT WARWICK in
"MISS PRINCESS"

MARIE CAHILL in
"THE OPERA BALL"

EDDIE FOY, MAUDE LAMBERT & CO. in
"OVER THE RIVER"

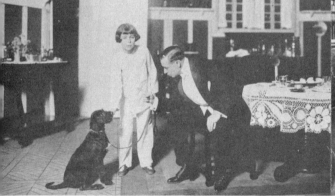

BUSTER COLLIER, WILLIAM COLLIER in
"NEVER SAY DIE"

JOHN EMERSON in
"CONSPIRACY"

LEWIS WALLER in
"THE EXPLORER"

EVA DAVENPORT, MARIE DORO, DE WOLF
HOPPER in "PATIENCE"

VIOLET HEMING

WILLIAM S. HART

RALPH KELLARD

PEGGY WOOD

DAVID C. MONTGOMERY

GAIL KANE

CHARLES RICHMAN

DOLLY SISTERS, MARTIN BROWN in
"THE MERRY COUNTESS"

MRS. FISKE, BARRETT CLARK, FREDERICK PERRY in
"THE HIGH ROAD"

JAMES T. POWERS, FRANCES CAMERON in
"TWO LITTLE BRIDES"

HENRY MILLER, RUTH CHATTERTON in
"THE RAINBOW"

WILLIAM MONTGOMERY, FLORENCE
MOORE in "HANKY PANKY"

DOUGLAS FAIRBANKS, IRENE FENWICK in
"HAWTHORNE OF THE U. S. A."

ANNIE RUSSELL, FRANK REICHER in
"MUCH ADO ABOUT NOTHING"

MARGARET GREENE, WILLIAM
COURTENAY in "READY MONEY"

LILLIE FISHER, GEORGE M. COHAN in
"45 MINUTES FROM BROADWAY"

RALPH AUSTIN, GERTRUDE HOFFMANN, JAMES C.
MORTON in "BROADWAY TO PARIS"

LEWIS WALLER, HENRY STANFORD in
"MONSIEUR BEAUCAIRE"

HARRY C. BROWN, FRANCES STARR,
ALBERT BRUNING in
"THE CASE OF BECKY"

DORIS KEANE in "ROMANCE"
with WILLIAM COURTENAY

AIL KANE, PURNELL B. PRATT, WALLACE EDDINGER, ROY FAIRCHILD MARTIN L. ALSOP, JOSEPH ALLEN, CLAUDE BROOKE in "SEVEN KEYS TO BALDPATE"

ALEXANDER CARR, BARNEY BERNARD in "POTASH AND PERLMUTTER"

FORREST WINANT, IRENE FENWICK in "THE FAMILY CUPBOARD"

MARY NASH, VINCENT SERRANO in "THE LURE"

LILLIAN GISH, WILDA BENNETT, CLAIRE BURKE, MARY PICKFORD, REGINA WALLACE, GEORGIA FURSMAN, EDNA GRIFFIN in "THE GOOD LITTLE DEVIL"

1913

"Romance," a sentimental drama by Edward Sheldon, proved to be one of the most popular plays of the decade, and the radiant performance of Doris Keane as Mme. Cavallini skyrocketed her to fame and stardom. She played it for two years in this country then went to London where she had a record-breaking run of four years. Returning to America, she toured again with it in 1919. William Courtenay created the role of Bishop Armstrong. In London the part was played by two popular English actors, Owen Nares and Basil Sydney who became Miss Keane's husband.

"Potash and Perlmutter," a comedy by Montague Glass based on stories in the Saturday Evening Post, achieved the longest run (441 performances) of any play opening in 1913. Barney Bernard played Abe Potash while Alexander Carr was Mawruss Perlmutter. "Seven Keys to Baldpate," a popular mystery farce by George M. Cohan and with Wallace Eddinger and Gail Kane, had the second longest run. Other successes of the year were "A Good Little Devil" with Mary Pickford, William Norris, Ernest Truex and Lillian Gish; "Joseph and His Brethren," a Biblical spectacle, with Pauline Frederick, Brandon Tynan and James O'Neill; Arthur Hopkins' initial production, "Poor Little Rich Girl" with Viola Dana; "The Family Cupboard" with Irene Fenwick, Alice Brady and Forrest Winant; "At Bay" with Chrystal Herne and Guy Standing; "The Master Mind" with Edmund Breese; "The Lure" with Mary Nash and Vincent Serrano; "Nearly Married," a farce written by Edgar Selwyn and with Bruce McRae, Ruth Shepley, Jane Grey and Virginia Pearson; "Today" with Emily Stevens and Edwin Arden; "The Marriage Game" with Alexandra Carlisle, Vivian Martin, Charles Trowbridge, and Alison Skipworth; "The Misleading Lady" with Lewis Stone and Inez Buck; "The Things That Count" with Alice Brady, Howard Estabrook and Edna Wallace Hopper; and "Fine Feathers," a Eugene Walter play, with Robert Edeson, Wilton Lackaye, Rose Coghlan and Max Figman.

As usual, the stars were playing in a variety of attractions. John Drew, assisted by Mary Boland and Laura Hope Crews, played "Much Ado About Nothing" before starring in "The Tyranny of Tears." Marie Doro and Charles Cherry co-starred in "The New Secretary." Chauncey Olcott was in Rida Johnson Young's "The Isle O' Dreams." May Irwin delighted her following in "Widow By Proxy." H. B. Warner was becoming a matinee idol in "The Ghost Breaker." John Mason had Martha Hedman as his leading lady in both "Liberty Hall" and "Indian Summer." Richard Bennett created quite a stir in "Damaged Goods," a drama about the effects of syphilis that

ELLIOTT DEXTER, KATHARINE LaSALLE, EDMUND BREESE in "THE MASTER MIND"

WILLIAM COLLIER   OLIVE WYNDHAM

JOHN DREW   EDNA GOODRICH

BRANDON TYNAN, PAULINE FREDERICK in "JOSEPH AND HIS BRETHREN"

91

MAX FIGMAN, WILTON LACKAYE, ROBERT EDESON,
LOLITA ROBERTSON in "FINE FEATHERS"

EDWIN ARDEN, EMILY STEVENS in
"TODAY"

RICHARD BENNETT, WILTON LACKAYE in
"DAMAGED GOODS"

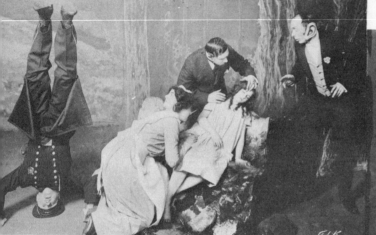

JOSEPH BINGHAM, GLADYS FAIRBANKS, HOWARD HALL, VIOLA
DANA, HARRY COWLEY, in "POOR LITTLE RICH GIRL"

BILLIE BURKE,
SHELLEY HULL in
"THE LAND OF PROMISE"

H. B. WARNER

BILLIE BURKE in
"THE AMAZONS"

INEZ BUCK, LEWIS S. STONE in
"THE MISLEADING LADY"

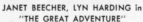

ETHEL BARRYMORE, CHARLES
CHERRY in "TANTE"

JANET BEECHER, LYN HARDING in
"THE GREAT ADVENTURE"

LEO DITRICHSTEIN, ISABEL IRVING in   WILLIAM COURTENAY, FLORENCE REED in
"THE TEMPERAMENTAL JOURNEY"   "THE GIRL AND THE PENNANT"

was backed by the Medical Review of Reviews. Olive Wyndham had the lead in the Owen Davis play "What Happened to Mary." Billie Burke was in "The Amazons," a Pinero play, and Shelley Hull was her leading man in both this and Somerset Maugham's "The Land of Promise" in which she starred later in the year. Marguerite Clark had little luck with "Are You A Crook?," a farce, but later she charmed her public in "Prunella," a fantasy. Her vis-a-vis was Ernest Glendinning. John Barrymore and Mary Young had the leads in "Believe Me, Xantippe."

Other stars and their vehicles were: Tom Wise in "The Silver Wedding," Julia Dean in "Her Own Money," Margaret Wycherly in "The Fight," Leo Ditrichstein with Isabel Irving in "The Temperamental Journey," William Collier in "Who's Who," Fannie Ward in "Madam President," Edna Goodrich in "Evangeline," Lyn Harding with Janet Beecher in "The Great Adventure," William Courtenay with Florence Reed in "The Girl and the Pennant," Ethel Barrymore in "Tante," Arnold Daly with Maire O'Neill in "General John Regan," Henrietta Crosman in "The Tongues of Men," Elsie Ferguson in "The Strange Woman," Fiske O'Hara in "In Old Dublin," Bertha Kalich in "Rachel" and Frances Starr with Robert Warwick in "The Secret."

Cyril Maude, famous English actor, made his American debut November 3rd in "The Second in Command," the same play John Drew acted in 1901. Two weeks later he opened in "Grumpy" with which he had great success. His daughter, Margery Maude, was in his company.

The Irish Players returned for another season of repertory. Sothern and

CYRIL MAUDE in
"GRUMPY"

MARGUERITE CLARK, ERNEST GLENDINNING in
"PRUNELLA"

MAY IRWIN

THOMAS CONKEY,
CHRISTIE MacDONALD in
"SWEETHEARTS"

RUTH SHEPLEY, JANE GREY, BRUCE McRAE, MARK SMITH,
JOHN WESTLEY in "NEARLY MARRIED"

KATHERINE EMMETT, H. B. WARNER in
"THE GHOST BREAKER"

CHRISTIE MacDONALD in
"SWEETHEARTS"

JOHN BARRYMORE, MARY YOUNG in
"BELIEVE ME, XANTIPPE"

MARIE DORO, CHARLES CHERRY in
"THE NEW SECRETARY"

Marlowe were playing Shakespearean repertory and J. Forbes-Robertson with Gertrude Elliott also played many of their famous roles in a season of repertory.

Holbrook Blinn organized what he called the Princess Players with Willette Kershaw, Francine Larrimore, Edward Ellis, Emilie Polini, Harrison Ford, Charlotte Ives, May Buckley and Harry Mestayer. They put on a series of one-act plays. During the spring season the plays presented were "The Switchboard," "Fear," "Fancy Free," "Any Night" and "A Tragedy of the Future." In the fall they did "The Eternal Mystery" by George Jean Nathan, "The Bride," "The Fountain," "A Pair of White Gloves" and others.

Among the revivals were Mrs. Leslie Carter in "The Second Mrs. Tanqueray," Edith Wynne Matthison and Ben Greet in "Everyman," Grace George in "Divorcons," William and Dustin Farnum with Elsie Ferguson, Chrystal Herne and Vincent Serrano in "Arizona," Fritzi Scheff in "Mlle. Modiste" with Peggy Wood in her cast, David Warfield in "The Auctioneer" with Marie Bates and George Le Guere, and "The Henrietta," originally produced and acted by Stuart Robson and William H. Crane, was retitled "The New Henrietta" with Crane playing his old role, Douglas Fairbanks in the Robson role and Amelia Bingham with Patricia Collinge in the cast.

The biggest musical hits were "High Jinks" and "Adele." Also popular were Christie MacDonald in Victor Herbert's "Sweethearts;" Julia Sanderson with Joseph Cawthorn in "The Sunshine Girl;" Donald Brian in "The Marriage Market;" "The Honeymoon Express" with Gaby Deslys, Al Jolson, Fannie Brice, Yanci Dolly and Harry Pilcer; "The Purple Road" featuring

ALICE GALE, TOM WISE in
"THE SILVER WEDDING"

CHAUNCEY OLCOTT, JENNIE
LAMONT in
"THE ISLE O' DREAMS"

93

FRED and
ADELE ASTAIRE

VIRGINIA
PEARSON

HENRY
WOODRUFF

PAULINE
FREDERICK

VIOLA
DANA

HARRISON
FORD

FRANCINE
LARRIMORE

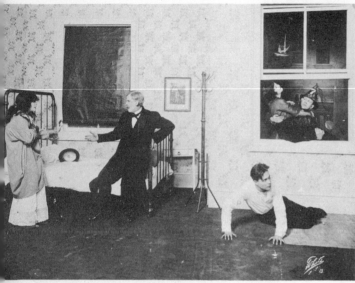

FRANCINE LARRIMORE, EDWARD ELLIS, HARRISON FORD,
WILLETTE KERSHAW in "ANY NIGHT"

HOLBROOK BLINN in
"THE BRIDE"

HOLBROOK BLINN, WILLETTE KERSHAW
WITH THE PRINCESS PLAYERS

JACK DEAN, FANNIE WARD in
"MADAM PRESIDENT"

HOWARD ESTABROOK, GRACE GEORGE, WM. COURTLEIGH in
"DIVORCONS"

FELIX KREMBS,
MARGARET WYCHERLY in
"THE FIGHT"

94   ELSIE FERGUSON,
DUSTIN FARNUM in
"ARIZONA"

JULIA DEAN, ERNEST GLENDINNING in
"HER OWN MONEY"

KATHLEEN
CLIFFORD

PATRICIA COLLINGE, WILLIAM H. CRANE, DOUGLAS FAIRBANKS,
AMELIA BINGHAM in "THE NEW HENRIETTA"

HARRY
HOUDINI

ANN
PENNINGTON

EDDIE CANTOR,
GEORGE JESSEL

FISKE
O'HARA

CARROLL
McCOMAS

HOWARD
ESTABROOK

DONALD
BRIAN

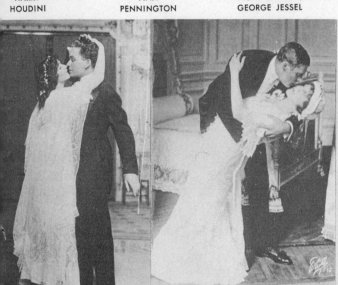

[M]IE FLYNN, JOSEPH SANTLEY in
[W]HEN DREAMS COME TRUE"

HAL FORDE, NATALIE ALT in
"ADELE"

LEW FIELDS in
"ALL ABOARD"

CHARES KING, GEORGIA CAINE, EDWIN STEVENS, PAULINE HALL, FRANK
POLLOCK, CARL GANTVOORT, (seated) ALICE ZEPPILLI, JAMES T.
POWERS, LINA ABARBANELL in 'THE GEISHA"

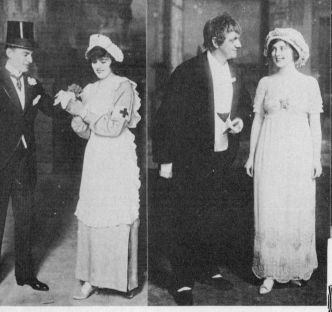

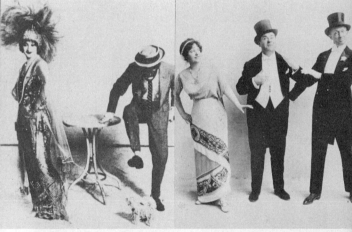

[B]URRELL BARBARETTO, ELAINE
[H]AMMERSTEIN in "HIGH JINKS"

JOSEPH CAWTHORN, JULIA
SANDERSON in "THE SUNSHINE GIRL"

VALLI VALLI, HARRISON
BROCKBANK in
"THE PURPLE ROAD"

GABY DESLYS, AL JOLSON in
"THE HONEYMOON EXPRESS"

HATTIE WILLIAMS, WILL WEST,
RICHARD CARLE in
"THE DOLL GIRL"

[H]UGH CAMERON, SALLY DALY, WM. MONTGOMERY, MYRTLE GILBERT, MAX
ROGERS, DOROTHY JARDON, BOBBY NORTH, FLORENCE MOORE, HARRY
COOPER, VIRGINIA EVANS, GEORGE WHITE, FLO MAY in
"THE PLEASURE SEEKERS"

Valli Valli and with Clifton Webb in a minor role; Lew Fields in "All Aboard" with Lawrence D'Orsay, Zoe Barnett, Carter De Haven and Flora Parker; "Ziegfeld Follies of 1913" with Bessie Clayton, Charles King, John Charles Thomas, Charlotte Greenwood, Mollie King and May Boley; Joseph Santley in "When Dreams Come True;" Richard Carle and Hattie Williams in "The Doll Girl;" Bessie Abbott in "Rob Roy;" "Her Little Highness" with Mitzi Hajos; "The Pleasure Seekers" with Florence Moore, Max Rogers, Dorothy Jardon and George White; "The Little Cafe" with Hazel Dawn; "The Madcap Duchess" with Ann Swinburne; De Wolf Hopper in "Hop O' My Thumb" with Texas Guinan in the cast; "The Girl in the Film" with Emmy Wehlen; Marie Dressler's All Star Gambol, arranged and compiled by Marie Dressler and starring her with Jefferson De Angelis; and a revival of "The Geisha" with James T. Powers, Lina Abarbanell, Edwin Stevens and Carl Gantvoort.

Vaudeville had come into its own with such illustrious headliners as Sarah Bernhardt, Lillian Russell, Olga Nethersole, Blanche Walsh, Henry Woodruff, Eva Tanguay, Alice Lloyd, Harry Houdini, also Belle Baker, Adele Ritchie, Joe Welch, Fred and Adele Astaire, Elizabeth Murray, Cissie Loftus, Valeska Suratt, Laddie Cliff, Adele Blood, Lulu Glaser, Sophie Tucker, Reine Davies, Kathleen Clifford and Rae Samuels.

JOHN DREW

WILL DEMING, SIDNEY SEAWARD, JOHN COPE,
GRANT MITCHELL, RUTH SHEPLEY in
"IT PAYS TO ADVERTISE"

MARY RYAN, CONSTANCE WOLFE,
FREDERICK PERRY in
"ON TRIAL"

MADGE KENNEDY, JOHN WESTLEY, GEORGIE LAWRENCE, CHARLES
JUDELS, MABEL ACKER, RAY COX, JOHN CUMBERLAND in
"TWIN BEDS"

SOPHIE
TUCKER

ELLA
SHIELDS

MAY
DE SOUSA

HAMILTON
REVELLE

CECILIA
LOFTUS

GRACE
VALENTINE

ERNEST
GLENDINNING

LOUISE
DREW

RALPH MORGAN, LILY CAHILL, WILLIAM COURTENAY in
"UNDER COVER"

INEZ PLUMMER, FRANK CRAVEN in
"TOO MANY COOKS"

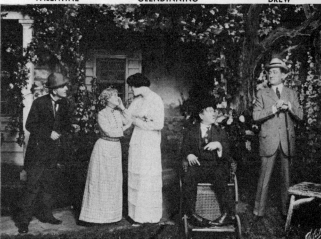

FRANK BACON, ADA GILMAN, GAIL KANE, JAMES C. MARLOWE,
GEORGE NASH in "THE MIRACLE MAN"

RUTH CHATTERTON in
"DADDY LONG-LEGS"

1914

"On Trial," besides being one of the outstanding hits of 1914, was the first play to employ the flashback technique being used in films. Elmer Reizenstein, a young lawyer, was so successful with his first play he gave up his law practice and, with his name shortened to Elmer Rice, took up playwriting as a profession. Other hits of the year were "Twin Beds," a farce that brought Madge Kennedy into the public eye; "It Pays To Advertise," a Cohan and Harris comedy with Ruth Shepley, Will Deming, Grant Mitchell and Louise Drew, John Drew's daughter, prominent in the cast; "Under Cover" with William Courtenay, Lola Fisher, Ralph Morgan, Phoebe Foster and Lucile Watson; "Daddy Long Legs," a dramatization of Jean Webster's popular book, with Ruth Chatterton in the lead; "The Law of the Land" with Julia Dean, George Fawcett and Milton Sills; "The Miracle Man" with Gail Kane, George Nash and Frank Bacon; "Too Many Cooks," a comedy by and with Frank Craven; "A Pair of Sixes," a farce with Ann Murdock, Hale Hamilton and Maude Eburne; "The Dummy," a comedy with Edward Ellis, Ernest Truex and Joyce Fair, a child actress who grew up to be Clare Booth Luce, playwright and politician; and "A Pair of Silk Stockings," a comedy produced by Winthrop Ames.

A. H. Woods, one of the outstanding producers of this period, had quite a few hits. In January, he produced "The Yellow Ticket" with John Mason, Florence Reed, John Barrymore, Em-

JOHN BARRYMORE, JOHN MASON,
MACY HARLAM, FLORENCE REED in
"THE YELLOW TICKET"

JOYCE FAIR, ERNEST TRUEX in
"THE DUMMY"

CAROLINE BAYLEY, KENNETH DOUGLAS in
"A PAIR OF SILK STOCKINGS"

JANE GREY, JOHN BARRYMORE, FORREST WINANT in
"KICK IN"

PAULINE FREDERICK
"INNOCENT"

EUGENE O'BRIEN, MOLLY McINTYRE in
"KITTY MAC KAY"

MILTON SILLS, JULIA DEAN in
"THE LAW OF THE LAND"

VIOLET HEMING,
MARGARET ILLINGTON
in "THE LIE"

MAUDE ADAMS, C. AUBREY SMITH in
"THE LEGEND OF LEONORA"

MARY BOLAND in
"MY LADY'S DRESS"

DAPHNE
POLLARD

VERA
MICHELENA

STEWART
BAIRD

EVELYN
VAUGHAN

JULIAN ELTINGE, MAIDEL TURNER, JAMES C. SPOTTSWOOD,
WALTER HORTON, CHARLES P. MORRISON in
"THE CRINOLINE GIRL"

mett Corrigan and Julian L'Estrange heading an imposing cast. Later in the year he presented John Barrymore in a crook melodrama, "Kick In," supported by Jane Grey, Forrest Winant and Katherine Harris who became the first Mrs. John Barrymore "The Song of Songs," put on in late December, also had a fine cast with Dorothy Donnelly, John Mason, Irene Fenwick, Tom Wise, Ernest Glendinning, Forrest Winant and Cyril Keightley. Julian Eltinge, Woods' greatest money-making star, was appearing in "The Crinoline Girl." Al Woods built and named the Eltinge Theatre after this bright star. He also starred Lew Fields in "The High Cost of Loving." His other attractions included "Innocent" with Pauline Frederick and "He Comes Up Smiling" with Douglas Fairbanks and Patricia Collinge.

William Elliott, popular young actor, turned producer with two successes to his credit. They were "Kitty MacKay," a Scotch comedy with Molly McIntyre and handsome Eugene O'Brien, and "Experience," an allegorical melodrama with Mr. Elliott playing the lead role of Youth. Later Ernest Glendinning took over the role for the road.

Charles Frohman's roster of stars were having a busy year. Maude Adams was appearing in Barrie's "The Legend of Leonora." John Drew and Ethel Barrymore were co-starring in a revival of "A Scrap of Paper" with Mary Boland. Later Mr. Drew appeared in "The Prodigal Husband" with Helen Hayes in his cast. William Gillette, Blanche Bates and Marie Doro were starring together in a revival of "Diplomacy." Ann Murdock

KER WHITESIDE
in "MR. WU"

PATRICIA COLLINGE, DOUGLAS FAIRBANKS in "HE COMES UP SMILING"

CHARLES RICHMAN, CHARLES RUGGLES, LOIS MEREDITH in "HELP WANTED"

HENRY KOLKER, GRACE VALENTINE in "HELP WANTED"

IS NEILSON-TERRY
'WELFTH NIGHT"

RITA JOLIVET, HENRY E. DIXEY, JEROME PATRICK in "A THOUSAND YEARS AGO"

CYRIL KEIGHTLEY, IRENE FENWICK in "THE SONG OF SONGS"

GUY BATES POST, JANE SALISBURY in "OMAR, THE TENTMAKER"

DOROTHY DONNELLY, LOU TELLEGEN in "MARIA ROSA"

with Charles Cherry, and Mrs. Thomas Whiffen were in "The Beautiful Adventure." Billie Burke still had Shelley Hull as her leading man in "Jerry." William Collier had Paula Marr, his wife, and Buster Collier, now billed as William Collier, Jr., with him in "A Little Water on the Side." G. B. Shaw's "Pygmalion" was having its first presentation in this country with Mrs. Patrick Campbell and Philip Merivale in the leading roles. "A Thousand Years Ago," a romantic fable of the ancient Orient, proved interesting theatre fare with Rita Jolivet, Henry E. Dixey, Fania Marinoff, Jerome Patrick and Sheldon Lewis. Mabel and Edith Taliaferro were co-starring together for the first time in "Young Wisdom," a Rachel Crothers' comedy. Guy Bates Post was having a successful starring engagement with "Omar, the Tentmaker." Lou Tellegen, Sarah Bernhardt's leading man, co-starred with Dorothy Donnelly in "Maria Rosa" and it was his first appearance in English. Chauncey Olcott's vehicle was "Shameen Dhu." William Faversham played Iago in a revival of "Othello" with Constance Collier, Cecilia Loftus and R. D. MacLean. Later he had success in "The Hawk" with Mlle. Gabrielle Dorziat, Conway Tearle and, in a lesser role, Richard Dix who became a film star. Phyllis Neilson-Terry made her first American appearance in "Twelfth Night" with Henry E. Dixey playing Malvolio. Jack Lait, a Chicago newspaperman, had written a play, "Help Wanted." With Henry Kolker and Grace Valentine, it had great success in that city. In New York, Charles Richman, Lois Meredith and Charles Ruggles were in the cast.

MARILYN MILLER

HARRY PILCER

HAL C. FORDE

BESSIE ABOTT

GEORGE W. HOWARD, IVY TROUTMAN, GEORGE PARSONS, HALE HAMILTON, ANN MURDOCK, MAUDE EBURNE in "A PAIR OF SIXES"

MARGARET ANGLIN,
SYDNEY GREENSTREET in
"AS YOU LIKE IT"

CONSTANCE COLLIER,
WILLIAM FAVERSHAM in
"OTHELLO"

MARIE DORO, WILLIAM GILLETTE,
BLANCHE BATES in
"DIPLOMACY"

ELSIE FERGUSON in "OUTCAST"

DOROTHY NEWELL, ERNEST GLENDINNING,
WILLIAM INGERSOLL, MARGOT WILLIAMS in
"EXPERIENCE"

CHARLES A. STEVENSON, WILLIAM ELLIOTT, BEN
JOHNSON, ROXANE BARTON, MARGOT WILLIAMS
in "EXPERIENCE"

GEORGE NASH, OLGA PETROVA, MILTON SILLS in
"PANTHEA"

MARY BOLAND, CHARLES DALTON, ETHEL BARRYMORE,
JOHN DREW in "A SCRAP OF PAPER"

MRS. PATRICK CAMPBELL, PHILIP MERIVALE,
MRS. EDMUND GURNEY in "PYGMALION"

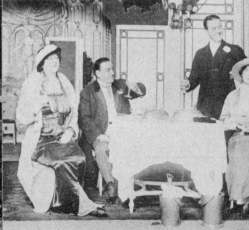

HELEN HAYES, JOHN DREW in
"THE PRODIGAL HUSBAND"

ROSE STAHL

VIVIAN MARTIN, LEW FIELDS in
"THE HIGH COST OF LOVING"

JOBYNA HOWLAND, WALTER JONES, TAYLOR HOLM
MARJORIE WOOD in "THE THIRD PARTY"

Margaret Anglin revived "As You Like It," "The Taming of the Shrew," "Twelfth Night" and later "Lady Windermere's Fan." Grace George was in a revival of "The Truth" with Conway Tearle, Isabel Irving, Zelda Sears and a young man named Guthrie McClintic playing a messenger. Taylor Holmes had a hit with "The Third Party." Fritzi Scheff was appearing in "Pretty Mrs. Smith."

Other stars and their plays were Leo Ditrichstein with Laura Hope Crews in "The Phantom Rival," Mary Boland in "My Lady's Dress," Walker Whiteside in "Mr. Wu," Rose Stahl in "A Perfect Lady," Elsie Ferguson in "Outcast," Nazimova in "That Sort," Otis Skinner in "The Silent Voice," Marie Tempest in a revival of "The Marriage of Kitty," Margaret Illington in "The Lie," Olga Petrova in "Panthea" and Marie Dressler in "A Mix-Up," a farce with Bert Lytell and Evelyn Vaughan, two young players who had great success in a San Francisco stock company.

The musical comedy hits were "Chin-Chin" starring Montgomery and Stone, Victor Herbert's "The Only Girl" with Wilda Bennett, Thurston Hall and Ernest Torrence, and "Watch Your Step" featuring Irene and Vernon Castle who had become the rage as a dance team. Other popular dance teams at this time were Maurice and Florence Walton, Carl Hyson and Dorothy Dickson and John Murray Anderson with his wife, Genevieve Lyon. Other musicals that scored were "Sari" with Mitzi Hajos; "The Whirl of the World" with Eugene and Willie Howard, Lillian Lorraine, Ralph Herz and Bernard Granville; "Queen of the Movies" with Valli Valli, Alice Dovey and Frank Moulan; Blanche Ring in "When Claudia Smiles;" "The Midnight Girl" with Margaret Romaine who was Hazel Dawn's sister; Gaby Deslys and Sam Bernard in "The Belle of Bond Street;" Raymond Hitchcock in "The Beauty Shop;" Julia Sanderson, Donald Brian and Joseph Cawthorn in "The Girl from Utah;" "Dancing Around" with Al Jolson, Doyle and Dixon, Kitty Doner, Earle Foxe and Clifton Webb; "The Lilac Domino" with Eleanor Painter and John E. Hazzard; Hazel Dawn in "The Debutante;" Emmy Wehlen in "Tonight's the Night" with Fay Compton and Iris Hoey, two well-known English actresses; George M. Cohan and William Collier in "Hello Broadway," and "Lady Luxury" with Ina Claire. The "Ziegfeld Follies of 1914" cast included Bert Williams, Ed Wynn, Ann Pennington, Vera Michelena, Gertrude Vanderbilt, Leon Errol, Kay Laurell and Gladys Feldman. "The Passing Show of 1914" featured Jose Collins, Bernard Granville and Marilyn Miller making her first New York appearance other than vaudeville.

The vaudeville headliners of the year included Gus Edwards' act featuring Cuddles, who became Lila Lee of films, and Georgie Price, and Victor Moore with his wife, Emma Littlefield.

MR. AND MRS. VERNON CASTLE

FLORENCE WALTON and MAURICE

DOROTHY DICKSON and CARL HYSON

GENEVIEVE LYON and JOHN MURRAY ANDERSON

MADGE KENNEDY in "TWIN BEDS"

DOUGLAS STEVENSON, HELEN FALCONER in "CHIN-CHIN"

LAURA HOPE CREWS, LEO DITRICHSTEIN in "THE PHANTOM RIVAL"

NAZIMOVA in "THAT SORT"

EDITH AND MABEL TALIAFERRO in "YOUNG WISDOM"

VICTOR MOORE & EMMA LITTLEFIELD

ELEANOR PAINTER, WILFRED DOUTHITT in "THE LILAC DOMINO"

ANNA ORR, RAYMOND HITCHCOCK, TESSA KOSTA in "THE BEAUTY SHOP"

BILLIE BURKE, SHELLEY HULL in "JERRY"

MRS. THOMAS WHIFFEN

MARIE DRESSLER, BERT LYTELL in "A MIX-UP"

101

HAZEL DAWN, STEWART BAIRD, MAUDE ODELL in "THE DEBUTANTE"

ELIZABETH BRICE, CHARLES KING, IRENE CASTLE, VERNON CASTLE, FRANK TINNEY, SALLIE FISHER, HARRY KELLY, ELIZABETH MURRAY in "WATCH YOUR STEP"

FRITZI SCHEFF, SYDNEY GRA "PRETTY MRS. SMITH"

SAM BERNARD, GABY DESLYS in "THE BELLE OF BOND STREET"

CHARLES MEAKINS, MITZI HAJOS in "SARI"

BERNARD GRANVILLE

THURSTON HALL, WILDA BENNETT in "THE ONLY GIRL"

FAY COMPTON, EMMY WEHL IRIS HOEY in "TONIGHT'S THE NIGHT"

MITZI HAJOS in "SARI"

GEORGE MacFARLANE, MARGARET ROMAINE in "THE MIDNIGHT GIRL"

CUDDLES (LILA LEE), GEORGIE PRICE

T. ROY BARNES, JOSE COLLINS in "THE PASSING SHOW OF 1914"

ALICE DOVEY, VALLI VALLI in "The QUEEN of the MOVIES"

BUSTER COLLIER, PAULA MARR, WILLIAM COLLIER

BLANCHE RI in "WHEN CLAUDIA

MONTGOMERY & STONE in "CHIN-CHIN"

JOSEPH CAWTHORN, JULIA SANDERSON, DONALD BRIAN in "THE GIRL FROM UTAH"

GEORGE M. COHAN in "HELLO, BROADWAY"

LEO DITRICHSTEIN in
"THE GREAT LOVER"

LOUIS MANN in
"THE BUBBLE"

ROBERT B. MANTELL

JULIA ARTHUR in
"THE ETERNAL MAGDALENE"

MARGARET ANGLIN in
"MEDEA"

OTIS SKINNER in
"COCK O' THE WALK"

1915

The First World War was raging in Europe, and while the United States still remained neutral, the troubled conditions somewhat affected our theatre. Fewer productions reached the boards and generally it was not a good year. An important event was the organization of the Washington Square Players by a group of ambitious amateurs and semi-professionals. They rented the small Bandbox Theatre on 57th Street and presented mostly one-act plays, charging only fifty cents admission. This venture resulted in the establishment of the Theatre Guild four years later. Among the plays presented were "Interior" and "A Miracle of St. Anthony" by Maeterlinck, "A Bear" by Tchekov, "My Lady's Honor" by Murdock Pemberton, "The Clod" by Lewis Beach, "Helena's Husband" by Philip Moeller, "Overtones" by Alice Gerstenberg and "The Red Cloak" by Josephine A. Meyer and Lawrence Langner. Among the players were Helen Westley, Philip Moeller, Florence Enright, Glenn Hunter, Frank Conroy, Mary Morris, Roland Young, Margaret Mower and Lydia Lopokova.

The hit plays of 1915 were: "The Boomerang," a comedy David Belasco produced with Wallace Eddinger, Ruth Shepley, Arthur Byron and Martha Hedman; "Fair and Warmer," a farce with Madge Kennedy, Ralph Morgan, Janet Beecher and Hamil-

GRACE GEORGE in
"MAJOR BARBARA"

JOHN ARTHUR,
FRANCINE LARRIMORE
in "SOME BABY"

ETHEL BARRYMORE
in
"THE SHADOW"

MARJORIE RAMBEAU,
PETER De CORDOBA in
"SADIE LOVE"

ROSE STAHL
in
"OUR MRS. McCHESNEY"

JOHN DREW,
ALEXANDRA CARLISLE
in "ROSEMARY"

GLENN HUNTER
in
"THE CLOD"

MR. & MRS. CHARLES
HOPKINS in
"TREASURE ISLAND"

RUTH SHEPLEY, ARTHUR BYRON, MARTHA HEDMAN, WALLACE
EDDINGER in "THE BOOMERANG"

WILLIAM BOYD, ETHEL BARRYMORE in
"OUR MRS. McCHESNEY"

JANE COWL, ORME CALDARA in
"COMMON CLAY"

HOLBROOK BLINN, LILLIAN ALBERTSON
in "MOLOCH"

WILLIAM BOYD, MARGARET ANGLIN in
"BEVERLY'S BALANCE"

FRANCES STARR, JEROME PATRICK in
"MARIE-ODILE"

ton Revelle; "Hit-the-Trail-Holiday," a farce written by George M. Cohan for his brother-in-law, Fred Niblo; "Common Clay," an A. H. Woods production with Jane Cowl and John Mason; "The Great Lover," a comedy by Frederick and Fanny Hatton starring Leo Ditrichstein; "The House of Glass" with Mary Ryan; "Sinners," an Owen Davis play with Alice Brady, Robert Edeson, Charles Richman, Emma Dunn, Florence Nash and John Cromwell who became a famous film director; "The Unchastened Woman" which Oliver Morosco produced with Emily Stevens, Willette Kershaw, Christine Norman and Hassard Short; "Abe and Mawruss," a sequel to "Potash and Perlmutter" and later retitled "Potash and Perlmutter in Society," and "Treasure Island" produced by Charles Hopkins with himself, Mrs. Charles Hopkins and Oswald Yorke.

In September Grace George began a season of repertory that ran into the spring of 1916. Among the plays presented were revivals of "Captain Brassbound's Conversion," "The Liars" and "The New York Idea," and, for the first time, Shaw's "Major Barbara" and "The Earth" by James Bernard Fagan. Miss George's company included Conway Tearle, Mary Nash, Robert Warwick, Louis Calvert, Charlotte Granville, Ernest Lawford, John Cromwell and Guthrie McClintic who became a famous

GLENN HUNTER, FLORENCE ENRIGHT, ROLAND YOUNG,
CHARLES EDWARDS with WASHINGTON SQUARE PLAYERS
in "THE RED CLOAK"

ARK TAYLOR,
AY IRWIN in
WASHINGTON SQ.

VIVIAN TOBIN
in
"ALICE IN WONDERLAND"

LENORE ULRIC
in
"THE MARK OF THE BEAST"

JASPER
in
"YOUNG AMERICA"

GARETH HUGHES
in
"MOLOCH"

CREIGHTON HALE
in
"MOLOCH"

MOLLY PEARSON,
WHITFORD KANE in
"HOBSON'S CHOICE"

JANET BEECHER, HAMILTON REVELLE, JOHN CUMBERLAND,
RALPH MORGAN, MADGE KENNEDY in "FAIR AND WARMER"

BENNY SWENNY, PERCY HELTON,
JASPER in "YOUNG AMERICA"

GRACE GEORGE, ERNEST LAWFORD in
"MAJOR BARBARA"

LOU TELLEGEN in
"THE WARE CASE"

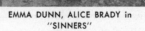

EMMA DUNN, ALICE BRADY in
"SINNERS"

FRED NIBLO, KATHERINE LaSALLE in
"HIT-THE-TRAIL-HOLIDAY"

producer and director and married Katharine Cornell.

There was a season of repertory at Wallack's Theatre with Shaw's "Androcles and the Lion" and "The Doctor's Dilemma," both presented for the first time in this country. Also given was Anatole France's "The Man Who Married a Dumb Wife" with the settings of Robert Edmond Jones starting him on the road to fame. Other repertoire included Robert B. Mantell and his company.

Arnold Daly revived Shaw's "Candida," "You Never Can Tell," and "Arms and the Man," while William Gillette revived "Sherlock Holmes" and "Secret Service" again.

William A. Brady presented a series of Gilbert and Sullivan revivals. Other revivals were "Rosemary" starring John Drew, "The Critic" with B. Iden Payne, Emilie Polini and Whitford Kane, "Trilby" with Phyllis Neilson-Terry, Wilton Lackaye, Leo Ditrichstein, Rose Coghlan, Burr McIntosh and Taylor Holmes; "A Celebrated Case" with Nat C. Goodwin, Otis Skinner, Florence Reed, Robert Warwick, Helen Ware, Eugene O'Brien and Ann Murdock, and Maude Adams in "Peter Pan" with Ruth Gordon making her first New York stage appearance in this revival.

The stars and their vehicles included: Effie Shannon and Her-

WILLETTE KERSHAW, LOUIS BENNISON, HASSARD SHORT,
EMILY STEVENS, CHRISTINE NORMAN, H. REEVES-SMITH in
"THE UNCHASTENED WOMAN"

105

ROBERT WARWICK, FLORENCE REED, FREDERIC de BELLEVILLE, HELEN WARE, NAT C. GOODWIN,
OTIS SKINNER, ANN MURDOCK, ELITA PROCTOR OTIS, EUGENE O'BRIEN,
MINNA GALE HAYNES in "A CELEBRATED CASE"

MARY ALDEN, GERTRUDE BECKLEY, NAZIMOVA in
"WAR BRIDES"

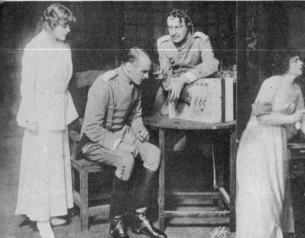

VIOLET HEMING, FELIX KREMBS, WILLIAM
COURTENAY in "UNDER FIRE"

MARY RYAN, THOMAS FINDLAY, FRANK M. THOMAS
in "THE HOUSE OF GLASS"

MARIE BATES, DAVID WARFIELD in
"VAN DER DECKEN"

WILLIAM HODGE, GERTRUDE HITZ
"THE ROAD TO HAPPINESS"

EUGENE
O'BRIEN

MARIE TEMPEST, REGINALD DENNY, KATE
SERJEANTSON in "ROSALIND"

JESSIE
BONSTELLE

ROSE COGHLAN, TAYLOR HOLMES, PHYLLIS NEILSON-TERRY, LEO
DITRICHSTEIN, GEORGE MacFARLANE, BURR McINTOSH, BRANDON
TYNAN, WILTON LACKAYE in "TRILBY"

bert Kelcey in "Children of Earth;" Frances Starr in "Marie-Odile;" Lou Tellegen in "Taking Chances" and later "The Ware Case;" Louis Mann in "The Bubble;" Margaret Anglin in "Beverly's Balance" and in August she won acclaim playing "Medea," "Electra" and "Iphigenia in Aulis" at the Greek Theatre in Berkeley, California; May Irwin in "No. 33 Washington Square;" Julian Eltinge in "Cousin Lucy;" William Hodge in "The Road to Happiness;" Marie Tempest in "The Duke of Killicrankie" and Barrie's one-act "Rosalind;" Holbrook Blinn in "Moloch;" E. H. Sothern in "The Two Virtues;" Ethel Barrymore in "The Shadow" and later the dramatized Edna Ferber stories, "Our Mrs. McChesney," which Rose Stahl also played on the road; Julia Arthur in "The Eternal Magdalene;" Otis Skinner in "Cock o' the Walk" and David Warfield in "Van Der Decken."

Other popular plays were: "The White Feather" with Leslie Faber; "Inside the Lines" with Lewis S. Stone and Carroll McComas; Alice Gerstenberg's version of "Alice in Wonderland" with Vivian Tobin; "A Full House" with May Vokes; "Under Fire" with William Courtenay, Violet Heming and Frank Craven; "Some Baby" with Francine Larrimore; "Rolling Stones"

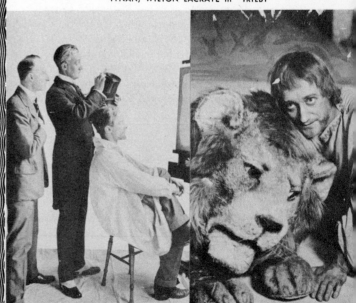

ARNOLD LUCY, O. P. HEGGIE, NICHOLAS
HANNEN in "THE DOCTOR'S DILEMMA"

O. P. HEGGIE in
"ANDROCLES AND THE LION"

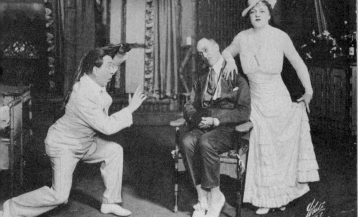

FRED WALTON, RICHARD CARLE, MARIE CAHILL in
"90 IN THE SHADE"

LLIE HOWARD, MARILYN MILLER in
"THE PASSING SHOW OF 1915"

PRUDENCE O'SHEA, ROBERT PITKIN in
"AROUND THE MAP"

JOSEPH SANTLEY, GABY DESLYS in
"STOP! LOOK! LISTEN!"

DE WOLF HOPPER in
"YEOMEN OF THE GUARD"

JANE OAKER, JULIAN ELTINGE, LEO DONNELLY in
"COUSIN LUCY"

NAT
WILLS

MARGUERITE NAMARA, JOHN CHARLES THOMAS,
JOSE COLLINS in "ALONE AT LAST"

WILL ROGERS

EMMA TRENTINI
in
HE PEASANT GIRL"

HARRISON FORD,
CHARLES RUGGLES in
"ROLLING STONES"

VIVIENNE SEGAL
in
"THE BLUE PARADISE"

with Harrison Ford, Charles Ruggles and Marie Carroll; "Young America" with Otto Kruger, Peggy Wood, Percy Helton and Jasper, a dog actor who scored; "Hobson's Choice" with Molly Pearson and Whitford Kane; "Sadie Love" with Marjorie Rambeau; "Ruggles of Red Gap" with Ralph Herz, and "The Mark of the Beast" which introduced Lenore Ulric to Broadway.

The musical hits were "The Blue Paradise" with Vivienne Segal, Cecil Lean, and Cleo Mayfield; "Very Good, Eddie" with Ernest Truex, Oscar Shaw, Alice Dovey and John E. Hazzard; "Alone At Last" with Jose Collins, John Charles Thomas and Marguerite Namara; "Katinka" with Edith Decker, Adele Rowland and Sam Ash; "A World of Pleasure" with Kitty Gordon, "Around the Map" with William Morris, Else Adler and Robert Pitkin; and "Stop! Look! Listen!" with Gaby Deslys, Joseph Santley, Harry Fox, Marion Davies and Harry Pilcer.

The musical comedy stars appearing on the boards were: Marie Cahill and Richard Carle in "90 in the Shade," Nora Bayes with Harry Fox in "Maid in America," Emma Trentini in "The Peasant Girl," William Norris with Ernest Glendinning and Leila Hughes in "A Modern Eve," Joseph Santley in "All Over Town," Eleanor Painter with Sam Hardy in "The Princess

107

CHARLOTTE in "HIP-HIP-HOORAY"   MARION DAVIES   HELEN ELEY   FRANKLYN ARDELL, MAY THOMPSON, SAM ASH in "KATINKA"   MAUDE LAMBERT   INA CLAIRE   OLIVE THOMAS

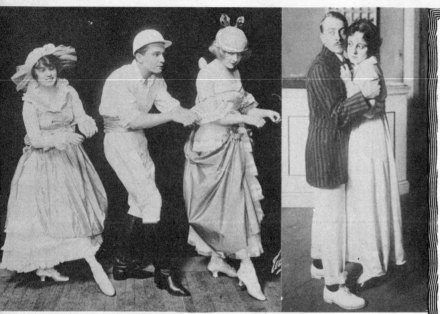

RUTH RANDALL, JOSEPH SANTLEY, BEATRICE ALLEN in "ALL OVER TOWN"   ERNEST TRUEX, ALICE DOVEY in "VERY GOOD, EDDIE"

Pat" and Elsie Janis in "Miss Information." A musical, "Hands Up," had Ralph Herz, Irene Franklin and Donald Macdonald in the cast, also a vaudevillian who was making his first appearance in the legitimate theatre, likeable, shy Will Rogers. The "Ziegfeld Follies of 1915" cast included Ina Claire, Ed Wynn, Ann Pennington, Bert Williams, W. C. Fields, Olive Thomas, Leon Errol, Bernard Granville, Mae Murray, George White, Justine Johnstone and Carl Randall. In the "Passing Show of 1915" cast were Willie and Eugene Howard, Marilyn Miller, John Charles Thomas, Daphne Pollard and Helen Ely. "Ned Wayburn's Town Topics" had Trixie Friganza, Clifton Webb, Blossom Seeley, Vera Michelena and Wellington Cross. "Hip-Hip-Hooray" was the Hippodrome attraction with John Philip Sousa and His Band, Charlotte, the skater Nat Wills and Toto.

The vaudeville headliners included Nazimova in "War Brides," a one-act play that was widely discussed, and Gertrude Hoffmann in "Sumurun."

NORA BAYES, HARRY FOX in "MAID IN AMERICA"   SAM B. HARDY, ELEANOR PAINTER in "THE PRINCESS PAT"   LEILA HUGHES, ERNEST GLENDINNING in "A MODERN EVE"   BLOSSOM SEELEY, TRIXIE FRIGANZA in "NED WAYBURN'S TOWN TOPICS"   GERTRUDE HOFFMANN RICHARD ORDYNSKE "SUMURUN"

FRANCES PRITCHARD, OLGA HEMPSTONE, DAPHNE POLLARD, JOHN T. MURRAY, JOHN CHARLES THOMAS, MARILYN MILLER, FRANCES DEMAREST, EUGENE HOWARD, ARTHUR HILL WILLIE HOWARD, GEORGE MONROE, HARRY FISHER, JULIETTE LIPPE, HELEN ELEY in "THE PASSING SHOW OF 1915"

ARNOLD DALY
in
"BEAU BRUMMELL"

MRS. CHARLES COBURN
in
"THE YELLOW JACKET"

CHARLES COBURN
in
"THE YELLOW JACKET"

ESTELLE WINWOOD
in
"HUSH"

McKAY MORRIS
with
PORTMANTEAU THEATRE

RICHARD BENNETT
in
"RIO GRANDE"

CALVIN THOMAS
in
"RIO GRANDE"

PATRICIA COLLINGE in
"POLLYANNA"

MARGARET WYCHERLY in
"THE THIRTEENTH CHAIR"

1916

In 1616, William Shakespeare died, and his tercentenary celebration saw quite a few of the Bard's plays on the boards. Sir Herbert Beerbohm Tree, in America because of the war abroad, was playing in "The Merchant of Venice" with Elsie Ferguson his Portia, and "King Henry VIII" with Lyn Harding, Edith Wynne Matthison and Willette Kershaw in his support. James K. Hackett won acclaim for his "Macbeth" while Viola Allen, his Lady Macbeth, also appeared with Henrietta Crosman and Tom Wise in "The Merry Wives of Windsor." "The Tempest" was acted by Louis Calvert, Jane Grey, Walter Hampden and Fania Marinoff who was particularly outstanding as Ariel.

Sarah Bernhardt was making another of her numerous farewell tours and among the plays she presented were "La Mort de Cleopatre," "Le Proces de Jeanne D'Arc" and scenes from "La Dame aux Camélias," "L'Aiglon" and "The Merchant of Venice."

There were many substantial hits and foremost among these were "Turn to the Right" with Forrest Winant and Lucy Cotton, "Cheating Cheaters" with Marjorie Rambeau and Cyril Keightley, "The Man Who Came Back" with Henry Hull and Mary Nash, "Nothing But The Truth" with William Collier, "Come Out of the Kitchen" with Ruth Chatterton, "The Thirteenth Chair" with Margaret Wycherly, and "Upstairs and Down" with Juliette Day, Christine Norman, Mary Servoss, Ida St. Leon and Leo Carillo.

Shelley Hull and Phoebe Foster were in "The Cinderella Man," Mrs. Fiske in "Erstwhile Susan," Elsie Ferguson in "Margaret Schiller" and "Shirley Kaye," Lenore Ulric in "The Heart of

RUTH ST. DENIS

MRS. FISKE in
"ERSTWHILE SUSAN"

CHARLOTTE
GREENWOOD

PAVLOWA

CHARLES CHERRY, HENRIETTA CROSMAN, HILDA SPONG, WILLIAM FAVERSHAM in "GETTING MARRIED"

STUART WALKER

LUCY COTTON, FORREST WINANT, RUTH CHESTER in "TURN TO THE RIGHT"

ROBERT AMES, BARBARA MILTON, CHARLES TROWBRIDGE, RUTH CHATTERTON in "COME OUT OF THE KITCHEN"

JOHN BARRYMORE in "JUSTICE"

JOHN BARRYMORE, CATHLEEN NESBITT, HENRY STEPHENSON, O. P. HEGGIE in "JUSTICE"

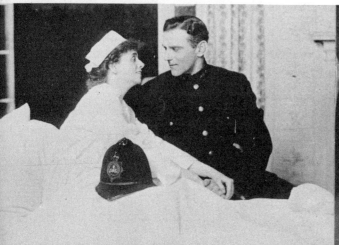

MAUDE ADAMS, NORMAN TREVOR in "A KISS FOR CINDERELLA"

TAYLOR HOLMES in "HIS MAJESTY BUNKER BEAN"

CYRIL KEIGHTLEY, MARJORIE RAMBEAU, WINIFRED HARRIS in "CHEATING CHEATERS"

LYNN FONTANNE, DION TITHERADGE, PHILIP MERIVALE, FFOLLIOTT PAGET, LAURETTE TAYLOR in "THE HARP OF LIFE"

FRANCES STARR, JEROME PATRICK in "LITTLE LADY IN BLUE"

HELEN MENKEN, JOHN DREW, HELEN MacKELLAR, BRANDON TYNAN in "MAJOR PENDENNIS"

WALTER HAMPDEN, LOUIS CALVERT, JANE GREY, FANIA MARINOFF in
"THE TEMPEST"

SIR HERBERT TREE, ELSIE FERGUSON in
"THE MERCHANT OF VENICE"

VIOLA ALLEN, REGGIE SHEFFIELD, HENRIETTA CROSMAN, TOM WISE in
"THE MERRY WIVES OF WINDSOR"

SIR HERBERT TREE, LYN HARDING, EDITH WYNNE MATTHISON in
"HENRY VIII"

Wetona," Taylor Holmes in "His Majesty Bunker Bean" and Patricia Collinge in "Pollyanna." "The Melody of Youth" was played by Lily Cahill, Eva Le Gallienne and Brandon Tynan, "A King of Nowhere" by Lou Tellegen and Olive Tell, "Rio Grande" by Richard Bennett and Lola Fisher, "Please Help Emily" by Ann Murdock, "Fixing Sister" by William Hodge, and "Seven Chances" by Frank Craven, Otto Kruger, Carroll McComas and Helen MacKellar.

The Dolly Sisters were in "His Bridal Night," Blanche Ring in "Broadway and Buttermilk," Marjorie Patterson in "Pierrot the Prodigal," Otis Skinner in "Mister Antonio" and Emma Dunn in "Old Lady 31."

"Good Gracious Annabelle" was played by Roland Young, Lola Fisher and Walter Hampden, "Getting Married" by William Faversham. Hilda Spong and Henrietta Crosman, a revival of "The Yellow Jacket" by the Charles Coburns, "Captain Kidd, Jr." by Edith Taliaferro and Otto Kruger, and "Our Little Wife" by Lowell Sherman and Margaret Illington.

"The Harp of Life" was acted by Laurette Taylor, Gail Kane, Lynn Fontanne and Philip Merivale, "Little Lady in Blue" by Frances Starr, and "The Pride of Race" by Robert Hilliard. Also George Arliss was appearing in "Paganini," Rose Stahl in "Moonlight Mary," Henry E. Dixey in "Mr. Lazarus" with Eva Le Gallienne, John Drew in "Major Pendennis," and Estelle Winwood was making her first American appearance in a slight comedy called "Hush."

Maude Adams revived "The Little Minister" and was also seen in "A Kiss for Cinderella." Marie Tempest appeared in "A Lady's Name" in which she was supported by Ruth Draper and Beryl Mercer. John Barrymore was highly effective in Galsworthy's "Justice" in which his leading lady was Cathleen Nesbitt.

Arnold Daly appeared in a revival of "Beau Brummell." Other revivals were E. H. Sothern in "David Garrick" and "If I Were King," David Warfield in "The Music Master," "Ben Hur" with A. H. Van Buren and Margaret Anglin, and Holbrook Blinn in "A Woman of No Importance."

Stuart Walker's Portmanteau Theatre played during the year, and among its actors were McKay Morris, Gregory Kelly and Mr. Walker. The Washington Square Players had a successful season of one and two-act plays including "Literature," "Plots and Playwrights," "Pariah" and "The Death of Tintagiles." Acting with this organization were Jose Ruben, Glenn Hunter, Helen Westley, Margaret Mower and Katharine Cornell who made her debut in "Bushido."

Charles Dillingham produced a spectacular entertainment at the Hippodrome called "The Big Show" with music by Raymond Hubbell. Prominent in the cast

JAMES K. HACKETT in
"MACBETH"

VIOLA ALLEN, JAMES K. HACKETT in
"MACBETH"

FANIA MARINOFF as ARIEL in
"THE TEMPEST"

111

MIRIAM COLLINS, WILLIAM HODGE in "FIXING SISTER"

JOHN CHARLES THOMAS in "HER SOLDIER BOY"

REGINALD BARLOW, EMMA DUNN in "OLD LADY 31"

ANN PENNINGTON in "ZIEGFELD FOLLIES"

GARETH HUGHES, IRENE FENWICK in "THE GUILTY MAN"

ANNA HELD in "FOLLOW ME"

E. H. SOTHERN, ALEXANDRA CARLISLE "DAVID GARRICK"

RUTH ROSE, OTIS SKINNER in "MISTER ANTONIO"

NANCY WINSTON, GREGORY KELLY, McKAY MORRIS in "THE LADY OF THE WEEPING WILLOW TREE"

MARY HARPER, VIVIAN WESSELL, WILLIAM COLLIER, RAPLEY HOLMES, MORGAN COMAN, NED A. SPARKS in "NOTHING BUT THE TRUTH"

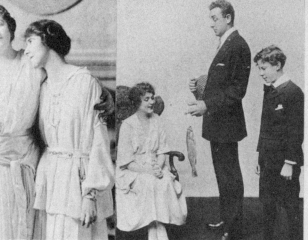

LOWELL SHERMAN, LENORE ULRIC in "THE HEART OF WETONA"

GEORGE LE GUERE, MARGARET ANGLIN, OTTOLA NESMITH in "A WOMAN OF NO IMPORTANCE"

LOLA FISHER, WALTER HAMPDEN, MAC MACOMBER in "GOOD GRACIOUS ANNABELLE"

RUBY CRAVEN, KATHARINE CORNELL "PLOTS AND PLAYWRIGHTS"

MARY NASH, HENRY HULL in "THE MAN WHO CAME BACK"

LOU TELLEGEN in "A KING OF NOWHERE"

PHOEBE FOSTER, SHELLEY HULL, FRANK BACON in "THE CINDERELLA MAN"

FRANK CRAVEN, HELEN MacKELLAR "SEVEN CHANCES"

THE DOLLY SISTERS in "HIS BRIDAL NIGHT"   IVY SAWYER, JOSEPH SANTLEY in "BETTY"   CHARLES PURCELL, LINA ABARBANELL in "FLORA BELLA"   JUSTINE JOHNSTONE in "ZIEGFELD FOLLIES"

ANTON ASCHER, ANN MURDOCK, JULES RAUCOURT in "PLEASE HELP EMILY"   MITZI HAJOS in "POM-POM"

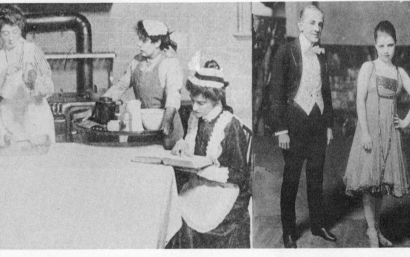

MARIE TEMPEST, BERYL MERCER, RUTH DRAPER in "A LADY'S NAME"   WILLIAM ROCK, FRANCES WHITE in "ZIEGFELD FOLLIES"

VALLI VALLI, FREDERIC SANTLEY, JAMES C. MARLOWE, RICHARD CARLE, LITTLE BILLY, JOHN HENDRICKS, HARRY DELF, CHARLES WINNINGER in "THE GREAT LOVER BURLESQUE" from "THE COHAN REVUE OF 1916"

JOSEPH CAWTHORNE, JULIA SANDERSON, DONALD BRIAN in "SYBIL"

was Anna Pavlowa who did part of the ballet "The Sleeping Beauty." Volinine danced the Prince, and the decor was by Bakst. The show also featured an ice-skating number and Toto, the Clown. Ruth St. Denis, another famous dancer, was appearing in vaudeville.

Outstanding musicals of the year were "Sybil" with Julia Sanderson, Donald Brian and Joseph Cawthorn, "The Cohan Revue of 1916" with Elizabeth Murray, Richard Carle, Charles Winninger and Valli Valli, "Pom-Pom" with Mitzi Hajos and Tom McNaughton, "Miss Springtime" with Sari Petrass, George MacFarlane, Georgia O'Ramey and John E. Hazzard, and "Her Soldier Boy" with Clifton Crawford, Adele Rowland and John Charles Thomas.

Al Jolson was in "Robinson Crusoe, Jr.," Lina Abarbanell in "Flora Bella," Raymond Hitchcock in "Betty" with Joseph Santley and Ivy Sawyer, Charlotte Greenwood in "So Long, Letty," and "Follow Me" proved to be the final starring vehicle for Anna Held. "Ziegfeld Follies of 1916" boasted a cast including Ina Claire, W. C. Fields, Fannie Brice, Bert Williams, Ann Pennington, Bernard Granville, Frances White, William Rock, Carl Randall, Emma Haig, Lilyan Tashman and Justine Johnstone, and "The Passing Show of 1916" featured Ed Wynn, James Hussey and Florence Moore.

Willie and Eugene Howard, George Monroe, Tom Lewis and Marilyn Miller were in "The Show of Wonders," and "The Century Girl" featured Elsie Janis, Sam Bernard, Hazel Dawn, Leon Errol, Frank Tinney and Van and Schenck.

114

SARAH BERNHARDT

Center: LEWIS STONE, EDMUND LOWE, MAUDE FULTON in
"THE BRAT"

EDMUND BREESE, LOTUS ROBB, ERNEST LAWFORD, ESTELLE WINWOOD,
SHELLEY HULL, NAT C. GOODWIN in "WHY MARRY?"

LAURETTE TAYLOR in
"OUT THERE"

1917

The United States entered World War I in 1917, and the theatre reflected this momentous event. War plays, soldier revues, all-star benefits were very much in evidence. This year also was the beginning of the Pulitzer Prize award for the best American play as picked by the trustees of Columbia University. "Why Marry?," a comedy by Jesse Lynch Williams, was the first play picked for this signal honor.

Of the hit plays that were stepping stones to stardom include "Eyes of Youth" for Marjorie Rambeau, "Polly With A Past" for Ina Claire, "Tiger Rose" for Lenore Ulric, "A Tailor-Made Man" for Grant Mitchell, "The Willow Tree" for Fay Bainter and "Parlor, Bedroom and Bath" for Florence Moore. Among the other successes were "Business Before Pleasure" with Barney Bernard and Alexander Carr; "Lombardi, Ltd." with Leo Carillo, Grace Valentine and Warner Baxter who went on to film fame; "Lilac Time" by Jane Cowl and Jane Murfin and starring Miss Cowl; "The Wanderer," a Biblical play based on the Prodigal Son, with William Elliott, Nance O'Neil, James O'Neill and Florence Reed; "A Successful Calamity," a Clare Kummer comedy, starring William Gillette; "The Brat" written by and starring Maude Fulton; "Our Betters," a Somerset Maugham comedy with Rose Coghlan, Chrystal Herne and Leonore Harris; "The Country Cousin" with Alexandra Carlisle and Eugene O'Brien; "DeLuxe Annie" with Jane Grey and Vincent Serrano;

FLORENCE MOORE in
"PARLOR, BEDROOM AND BATH"

MAUDE FULTON in
"THE BRAT"

GRANT MITCHELL in
"A TAILOR-MADE MAN"

JEANNE EAGELS in
"HAMILTON"

SHELLEY HULL in
"THE WILLOW TREE"

INA CLAIRE in
"POLLY WITH A PAST"

115

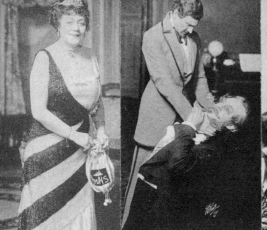

ROSE COGHLAN in "OUR BETTERS" JOHN AND LIONEL BARRYMORE in "PETER IBBETSON" Scene from "PETER IBBETSON" CONSTANCE COLLIER, LAURA HOPE CREWS in "PETER IBBETSON" MRS. FISKE in "MADAME SAND"

IRENE FENWICK in "LORD AND LADY ALGY" ERNEST GLENDINNING, PHOEBE FOSTER in "THE GIPSY TRAIL" ORME CALDARA, JANE COWL, HENRY STEPHENSON in "LILAC TIME" FLORENCE REED in "CHU CHIN CHOW"

HELEN MENKEN PEGGY WOOD CHARLES COBURN KATHARINE CORNELL FRANK TINNEY JOHN CRAIG HELEN HAYES BRUCE McRAE ANNA WHEATON

MR. AND MRS. GEORGE ARLISS in "HAMILTON" WARNER BAXTER, LEO CARILLO, GRACE VALENTINE in "LOMBARDI, LTD."

"The Gipsy Trail" with Ernest Glendenning, Phoebe Foster and Roland Young; "Yes or No" with Willette Kershaw; "Johnny, Get Your Gun" with Louis Bennison; "Magic," a fantasy by G. K. Chesterton, with O. P. Heggie and Cathleen Nesbitt; "Mary's Ankle," an Al Woods farce, with Irene Fenwick and Bert Lytell; and "Chu Chin Chow," a spectacular musical tale of the East, with Tyrone Power, Florence Reed, Henry E. Dixey, Tessa Kosta and George Rosely.

Laurette Taylor had success with three of J. Hartley Manners' plays: "Out There," "The Wooing of Eve" and "Happiness." Lynn Fontanne was in all three.

The stars and their attractions included Julia Arthur in "Seremonda," Marie Tempest in "Her Husband's Wife," Nazimova in " 'Ception Shoals," William Courtenay and Tom Wise in "Pals First," Emily Stevens in "The Fugitive," Guy Bates Post in "The Masquerader," Robert Hilliard in "The Scrap of Paper," Edith Taliaferro in "Mother Carey's Chickens," Maclyn Arbuckle in "Misalliance," Billie Burke in "The Rescuing Angel," Mrs. Fiske in "Madame Sand," Leo Ditrichstein in "The King" with William Powell of film fame in a small role, Lou Tellegen in "Blind Youth," Margaret Anglin in "Billeted," Ethel Barrymore in "The Lady of the Camellias" with Conway Tearle and Holbrook Blinn, Francine Larrimore with Otto Kruger in "Here Comes the Bride," and George Arliss in "The Professor's Love Story,"

MARGARET ANGLIN
in
"BILLETED"

WILLIAM ELLIOTT
in
"THE WANDERER"

Left: WILLIAM ELLIOTT, FLORENCE REED in
"THE WANDERER"

NANCE O'NEIL
in
"THE WANDERER"

SIR HERBERT TREE
in
"COLONEL NEWCOME"

INA CLAIRE, HERBERT YOST, CYRIL SCOTT in
"POLLY WITH A PAST"

FAY BAINTER, SHELLEY HULL in
"THE WILLOW TREE"

O. P. HEGGIE, CATHLEEN
NESBITT in "MAGIC"

LOU TELLEGEN in
"BLIND YOUTH"

EMMA
CARUS

CLIFTON
WEBB

LILYAN
TASHMAN

FREDERIC
SANTLEY

GRACE
LA RUE

JOSEPH
SANTLEY

GEORGIA
O'RAMEY

OSCAR
SHAW

WILDA
BENNETT

"Hamilton," and a revival of "Disraeli" with Mrs. Arliss and Jeanne Eagles supporting him.

One of the most talked about plays of the year was "Peter Ibbetson" which the Messrs. Shubert produced with John and Lionel Barrymore, Constance Collier, Laura Hope Crews and Madge Evans, then a child actress. An artistic failure was Arthur Hopkins' production of "The Deluge" with Pauline Lord, Henry E. Dixey and Edward G. Robinson. "The Old Lady Shows Her Medals," a one-act Barrie play with Beryl Mercer, made quite a hit when given with two other one-act plays. Robert B. Mantell was still trouping with his repertoire company. Helen Hayes was touring in the title role in "Pollyanna." John Craig, who had great success with the Boston Castle Square Stock Company, was winning laurels for his performance of "Hamlet," and so was his wife, Mary Young, as Ophelia. Alfred Lunt, who had toured with Margaret Anglin and played in vaudeville with Mrs. Langtry, was with Laura Hope Crews in "Romance and Arabella," noted only as Lunt's first play on Broadway.

Two outstanding musicals that ran for over a year were "Maytime" with Sigmund Romberg music and Peggy Wood, Charles Purcell and William Norris in the original cast, and "Oh, Boy," a Princess Theatre musical with Anna Wheaton, Tom Powers, Edna May Oliver, Hal Forde. Marion Davies, Justine Johnstone and Marie Carroll. Other musicals which had long runs were

LENORE ULRIC, WILLARD MACK
in
"TIGER ROSE"

MARJORIE RAMBEAU, RALPH KELLARD
in
"EYES OF YOUTH"

CHARLES BRYANT,
NAZIMOVA in
"'CEPTION SHOALS"

JULIA ARTHUR
in
"SEREMONDA"

DOROTHY MORTIMER,
LEO DITRICHSTEIN in
"THE KING"

MAXINE ELLIOTT
in
"LORD and LADY ALGY"

LOTTIE LINTHICUM, GRANT MITCHELL, FRANK BURBECK,
GUS C. WEINBERG, L. E. CONNESS in
"A TAILOR-MADE MAN"

ALFRED LUNT in
"ROMANCE AND ARABELLA"

CONWAY TEARLE, ETHEL BARRYMORE in
"THE LADY OF THE CAMELLIAS"

LAURETTE TAYLOR, FRANK KEMBLE COOPER, LEWIS EDGARD,
LYNN FONTANNE, DAISY BELMORE in "OUT THERE"

WILLIAM GILLETTE, ESTELLE WINWOOD in
"A SUCCESSFUL CALAMITY"

EMILY STEVENS, CONWAY TEARLE in
"THE FUGITIVE"

EDITH TALIAFERRO, LORIN RAKER,
DORIS EATON in
"MOTHER CAREY'S CHICKENS"

EUGENE O'BRIEN, DONALD GALLAN
MARION COAKLEY, ALEXANDRA
CARLISLE in "THE COUNTRY COUS

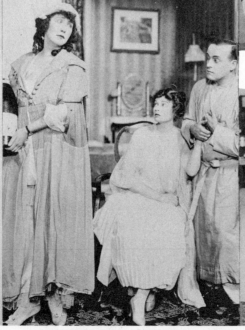

GUY BATES POST in his dual role of
CHILCOTE and LODER in
"THE MASQUERADER"

FLORENCE MOORE, SYDNEY SHIELDS,
JOHN CUMBERLAND in
"PARLOR, BEDROOM and BATH"

ALEXANDER CARR, CLARA JOEL,
BARNEY BERNARD in
"BUSINESS BEFORE PLEASURE"

CARROLL McCOMAS, MARGALO GIL
ROBERT HILLIARD in
"THE SCRAP OF PAPER"

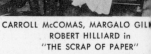

EWART BAIRD, JOSEPH CAWTHORN
in "RAMBLER ROSE"

WILDA BENNETT, CARL GANTVOORT
in "THE RIVIERA GIRL"

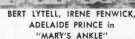
BERT LYTELL, IRENE FENWICK,
ADELAIDE PRINCE in
"MARY'S ANKLE"

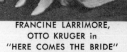
GLORIA GOODWIN,
CLIFTON WEBB in
"LOVE O' MIKE"

FRANCINE LARRIMORE,
OTTO KRUGER in
"HERE COMES THE BRIDE"

TRIXIE FRIGANZA, HERBERT CORTHELL, CHARLES RUGGLES in
"CANARY COTTAGE"

WILLIAM NORRIS, PEGGY WOOD, CHARLES PURCELL in
"MAYTIME"

FRED STONE in
"JACK O'LANTERN"

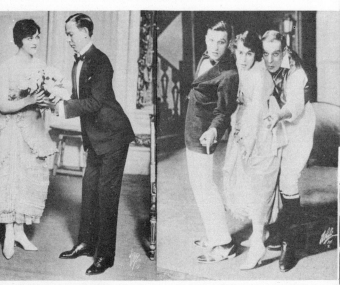

EDITH DAY, FRANK CRAVEN in
"GOING UP"

TOM POWERS, ANNA WHEATON,
HAL FORDE in "OH, BOY!"

LEON ERROL, RAYMOND HITCHCOCK
in "HITCHY-KOO"

OSCAR SHAW, GEORGIA O'RAMEY
in "LEAVE IT TO JANE"

"Going Up" with Frank Craven and Edith Day, "Jack O'Lantern," Fred Stone's first solo starring vehicle after the death of his partner David C. Montgomery, and "Hitchy-Koo," produced by and starring Raymond Hitchcock with a cast that included Grace LaRue, Irene Bordoni, Frances White and Leon Errol.

Other popular musicals of the year were "Love O' Mike" with Molly McIntyre and Clifton Webb, "Canary Cottage" with Trixie Friganza and Charles Ruggles, "Have A Heart" with Billy B. Van and Louise Dresser, "His Little Widows" with Carter De Haven and Flora Parker, "The Passing Show of 1917" with De Wolf Hopper, Irene Franklin, Jefferson De Angelis and Stafford Pemberton, "Ziegfeld Follies of 1917" with W. C. Fields, Fannie Brice, Eddie Cantor, Will Rogers, Bert Williams, Lilyan Tashman and Peggy Hopkins (Joyce was added later), "Leave It To Jane" with Oscar Shaw and Georgia O'Ramey, "Rambler Rose" starring Julia Sanderson and Joseph Cawthorn, "The Riviera Girl" with Juliette Day, Wilda Bennett and Sam B. Hardy, "Doing Our Bit" with Ed Wynn, Frank Tinney, Ada Lewis and the Duncan Sisters—Rosetta and Vivian, "Miss 1917" with Lew Fields, Vivienne Segal, Cecil Lean, Irene Castle, Bert Savoy, George White, Ann Pennington, Bessie McCoy, Van and Schenck, Charles King and Marion Davies, "Her Regiment" starring Donald Brian, "Over The Top" with Justine Johnstone, and "The Cohan Revue of 1918" with Nora Bayes, Charles Winninger and Frederic Santley.

WILTON
LACKAYE

NITA
NALDI

CYRIL
KEIGHTLEY

TALLULAH
BANKHEAD

CHAUNCEY
OLCOTT

MARJORIE
RAMBEAU

CONRAD
NAGEL

GENEVIEVE
HAMPER

FAY BAINTER in
"EAST IS WEST"

1918

The biggest hit of 1918 was "Lightnin' " by Winchell Smith and Frank Bacon. It chalked up a total of 1,291 performances, and gave Frank Bacon the best role of his career. Long runs were also achieved by "Friendly Enemies" with Louis Mann and Sam Bernard, and by "East is West" which brought fame to Fay Bainter.

"The Better 'Ole" by Capt. Bruce Bairnsfather and Capt. Arthur Elliott was the top war comedy with Charles Coburn as the original Old Bill, Colin Campbell as Alf, and Charles McNaughton as Bert. The role of Old Bill was also played by James K. Hackett, De Wolf Hopper and Maclyn Arbuckle, and the play was a huge success throughout the country.

John Barrymore gave a memorable performance in Tolstoi's "Redemption;" Lionel Barrymore was successful in "The Copperhead" by Augustus Thomas, and Ethel Barrymore was seen in "The Off Chance" and "Belinda."

Nazimova scored an artistic triumph in a series of Ibsen plays: "A Doll's House," "The Wild Duck" and "Hedda Gabler." Lionel Atwill was the leading man in all these plays. Laurette Taylor appeared in "Scenes From Shakespeare" and in her support

INA HAWLEY, LOUIS MANN, NATALIE MANNING, SAM BERNARD, MATHILDE COTTRELLY,
RICHARD BARBEE, REGINA WALLACE in "FRIENDLY ENEMIES"

FORREST WINANT, FAY BAINTER, MARTHA MAYO, FRANK KEMBLE
COOPER, ETHEL INTROPIDI in "EAST IS WEST"

CLAUDE GILLINGWATER, HARRY
DAVENPORT, WILLIAM
INGERSOLL in
"THREE WISE FOOLS"

ARTHUR BYRON, MARGARET LAWRENCE, FREDERICK PERRY in
"TEA FOR THREE"

EDITH TALIAFERRO   ROBERT HILLIARD   CONSTANCE BINNEY   THURSTON HALL   CARL RANDALL   LOLA FISHER   SHELLEY HULL   MARY NASH

were Shelley Hull, Jose Ruben, O. P. Heggie and Lynn Fontanne. Robert B. Mantell appeared in Shakespearean repertory with Genevieve Hamper and Fritz Leiber in his company.

Ruth Gordon and Gregory Kelly were in "Seventeen," Billie Burke and Henry Miller in "A Marriage of Convenience," Mr. and Mrs. Sidney Drew in "Keep Her Smiling," and Shelley Hull and Effie Shannon in "Under Orders." Richard Bennett and Helen MacKellar played in "The Unknown Purple," Arthur Byron and Margaret Lawrence in "Tea for Three," H. B. Warner and Irene Bordoni in "Sleeping Partners" and Alice Brady and Conrad Nagel in "Forever After."

Violet Heming was in "Three Faces East," Mary Ryan in "The Little Teacher," Mary Boland in "Sick-a-Bed," William Hodge in "A Cure for Curables," William Collier in "Nothing But Lies" and Cyril Maude in "The Saving Grace." Bertha Kalich appeared in "The Riddle: Woman," Florence Reed in "Roads of Destiny," George M. Cohan in "A Prince There Was," Virginia Harned in "Josephine," Frances Starr in "Tiger! Tiger!" and Tallulah Bankhead made her debut in "The Squab Farm."

"Daddies" featured Jeanne Eagels and Bruce McRae; "Seven

FRANK BACON in
"LIGHTNIN'"

LIONEL ATWILL, NILA MAC, NAZIMOVA, CHARLES BRYANT in
"HEDDA GABLER"

EMMETT CORRIGAN, VIOLET HEMING, JOSEPH SELMAN in
"THREE FACES EAST"

NAZIMOVA, LIONEL ATWILL in
"THE WILD DUCK"

JESSIE PRINGLE, FRANK BACON, RALPH MORGAN in
"LIGHTNIN'"

E. J. BALLANTINE, JOHN BARRYMORE, THOMAS MITCHELL in "REDEMPTION"

SYLVIA FIELD, REGGIE SHEFFIELD in "THE BETROTHAL"

JEANNE EAGELS, BRUCE McRAE in "DADDIES"

CHARLES McNAUGHTON, CHARLES COBURN, MRS. CHAS. COBURN, COLIN CAMPBELL in "THE BETTER 'OLE"

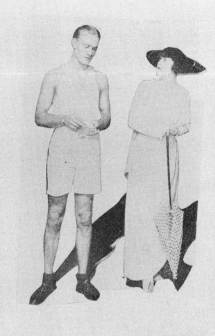

JOHN BARRYMORE in "REDEMPTION"

LIONEL ATWILL, FRANCES STARR in "TIGER! TIGER!"

CONRAD NAGEL, ALICE BRADY in "FOREVER AFTER"

HELEN HAYES, WILLIAM GILLETTE in "DEAR BRUTUS"

MR. AND MRS. SIDNEY DREW in "KEEP HER SMILING"

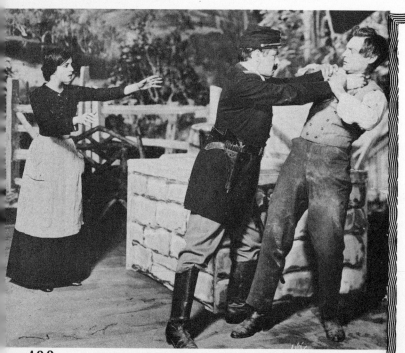

DORIS RANKIN, ALBERT PHILLIPS, LIONEL BARRYMORE in "THE COPPERHEAD"

Days Leave" was played by Elisabeth Risdon, Frederick Perry and Evelyn Varden; "An Ideal Husband" by Constance Collier and Norman Trevor, and "The Big Chance" by Willard Mack, Katherine Harris Barrymore, Mary Nash and John Mason. "Three Wise Fools" was acted by Claude Gillingwater, Harry Davenport, William Ingersoll and Helen Menken; "Be Calm, Camilla" by Walter Hampden, Hedda Hopper and Lola Fisher; "A Little Journey" by Jobyna Howland, Cyril Keightley, Gilda Varesi and Estelle Winwood, and "Dear Brutus" by William Gillette and Helen Hayes.

Jane Cowl appeared in "The Crowded Hour," and the feminine lead was also played by Willette Kershaw with great success. "Getting Together" starred Holbrook Blinn and Blanche Bates, and "Where Poppies Bloom" had Marjorie Rambeau and Lewis S. Stone. "Out There" was revived by the American Red Cross with an all-star cast including Laurette Taylor, Helen Ware, Beryl Mercer, H. B. Warner, James T. Powers, George Arliss, Chauncey Olcott, James K. Hackett and George M. Cohan.

JAMES K. HACKETT, CHARLES COBURN, DE WOLF HOPPER, MACLYN ARBUCKLE as OLD BILL in "THE BETTER 'OLE"

MARJORIE RAMBEAU, PEDRO DE CORDOBA, LEWIS STONE in "WHERE POPPIES BLOOM"

CHARLOTTE GRANVILLE, CYRIL MAUDE, LAURA HOPE CREWS in "THE SAVING GRACE"

CURTIS COOKSEY, EDWARD G. ROBINSON, MARY RYAN in "THE LITTLE TEACHER"

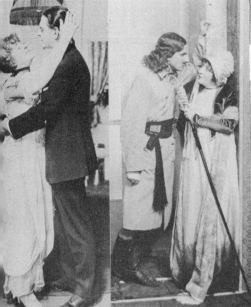

AMELIA BINGHAM, A. H. VAN BUREN in "THE MAN WHO STAYED AT HOME"

VIRGINIA HARNED, JOHN McMANUS in "JOSEPHINE"

LOLA FISHER, WALTER HAMPDEN in "BE CALM, CAMILLA"

EFFIE SHANNON, SHELLEY HULL in "UNDER ORDERS"

CLAY CLEMENT, MINNA GOMBEL, LIONEL ATWILL in "THE INDESTRUCTIBLE WIFE"

MALCOLM WILLIAMS, EDMUND LOWE, FLORENCE REED in "ROADS OF DESTINY"

OLIVE WYNDHAM, WILLIAM COLLIER in "NOTHING BUT LIES"

EVELYN VARDEN, ELISABETH RISDON in "SEVEN DAYS LEAVE"

HELEN HAYES, PAUL KELLY in "PENROD"

Other new plays of the year were "The Betrothal," "The Indestructible Wife," "Once Upon a Time," "Penrod," "The Man Who Stayed at Home," "Perkins," "The Little Brother," "A Place in the Sun" and "Why Worry?" which was the first non-musical play to be done by Fannie Brice.

The year also offered many long run musicals, and among the favorites were "Oh, Lady! Lady!!" with Constance Binney and Vivienne Segal, "Sinbad" with Al Jolson, and "Ziegfeld Follies of 1918" with Eddie Cantor, Marilyn Miller, Will Rogers, Dolores, Ann Pennington, W. C. Fields and Lillian Lorraine, also "The Passing Show of 1918" with Fred and Adele Astaire, Charles Ruggles, Frank Fay, the Howard Brothers and Nita Naldi and "Everything", a Hippodrome show, with De Wolf Hopper and Belle Story.

Billy B. Van was in "The Rainbow Girl," Fay Bainter in "The Kiss Burglar," Mitzi (she had dropped the Hajos) in "Head Over Heels," Donald Brian in "The Girl Behind the Gun," and Ed Wynn in "Sometime" with Francine Larrimore and Mae

IRENE BORDONI, H. B. WARNER in "SLEEPING PARTNERS"

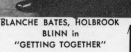

BLANCHE BATES, HOLBROOK BLINN in "GETTING TOGETHER"

DOROTHY KLEWER,
RAYMOND BLOOMER in
"THE SQUAB FARM"

FRITZ
LEIBER

O. P. HEGGIE, LAURETTE
TAYLOR in "SCENES
FROM SHAKESPEARE"

PEGGY O'NEIL in
"PATSY ON THE WING"

MABEL BUNYEA, WALKER
WHITESIDE in
"THE LITTLE BROTHER"

WILLETTE
KERSHAW

ANDREW LAWLOR,
"PENROD"

EVA LE GALLIENNE, CYRIL KEIGHTLEY, ETHEL BARRYMORE,
E. LYALL SWETE, RICHARD HATTERAS in "BELINDA"

WILLIAM HODGE in
"A CURE FOR CURABLES"

PEGGY HOPKINS in
"A PLACE IN THE SUN"

CHRISTINE NORMAN, HENRY STEPHENSON, ORME
CALDARA, JANE COWL in "THE CROWDED HOUR"

ROBERT EDESON, BERTHA KALICH in
"THE RIDDLE: WOMAN"

EDWIN NICANDER, MARY BOLAND in
"SICK-A-BED"

Standing: GEORGE MacFARLANE, BURR McINTOSH, LAURETTE TAYLOR, H. B. WARNER,
GEORGE M. COHAN, CHAUNCEY OLCOTT, HELEN WARE, O. P. HEGGIE. Seated:
ELEANORA de CISNEROS, MRS. FISKE, GEORGE ARLISS, JULIA ARTHUR,
JAMES T. POWERS, ROSE STAHL, JAMES K. HACKETT, J. HARTLEY
MANNERS in "OUT THERE"

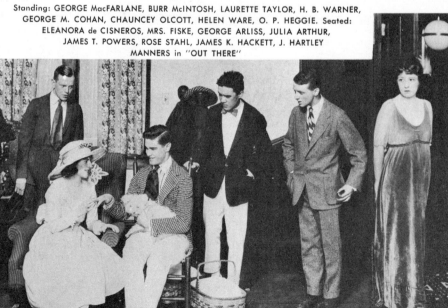

BILLIE BURKE, HENRY MILLER in
"A MARRIAGE OF CONVENIENCE"

NEIL MARTIN, RUTH GORDON, PAUL KELLY, GREGORY KELLY,
MORGAN FARLEY in "SEVENTEEN"

HELEN MACKELLAR, RICHARD BENNETT,
EARLE BROWNE in
"THE UNKNOWN PURPLE"

BILLY B.
VAN

KOLB AND
DILL

ELIZABETH
MURRAY

FLORA PARKER
and
CARTER DE HAVEN

ELEANOR
PAINTER

DONALD MACDONALD,
LOUISE ALLEN in
"TOOT-TOOT!"

FRANK TINNEY in
"ATTA-BOY"

MORGAN, LOUISE DRESSER, EDNA HIBBARD in
"ROCK-A-BYE BABY"

VIVIENNE SEGAL, CARL RANDALL in
"OH, LADY! LADY!!"

STEWART BAIRD, MARJORIE GATESON, WALTER
CATLETT in "LITTLE SIMPLICITY"

ON COMEDY FOUR, FANNIE BRICE, GEORGE SIDNEY,
MAY BOLEY in "WHY WORRY?"

FISKE O'HARA in
"THE ROSE OF KILDARE"

NORA BAYES in
"LADIES FIRST"

JACK HAZZARD, DONALD BRIAN, WILDA BENNETT,
FRANK DOANE in "THE GIRL BEHIND THE GUN"

MITZI in
"HEAD OVER HEELS"

GERTRUDE VANDERBILT, JOHN DOOLEY,
ADA MAE WEEKS, CLIFTON WEBB in
"LISTEN, LESTER"

West. Nora Bayes was in "Ladies First," Eleanor Painter in "Glorianna," Joseph Cawthorn and Julia Sanderson in "The Canary," and Marjorie Gateson in "Little Simplicity."

"Oh, My Dear" featured Joseph Santley and Ivy Sawyer, while "Listen, Lester" was played by Johnny Dooley, Clifton Webb, Ada Lewis, Ada Mae Weeks and Gertrude Vanderbilt. Frank Morgan and Louise Dresser were in "Rock-a-Bye Baby" and Raymond Hitchcock and Leon Errol were in "Hitchy Koo of 1918." Other musical shows of the year were "Girl O' Mine," "Oh, Look!," "Fancy Free," "The Maid of the Mountains" and "Somebody's Sweetheart." Kolb and Dill were extremely popular in musicals out on the West Coast.

"Biff! Bang!" was a musical show written and presented by the sailors of the Naval Training Camp, and "Yip, Yip, Yaphank" was a 'musical mess cooked up by the boys of Camp Upton' with words and music by Sergeant Irving Berlin.

LOWELL SHERMAN, MARY RYAN in
"THE SIGN ON THE DOOR"

JENNIE E. EUSTACE, FRANK McGLYNN in
"ABRAHAM LINCOLN"

EDMUND LOWE, LENORE ULRIC in
"THE SON-DAUGHTER"

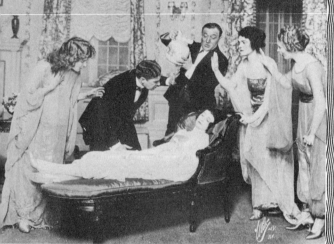

HAZEL DAWN, DUDLEY HAWLEY, ENID MARKEY, WALTER JONES,
LUCY COTTON, EVELYN GOSNELL in "UP IN MABEL'S ROOM"

MARGALO GILLMORE, HENRY MILLER, BLANCHE BATES,
JACK DEVEREAUX in "THE FAMOUS MRS. FAIR"

1919 The year 1919 was significant in the theatre as the year of the actors' strike, the termination of which led to the betterment of working conditions for actors through membership in Actors' Equity Association.

This year also saw the formation of the Theatre Guild, a producing organization run on a subscription basis which was an outgrowth of the Washington Square Players. Their first production, Benavente's "Bonds of Interest" was unsuccessful, but their next offering, St. John Ervine's "John Ferguson," furnished a foundation of commercial success on which the organization was able to grow and prosper. The leading roles in this play were acted by Augustin Duncan, Rollo Peters and Dudley Digges. The Guild also produced a dramatization of William Dean Howell's celebrated novel, "The Rise of Silas Lapham," and prominent in the cast were James K. Hackett and Helen Westley.

Many comedies had outstanding runs. Among these were "Up In Mabel's Room" with Hazel Dawn and Enid Markey, "Adam and Eva" with Ruth Shepley and Otto Kruger, and "Clarence" with Mary Boland, Glenn Hunter, Helen Hayes and Alfred Lunt. Also: "The Gold Diggers" with Ina Claire, "His Honor, Abe Potash" with Barney Bernard, "My Lady Friends"

HENRY MILLER, BLANCHE BATES, HOLBROOK
BLINN in "MOLIERE"

FRANCINE LARRIMORE in
"SCANDAL"

INA CLAIRE, BRUCE McRAE in
"THE GOLD DIGGERS"

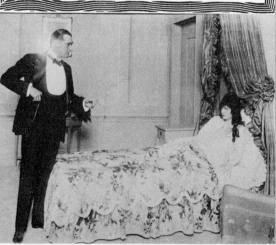

CHARLES CHERRY, FRANCINE LARRIMORE in
"SCANDAL"

GEORGE M. COHAN

SUZANNE WILLA CHIC SALE MARGALO GILLMORE GEORGE LE GUERE PEGGY O'NEIL TIM MURPHY ANN ANDREWS BARNEY BERNAR

DUDLEY DIGGES, EDNA ST. VINCENT MILLAY, ROLLO PETERS in "BONDS OF INTEREST"

MARILYN MILLER in "ZIEGFELD FOLLIES"

OTTO KRUGER, RUTH SHEPLEY, FERDINAND GOTTSCHALK in "ADAM AND EVA"

HENRY HERBERT, AUGUSTIN DUNCAN, HELEN WESTLEY, HELEN FREEMAN, DUDLEY DIGGES, MICHAEL CARR, ROLLO PETERS in "JOHN FERGUSON"

JACK SQUIRES in "MONTE CRISTO, JR."

McKAY MORRIS, DOROTHY DALTON in "APHRODITE"

LIONEL BARRYMORE, JOHN BARRYMORE in "THE JEST"

with Clifton Crawford, June Walker, Frank Morgan, and "Scandal" with Charles Cherry and Francine Larrimore.

Lenore Ulric appeared in "The Son-Daughter," Jane Cowl in "Smilin' Through," Mrs. Fiske in "Mis' Nelly of N'Orleans," Ruth Chatterton in "Moonlight and Honeysuckle," Patricia Collinge in "Tillie," and Billie Burke in "Caesar's Wife." Wallace Eddinger and Margaret Lawrence were in "Wedding Bells," Laurette Taylor and Philip Merivale in "One Night in Rome," and Mary Ryan and Lowell Sherman in "The Sign on the Door." "Cappy Ricks" starred William Courtenay and Tom Wise. "Toby's Bow" was played by Norman Trevor and George Marion, and "39 East" by Henry Hull, Alison Skipworth and Constance Binney.

Ethel Barrymore was highly successful in "Declassee," and John and Lionel Barrymore co-starred with distinction in Sem Benelli's tragi-comedy, "The Jest."

"Moliere" was played by Holbrook Blinn, Estelle Winwood, Henry Miller and Blanche Bates, and the spectacular "Aphrodite" had a large cast including Dorothy Dalton, McKay Morris and Nita Naldi.

Edward Arnold and Helen MacKellar were seen in "The Storm," Wilton Lackaye and Genevieve Tobin in "Palmy Days,"

| WILLIAM DANFORTH | LENORE ULRIC | LOWELL SHERMAN | TESSA KOSTA | CHARLES CHERRY | RUTH SHEPLEY | JOHN CHARLES THOMAS | MOLLIE KING |

EDITH DAY, DOROTHY WALTERS in "IRENE"

MARY EATON in "THE ROYAL VAGABOND"

FREDERIC SANTLEY, FRANCES DEMAREST, ROBINSON NEWBOLD in "THE ROYAL VAGABOND"

HENRY STEPHENSON, JANE COWL, ORME CALDARA in "SMILIN' THROUGH"

PATRICIA COLLINGE in "TILLIE"

DORIS KENYON, FRANK THOMAS, JOHN CUMBERLAND, VIVIAN RUSHMORE, CHARLES RUGGLES, CLAIBORNE FOSTER, ZELDA SEARS in "THE GIRL IN THE LIMOUSINE"

Pauline Lord in "Night Lodging" and Frank McGlynn in "Abraham Lincoln." Blanche Bates, Margalo Gillmore and Henry Miller were in "The Famous Mrs. Fair," Janet Beecher, Lowell Sherman and Gail Kane in "The Woman in Room 13," Doris Kenyon, Charles Ruggles, John Cumberland and Zelda Sears in "The Girl in the Limousine," Thurston Hall, Glenn Anders and Olive Tell in "Civilian Clothes," Suzanne Willa and Francis Byrne in "Nighty-Night," and Eileen Huban and Thomas Mitchell in "Dark Rosaleen."

Otis Skinner revived "The Honor of the Family," and Sothern and Marlowe played Shakespearean repertoire. Appearing with Stuart Walker's Portmanteau Theatre were McKay Morris, George Gaul, Elizabeth Patterson, Margaret Mower and Morgan Farley.

Successful musicals of the year were "The Royal Vagabond" with Frederic Santley, Tessa Kosta and Mary Eaton, "Greenwich Village Follies" with James Watts and Bessie McCoy Davis, "Apple Blossoms" with Wilda Bennett, John Charles Thomas and Fred and Adele Astaire, "The Magic Melody" with Julia Dean, Charles Purcell and Carmel Myers, and "Buddies" with Donald Brian, Peggy Wood and Roland Young.

Edith Day scored a personal hit in "Irene," Vivienne Segal

HELEN HAYES, ALFRED LUNT, MARY BOLAND in "CLARENCE"

GLENN HUNTER, HELEN HAYES in "CLARENCE"

HENRY HULL, CONSTANCE BINNEY in
"39 EAST"

McKAY MORRIS, MARGARET MOWER in
"THE LAUGHTER OF THE GODS"

EDWARD ARNOLD, HELEN MACKELLAR, ROBERT
RENDEL in "THE STORM"

BILLIE BURKE, NORMAN TREVOR
"CAESAR'S WIFE"

BARRY BAXTER, LAURETTE TAYLOR, HELEN BLAIR, GRETA KEMBLE COOPER,
VALENTINE CLEMOW in "ONE NIGHT IN ROME"

IRENE HAISMAN, GEORGES RENAVENT, FREDERIC BURT, MRS. FISKE, ZOLYA
TALMA, HAMILTON REVELLE in "MIS' NELLY OF N'ORLEANS"

GEORGE LE GUERE, GENEVIEVE TOBIN in
"PALMY DAYS"

MARGARET LAWRENCE, WALLACE EDDINGER in
"WEDDING BELLS"

CHARLOTTE
WALKER

A BEN ALI HAGGIN TABLEAU in
"ZIEGFELD FOLLIES OF 1919"

TOM WISE, WILLIAM COURTENAY in
"CAPPY RICKS"

OSCAR SHAW, JANE RICHARDSON, FRANK
McINTYRE in "THE ROSE OF CHINA"

EILEEN HUBAN, HENRY
DUFFY in
"DARK ROSALEEN"

DONALD MACDONALD
in
"THE LADY IN RED"

RUTH CHATTERTON in
"MOONLIGHT AND
HONEYSUCKLE"

MOLLIE KING, CHA
KING in
"GOOD MORNING,

McINTYRE AND HEATH in "HELLO, ALEXANDER"

FRANCES VICTORY, CHARLOTTE GREENWOOD, BERNICE KIRSCH in "LINGER LONGER, LETTY"

THURSTON HALL, MARION VANTINE, OLIVE TELL in "CIVILIAN CLOTHES"

FRED HILLEBRAND, VERA MICHELENA in "TAKE IT FROM ME"

QUEENIE SMITH, EDDIE LEONARD in "ROLY-BOLY EYES"

ZANNE WILLA, FRANCIS BYRNE in "NIGHTY-NIGHT"

JULIA DEAN, CHARLES PURCELL in "THE MAGIC MELODY"

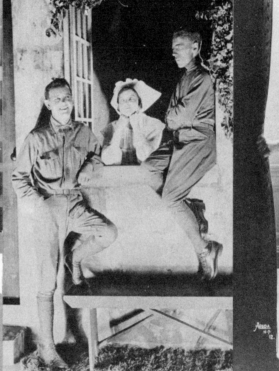

DONALD BRIAN, PEGGY WOOD, ROLAND YOUNG in "BUDDIES"

ETHEL BARRYMORE in "DECLASSÉE"

GEORGE WHITE,   in   ANN PENNINGTON "SCANDALS OF 1919"

SEPH SANTLEY, Y SAWYER in HE'S A GOOD FELLOW"

DOLORES in "ZIEGFELD FOLLIES"

FLO LEWIS, JAY GOULD in "TICK-TACK-TOE"

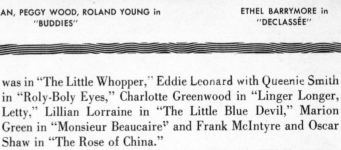

was in "The Little Whopper," Eddie Leonard with Queenie Smith in "Roly-Boly Eyes," Charlotte Greenwood in "Linger Longer, Letty," Lillian Lorraine in "The Little Blue Devil," Marion Green in "Monsieur Beaucaire" and Frank McIntyre and Oscar Shaw in "The Rose of China."

Charles Ruggles, Edna Hibbard and Peggy O'Neil were in "Tumble In," Joseph Santley, Ivy Sawyer and the Duncan Sisters in "She's A Good Fellow," Fred Hillebrand, Jack McGowan and Vera Michelena in "Take It From Me," Ralph Herz and Jack Squires in "Monte Cristo, Jr.," and Mollie King, Charles King and Margaret Dale in "Good Morning, Judge."

"Happy Days" was the Hippodrome show with Clyde Cook and the Hanneford Family; "Ziegfeld Midnight Frolic" featured Frances White, Fannie Brice, Chic Sale, Ted Lewis, Martha Mansfield and W. C. Fields; "Hello, Alexander" had McIntyre and Heath and Gilda Gray; and "The Passing Show of 1919" was played by Walter Woolf, James Barton, Blanche Ring and Charles Winninger.

"Scandals of 1919" was the first of this series produced by George White. The cast included Ann Pennington, Lester Allen and Mr. White himself.

131

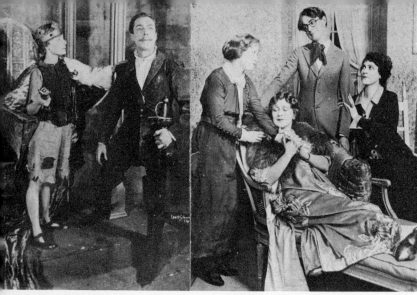

RUTH FINDLAY, WILLIAM FAVERSHAM in
"THE PRINCE AND THE PAUPER"

IDA ST. LEON, EFFIE SHANNON, GEORGE LE GUERE,
KATHERINE KAELRED in "MAMMA'S AFFAIR"

ORVILLE CALDWELL, HANNAH TOBACK in
"MECCA"

MARY FOWLER, JOHN HALLIDAY,
MARGARET ANGLIN in
"THE WOMAN OF BRONZE"

JOHN BARRYMORE in
"RICHARD III"

1920 The year 1920 saw the production of Eugene O'Neill's first full-length play, "Beyond the Horizon," win the Pulitzer Prize for 1919-20. Richard Bennett played the leading role. "Miss Lulu Bett," a comedy by Zona Gale, won the 1920-21 Pulitzer Prize and acting honors went to Carroll McComas in the title role. Another O'Neill play that was widely discussed was "The Emperor Jones" with Charles S. Gilpin.

"The Bat," a mystery play by Mary Roberts Rinehart and Avery Hopwood, had a run of 867 performances. Other plays that were hits and achieved long runs included an Al Woods farce, "Ladies Night;" "Enter Madame" with Gilda Varesi; "Spanish Love" with James Rennie; "Little Old New York" with Genevieve Tobin and Ernest Glendinning; "The Tavern" starring Arnold Daly; Holbrook Blinn in one of his greatest hits, "The Bad Man;" Margaret Anglin in "The Woman in Bronze;" Frank Craven in his own play, "The First Year;" "Rollo's Wild Oat" with Roland Young; Florence Reed in "The Mirage;" also "Three Live Ghosts," "The Meanest Man in the World" and "Welcome Stranger."

John Barrymore was gaining in stature as an actor with his first Shakespearean role in "The Tragedy of Richard III." Nance O'Neil won acclaim for her performance in "The Passion

FRANK CRAVEN, HALE NORCROSS, LELIA BENNETT, ROBERTA ARNOLD,
MERCEITA ESMONDE in "THE FIRST YEAR"

CARROLL McCOMAS in
"MISS LULU BETT"

NANCE O'NEIL in
"THE PASSION FLOWER"

FANNIE BRICE singing
"MY MAN" in
"ZIEGFELD FOLLIES"

ARNOLD DALY in
"THE TAVERN"

RICHARD BENNETT in
"BEYOND THE HORIZON"

GENEVIEVE TOBIN in
"LITTLE OLD NEW YORK"

MALCOLM WILLIAMS, FLORENCE REED,
ALAN DINEHART in "THE MIRAGE"

Flower;" "Jane Clegg" was well acted by Margaret Wycherly, Helen Westley and Dudley Digges; and "The Tragedy of Nan" by Alexandra Carlisle. "Medea" was produced by Maurice Browne with Ellen Van Volkenburg in the lead, while Tolstoi's tragedy, "The Power of Darkness," was presented by the Theatre Guild.

The stars and the plays they appeared in were: John Drew in "The Cat Bird," William Faversham in "The Prince and the Pauper," Effie Shannon in "Mamma's Affair," Lionel Atwill in "Deburau," Frances Starr in "One," William Collier in "The Hottentot," Jeanne Eagels in "The Wonderful Thing," Leo Ditrichstein in "The Purple Mask," Chrystal Herne in "The Acquittal," Maxine Elliott in "Trimmed in Scarlet," William Hodge in "The Guest of Honor," Grace George in "The 'Ruined' Lady," George Arliss with Julia Dean in "Poldekin," Jacob Ben-Ami and Pauline Lord in "Samson and Delilah," Elsie Ferguson in "Sacred and Profane Love," Florence Moore in "Breakfast in Bed," Madge Kennedy in "Cornered," Harry Beresford in "Shavings," Alice Brady with Rod La Roque in "Anna Ascends," Mary Young in "The Outrageous Mrs. Palmer," Emily Stevens in "Footloose," Minnie Dupree in "The Charm School" and Patricia Collinge in "Just Suppose" with Leslie

WILLIAM COLLIER in
"THE HOTTENTOT"

ROLAND YOUNG in
"ROLLO'S WILD OAT"

HOLBROOK BLINN in
"THE BAD MAN"

MARILYN MILLER in "SALLY"
with LEON ERROL

133

WILLIAM HODGE in
"THE GUEST OF HONOR"

LOUIS MANN in
"THE UNWRITTEN CHAPTER"

ELSIE MACKAY, JOHN ROCHE, GEORGIE RYAN,
LIONEL ATWILL in "DEBURAU"

"THE EMPEROR JONES"

EARLE FOXE, GAIL
KANE in
"COME SEVEN"

MARIE CARROLL, JAMES
GLEASON in
"THE CHARM SCHOOL"

GAVIN MUIR, GILDA VARESI in
"ENTER MADAME"

CLARA MOORES, HARRY
BERESFORD in "SHAVINGS"

PATRICIA COLLINGE, GEOFF
KERR in "JUST SUPPOSE"

ALICE BRADY in
"ANNA ASCENDS"

BERYL MERCER in
"THREE LIVE GHOSTS"

FLORENCE MOORE, LEON
GORDON in
"BREAKFAST IN BED"

PHILIP MERIVALE, WILLIAM
MORRIS, JANET BEECHER in
"CALL THE DOCTOR"

CARROLL McCOMAS, LOUISE CLOSSER HALE, WILLARD
ROBERTSON in "MISS LULU BETT"

GEORGES
RENAVENT

LOUISE CLOSSER
HALE

Howard who was making his first American stage appearance.

Theda Bara, who had been wrecking homes in the movies, was starring on Broadway in a hackneyed play, "The Blue Flame." George M. Cohan was starring Georges Renavent for the one and only time during his career in "Genius and the Crowd." Ruth Chatterton was having a mild success with Barrie's "Mary Rose," and "Bab" featured Helen Hayes and Tom Powers.

"Mixed Marriage" was played by Margaret Wycherly and Rollo Peters, "Heartbreak House" by Lucile Watson, Effie Shannon, Dudley Digges and Helen Westley, "Not So Long Ago" by Eva Le Gallienne and Sidney Blackmer, "He and She" by Cyril Keightley, Rachel Crothers and Faire Binney, "Thy Name Is Woman" by Mary Nash and Jose Ruben, "Come Seven" by Gail Kane and Earle Foxe, "Opportunity" by James Crane, Lily Cahill and Nita Naldi, "Call the Doctor" by Janet Beecher, Philip Merivale, Charlotte Walker and Fania Marinoff, and "Scrambled Wives" by Glenn

MAXINE ELLIOTT in
"TRIMMED IN SCARLET"

PAULINE LORD in
"SAMSON AND DELILAH"

ROBERT VAUGHAN, EFFIE ELLSLER, ANNE MORRISON,
MAY VOKES, STUART SAGE in "THE BAT"

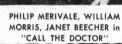

WILLIAM POWELL (second upper left) in "SPANISH LOVE"

GUY BUCKLEY, RUTH CHATTERTON, TOM NESBITT in "MARY ROSE"

GEORGE ARLISS in "POLDEKIN"

THEDA BARA in "THE BLUE FLAME"

ARTHUR ELDRED, HELEN HAYES in "BAB"

CHRYSTAL HERNE, WILLIAM HARRIGAN, EDWARD H. ROBINS in "THE ACQUITTAL"

EVA LE GALLIENNE, SIDNEY BLACKMER, MARY KENNEDY in "NOT SO LONG AGO"

MARGARET WYCHERLY in "MIXED MARRIAGE"

MRS. THOMAS WHIFFEN in "JUST SUPPOSE"

LILY CAHILL, LEO DITRICHSTEIN in "THE PURPLE MASK"

JAMES CRANE, LILY CAHILL in "OPPORTUNITY"

CHARLES GILPIN in "THE EMPEROR JONES"

JAMES RENNIE in "SPANISH LOVE"

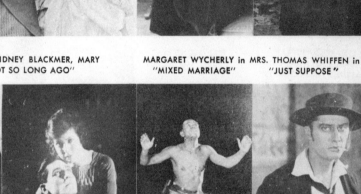

DUDLEY DIGGES, HELEN WESTLEY, HENRY TRAVERS, MARGARET WYCHERLY in "JANE CLEGG"

CLARA JOEL

IDA ST. LEON

Anders, Roland Young and Juliette Day.

Marilyn Miller danced her way to the greatest of all her successes in "Sally," ably supported by Leon Errol. Fred Stone with "Tip Top," Mitzi with "Lady Billy," and Frank Tinney with "Tickle Me" were big hits, and so were "Mary" with Jack McGowan and Janet Velie, "Afgar" with Alice Delysia and Lupino Lane, "The Night Boat" with Hal Skelly, and "Honey Girl" with Lynne Overman.

"Mecca," a musical spectacle with Orville Caldwell and Gladys Hanson, drew crowds. J. J. Shubert revived "Florodora" with Christie MacDonald, Walter Woolf, Eleanor Painter and Harry Fender. Irene Bordoni, Sam Bernard and Clifton Webb were a delightful threesome in "As You Were;" Cecil Lean and Cleo Mayfield were in "Look Who's Here;" Tessa Kosta was in "Lassie;" Ed Wynn in "Ed Wynn Carnival;" Frances White in "Jimmie;" Nora Bayes in "Her Family Tree;" Joe E. Brown and Frank Fay in "Jim Jam Jems," and "The Sweetheart Shop" had Harry K. Morton, Esther Howard and Helen Ford.

CURTIS COOKSEY, MARY NASH, JOSE RUBEN in "THY NAME IS WOMAN"

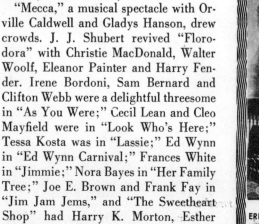

ERNEST GLENDINNING in "LITTLE OLD NEW YORK"

JEANNE EAGELS in "THE WONDERFUL THING"

FRANK FAY and girls in
"JIM JAM JEMS"

JANET VELIE, JACK
McGOWAN in "MARY"

JUDITH VOSSELLI, CHARLES RUGGLES, EDWARD
DOUGLAS in "LADIES NIGHT"

RALPH SIPPERLY, RUTH DONNELLY, GEORGE M. COHAN, MARION
COAKLEY in "THE MEANEST MAN IN THE WORLD"

J. HAROLD MURRAY,
GRACE KEESHON in
"PASSING SHOW OF 1921"

FRED STONE in
"TIP TOP"

IRENE BORDONI, CLIFTON WEBB, SAM BERNARD in
"AS YOU WERE"

JULIUS TANNEN, NORA BAYES in
"HER FAMILY TREE"

ESTHER HOWARD, HARRY K.
MORTON in
"THE SWEETHEART SHOP"

THE DUNCAN SISTERS in
"TIP TOP"

ED WYNN, LILLIAN
FITZGERALD in
"ED WYNN CARNIVAL"

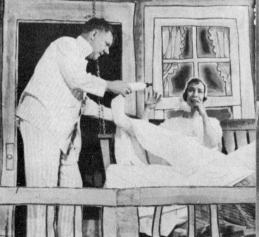

HILDA
SPONG

MARGUERITE
NAMARA

W. C. FIELDS, RAY DOOLEY in
"ZIEGFELD FOLLIES"

JOSEPH SANTLEY, IVY SAWYER,
JOSEPH CAWTHORN in
"THE HALF MOON"

BOYD MARSHALL, MITZI in
"LADY BILLY"

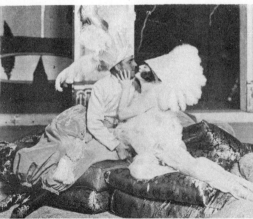

GEORGE SIDNEY in
"WELCOME STRANGER"

TESSA KOSTA in
"LASSIE"

ALICE DELYSIA, IRVING BEEBE in
"AFGAR"

ARTHUR WYNN, SYLVIA NELIS,
LENA MAITLAND in
"THE BEGGAR'S OPERA"

BEN WELCH, FRANCES WHITE i
"JIMMIE"

EFFIE SHANNON in "THE DETOUR"

MARY BLAIR, EUGENE LINCOLN in "DIFF'RENT"

HELEN HAYES, LESLIE HOWARD in "THE WREN"

WALTER HAMPDEN as "MACBETH"

JOSEPHINE DRAKE, MARIE DORO in "LILIES OF THE FIELD"

NA ABARBANELL, ONEL ATWILL in E GRAND DUKE"

GLENN ANDERS, HAZEL DAWN in "THE DEMI-VIRGIN"

1921

The year was late getting started as there were no productions opening during the month of January. Eugene O'Neill's two-act drama, "Diff'rent," was the first arrival on February 4th. Other O'Neill plays produced this year were "Gold," "The Straw" and "Anna Christie" which won the Pulitzer Prize, and in it Pauline Lord scored the greatest triumph of her career. It was also the year of Clemence Dane's "A Bill of Divorcement" with Allan Pollock, Janet Beecher and young Katharine Cornell who received great acclaim; of Molnar's "Liliom" which brought Joseph Schildkraut and Eva Le Gallienne fine notices; and of Lenore Ulric's great success with "Kiki."

"Lightnin'," with Frank Bacon its veteran star, was still on Broadway, and when it finally closed its New York run on June 15, 1921, it had clocked up 1,291 performances, a record at that time which has since been broken by ten other plays.

Other successes of the year were "Six-Cylinder Love" with Ernest Truex and June Walker, "Dulcy" with Gregory Kelly, Lynn Fontanne and in a small role, Elliott Nugent, "The Circle" with John Drew and Mrs. Leslie Carter, Estelle Winwood and John Halliday, "Thank You" with Harry Davenport, Edith King and Donald Foster, "The Demi-Virgin" with Hazel Dawn, Charles Ruggles and Glenn Anders, and "Captain Applejack" with Wallace Eddinger, Mary Nash and Hamilton Revelle.

HEDDA HOPPER in "SIX-CYLINDER LOVE"

CILE WATSON in MARCH HARES"

WILLIAM GILLETTE in "THE DREAM MAKER"

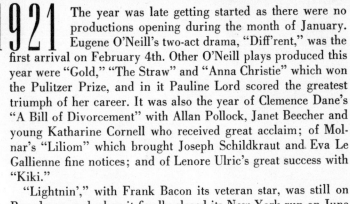

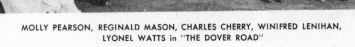

JOHN BARRYMORE in "CLAIR DE LUNE"

LGA PETROVA in E WHITE PEACOCK"

RONALD ADAIR in "TARZAN OF THE APES"

MOLLY PEARSON, REGINALD MASON, CHARLES CHERRY, WINIFRED LENIHAN, LYONEL WATTS in "THE DOVER ROAD"

LOU TELLEGEN in "DON JUAN"

HELEN HAYES, DONALD GALLAHER in "GOLDEN DAYS"

ROLLO PETERS, ELSIE FERGUSON, CHARLES FRANCIS in "THE VARYING SHORE"

JOHN BARRYMORE, JANE COOPER, HERBERT GRIMWOOD, ETHEL BARRYMORE in "CLAIR DE LUNE"

DORIS EATON in "ZIEGFELD FOLLIES"

137

LENORE ULRIC in
"KIKI"

AL JOLSON in
"BOMBO"

FRANCINE LARRIMORE in
"NICE PEOPLE"

EMILIE
POLINI

NORMAN
TREVOR

FAIRE
BINNEY

EMMETT
CORRIGAN

The star system was still going strong. Mrs. Fiske was playing in "Wake up, Jonathan!," George Arliss was in "The Green Goddess," Otis Skinner in "Blood and Sand," Ina Claire in "Bluebeard's Eighth Wife," Grace George in "Marie Antoinette," Leo Ditrichstein in "Toto," Elsie Ferguson in "The Varying Shore," William Gillette in "The Dream Maker," Marjorie Rambeau in "Daddy's Gone A-Hunting," William Faversham in "The Silver Fox," Lionel Atwill in "The Grand Duke," William Hodge in "Beware of Dogs," Effie Shannon in "The Detour," Lou Tellegen in "Don Juan," Mary Ryan in "Only 38" and Grant Mitchell in "The Champion."

Sothern and Marlowe appeared in Shakespearean repertoire and so did Robert B. Mantell; Lionel Barrymore and Julia Arthur co-starred in "Macbeth," and Margaret Anglin was seen in "Iphigenia in Aulis" and "The Trial of Joan of Arc." Marie Doro was in "Lilies of the Field" which proved to be her last appearance on the stage as she retired into private life. Ethel and John Barrymore appeared in Michael Strange's "Clair De Lune" supported by Violet Kemble Cooper and Dennis King, while Lionel Barrymore was appearing in "The Claw" with Irene Fenwick and Doris Rankin. Billie Burke was starring in Booth Tarkington's "The Intimate Strangers" supported by Alfred Lunt, Glenn Hunter and Frances Howard who married film mogul Samuel Goldwyn. Francine Larrimore's starring

HELEN WESTLEY, DUDLEY DIGGES, O. P. HEGGIE, LAURA HOPE CREWS in
"MR. PIM PASSES BY"

JOHN DREW, MRS. LESLIE CARTER in
"THE CIRCLE"

WALLACE EDDINGER in
"CAPTAIN APPLEJACK"

vehicle was "Nice People" supported by Katharine Cornell and Tallulah Bankhead. Vivian Martin with Lynne Overman had a hit with "Just Married," while Grace LaRue with Hale Hamilton was also successful with "Dear Me." Helen Hayes was starring now in "The Wren" supported by Leslie Howard, but the play was a flop so she turned to "Golden Days." A. E. Matthews was in "Bulldog Drummond," a play H. B. Warner later took on tour.

Otto Kruger and Violet Heming were in "Sonya," Lola Fisher and William Courtenay in "Honors Are Even" and Lucile Watson in "March Hares." "The Wandering Jew" was played by Tyrone Power, Helen Ware and Belle Bennett; "The White-Headed Boy" by Arthur Shields and Maire O'Neill; "Mary Stuart" by Clare Eames; "The White Peacock" by Olga Petrova and "The Mountain Man" by Sidney Blackmer and George Fawcett.

Gilbert Emery's "The Hero" was given two productions during the year. It was first played by Grant Mitchell, Jetta Goudal and Robert Ames for only five performances and later it ran 80 times with Richard Bennett, Fania Marinoff and Robert Ames. Laura Hope Crews, Phyllis Povah and Dudley Digges were in "Mr. Pim Passes By" and Charles Cherry and Winifred Lenihan in "The Dover Road." Hazel Dawn also appeared in another Al Woods farce, "Getting Gertie's Garter." "Tarzan of the Apes," dramatized from the popular book, was unsuccessful.

KATHARINE
CORNELL

ALLAN
POLLOCK

EVA
LE GALLIENNE

GRANT
MITCHELL

JUNE WALKER, ERNEST TRUEX (right) in
"SIX-CYLINDER LOVE"

139

KATHARINE CORNELL, FRANCINE LARRIMORE,
TALLULAH BANKHEAD in "NICE PEOPLE"

KATHARINE CORNELL, ALLAN POLLOCK in
"A BILL OF DIVORCEMENT"

VIVIAN MARTIN, LYNNE OVERMAN in
"JUST MARRIED"

LYNN FONTANNE, JOHN WESTLEY in
"DULCY"

CATHERINE CALVERT, OTIS SKINNER, CORNELIA
OTIS SKINNER in "BLOOD AND SAND"

ELIZABETH PATTERSON, GLENN HUNTER, CLARE WELDON, BILLIE BURKE,
FRANCES HOWARD, ALFRED LUNT in "THE INTIMATE STRANGERS"

GEORGE FAWCETT, SIDNEY BLACKMER in
"THE MOUNTAIN MAN"

JOE SCHENCK, BERT WILLIAMS, GUS VAN, EDDIE DOWLING,
RAY DOOLEY in "ZIEGFELD FOLLIES"

Revivals of the year included Laurette Taylor in "Peg O' My Heart," Doris Keane in "Romance," David Warfield in "The Return of Peter Grimm," Frances Starr in "The Easiest Way," William Faversham in "The Squaw Man" and Wilton Lackaye and Charlotte Walker in "Trilby."

"Blossom Time" was destined to prove the most durable of the year's musical productions with Bertram Peacock and Olga Cook heading the original cast. Ed Wynn was in "The Perfect Fool" and Al Jolson in "Bombo." Other musicals included "Tangerine," a big hit, starring Julia Sanderson and Frank Crumit who became husband and wife; "The Last Waltz" with Eleanor Painter and Walter Woolf; "Shuffle Along" with Sissle and Blake; "The Love Letter" with John Charles Thomas, Fred and Adele Astaire, Marjorie Gateson and Alice Brady; "Good Morning Dearie" with Louise Groody and Oscar Shaw; and "The O'Brien Girl" with Elizabeth Hines.

Among the revues, the "Ziegfeld Follies of 1921" cast included Raymond Hitchcock, Fannie Brice, W. C. Fields, Ray Dooley, Vera Michelena and Mary Eaton; "George White's Scandals" had Ann Pennington, Charles King, Lester Allen and Aunt Jemima; "Music Box Revue" had William Collier, Sam Bernard, Florence Moore, Joseph Santley, Ivy Sawyer and Wilda Bennett; and the "Greenwich Village Follies" had Irene Franklin, Ted Lewis, James Watts and Al Herman.

FRANK CRUMIT, JULIA SANDERSON in
"TANGERINE"

BERTRAM PEACOCK, OLGA COOK, COLIN O'MOORE in
"BLOSSOM TIME"

GEORGE ARLISS in
"THE GREEN GODDESS"

RICHARD BENNETT, FANIA MARINOFF, ROBERT AMES,
JOSEPH DEPEW, ALMA BELWIN, BLANCHE FRIDERICI in
"THE HERO"

INA CLAIRE, BARRY BAXTER in
"BLUEBEARD'S EIGHTH WIFE"

OSCAR SHAW, OLIN HOWLAND, FREDERIC SANTLEY
with the FAIRBANKS TWINS in
"TWO LITTLE GIRLS IN BLUE"

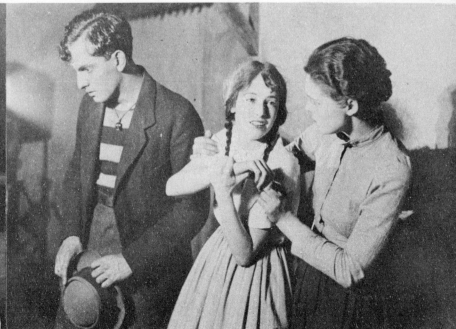

MRS. FISKE in
"WAKE UP,
JONATHAN!"

GEORGE M. COHAN in
"THE TAVERN"

HELEN WARE in
"THE WANDERING
JEW"

JOSEPH SCHILDKRAUT, EVELYN CHARD, EVA LE GALLIENNE in
"LILIOM"

141

E. H. SOTHERN as PETRUCHIO in
"THE TAMING OF THE SHREW"

JULIA MARLOWE as VIOLA in
"TWELFTH NIGHT"

EDITH KING, FRANK MONROE in
"THANK YOU"

SAM BERNARD, JOSEPH SANTLEY, WILLIAM COLLIER, IVY SAWYER,
WILDA BENNETT, FLORENCE MOORE in "MUSIC BOX REVUE"

IRENE FENWICK, LIONEL BARRYMORE in
"THE CLAW"

JEFFERSON ANGELIS   EVA DAVENPORT   WILLIAM KENT   ELIZABETH HINES   CHARLES PURCELL   ADA-MAE WEEKS   JAY GOULD   KATHRYN PERRY   TYRONE POWER

VIOLET KEMBLE COOPER, IAN KEITH in "THE SIVER FOX"

MARGARET ANGLIN in "THE TRIAL OF JOAN OF ARC"

VIOLET HEMING, OTTO KRUGER in "SONYA"

JOSEPH ALLEN in "THE TAVERN"

GRACE GEORGE in "MARIE ANTOINETTE"

GRACE LaRUE in "DEAR ME"

GRANT MITCHELL AND COMPANY in "THE CHAMPION"

TRUMAN STANLEY, ELIZABETH HINES, ANDREW TOMBES, ADA-MAE WEEKS, EDWIN FORSBERG, FINITA DE SORIA, ROBINSON NEWBOLD, GEORGIA CAINE in "THE O'BRIEN GIRL"

TRUE RICE, JOHN DALE, ED WYNN in "THE PERFECT FOOL"

Front Line: FRANK BACON, LILLIAN ALBERTSON, FLORENCE REED, LILLIAN RUSSELL, NANCE O'NEIL, JANE COWL, HELEN WARE, MABEL TALIAFERRO, JOHN CHARLES THOMAS.
Second Line: JANE GREY, HELEN MacKELLAR, FRANCINE LARRIMORE, PEGGY WOOD, MARJORIE RAMBEAU, FANIA MARINOFF, ETHEL BARRYMORE, MARTHA HEDMAN, CHRYSTAL HERNE, MARGALO GILLMORE, BLANCHE RING.   Top: ELSIE FERGUSON in SHAKESPEAREAN PAGEANT FOR ACTORS' EQUITY BENEFIT.

PAULINE LORD in
"ANNA CHRISTIE"

CILE WATSON,
ETH MacKENNA in
"THE NEST"

ALEXANDER CARR,
BARNEY BERNARD in
"PARTNERS AGAIN"

YNA HOWLAND in
EXAS NIGHTINGALE"

WALKER WHITESIDE in
"THE HINDU"

ARET LAWRENCE in
"SECRETS"

MARY SERVOSS in
"THE MERCHANT
OF VENICE"

NIKITA
BALIEFF

MARY
EATON

1922

The greatest dramatic triumph of 1922 was "Rain" with Jeanne Eagels in the role of Sadie Thompson, and the top comedy was "Merton of the Movies" with Glenn Hunter. It was an exciting theatrical year, and one of its most memorable events was John Barrymore's record-breaking production of "Hamlet" in which he was supported by Rosalind Fuller, Blanche Yurka, Tyrone Power and Whitford Kane. The longest run play of the year was "Abie's Irish Rose" by Anne Nichols. It had a sensational run and chalked up 2,327 performances in spite of generally bad notices.

Among the outstanding hits of the year were "Seventh Heaven" with Helen Menken and George Gaul, "He Who Gets Slapped" with Richard Bennett and Margalo Gillmore, "The Torchbearers" with Mary Boland and Alison Skipworth, "Partners Again" with Barney Bernard and Alexander Carr, "Loyalties" with James Dale and "The Hairy Ape" with Louis Wolheim.

Other popular plays were "Shore Leave" starring Frances Starr, "The Awful Truth" played by Ina Claire and Bruce McRae, "To The Ladies" played by Helen Hayes and Otto Kruger, "The Goldfish" by Marjorie Rambeau, Wilton Lackaye and Wilfred Lytell, "The Old Soak" by Harry Beresford, "Lawful Larceny" by Lowell Sherman, Margaret Lawrence, Gail Kane and Alan Dinehart, "The Truth About Blayds" by Alexandra Carlisle, "East of Suez" by Florence Reed, "Fashions For Men" by Helen Gahagan, O. P. Heggie and Beth Merrill and "Up The Ladder" by Paul Kelly and Doris Kenyon.

Bernard Shaw's lengthy fantasy, "Back to Methuselah," was produced by the Theatre Guild in three divisions and acted by George Gaul, Ernita Lascelles, Dennis King and Margaret Wycherly. The Guild also produced Karel Capek's robot melodrama, "R.U.R." and a medieval mystery play called "The Tidings Brought to Mary." The season also saw the first productions of Pirandello's "Six Characters in Search of an Author" and Josef and Karel Capek's insect comedy, "The World We Live In." "The Cat and the Canary" with Henry Hull and Florence Eldridge and "Whispering Wires" with Paul Kelly and Olive Tell were long run mystery plays. Other plays stressing horror and mystery were "The Last Warning," "The Monster" and "The Charlatan."

David Warfield played "The Merchant of Venice" with Mary Servoss as Portia, while Robert B. Mantell and Fritz Leiber were trouping the country with their Shakespearean repertoire companies. Ethel Barrymore had an unhappy experience with "Romeo and Juliet" and no better luck earlier when she appeared in "Rose Bernd."

Other stars and their vehicles were Doris Keane in "The Czarina," Laurette Taylor in "The National Anthem," Henry Miller and Ruth Chatterton in "La Tendresse," Billie Burke in "Rose Briar,"

"R. U. R."

TOM NESBITT, MARGARET
LAWRENCE in
"SECRETS"

DORIS KENYON, PAUL
KELLY in
"UP THE LADDER"

CHARLES QUARTERMAINE, LAURENCE HANRAY, FELIX
AYLMER, JAMES DALE in "LOYALTIES"

"FASHIONS FOR MEN"
with HELEN GAHAGAN (extreme left)

145

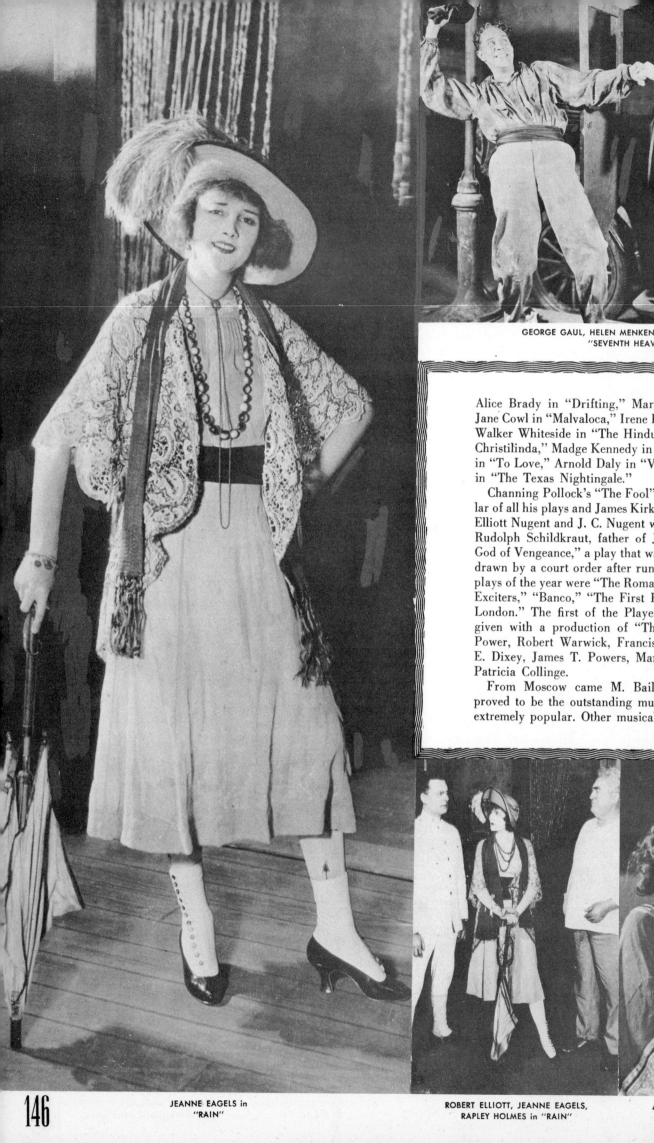

JEANNE EAGELS in "RAIN"

GEORGE GAUL, HELEN MENKEN, HERBERT DRUCE in "SEVENTH HEAVEN"

Alice Brady in "Drifting," Margaret Lawrence in "Secrets," Jane Cowl in "Malvaloca," Irene Bordoni in "The French Doll," Walker Whiteside in "The Hindu," Fay Bainter in "The Lady Christilinda," Madge Kennedy in "Spite Corner," Grace George in "To Love," Arnold Daly in "Voltaire" and Jobyna Howland in "The Texas Nightingale."

Channing Pollock's "The Fool" proved one of the most popular of all his plays and James Kirkwood headed the original cast. Elliott Nugent and J. C. Nugent wrote and played in "Kempy." Rudolph Schildkraut, father of Joseph, was starring in "The God of Vengeance," a play that was declared immoral and withdrawn by a court order after running eleven weeks. Other new plays of the year were "The Romantic Age," "Why Not?," "The Exciters," "Banco," "The First Fifty Years" and "So This Is London." The first of the Players' Club all-star revivals was given with a production of "The Rivals" played by Tyrone Power, Robert Warwick, Francis Wilson, John Craig, Henry E. Dixey, James T. Powers, Mary Shaw, Violet Heming and Patricia Collinge.

From Moscow came M. Baileff's "Chauve-Souris" which proved to be the outstanding musical novelty of the year and extremely popular. Other musical hits were "The Lady in Er-

ROBERT ELLIOTT, JEANNE EAGELS, RAPLEY HOLMES in "RAIN"

ALICE BRADY, ROBERT WARWICK in "DRIFTING"

IDA KRAMER, ALFRED WHITE, HAROLD SHUBERT, JACK BERTIN, MILTON WALLACE
IN ONE OF THE MANY COMPANIES OF "ABIE'S IRISH ROSE"

GLENN HUNTER in
"MERTON OF THE MOVIES"

...ine" with Wilda Bennett and Walter Woolf, "The Gingham
...irl" with Helen Ford and Eddie Buzzell, "Sally, Irene and
...ary" with Eddie Dowling and Hal Van Rensselaer, and "The
...eenwich Village Follies" with Carl Randall, Marjorie Peter-
...n and Savoy and Brennan.

Elsie Janis appeared in "Elsie Janis and Her Gang," Peggy
...ood was in "The Clinging Vine," Edith Day, Queenie Smith
...d Hal Skelly were in "Orange Blossoms," Elizabeth Hines and
...harles King in "Little Nellie Kelly," and Frank Tinney in
...Daffy Dill." Eddie Cantor was in "Make It Snappy" and Nora
...ayes in "Queen o' Hearts."

Vivienne Segal, Mary Eaton, Gilda Gray, Gallagher and
...hean and Mary Lewis were in "Ziegfeld Follies, 1922," George
...hite, Lester Allen, W. C. Fields and Paul Whiteman's orches-
...a in "Scandals," Willie and Eugene Howard, Arthur Margetson
...d Francis Renault in "The Passing Show of 1922," and Clark
...d McCullough, Grace LaRue, Charlotte Greenwood and John
...eel in "Music Box Revue."

Other musicals of the year were "Up In The Clouds," "The
...lue Kitten," "The Hotel Mouse," "Marjolaine" and "Letty
...epper." Howard Thurston, the Magician, was seen in a one
...an show of magic acts.

...ALPH MORGAN, LAURETTE TAYLOR in
"THE NATIONAL ANTHEM"

JAMES RENNIE, FRANCES STARR in
"SHORE LEAVE"

HELEN HAYES, OTTO KRUGER in
"TO THE LADIES"

FLORENCE NASH, GLENN HUNTER in
"MERTON OF THE MOVIES"

147

MARJORIE RAMBEAU in
"THE GOLDFISH"

DORIS KEANE in
"THE CZARINA"

DAVID WARFIELD in
"THE MERCHANT OF VENICE"

IRENE BORDONI in
"THE FRENCH DOLL"

BLANCHE FRIDERICI, HENRY HULL, BETH FRANKLYN,
JANE WARRINGTON, FLORENCE ELDRIDGE in
"THE CAT AND THE CANARY"

FAY BAINTER in
"THE LADY CRISTILINDA"

ROBERT E. O'CONNOR, HARRY BERESFORD, EVA
WILLIAMS in "THE OLD SOAK"

BILLIE BURKE, ALAN DINEHART in
"ROSE BRIAR"

JAMES T. POWERS, JOHN CRAIG, MARY SHAW, TYRONE POWER,
HENRY E. DIXEY in "THE RIVALS"

MARGALO GILLMORE, RICHARD BENNETT
"HE WHO GETS SLAPPED"

148

WALTER WOOLF in
"THE LADY IN ERMINE"

ADELE AND FRED ASTAIRE in
"FOR GOODNESS SAKE"

ELSIE JANIS in
"ELSIE JANIS AND HER GANG"

NORA BAYES in
"QUEEN O' HEARTS"

"SIX CHARACTERS IN SEARCH OF AN AUTHOR"
with MARGARET WYCHERLY

FLORENCE REED in
"EAST OF SUEZ"

KENNETH MacKENNA, BEATRICE MAUDE in
"THE WORLD WE LIVE IN"

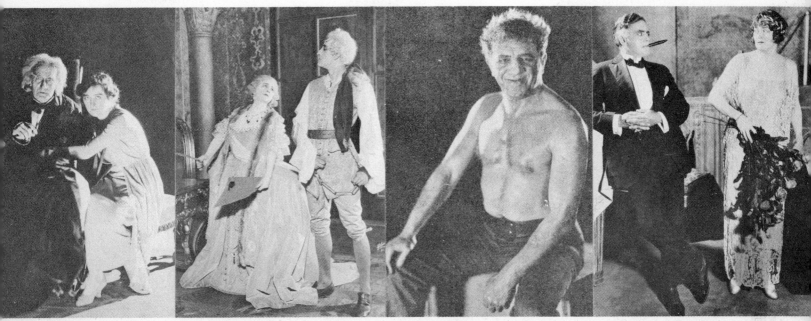

P. HEGGIE, ALEXANDRA CARLISLE in
"THE TRUTH ABOUT BLADYS"

DORIS KEANE, BASIL RATHBONE in
"THE CZARINA"

LOUIS WOLHEIM in
"THE HAIRY APE"

ARTHUR SHAW, MARY BOLAND in
"THE TORCHBEARERS"

WILFRED LYTELL McKAY MORRIS TALLULAH BANKHEAD in "THE EXCITERS" RUDOLPH SCHILDKRAUT CHRISTINE NORMAN DOUGLAS STEVENSON CLEO MAYFIE... "THE BLUSHING...

GEORGE GAUL, ERNITA LASCELLES in "BACK TO METHUSELAH"

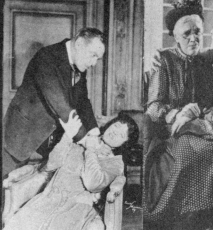
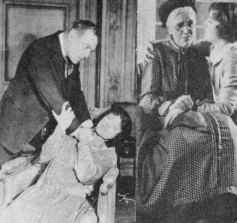

WILL ROGERS in "ZIEGFELD FOLLIES OF 1922" GILDA GRAY in "ZIEGFELD FOLLIES OF 1922" HENRY MILLER, RUTH CHATTERTON in "LA TENDRESSE" MARIE L. DAY, MA... KENNEDY in "SPITE CORNER...

BRUCE McRAE, INA CLAIRE in "THE AWFUL TRUTH" JAMES KIRKWOOD, SARA SOTHERN in "THE FOOL" DONALD GALLAHER, LEAH WINSLOW, EDMUND BREESE in "SO THIS IS LONDON" OLIVE TELL, PAUL KELLY in "WHISPERING WIVES"

HOWARD
THURSTON

VINTON FREEDLEY in
"FOR GOODNESS SAKE"

MARION GREEN in
"THE ROSE OF STAMBOUL"

FAY MARBE, AL SEXTON in
"THE HOTEL MOUSE"

CHARLOTTE GREENWOOD
in "MUSIC BOX REVUE"

FRANCIS RENAULT in
"PASSING SHOW OF 1922"

HAL VAN RENSSELAER in
"UP IN THE CLOUDS"

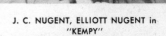

_LAN DINEHART, GAIL KANE, MARGARET LAWRENCE in
"LAWFUL LARCENY"

VICTOR MORLEY, JOSEPH CAWTHORN, MARION SUNSHINE,
LILLIAN LORRAINE, ROBERT WOOLSEY, DOUGLAS
STEVENSON in "THE BLUE KITTEN"

J. C. NUGENT, ELLIOTT NUGENT in
"KEMPY"

_HARLOTTE MONTEREY,
ARNOLD DALY in
"VOLTAIRE"

FRANCES WHITE,
TAYLOR HOLMES in
"THE HOTEL MOUSE"

Above: KATINKA; Lower: THE WOODEN SOLDIERS
From "CHAUVE-SOURIS"

NANCY WELFORD,
HAL SKELLY in
"ORANGE BLOSSOMS"

IRENE OLSEN,
GUY ROBERTSON in
"DAFFY DILL"

ELIZABETH HINES,
_RRETT GREENWOOD in
_ITTLE NELLIE KELLY"

BERT SAVOY, JAY BRENNAN in
"GREENWICH VILLAGE FOLLIES"

EDDIE BUZZELL, HELEN FORD in
"THE GINGHAM GIRL"

PEGGY WOOD, LOUISE GALLOWAY in
"THE CLINGING VINE"

EDDIE CANTOR in
"MAKE IT SNAPPY"

JOHN BARRYMORE as "HAMLET" with
BLANCHE YURKA as THE QUEEN

IVAN MOSKVINE in "TSAR FYODOR IVANOVITCH"

HELEN GAHAGAN, PAUL KELLY in "CHAINS"

ALFRED LUNT, LAURETTE TAYLOR in "SWEET NELL OF OLD DRURY"

MRS. FISKE, FRANCIS LISTER in "MARY, MARY, QUITE CONTRARY"

HENRIETTA CROSMAN, FLORENCE JOHNS in "CHILDREN OF THE MOON"

SIR JOHN MARTIN HARVEY as "OEDIPUS"

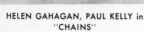

1923 Jane Cowl scoring one of the major successes of her career in "Romeo and Juliet" with Rollo Peters as Romeo, and Walter Hampden appearing in the new Brian Hooker version of Rostand's "Cyrano de Bergerac" with Carroll McComas as Roxane were two of the major events of the year 1923. Later in the year, Miss Cowl appeared with Mr. Peters in Maeterlinck's "Pelleas and Melisande."

The Theatre Guild was having an impressive year with fine revivals of "Peer Gynt" with Joseph Schildkraut, "The Devil's Disciple" with Basil Sydney and Roland Young, and the first American production of Shaw's "Saint Joan" with Winifred Lenihan. Julia Arthur played the title role in this on the road.

Eleonora Duse began her farewell American tour with "The Lady From the Sea," "Ghosts," "Cosi Sia," "La Porta Chiusa" and "La Citta Morta" in her repertory. It was a tour that ended tragically with her death from pneumonia in Pittsburgh.

The Moscow Art Players arrived from Russia and were an artistic success with such plays as "The Lower Depths," "The Cherry Orchard," "The Three Sisters," "Tsar Fyodor Ivanovitch" and "The Brothers Karamazoff." Sir John Martin Harvey, over from London, was impressing audiences with "Oedipus Rex." Sothern and Marlowe were including the seldom produced

WINIFRED LENIHAN as "SAINT JOAN"

LOWELL SHERMAN

ALISON SKIPWORTH

ALAN DINEHART

EMILY ANN WELLMAN

TOM POWERS

ROBERTA ARNOLD

BASIL RATHBONE

JUNE WALKER

A LE GALLIENNE in "THE SWAN"

RALPH MORGAN, HENRY HULL, LYNN FONTANNE, ROBERT STRANGE in "IN LOVE WITH LOVE"

LUCILE WATSON, H. B. WARNER, GEOFFREY KERR in "YOU AND I"

McKAY MORRIS in "THE RIVALS"

JANE COWL as JULIET

JANE COWL, ROLLO PETERS in
"PELLEAS AND MELISANDE"

JANE COWL and ROLLO PETERS in
"ROMEO AND JULIET"

"Cymbeline" in their Shakespearean repertoire while Marjorie Rambeau failed as Rosalind in "As You Like It" with Ian Keith as her Orlando. The Players' Club revived "The School for Scandal" with John Drew, Ethel Barrymore and Robert B. Mantell heading an all-star cast.

The Pulitzer Prize was awarded to "Icebound" by Owen Davis. Other important new plays were Molnar's "The Swan" with Eva Le Gallienne, Basil Rathbone and Philip Merivale, Gilbert Emery's "Tarnish" with Tom Powers, Ann Harding and Fania Marinoff, and Lee Wilson Dodd's "The Changelings" with Blanche Bates, Henry Miller, Laura Hope Crews, Ruth Chatterton and Geoffrey Kerr.

Lula Vollmer was represented by "Sun Up" in which Lucille LaVerne played the Widow Cagle, and also by "The Shame Woman" which featured Florence Rittenhouse. This year also saw productions of "You and I" by Philip Barry, "The Adding Machine" by Elmer Rice, "Robert E. Lee" by John Drinkwater and "Windows" by John Galsworthy.

Katharine Cornell appeared with Otto Kruger in "Will Shakespeare," Louise Huff with Ben Lyon in "Mary the Third," Judith Anderson with Frank Keenan in "Peter Weston," Helen Gahagan with Paul Kelly in "Chains" and June Walker with Otto Kruger in "The Nervous Wreck."

LUCILLE LA VERNE in
"SUN UP"

WALTER HAMPDEN as "CYRANO DE BERGERAC"

Irene Bordoni played in "Little Miss Bluebeard," Nazimova in "Dagmar," Genevieve Tobin in "Polly Preferred," Pauline Frederick in "The Guilty One," Laurette Taylor in "Humoresque," and Ethel Barrymore in "The Laughing Lady." Alice Brady appeared in "Zander the Great," Norman Trevor in "The Mountebank," Ruth Gordon in "Tweedles" and Grant Mitchell in "The Whole Town's Talking."

Maude Fulton was in "The Humming Bird," Florence Reed in "The Lullaby," William Hodge in "For All of Us" and Beryl Mercer in "Queen Victoria." Mary Nash appeared in "The Lady," Olga Petrova in "Hurricane," Mary Ryan in "Red Light Annie" and George M. Cohan in "The Song and Dance Man."

"Sweet Nell of Old Drury" was played by Laurette Taylor, Lynn Fontanne and Alfred Lunt; "Aren't We All?" by Cyril Maude, Alma Tell and Leslie Howard; "Two Fellows and a Girl" by Alan Dinehart, Ruth Shepley and John Halliday, and "Children of the Moon" by Henrietta Crosman. "In Love With Love" was acted by Lynn Fontanne, Henry Hull and Ralph Morgan; "Casanova" by Lowell Sherman, Katharine Cornell and Mary Ellis; "Spring Cleaning" by Violet Heming, A. E. Matthews, Arthur Byron and Estelle Winwood, and "The Woman on the Jury" by Mary Newcomb.

ROBERT AMES, EDNA MAY OLIVER in
"ICEBOUND"

CARROLL McCOMAS as
ROXANE

CYRIL MAUDE, ALMA TELL in
"AREN'T WE ALL"

155

PHILIP MERIVALE, EVA LE GALLIENNE, BASIL RATHBONE in "THE SWAN"

JUNE WALKER, OTTO KRUGER in "THE NERVOUS WRECK"

MARY BOLAND, CLIFTON WEBB in "MEET THE WIFE"

SELENA ROYLE, JOSEPH SCHILDKRAUT in "PEER GYNT"

BASIL SYDNEY, LOTUS ROBB, ROLAND YOUNG in "THE DEVIL'S DISCIPLE"

FRANK KEENAN, JUDITH ANDERSON in "PETER WESTON"

JOHN HALLIDAY, CLAIBORNE FOSTER, RUTH SHEPLEY, ALAN DINEHART in "TWO FELLOWS AND A GIRL"

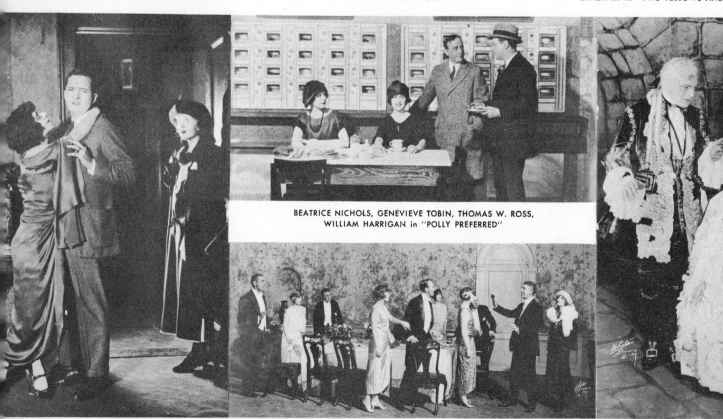

BEATRICE NICHOLS, GENEVIEVE TOBIN, THOMAS W. ROSS, WILLIAM HARRIGAN in "POLLY PREFERRED"

FANIA MARINOFF, TOM POWERS, ANN HARDING in "TARNISH"

ROBERT NOBLE, VIOLET HEMING, A. E. MATTHEWS, BLYTHE DALY, GORDON ASH, MAXINE McDONALD, PAULINE WHITSON, C. HAVILAND CHAPELLE, ARTHUR BYRON, ESTELLE WINWOOD in "SPRING CLEANING"

LOWELL SHERMAN, KATHARINE CORNELL in "CASANOVA"

ALICE BRADY, JEROME PATRICK in "ZANDER THE GREAT"

IRENE FENWICK, IAN KEITH, LIONEL BARRYMORE in "LAUGH, CLOWN, LAUGH!"

MARJORIE RAMBEAU as ROSALIND

FRANK MORGAN, FLORENCE REED in "THE LULLABY"

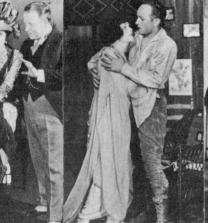

MARY NASH. ELISABETH RISDON in "THE LADY"

FANIA MARINOFF, ERNEST COSSART in "THE LOVE HABIT"

GAIL KANE, McKAY MORRIS in "THE BREAKING POINT"

RICHARD STEVENSON, BETTY PIERCE in "WHITE CARGO"

HENRY MILLER, BLANCHE BATES, RUTH CHATTERTON in "THE CHANGELINGS"

DUDLEY DIGGES, MARGARET WYCHERLY in "THE ADDING MACHINE"

BEN LYON, LOUISE HUFF in "MARY THE THIRD"

EUGENE O'BRIEN in "STEVE"

Otis Skinner was seen in "Sancho Panza," Mrs. Fiske in "Mary, Mary, Quite Contrary." Mary Boland starred in "Meet the Wife," Eugene O'Brien in "Steve," and "Laugh, Clown, Laugh" starred Lionel Barrymore. "White Cargo," a lurid drama, caught the public fancy and so did the comedy "The Potters" which started Raymond Guion, better known as Gene Raymond, on the road to fame.

Foremost among the tuneful entertainment were "Wildflower" with Edith Day and Guy Robertson, "Poppy" with Madge Kennedy and W. C. Fields, "Kid Boots" with Eddie Cantor and Mary Eaton, and "Little Jessie James" with Nan Halperin, Miriam Hopkins and Allen Kearns.

Other musicals were "The Dancing Girl" with Trini and Marie Dressler, "Helen of Troy, N.Y." with Queenie Smith, "Battling Buttler" with Charles Ruggles, "Dew Drop Inn" with James Barton. "Stepping Stones" with Fred and Dorothy Stone.

Joe Cook and Peggy Hopkins Joyce were in the "Vanities," Frank Fay in "Artists and Models," Frank Tinney, Joseph Santley, Ivy Sawyer, Florence Moore, Grace Moore and John Steel in "Music Box Revue," Alice Delysia in "Topics of 1923," Miller and Lyles in "Runnin' Wild," "Nifties of 1923" featured William Collier, Sam Bernard, Hazel Dawn and the Tiller Girls, and in the "Ziegfeld Follies" cast were Fannie Brice, Bert and Betty Wheeler, and Paul Whiteman and his orchestra.

RUTH GORDON

BRUCE McRAE, IRENE BORDONI in "LITTLE MISS BLUEBEARD"

DENNIS KING as MERCUTIO

BERYL MERCER in "QUEEN VICTORIA"

OTIS SKINNER in "SANCHO PANZA"

NORMAN TREVOR in "THE MOUNTEBANK"

LOUISE HUFF

W. C. FIELDS, MADGE KENNEDY in "POPPY"

MARY EATON in "KID BOOTS"

JOBYNA HOWLAND, EDDIE CANTOR in "KID BOOTS"

ANN HARDING

MIRIAM HOPKINS

CHARLES COLUMBUS, FLORENCE O'DENISHAWN, NELSON SNOW in "MUSIC BOX REVUE"

FLORENCE MOORE, JOHN STEEL, IVY SAWYER, JOSEPH SANTLEY, GRACE MOORE, FRANK TINNEY, singing "YES, WE HAVE NO BANANAS" in "MUSIC BOX REVUE"

CHARLES RUGGL "BATTLING BUT

QUEENIE
SMITH

EDITH
DAY

BETTY & BERT WHEELER in
"ZIEGFELD FOLLIES"

JACK McGOWAN, VIRGINIA
O'BRIEN in "THE RISE OF
ROSIE O'REILLY"

NAN
HALPERIN

JAMES
BARTON

MARIE
CAHILL

DOROTHY STONE, FRED STONE, ALLENE CRATER in
"STEPPING STONES"

W. C. FIELDS in
"POPPY"

EDITH DAY, GUY ROBERTSON in
"WILDFLOWER"

ROY
ATWELL

ETHELIND
TERRY

HARRY
FENDER

WINNIE
LIGHTNER

JOHN
BYAM

EDYTHE
BAKER

ROY
HOYER

ESTHER
HOWARD

ALAN
EDWARDS

MITZI in
"THE MAGIC RING"

OSCAR SHAW, LOUISE GROODY in
"ONE KISS"

BEN BARD, MARIE DRESSLER, JACK
PEARL in "THE DANCING GIRL"

JOE SCHENCK, HAZEL DAWN,
FLORENZ AMES in "PARODY ON
RAIN" in "NIFTIES OF 1923"

ALLEN KEARNS, MIRIAM HOPKINS in
"LITTLE JESSIE JAMES"

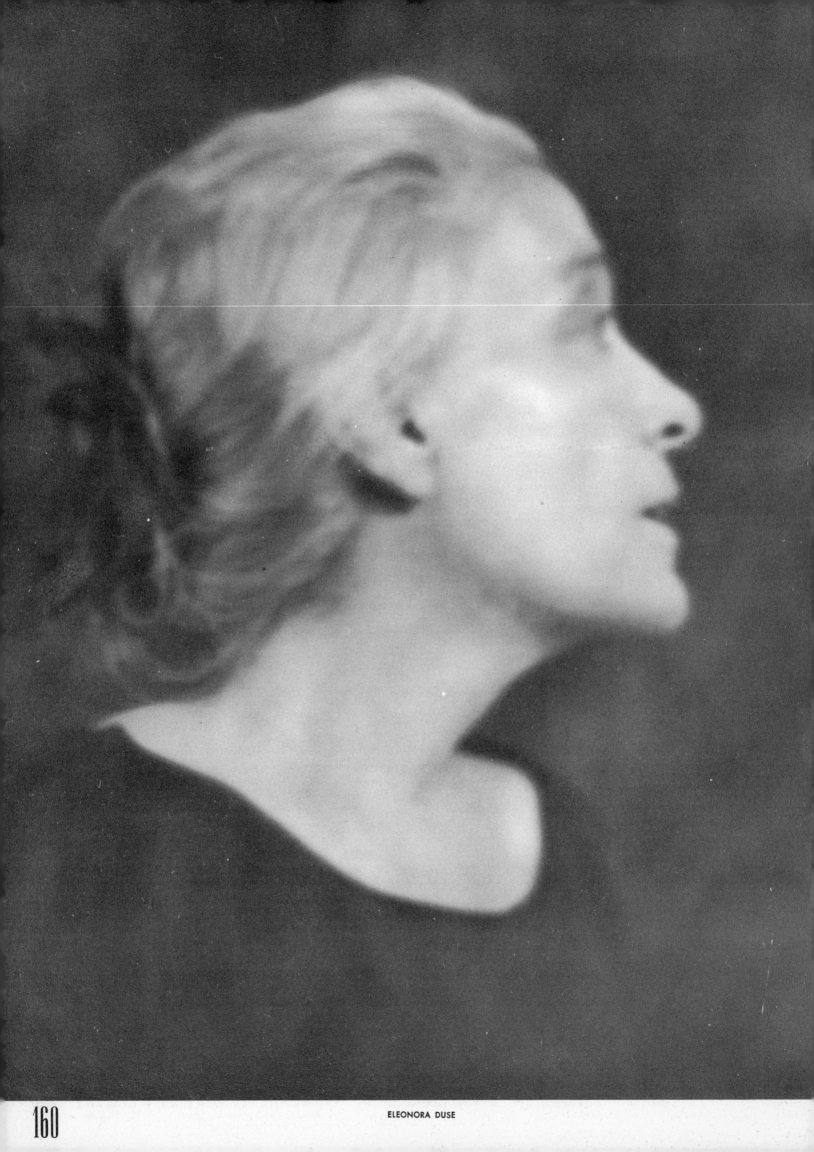

ELEONORA DUSE

MARGARET
DALE

FRANK
McGLYNN

LUCILE
WATSON

WHITFORD
KANE

JANET
BEECHER

JOHN
CRAIG

CLARE
EAMES

ROBERT
WARWICK

ALEXANDRA
CARLISLE

WILLETTE
KERSHAW

JAMES
CRANE

WILLIAM
COURTENAY

CHARLOTTE
IVES

GREGORY
KELLY

ALINE
MacMAHON

ROLAND
YOUNG

BLANCHE
YURKA

LOU
TELLEGEN

KATHERINE
ALEXANDER

PAUL
KELLY

NEDDA
HARRIGAN

GEORGE
GAUL

HELEN
WESTLEY

OTTO
KRUGER

MARGARET
WYCHERLY

IAN
KEITH

HEDDA
HOPPER

HELEN
MacKELLAR

WILLARD
MACK

ALMA TELL

OLIVE TELL

FRANK KEENAN

HELEN MENKEN

VIOLET KEMBLE
COOPER

GEOFFREY
KERR

PLAYERS OF THE PERIOD

161

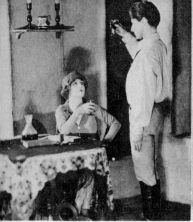

EMILY STEVENS, MORGAN FARLEY in "FATA MORGANA"

PHYLLIS POVAH, O. P. HEGGIE, FREDERIC BURT in "MINICK"

PAULINE LORD, RICHARD BENNETT, GLENN ANDERS in "THEY KNEW WHAT THEY WANTED"

MARY YOUNG in "DANCING MOTHERS"

PHILIP MERIVALE, INA CLAIRE in "GROUNDS FOR DIVORCE"

GRETA NISSEN in "BEGGAR ON HORSEBACK"

1924

There were many distinguished plays produced in 1924. Among them were two Pulitzer Prize plays: Hatcher Hughes' "Hell-Bent fer Heaven" for the 1923-24 season and Sidney Howard's "They Knew What They Wanted" for the 1924-25 season. Pauline Lord and Richard Bennett were starred in the latter play while Glenn Anders appeared to advantage in both plays. Others were the Maxwell Anderson-Laurence Stallings war play, "What Price Glory?" with Louis Wolheim as Capt. Flagg and William Boyd as Sgt. Quirt, George Kelly's "The Show Off" with Louis John Bartels in the title role, Eugene O'Neill's "Desire Under the Elms" acted by Walter Huston and Mary Morris, and Sutton Vane's "Outward Bound" with Alfred Lunt, Leslie Howard, Beryl Mercer, Margalo Gillmore, Dudley Digges and Charlotte Granville.

Among the stars, George Arliss appeared in "Old English," Ina Claire in "Grounds For Divorce," H. B. Warner in "Silence," Elsie Ferguson in "The Moonflower," Emily Stevens with Morgan Farley in "Fata Morgana," Lenore Ulric with William Courtenay in "The Harem," Louis Mann in "Milgrim's Progress," Doris Keane with Jacob Ben-Ami in "Welded," Mrs. Fiske in "Helena's Babies" and Grace George with Laura Hope Crews in "The Merry Wives of Gotham."

OSGOOD PERKINS, MARION BALLOU, GEORGE W. BARBIER, ANNE CARPENGER, ROLAND YOUNG in "BEGGAR ON HORSEBACK"

WM. COURTENAY, LENORE ULRIC in "THE HAREM"

ETHEL BARRYMORE, HENRY DANIELL in "THE SECOND MRS. TANQUERAY"

EUGENE POWERS, BERYL MERCER, CHARLOTTE GRANVILLE, LYONEL WATTS, ALFRED LUNT, LESLIE HOWARD, MARGALO GILLMORE in "OUTWARD BOUND"

KATHERINE GREY, NORMAN TREVOR, MRS. THOMAS WHIFFEN in "THE GOOSE HANGS HIGH"

WALTER HUSTON, MARY MORRIS, CHARLES ELLIS in "DESIRE UNDER THE ELMS"

BURKE CLARKE, GLENN ANDERS, CLARA BLANDICK, AUGUSTIN DUNCAN in "HELL-BENT FER HEAVEN"

Ethel Barrymore revived "The Second Mrs. Tanqueray." Other revivals were Marilyn Miller in "Peter Pan" with Leslie Banks as Capt. Hook; Jane Cowl with Rollo Peters in "Antony and Cleopatra;" Bertha Kalish in "The Kreutzer Sonata;" James K. Hackett with Clare Eames in "Macbeth;" Miss Ames also revived "Hedda Gabler;" "She Stoops to Conquer" was presented by The Players' Club with an all-star cast.

Alfred Lunt and Lynn Fontanne were having their first great success as a team with "The Guardsman," while Judith Anderson was also receiving applause for her performance in "Cobra" with Louis Calhern. After his success in "Liliom," Joseph Schildkraut won new laurels and stardom for his performance in "The Firebrand." Katharine Cornell and Helen Hayes were both advancing rapidly and both had a very active year. Miss Hayes first appeared in "We Moderns," then "Dancing Mothers" with Mary Young and John Halliday, and in December she co-starred with Sidney Blackmer in "Quarantine." Miss Cornell appeared in "The Way Things Happen," was Lionel Atwill's leading lady in "The Outsider," Robert Loraine's vis-a-vis in "Tiger Cats," and also in December had great success with a revival of "Candida." She has since revived it several times. In this production Richard Bird played Marchbanks, Pedro De Cordoba was Morell and Clare Eames, Prosey.

JUDITH ANDERSON in "COBRA"

ELSIE FERGUSON, SIDNEY BLACKMER in "THE MOONFLOWER"

H. B. WARNER in "SILENCE"

HELEN LOWELL, REGINA WALLACE, LOUIS JOHN BARTELS, C. W. GOODRICH, GUY D'ENNERY, LEE TRACY, JULIETTE CROSBY in "THE SHOW OFF"

LOUIS WOLHEIM, WILLIAM BOYD in "WHAT PRICE GLORY?"

FRANCES HOWARD, JAMES RENNIE, CHARLES RICHMAN in "THE BEST PEOPLE"

NYDIA WESTMAN, WALLACE FORD in "PIGS"

JOSEPH SCHILDKRAUT in
"THE FIREBRAND"

TOP: ORVILLE CALDWELL, ROSAMUND PINCHOT,
LADY DIANA MANNERS AND A SCENE from
"THE MIRACLE"

MARILYN MILLER
as "PETER PAN"

NANA BRYANT, FRANK MORGAN, HORTENSE ALDEN (left)
JOSEPH SCHILDKRAUT (center) EDWARD G. ROBINSON (right)
in "THE FIREBRAND"

JANE COWL in
"ANTONY AND CLEOPATRA"

BERNARD A. REINOLD, SIDNEY BLACKMER, HELEN HAYES,
BERYL MERCER in "QUARANTINE"

KATHARINE CORNELL, PEDRO
DE CORDOBA in
"CANDIDA"

LIONEL ATWILL, PAT SOMERSET,
KATHARINE CORNELL in
"THE OUTSIDER"

GEORGE ARLISS
in
"OLD ENGLISH"

JOHN HALLIDAY, HELEN HAYES
in
"DANCING MOTHERS"

The Century Theatre was effectively redecorated to look like a cathedral for the Morris Gest and Ray Comstock production of "The Miracle," a religious legend spectacularly staged by Max Reinhardt. It was one of the theatrical events of the year. Lady Diana Manners played the Madonna, Rosamond Pinchot was the Nun, Orville Caldwell, the Knight and others in the cast were Rudolph Schildkraut, Schuyler Ladd, Werner Krauss and Fritz Feld.

"Beggar on Horseback" by George S. Kaufman and Marc Connelly was an unusual play. Roland Young played the lead, supported by Kay Johnson, Osgood Perkins, Spring Byington and Grethe Ruzt-Nissen (Greta Nissen).

Other new plays were "The Goose Hangs High" by Lewis Beach, "Expressing Willie" by Rachel Crothers, "The Youngest" by Philip Barry and "Minick" by George S. Kaufman and Edna Ferber. Also there were "Pigs" with Wallace Ford and Nydia Westman, "Ladies of the Evening" with Beth Merrill, Edna Hibbard and Vernon Steele, "The Best People" with James Rennie and Frances Howard, "High Stakes" with Lowell Sherman and Wilton Lackaye, "Cheaper to Marry" with Robert Warwick, Claiborne Foster and Alan Dinehart and "Conscience" in which Lillian Foster scored.

Billie Burke, Ruth Chatterton and Fay Bainter were all appearing in musical comedies, which was an event, since they usually appeared only in straight plays. Miss Burke with Ernest Truex was in "Annie Dear," Miss Bainter with Walter Woolf was in "The Dream Girl," while Miss Chatterton had her newly acquired husband, Ralph Forbes, as her leading man in "The Magnolia Lady."

And the year offered two musical comedies of exceptional popularity: "Rose Marie" and "The Student Prince." Mary Ellis played the title role in the former with Dennis King as her leading man, and in the latter, Howard Marsh was the original Prince Karl to the Kathie of Ilse Marenga.

"Charlot's Revue" was the most distinguished offering in its field, and served to introduce the rare talents of Jack Buchanan, Gertrude Lawrence and Beatrice Lillie.

Many other musical shows were presented during the year, and the quality was high. The Duncan Sisters appeared in "Topsy and Eva," Wilda Bennett in "Mme. Pompadour," the Marx Brothers in "I'll Say She Is," Fred and Adele Astaire in "Lady, Be Good," Ed Wynn in "The Grab Bag" and Eleanor Painter in "The Chiffon Girl."

Will Rogers, Ann Pennington, Lupino Lane and Imogene Wilson were in the "Ziegfeld Follies," Lester Allen and Winnie Lightner in the "George White's Scandals," Joe Cook and Sophie Tucker in the "Vanities," Grace Moore, Fannie Brice and Clark and McCullough in the "Music Box Revue." Moran and Mack and the Dolly Sisters were in "Greenwich Village Follies."

OSCAR SHAW in "DEAR SIR"   MISTINGUETT in "INNOCENT EYES"   ERNEST TRUEX in "ANNIE DEAR"   IRENE DUNNE in "LOLLIPOP"   JACK BUCHANAN

GENEVIEVE TOBIN, KATHERINE ALEXANDER, WALKER ELLIS, HENRY HULL, EFFIE SHANNON in "THE YOUNGEST"   BETH MERRILL, ROBERT O'CONNOR, JOHN CARMODY, EDNA HIBBARD in "LADIES OF THE EVENING"

JIMMY HUSSEY   ROBERT WARWICK, CLAIBORNE FOSTER, ALAN DINEHART in "CHEAPER TO MARRY"   LILLIAN FOSTER   JACK OSTERMAN

LOU HOLTZ   MARY MORRIS

LOWELL SHERMAN, WILTON LACKAYE, PHOEBE FOSTER, FLEMING WARD in "HIGH STAKES"

ANN PENNINGTON in "ZIEGFELD FOLLIES"   MOLLY McINTYRE, CHRYSTAL HERNE, ALAN BROOKS, RICHARD STERLING, JOHN GERARD, LOUISE CLOSSER HALE, DOUGLAS GARDEN, MERLE MADDERN, WARREN WILLIAM in "EXPRESSING WILLIE"   FRANCES WHITE

THE MARX BROTHERS, LOTTA MILES in
"I'LL SAY SHE IS"

HOWARD MARSH, GREEK EVANS in
"THE STUDENT PRINCE"

DENNIS KING, MARY ELLIS in
"ROSE-MARIE"

BEATRICE LILLIE in
"CHARLOT'S REVUE OF 1924"

JAY GOULD, LORRAINE MANVILLE in
"PLAIN JANE"

VIVIAN and ROSETTA DUNCAN in
"TOPSY AND EVA"

JACK DONAHUE, QUEENIE SMITH in
"BE YOURSELF"

FAY BAINTER, WALTER WOOLF in
"THE DREAM GIRL"

GERTRUDE LAWRENCE in
"CHARLOT'S REVUE OF 1924"

ADA-MAY WEEKS,
HARRY PUCK in
"LOLLIPOP"

ED WYNN
in
"THE GRAB BAG"

FRED ASTAIRE, ADELE ASTAIRE, CLIFF EDWARDS
in
"LADY, BE GOOD"

ROY ROYSTON,
ELIZABETH HINES in
"MARJORIE"

PHILIP McCULLOUGH
BOBBY CLARK in
"MUSIC BOX REVU

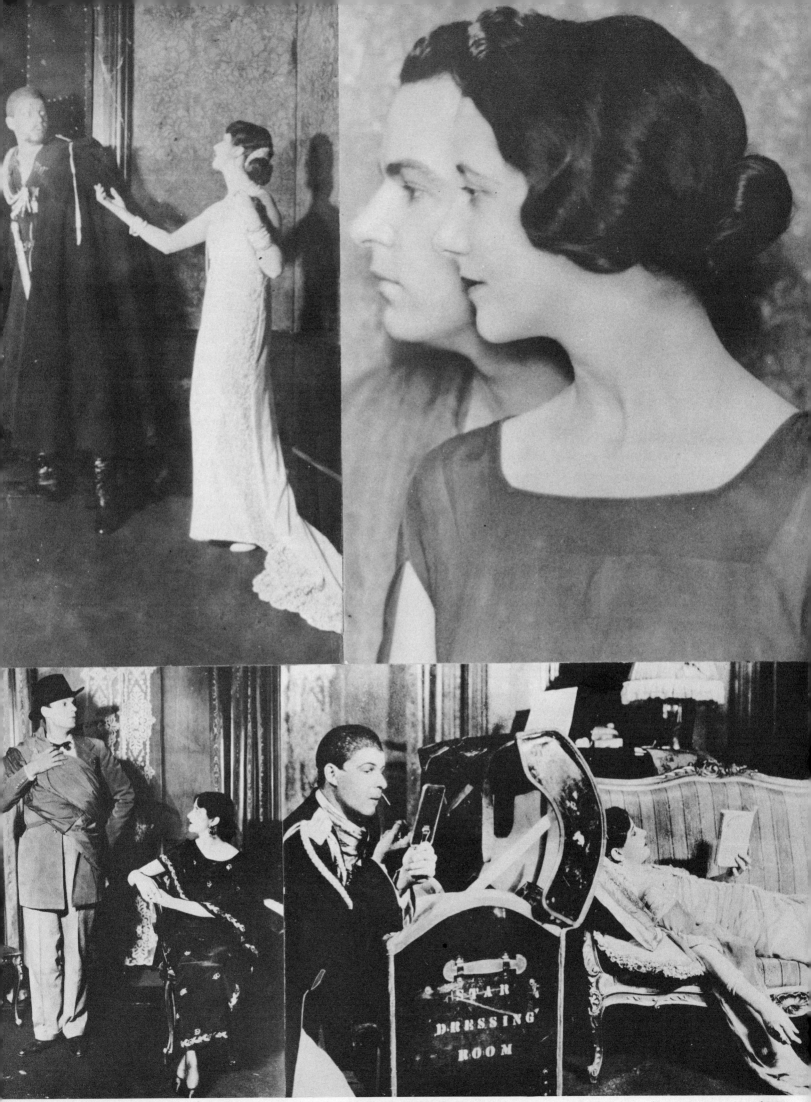

ALFRED LUNT and LYNN FONTANNE in
"THE GUARDSMAN"

167

LAURA HOPE
CREWS

ESTELLE WINWOOD,
WILLIAM FARNUM in
"THE BUCCANEER"

GLENN
HUNTER

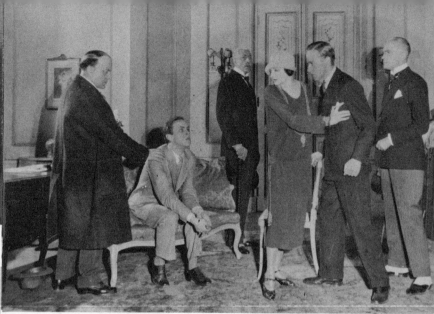

A. P. KAYE, PAUL GUILFOYLE, EUGENE POWERS, KATHARINE CORNELL, LESLIE HOWARD, GORDON AS
"THE GREEN HAT"

VICTOR MOORE,
OTTO KRUGER in
"EASY COME, EASY GO"

MILDRED FLORENCE, WARREN
WILLIAM, JOHN WESTLEY in
"12 MILES OUT"

GARETH HUGHES
in
"THE DUNCE BOY"

MARY NEWCOMB
in
"NIGHT HAWK"

RALPH FORBES,
RUTH CHATTERTON in
"THE LITTLE MINISTER"

ELLIOTT NUGENT
in
"THE POOR NUT"

1925 The first New York productions of 1925 opened on the same night and were both well received. "Mrs. Partridge Presents," a pleasant comedy, was acted by Blanche Bates, Ruth Gordon and Eliot Cabot. "Is Zat So?" an overnight success, was played by Robert Armstrong and James Gleason, and the latter co-authored this comedy with Richard Taber. Later in the season, "The Fall Guy," a writing collaboration by Mr. Gleason and George Abbott became another hit, providing an excellent role for Ernest Truex.

"Craig's Wife" by George Kelly was the Pulitzer Prize winner with Chrystal Herne scoring. Other successes were Channing Pollock's "The Enemy" starring Fay Bainter, "The Dove" brilliantly played by Holbrook Blinn and Judith Anderson, "The Cradle Snatchers" with Mary Boland and Edna May Oliver, "The Jazz Singer" with George Jessel, "The Poor Nut" with Elliot Nugent, also "Aloma of the South Seas" and "The Gorilla."

Among the comedies of the year were "The Butter and Egg Man" with Gregory Kelly, "The Patsy" with Claiborne Foster, "Alias the Deacon" with Berton Churchill, "The Grand Duchess and the Waiter" wtih Elsie Ferguson, Basil Rathbone and Alison Skipworth, and "Hell's Bells" with Humphrey Bogart and Shirley Booth making her Broadway debut.

Ina Claire scored a great success in "The Last of Mrs. Cheyney" with A. E. Matthews and Roland Young, while Glenn Hunter was outstanding in "Young Woodley," a play of English school

ALFRED LUNT, LYNN FONTANNE in
"ARMS AND THE MAN"

LIONEL ATWILL, HELEN HAYES in
"CAESAR AND CLEOPATRA"

RAYMOND HACKETT, MARGARET DALE, HUMPHREY BOGART, MARY BOLAND, EDNA MAY OLIVER,
RAYMOND GUION (GENE RAYMOND) in "THE CRADLE SNATCHERS"

JUDITH ANDERSON, HOLBROOK BLINN (left), WILLIAM HARRIGAN (right) in "THE DOVE"

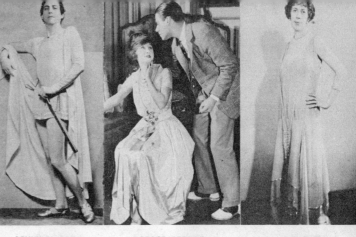

SCHUYLER LADD in "CAESAR AND CLEOPATRA"

GRACE GEORGE, EDWARD H. WEVER in "SHE HAD TO KNOW"

EDNA MAY OLIVER

RUTH GORDON

JANE COWL, JOYCE CAREY in "EASY VIRTUE"

DORIS KEANE, BORDEN HARRIMAN in "STARLIGHT"

GEORGE M. COHAN in "AMERICAN BORN"

CLARK SILVERNAIL, CORNELIA OTIS SKINNER in "WHITE COLLARS"

WALTER GILBERT in "ALOMA OF THE SOUTH SEAS"

life written by John Van Druten.

The fad for Michael Arlen was at its height, and he made his own dramatization of "The Green Hat" in which Katharine Cornell portrayed his celebrated Iris March. She was supported by Leslie Howard and Margalo Gillmore. Mr. Arlen was also represented on the boards by "These Charming People" with Cyril Maude, Alma Tell, Edna Best and Herbert Marshall.

Noel Coward, then in his mid-twenties, created a furore among sophisticates by his first American production: "The Vortex." Mr. Coward himself played the lead opposite Lilian Braithwaite. Less than a month later another Coward comedy, "Hay Fever," was produced with Laura Hope Crews, and before the year was over Jane Cowl was appearing in his "Easy Virtue."

Shaw's "Caesar and Cleopatra" was chosen as the opening attraction for the new Guild Theatre. The production was outstanding, and both Helen Hayes and Lionel Atwill won critical acclaim.

Other Theatre Guild productions of the year were "Processional"—a jazz symphony of American life, done in the impressionistic manner — and a refreshing revue called "Garrick Gaieties" with a score by Rodgers and Hart, and whose young hopefuls included Sterling Holloway, Romney Brent, Philip Loeb, Edith Meisner, Hildegarde Halliday and Libby Holman. Alfred Lunt and Lynn Fontanne appeared in "Arms and the Man," and the double bill of "A Man of Destiny" and "Androcles

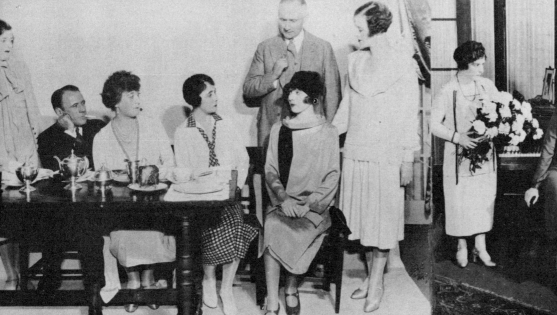

NANCY RYAN, ROLAND YOUNG, WINIFRED HARRIS, MAY BUCKLEY, FELIX AYLMER, INA CLAIRE, HELEN HAYE, in "THE LAST OF MRS. CHEYNEY"

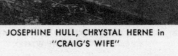

JOSEPHINE HULL, CHRYSTAL HERNE in "CRAIG'S WIFE"

GEORGE JESSEL in "THE JAZZ SINGER"

HELEN GAHAGAN, GLENN HUNTER,
HERBERT BUNSTON in
"YOUNG WOODLEY"

ADRIENNE MORRISON, BASIL SYDNEY,
ERNEST LAWFORD in
"HAMLET"

IRENE BORDONI,
HENRY KENDALL in
"NAUGHTY CINDERELLA"

GAVIN MUIR, LAURA HOPE CREWS,
FRIEDA INESCORT in
"HAY FEVER"

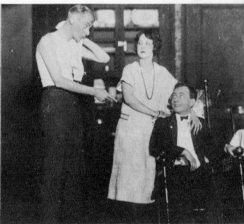

TOM POWERS, CLARE EAMES in
"THE MAN OF DESTINY"

MRS. FISKE, TOM WISE in
"THE RIVALS"

RALPH SIPPERLY, BEATRICE NOYES, ERNEST TRUEX in
"THE FALL GUY"

CHARLES
TROWBRIDGE

CORA
WITHERSPOON

ROLLO
PETERS

CHAUNCEY OLCOTT,
JAMES T. POWERS in
"THE RIVALS"

ANNE
SUTHERLAND

WALTER
HUSTON

ELIZABETH
PATTERSON

JAMES GLEASON, SIDNEY RIGGS, ROBERT
ARMSTRONG in "IS ZAT SO?"

NOEL COWARD, LILIAN BRAITHWAITE in
"THE VORTEX"

JUNE WALKER, BEN GRAUER,
"PROCESSIONAL"

BLANCHE FRIDERICI, GEORGE ABBOTT in
"PROCESSIONAL"

EDWARD EMERY, RUTH GORDON, SYLVIA FIELD, BLANCHE BATES, ELIOT CABOT in
"MRS. PARTRIDGE PRESENTS"

PEGGY WOOD as
"CANDIDA"

NEL BARRYMORE, WALTER HAMPDEN
in "THE MERCHANT OF VENICE"

GREGORY KELLY in
"THE BUTTER AND EGG MAN"

and the Lion" also clicked. Ruth Chatterton with Ralph Forbes appeared in "The Man With A Load of Mischief" and a revival of "The Little Minister." Mary Newcomb played in "Night Hawk," Gareth Hughes was in "The Dunce Boy," Laurette Taylor did "Pierre the Prodigal" and Peggy Wood won great acclaim in "Candida."

Other stars and their plays included George M. Cohan in "American Born," E. H. Sothern in "Accused," Grace George in "She Had To Know," Irene Bordoni in "Naughty Cinderella," Alice Brady in "Oh, Mama," William Farnum with Estelle Winwood in "The Buccaneer," Marjorie Rambeau in "The Valley of Content," Lionel Barrymore in "The Piker" and Doris Keane in "Starlight."

Eugene O'Neill's "The Fountain" had a short run, and so did Maxwell Anderson's Hobo play, "Outside Looking In" and "Wild Birds" by Dan Totheroh.

Walter Hampden did Shakespearean revivals including "Othello" and "The Merchant of Venice" and "Hamlet" with Ethel Barrymore. A Modern Dress Version of "Hamlet" was also done by Basil Sydney. There were outstanding revivals of "The Wild Duck" with Blanche Yurka, Tom Powers and Helen Chandler, and "The Rivals" with an all-star cast headed by Mrs. Fiske which toured the country with great success.

The Moscow Art Theatre Musical Studio presented in their repertoire an exciting "Carmencita and the Soldier" and a version of "Lysistrata" with music by Gliere. Olga Baclanova scored a personal triumph in both of these plays.

Musical fare was abundant and hits were numerous. Dennis King had a tremendous success in "The Vagabond King" and Marilyn Miller had a smash in "Sunny." "No, No, Nanette" and "Dearest Enemy" were also big hits.

Other popular shows were "Louis the 14th" with Leon Errol, "Big Boy" with Al Jolson, "Puzzles of 1925" with Elsie Janis, "Tip Toes" with Queenie Smith, "Captain Jinks" with Joe E.

HOLBROOK BLINN in
"THE DOVE"

OM POWERS, WARBURTON GAMBLE, BLANCHE YURKA,
ELEN CHANDLER, THOMAS CHALMERS, PHILIP LEIGH in
"THE WILD DUCK"

VIVIENNE OSBORNE, FRANK THOMAS, GEORGE GAUL in
"ALOMA OF THE SOUTH SEAS"

BASIL RATHBONE, ELSIE FERGUSON,
ALISON SKIPWORTH, FREDERICK WORLOCK in
"THE GRAND DUCHESS AND THE WAITER"

IRENE
FRANKLIN

MARGARET IRVING,
JOHN BOLES in
"MERCENARY MARY"

TESS GARDELLA
as
AUNT JEMIMA

HARRY WELCHMAN,
EVELYN HERBERT in
"PRINCESS FLAVIA"

IRENE
DELROY

FLORENCE
MILLS

ODETTE
MYRTIL

LOUISE GROODY, CHARLES WINNINGER, WELLINGTON CROSS,
JOSEPHINE WHITTLE in "NO, NO, NANETTE"

JAY C. FLIPPEN,
ROY ROYSTON in
"JUNE DAYS"

PAT ROONEY, JR., MARION BRENT and
PAT ROONEY

DAVE
CHASEN

SHIRLEY
BOOTH

ED   AL
GALLAGHER & SHEAN

MARJORIE
PETERSON

JOHN D.
SEYMOUR

MARIE
CAHILL

JOE E. BROWN in
"CAPTAIN JINKS"

EVA
TANGUAY

ESTHER HOWARD, JOSEPH CAWTHORN, DOROTHY FRANCIS, CLIFTON WEBB, MARILYN MILLER, PAUL FRAWLEY,
MARY HAY, JACK DONAHUE in "SUNNY"

AL JOLSON in
"BIG BOY"

HILDEGARD HALLIDAY   ROMNEY BRENT   STERLING HOLLOWAY   JAMES NORRIS   EDITH MEISER
"GARRICK GAITIES"

CHARLES PURCELL, HELEN FORD in "DEAREST ENEMY"

CLARA KIMBALL YOUNG

LEON ERROL

VIVIAN HART in "VANITIES"

STERLING HOLLOWAY

PAUL and GRACE HARTMAN

QUEENIE SMITH in "TIP-TOES"

DENNIS KING, CAROLYN THOMSON in "THE VAGABOND KING"

CICELY COURTNEIDGE, JACK HULBERT in "BY THE WAY"

JACK BARKER, MABEL WITHEE in "THE COCOANUTS"

DENNIS KING

OLGA BACLANOVA in "CARMENCITA AND THE SOLDIER"

CICELY COURTNEIDGE

TESSA KOSTA, GUY ROBERTSON in SONG OF THE FLAME"

WALTER PIDGEON, ELSIE JANIS, BORAH MINEVITCH in "PUZZLES OF 1925"

Brown, J. Harold Murray and Louise Brown, "The Cocoanuts" with the Marx Brothers, "Song of the Flame" with Guy Robertson and Tessa Kosta and "Sky High" starring Willie Howard.

Cicely Courtneidge and Jack Hulbert delighted audiences in the British import "By the Way," and another "Charlot's Revue" with Beatrice Lillie, Gertrude Lawrence and Jack Buchanan was welcomed with open arms, as was Balieff's "Chauve Souris" in a revised version. "The Grand Street Follies" was also popular with a cast which included Albert Carroll, Dorothy Sands, Paula Trueman, Whitford Kane, Marc Lobell and Danton Walker.

Less intimate types of revue also flourished, such as "George White's Scandals" with Helen Morgan, Harry Fox and Tom Patricola, "Earl Carroll Vanities" with Ted Healy, Vivian Hart, Marjorie Peterson, Julius Tannen and Dave Chasen, "Artists and Models" with Lulu McConnell, Walter Woolf, Phil Baker and Aline MacMahon, and "The Greenwich Village Follies" with Florence Moore, Frank McIntyre, Tom Howard, Irene Delroy and William Ladd.

Vaudeville still flourished, and among the year's headliners were May Irwin, Houdini, Julian Eltinge, Eva Tanguay, Pat Rooney, Marie Cahill, Gilda Gray, Clara Kimball Young (famous film star), Aunt Jemima, Cissie Loftus and out on the West Coast, two youngsters, Paul and Grace Hartman, were starting their careers.

ROSE McCLENDON in
"IN ABRAHAM'S BOSOM"

RAQUEL MELLER

VIVIAN MARTIN in
"PUPPY LOVE"

BERTHA KALICH in
"MAGDA"

YVONNE PRINTEMPS, SACHA GUITRY in
"MOZART"

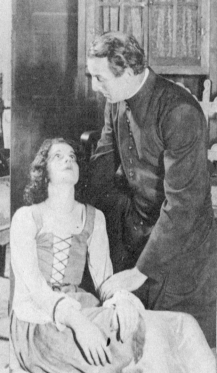

EDITH BARRETT, WALTER HAMPDEN in
"CAPONSACCHI"

ALFRED LUNT, CLARE EAMES in
"JUAREZ AND MAXIMILIAN"

FRANCINE LARRIMORE in
"CHICAGO"

JUNE WALKER, FRANK MORGAN in
"GENTLEMEN PREFER BLONDES"

MIRIAM HOPKINS, MORGAN FARLEY in
"AN AMERICAN TRAGEDY"

1926 The year 1926 saw the opening of Eva Le Gallienne's Civic Repertory Theatre on 14th. Street, where outstanding plays were presented at low admission. Benavente's "Saturday Night" was the initial offering, followed by "Three Sisters," "The Master Builder," "John Gabriel Borkman," "La Locandiera" and "Twelfth Night." Supporting Miss Le Gallienne at this period were Leona Roberts, Rose Hobart, Hardie Albright, Beatrice de Neergaard, Egon Brecher, Paul Leyssac, Sayre Crawley and Josephine Hutchinson.

All in all, it was a booming year in the theatre, and there were many hits, such as the fast-moving "Broadway" which sky-rocketed Lee Tracy to fame; the Gershwin musical "Oh, Kay" with Gertrude Lawrence, Victor Moore and Oscar Shaw; "The Shanghai Gesture" which starred Florence Reed in the sensational role of Mother Goddam; also Lenore Ulric was enthusiastically received in "Lulu Belle," as was Francine Larrimore in "Chicago." Holbrook Blinn had a hit with "The Play's the Thing," and Ethel Barrymore was popular in "The Constant Wife." The Pulitzer Prize was awarded to "In Abraham's Bosom."

The law interfered and caused the closing of "The Captive" and "Sex." The former, a sensitive study in abnormal psychology, was played by Helen Menken and Basil Rathbone, and the latter,

WALTER HUSTON in "KONGO"

ETHEL BARRYMORE in "THE CONSTANT WIFE"

EMILY STEVENS in "HEDDA GABLER"

HOLBROOK BLINN in "THE PLAY'S THE THING"

LEONA HOGARTH, WILLIAM HARRIGAN in "THE GREAT GOD BROWN"

SYLVIA FIELD, LEE TRACY in "BROADWAY"

CRANE WILBUR, ALICE BRADY in "THE BRIDE OF THE LAMB"

HELEN MENKEN in "THE CAPTIVE"

a less sensitive investigation of matters suggested by its title, brought overnight fame to its star, Mae West, along with a ten day sentence in the workhouse.

Raquel Meller, the Spanish diseuse, repeated her European triumphs in this country. The Habima Players of Moscow offered "The Dybbuk" in its original Hebrew version, and "Mozart," a comedy by Sacha Guitry, was played by M. Guitry and Yvonne Printemps.

Sean O'Casey's "Juno and the Paycock" was given its first American performance with a cast headed by Augustin Duncan and Louise Randolph. Other important dramas were "The Bride of the Lamb" by William Hurlbut with Alice Brady and Crane Wilbur, and Eugene O'Neill's "The Great God Brown" which employed the Greek mask in a modernized form.

Two outstanding revivals of the year were "Pygmalion" with Lynn Fontanne and Reginald Mason, and "What Every Woman Knows" with Helen Hayes and Kenneth MacKenna. Other revivals were Emily Stevens in "Hedda Gabler," Bertha Kalich in "Magda," Walter Hampden in "Cyrano de Bergerac," Lucile Watson in "Ghosts," Basil Sydney in "The Jest," and a star-studded production of "The Two Orphans" with Robert Loraine,

LINDA WATKINS, FREDRIC MARCH in "THE DEVIL IN THE CHEESE"

BLANCHE YURKA, HORACE BRAHAM in "THE SQUALL"

175

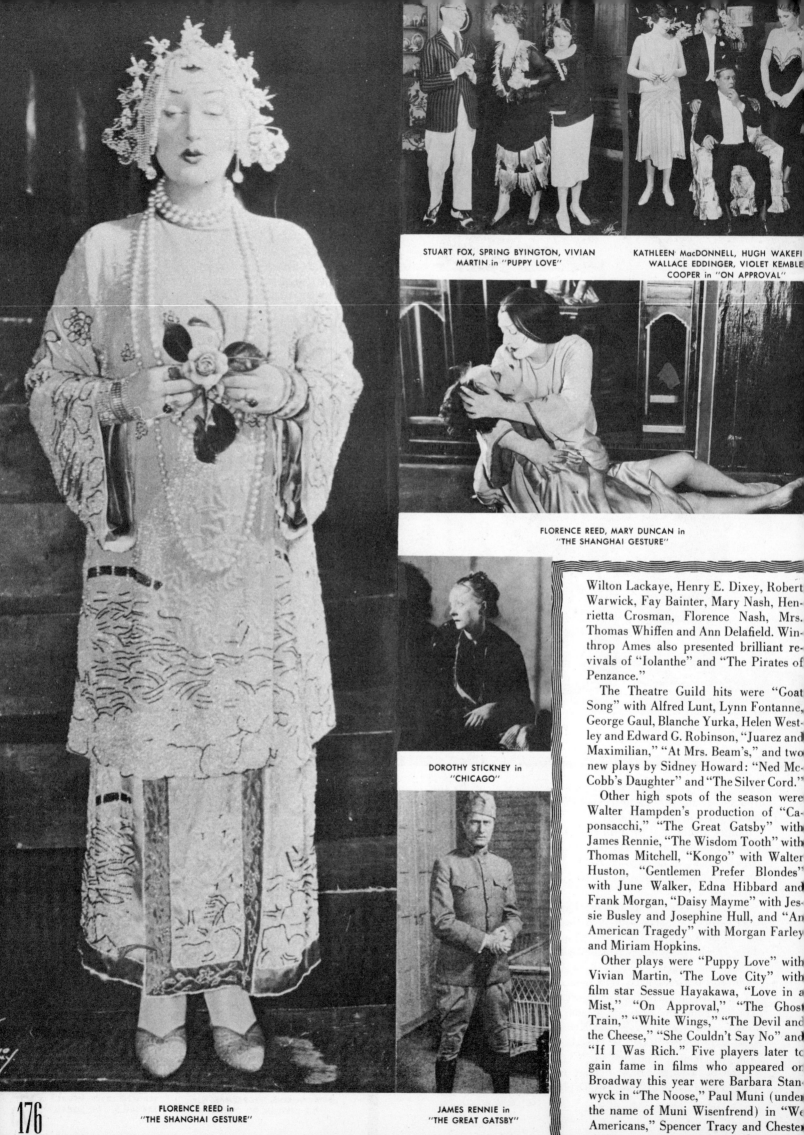

STUART FOX, SPRING BYINGTON, VIVIAN MARTIN in "PUPPY LOVE"

KATHLEEN MacDONNELL, HUGH WAKEFI WALLACE EDDINGER, VIOLET KEMBLE COOPER in "ON APPROVAL"

FLORENCE REED, MARY DUNCAN in "THE SHANGHAI GESTURE"

DOROTHY STICKNEY in "CHICAGO"

FLORENCE REED in "THE SHANGHAI GESTURE"

JAMES RENNIE in "THE GREAT GATSBY"

Wilton Lackaye, Henry E. Dixey, Robert Warwick, Fay Bainter, Mary Nash, Henrietta Crosman, Florence Nash, Mrs. Thomas Whiffen and Ann Delafield. Winthrop Ames also presented brilliant revivals of "Iolanthe" and "The Pirates of Penzance."

The Theatre Guild hits were "Goat Song" with Alfred Lunt, Lynn Fontanne, George Gaul, Blanche Yurka, Helen Westley and Edward G. Robinson, "Juarez and Maximilian," "At Mrs. Beam's," and two new plays by Sidney Howard: "Ned McCobb's Daughter" and "The Silver Cord."

Other high spots of the season were Walter Hampden's production of "Caponsacchi," "The Great Gatsby" with James Rennie, "The Wisdom Tooth" with Thomas Mitchell, "Kongo" with Walter Huston, "Gentlemen Prefer Blondes" with June Walker, Edna Hibbard and Frank Morgan, "Daisy Mayme" with Jessie Busley and Josephine Hull, and "An American Tragedy" with Morgan Farley and Miriam Hopkins.

Other plays were "Puppy Love" with Vivian Martin, 'The Love City' with film star Sessue Hayakawa, "Love in a Mist," "On Approval," "The Ghost Train," "White Wings," "The Devil and the Cheese," "She Couldn't Say No" and "If I Was Rich." Five players later to gain fame in films who appeared on Broadway this year were Barbara Stanwyck in "The Noose," Paul Muni (under the name of Muni Wisenfrend) in "We Americans," Spencer Tracy and Chester

DGE KENNEDY, SIDNEY BLACKMER in
"LOVE IN A MIST"

HENRY MOWBRAY, ARTHUR BARRY, ERIC BLORE,
ISOBEL ELSOM in "THE GHOST TRAIN"

"LULU BELLE"

Morris in "Yellow" and Claudette Colbert in "The Pearl of Great Price."

"The Ladder," a play about reincarnation, opened October 22, 1926, and ran into 1927, chalking up 789 performances. Despite its long run, the play could not be termed a success. It was backed by Edgar B. Davis, a Texas oil man, who spent more than half a million dollars trying to put its message across to the public. Later in its run people could see the play free of charge.

The Ziegfeld show of the year was called "No Foolin'," and the cast included James Barton, Claire Luce, Moran and Mack, Ray Dooley and Greta Nissen. Hazel Dawn and Jack Benny were in "Great Temptations," and Ann Pennington, Frances Williams, Eugene and Willie Howard and Harry Richman were featured in "George White's Scandals." Frank Tinney was in the "Vanities," and Clark and McCullough were cavorting in "The Ramblers," and so was Fred Stone in "Criss Cross."

"Americana" was a bright revue featuring Roy Atwell and Charles Butterworth, and there were new editions of "Garrick Gaieties" and "Grand Street Follies." Beatrice Lillie was starred in "Oh, Please!"

Two musical comedies of great durability opened during the year: "The Desert Song" with Robert Halliday and Vivienne Segal, and "Countess Maritza" with Yvonne D'Arle, Odette Myrtil and Walter Woolf.

HENRY HULL in
"LULU BELLE"

ROSS ALEXANDER,
IRENE PURCELL in
"THE LADDER"

LENORE ULRIC in
"LULU BELLE"

177

JEAN CADELL in
"AT MRS. BEAM'S"

JOSEPHINE
HULL

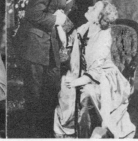
VIVIENNE SEGAL in
"THE DESERT SONG"

JOSE RUBEN, LUCILE
WATSON in "GHOSTS"

SESSUE HAYAKAWA in
"THE LOVE CITY"

NYDIA
WESTMAN

JESSIE BUSH
JOSEPHINE HU
"DAISY MAY

VERNON STEELE in
"THE LADDER"

FRANCINE LARRIMORE, EDWARD ELLIS (left) and JURY in
"CHICAGO"

CATHERINE DALE OWEN, HOLBROOK BLINN, REGINALD OWEN in
"THE PLAY'S THE THING"

WINIFRED LENIHAN,
TOM POWERS in
"WHITE WINGS"

ALFRED LUNT, LYNN FONTANNE in
"GOAT SONG"

ALFRED LUNT, LESLIE BARRIE, LYNN
FONTANNE in "AT MRS. BEAM'S"

KENNETH MacKENNA, HELEN HAYES in
"WHAT EVERY WOMAN KNOWS"

WILLIAM FORAN, KATE MAYH
THOMAS MITCHELL in
"THE WISDOM TOOTH"

HENRIETTA CROSMAN in
"THE TWO ORPHANS"

VIOLET HEMING, ALPHONZ ETHIER, BASIL SYDNEY in
"THE JEST"

ELISABETH RISDON, ELIOT CABOT, MARGALO GILLMORE, EARLE LARRIMORE
LAURA HOPE CREWS in "THE SILVER CORD"

HUMPHREY
BOGART

MAE
WEST

SPENCER
TRACY

RALPH KELLARD,
FLORENCE MOORE in
"SHE COULDN'T SAY NO"

BARBARA
STANWYCK

MUNI WISENFREND
(PAUL MUNI)

CLAUDETTE
COLBERT

BERYL MERCER, LYNN FONTANNE, HENRY TRAVERS, REGINALD
MASON in "PYGMALION"

ALFRED LUNT, CLARE EAMES in
"NED McCOBB'S DAUGHTER"

EDITH VAN CLEVE in
"BROADWAY"

JOSE RUBEN, FAY BAINTER, HENRIETTA CROSMAN, WILTON LACKAYE, MARY
NASH, ROBERT LORAINE, HENRY E. DIXEY in "THE TWO ORPHANS"

JOE LAURIE, JR. in
"IF I WAS RICH"

X CHERRYMAN, GEORGE NASH,
ARA STANWYCK in "THE NOOSE"

SPENCER TRACY, MARJORIE WOOD,
SHIRLEY WARDE in "YELLOW"

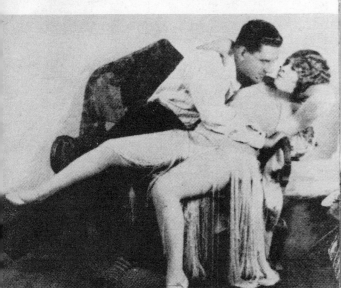

MAE WEST in "SEX"

ALICE BRADY

CECILIA LOFTUS

179

as KING LEAR   "JULIUS CAESAR" SCENE   MISS HAMPER   MR. MANTELL   as MACBETH   as OTHELLO

ROBERT B. MANTELL and GENEVIEVE HAMPER (MRS. MANTELL)

HARRY RICHMAN in GEORGE WHITE'S "SCANDALS"   STANLEY LUPINO, MITZI in "NAUGHTY RIQUETTE"   MORAN & MACK in EARL CARROLL'S "VANITIES"   PAULINE MASON, EDDIE DOWLING in "HONEYMOON LANE"   KARYL NORMAN "THE CREOLE FASHION PLATE"

WILLIAM WILLIAMS   CLAIRE LUCE   CHARLES BUTTERWORTH in "AMERICANA"   ROY CROPPER   ZOE BARNETT

CHARLES WINNINGER   FRANCES WILLIAMS   CHARLES KING

180   VERA ROSS, WILLIAM WILLIAMS, ADELE SANDERSON in "IOLANTHE"   ANN DELAFIELD   KITTY AND FANNIE WATSON   NANCY WELFORD   WILLIAM O'NEAL, MARGARET IRVING, LYLE EVANS in "THE DESERT SONG"

TTE MYRTIL, WALTER WOOLF MARJORIE PETERSON, CARL RANDALL in "COUNTESS MARITZA"

KATE SMITH in "HONEYMOON LANE"

VIVIENNE SEGAL, J. HAROLD MURRAY in "CASTLES IN THE AIR"

CLARK & McCULLOUGH in "THE RAMBLERS"

BERT CARROLL in ARRICK GAIETIES"

GERTRUDE LAWRENCE in "OH, KAY"

ALBERT CARROLL, JOHN SCOTT, PAULA TRUEMAN in "GRAND STREET FOLLIES"

BEATRICE LILLIE in "OH, PLEASE!"

CHARLES RUGGLES, LUELLA GEAR in "QUEEN HIGH"

RAY DOOLEY as COUNTESS OF CATHCART, PEGGY FEARS as RAQUEL MELLER, EDNA LEEDOM as PEGGY JOYCE, POLLY WALKER as ELLEN MACKAY, CLAIRE LUCE as "LULU BELLE", PAULETTE GODDARD as PEACHES in ZIEGFELD'S REVUE "NO FOOLIN'"

ANN PENNINGTON in "GEORGE WHITE'S SCANDALS"

EUGENE and WILLIE HOWARD in "GEORGE WHITE'S SCANDALS"

FRANK TINNEY in "EARL CARROLL'S VANITIES"

181

EVA LE GALLIENNE AND SOME OF HER CIVIC REPERTORY THEATRE PRODUCTIONS. Top right: MISS LE GALLIENNE in "JOHN GABRIEL BORKMAN". Center: "THE THREE SISTERS" with EVA LE GALLIENNE, JOSEPHINE HUTCHINSON, BEATRICE TERRY. Bottom left: "TWELFTH NIGHT" with BEATRICE TERRY, ALAN BIRMINGHAM, SAYRE CRAWLEY. Right: "THE CRADLE SONG" with EVA LE GALLIENNE, JOSEPHINE HUTCHINSON.

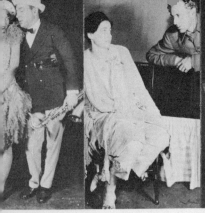

RIS EATON,
NK McHUGH in
ESS BAGGAGE"

FRIEDA INESCORT,
LESLIE HOWARD in
"ESCAPE"

JAMES RENNIE, SYLVIA SIDNEY, DOUGLAS
MONTGOMERY, CHESTER MORRIS in "CRIME"

MAX REINHARDT REHEARSING HIS PRODUCTION OF
"A MIDSUMMER NIGHT'S DREAM" with VLADIMIR SOKOLOFF,
HERMAN THIMIG, LILI DARVAS, HANS THIMIG and STAGE MANAGER

ALFRED LUNT, EDWARD G. ROBINSON in
"THE BROTHERS KARAMAZOV"

ROSE McCLENDON, FRANK WILSON,
EVELYN ELLIS in "PORGY"

ELLE WINWOOD, HELEN GAHAGAN, PAULINE
LORD in "TRELAWNEY OF THE WELLS"

1927

In 1927 the theatre was at its peak. There were 268 attractions produced on Broadway during the year; an impressive number that has not been repeated since, and is never likely to be in our time. The number of plays produced annually since has declined from year to year.

With so many productions there were many and varied smash hits to whet the theatregoer's appetite. Among them were "Burlesque" with Hal Skelly and Barbara Stanwyck, "Coquette" with Helen Hayes, "The Road to Rome" with Jane Cowl, "The Barker" with Walter Huston, Claudette Colbert and Norman Foster, "The Trial of Mary Dugan" with Ann Harding, "The Royal Family" with Otto Kruger, Haidee Wright and Ann Andrews, "Saturday's Children" with Ruth Gordon and "Paris Bound" with Madge Kennedy.

Other plays that were successful include "Tommy," "Interference" with A. E. Matthews, "The Command to Love" with Mary Nash and Basil Rathbone, "Her Cardboard Lover" with Jeanne Eagels and Leslie Howard, "The Letter" with Katharine Cornell, "The Ivory Door" with Henry Hull, "Escape" with Leslie Howard, "The Shannons of Broadway" with James Gleason and his wife, Lucile Webster, "And So To Bed" with Yvonne Arnaud, Wallace Eddinger and Emlyn Williams, "Crime" with James Rennie, Chester Morris, Sylvia Sidney and Douglas Montgomery and "Excess Baggage" with Miriam Hopkins, Frank McHugh, Suzanne Willa and Morton Downey. "Dracula," a horror play with Bela Lugosi, had a long run, and so did "The Spider," a mystery play with John Halliday.

The Theatre Guild had a good year with "Porgy," "The Brothers Karamazov," "The Second Man" and a revival of "The Doctor's Dilemma." Alfred Lunt and Lynn Fontanne appeared in the last three plays. Eva Le Gallienne's productions of "The Cradle Song" and "The Good Hope" were well received.

George C. Tyler had a sensational success with his all-star revival of "Trelawney of the Wells." Its cast included John Drew, Pauline Lord, Henrietta Crosman, Wilton Lackaye, Effie Shannon, Mrs. Thomas Whiffen, Estelle Winwood, Otto

ALFRED LUNT, LYNN FONTANNE in
"THE DOCTOR'S DILEMMA"

MARGARET ANGLIN in
"ELECTRA"

ALFRED LUNT, LYNN FONTANNE, EARLE LARIMORE,
MARGALO GILLMORE in "THE SECOND MAN"

J. W. AUSTIN, KATHARINE CORNELL, ALLAN JEAYES,
JOHN BUCKLER in "THE LETTER"

RUTH GORDON, FREDERICK PERRY, ROGER PRYOR in
"SATURDAY'S CHILDREN"

SARA ALLGOOD in
"JUNO AND THE PAYCOCK"

REX CHERRYMAN, ANN HARDING in
"THE TRIAL OF MARY DUGAN"

HELEN HAYES, ELIOT CABOT in
"COQUETTE"

BASIL RATHBONE, MARY NASH, HENRY STEPHENSON in
"THE COMMAND TO LOVE"

WALTER HUSTON in
"THE BARKER"

CLAUDETTE COLBERT in
"THE BARKER"

JEANNE EAGELS, LESLIE HOWARD in
"HER CARDBOARD LOVER"

184

SIDNEY TOLER, WILLIAM JANNEY in
"TOMMY"

JAMES GLEASON, LUCILE WEBSTER in
"THE SHANNONS OF BROADWAY"

Kruger, Lawrence D'Orsay, Helen Gahagan and Rollo Peters. For the road tour Peggy Wood replaced Miss Lord. Mr. Tyler also brought over the Irish Players including Sara Allgood, Maire O'Neill and Arthur Sinclair in Sean O'Casey's new play "The Plough and the Stars" and a revival of "Juno and the Paycock."

Max Reinhardt brought his company over from Germany. The players included Alexander Moissi, Lili Darvas, Tilly Losch and Arnold Korff, and in their repertoire were "A Midsummer Night's Dream," "Everyman" and "Danton's Death."

Billie Burke was appearing in Noel Coward's "The Marquise." Another Coward play, "Fallen Angels," with Fay Bainter and Estelle Winwood was a flop. Mary Boland was in "Women Go On Forever" with James Cagney in a small role. Louis Mann and Clara Lipman co-starred in "That French Lady." Frank Craven wrote and starred in "The 19th Hole." Muni Wisenfrend (Paul Muni) was in "Four Walls," Glenn Hunter was in "Behold This Dreamer," Frances Starr in "Immoral Isabella?," Walker Whiteside in "The Arabian," Mae West in "The Wicked Age," Judith Anderson in "Behold the Bridegroom," and Nance O'Neil co-starred with Elsie Ferguson in "The House of Women." Pauline

BASIL SYDNEY, MARY ELLIS in
"THE TAMING OF THE SHREW"

JANE COWL, PHILIP MERIVALE in
"THE ROAD TO ROME"

A. E. MATTHEWS in
"INTERFERENCE"

HAL SKELLY, BARBARA STANWYCK in
"BURLESQUE"

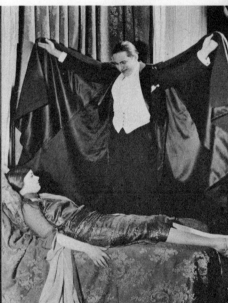

TO KRUGER, HAIDEE WRIGHT, ANN ANDREWS in
"THE ROYAL FAMILY"

HENRY HULL, LINDA WATKINS in
"THE IVORY DOOR"

JOHN HALLIDAY in
"THE SPIDER"

DOROTHY PETERSON, BELA LUGOSI in
"DRACULA"

Lord was artistically successful in "Mariners" and "Spellbound," but both plays were short-lived. There were many revivals ranging from Margaret Anglin in "Electra" to Roscoe Arbuckle in "Baby Mine." Mrs. Fiske was seen in "Ghosts," Grace George revived "The Legend of Leonora," the Players' Club did "Julius Caesar," the Winthrop Ames Gilbert and Sullivan festival continued with a new and stunning production of "The Mikado" and Walter Hampden played "An Enemy of the People." There was also a revival of "Madame X" with Carroll McComas, and one of "L'Aiglon" with Michael Strange, while Basil Sydney and Mary Ellis had great success playing "The Taming of the Shrew" in modern dress, as well as "The Crown Prince," a new play.

Florenz Ziegfeld opened the theatre bearing his name with a rousing musical, "Rio Rita," and towards the end of the year followed it with an even greater success: "Show Boat" with Jerome Kern music. The original cast included Charles Winninger, Edna May Oliver, Aunt Jemima, Sammy White, Eva Puck, Howard Marsh, Norma Terris, Jules Bledsoe and Helen Morgan.

The other major musical shows of the year were "Good News" with Gus Shy and Zelma O'Neal, "Hit the Deck" with Charles

WALTER HAMPDEN, MABEL MOORE in
"AN ENEMY OF THE PEOPLE"

MADGE KENNEDY, DONALD COOK in
"PARIS BOUND"

DONALD
MACDONALD

RUTH
HAMMOND

ALEXANDER
MOISSI

INEZ
COURTNEY

WILLIAM COLLIER, MARIE CAHILL in
"MERRY-GO-ROUND"

A BEN ALI HAGGIN TABLEAU in
"ZIEGFELD FOLLIES"

GLORIFYING THE AMERICAN GIRL in
"ZIEGFELD FOLLIES"

MORTON
DOWNEY

HOPE
HAMPTON

VINCENT
SERRANO

MADELINE
CAMERON

EDDIE CANTOR in
"ZIEGFELD FOLLIES"

RUBY KEELER in
"SIDEWALKS OF
NEW YORK"

TEXAS GUINAN in
"PADLOCKS OF 1927"

ALBERT CARROLL in
"GRAND STREET FOLLIES"

ED WYNN in
"MANHATTAN MARY"

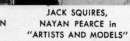

GUY
ROBERTSON

JACK SQUIRES,
NAYAN PEARCE in
"ARTISTS AND MODELS"

RAY DOOLEY in
"SIDEWALKS OF
NEW YORK"

GREEK EVANS, TRINI, WILL
MAHONEY, DOROTHY DILLEY
in "TAKE THE AIR"

OSCAR SHAW, MARY
EATON in
"FIVE O'CLOCK GIRL"

EVELYN HERBERT,
NATHANIEL WAGNER in
"MY MARYLAND"

ETHELIND TERRY
"RIO RITA"

LOUISE GROODY, CHARLES KING in
"HIT THE DECK"

WILLIAM WILLIAMS, LOIS BENNETT in
"THE MIKADO"

SHIRLEY VERNON, JOHN PRICE JONES in
"GOOD NEWS"

DESIREE TABOR, GUY ROBERTSON in
"THE CIRCUS PRINCESS"

NORMA TERRIS, HOWARD MARSH in
"SHOW BOAT"

LEON ERROL in
"YOURS TRULY"

HELEN MORGAN in
"SHOW BOAT"

J. HAROLD MURRAY in
"RIO RITA"

King, Louise Groody and Stella Mayhew, "The Five O'Clock Girl" with Mary Eaton and Oscar Shaw, and "A Connecticut Yankee" with William Gaxton, William Norris and Constance Carpenter.

Texas Guinan was seen in "Padlocks of 1927," Leon Errol was in "Yours Truly," Guy Robertson was in "The Circus Princess," Eddie Cantor was in "Ziegfeld Follies," Evelyn Herbert and Warren Hull were in "My Maryland" and Victor Moore and Charles Butterworth were in "Allez-Oop." Other popular musicals were "Merry-Go-Round" with Marie Cahill and William Collier, "Manhattan Mary" with Ed Wynn, "The Merry Malones" with George M. Cohan, "Artists and Models" with Florence Moore, Ted Lewis and Jack Pearl, "Yes, Yes, Yvette" with Jeanette Mac-Donald and Jack Whiting, "A Night in Spain" with Ted Healy, Phil Baker, Helen Kane and Grace Hayes, "The Nightingale" with Eleanor Painter and Stanley Lupino, "Take the Air" with Will Mahoney, "Sidewalks of New York" with Ray Dooley, Ruby Keeler and Fiske O'Hara, "Just Fancy" with Raymond Hitchcock, Joseph Santley and Ivy Sawyer and "Funny Face" with Fred and Adele Astaire.

EDNA MAY OLIVER, NORMA TERRIS, CHARLES WINNINGER
in
"SHOW BOAT"

187

| JEANNE EAGELS | MARGARET LAWRENCE | GLENN HUNTER | CHRYSTAL HERNE | SIDNEY BLACKMER | VIOLET HEMING | MARGARET ILLINGTON |

| GAIL KANE | ELSIE FERGUSON | MADGE KENNEDY | WILLIAM HODGE | JOSEPHINE HULL | CONSTANCE BINNEY | CHARLOTTE WALKER |

| JULIAN ELTINGE | MARION HARRIS | TED HEALY | CHARLOTTE GREENWOOD | WILLIE HOWARD | GERTRUDE HOFFMANN | GEORGE JESSEL |

| JOHN STEEL | TRIXIE FRIGANZA | WALTER WOOLF | JOSEPH SANTLEY and IVY SAWYER | GUY ROBERTSON | SOPHIE TUCKER | JACK DONAHUE |

VIVIAN HART | TED LEWIS | TEXAS GUINAN | RAYMOND HITCHCOCK | BELLE BAKER | J. HAROLD MURRAY | BLOSSOM SEELE

POPULAR PLAYERS

928

These were lush days in the theatre during the 'Twenties when over two hundred fifty productions reached the Broadway boards each year, and the road was in a healthy condition; when many plays could attain a moderate run with the help of the cut-rate ticket agency; when there were many promising young players trodding the boards assured of theatre stardom, futures that were nipped in the Broadway bud with the event of talkies; when such hopefuls as Claudette Colbert, Clark Gable, Spencer Tracy, Barbara Stanwyck, Archie Leach (Cary Grant), Muni Wisenfrend (Paul Muni), Chester Morris, Lee Tracy, Miriam Hopkins and others were all whisked off to Hollywood before they ever achieved Broadway stardom.

The Pulitzer Prize for 1928 was awarded to Eugene O'Neill's "Strange Interlude." Produced by the Theatre Guild, it was in nine short acts, and, because of its length, performances began at 5:15, adjourned for a dinner recess, and resumed at 8:30. The aside and soliloquy, commonly used in drama of the past, was restored and the characters spoke their private thoughts in addition to their normal speech. The original cast included Lynn Fontanne, Tom Powers, Glenn Anders, Earle Larimore and Helen Westley. The leading role of Nina Leeds was also played by Pauline Lord and Judith Anderson. The Theatre Guild offered another O'Neill play, "Marco Millions," also "Wings Over Europe," "Caprice," the Stefan Zweig version of Ben Jonson's "Volpone" and revivals of "Major Barbara" and "Faust."

Ethel Barrymore opened the new theatre bearing her name with "The Kingdom of God." Katharine Cornell assisted by Rollo Peters and Franchot Tone appeared in "The Age of Innocence." Ina Claire sparkled in a revival of "Our Betters" supported by Constance Collier, Hugh Sinclair and Edward Crandall. A minor Molnar comedy, "Olympia," brought Fay Compton over from London to act with Laura Hope Crews and Ian Hunter. David Belasco went to great expense transforming his playhouse into a steel-sheeted Hades for a play called "Mima" which starred Lenore Ulric, but the play, unfortunately, was considerably less impressive than its sets.

Mae West made a dent in theatrical history with "Diamond Lil," a play of her own authorship. "Pleasure Man," another play by Miss West (in which she did not appear), boasted a piece of off-stage action as flagrant as any ever attempted. A "Black Maria" awaited the entire cast after the second performance. Another play closed by the police was "Maya," a symbolic biography of a Marseilles prostitute played to critical acclaim by Aline MacMahon.

The biggest hit in the comedy class was "The Front Page" by Charles MacArthur

JOHN CROMWELL, HELEN FLINT in "GENTLEMEN OF THE PRESS"

OSGOOD PERKINS, WALTER BALDWIN, LEE TRACY in "THE FRONT PAGE"

ROLLO PETERS, KATHARINE CORNELL in "THE AGE OF INNOCENCE"

ERNEST COSSART, MARGALO GILLMORE, ALFRED LUNT, DUDLEY DIGGES in "VOLPONE"

DOUGLAS MONTGOMERY, LYNN FONTANNE, ALFRED LUNT, LILY CAHILL in "CAPRICE"

DONALD OGDEN STEWART, HOPE WILLIAMS, BEN SMITH, BARBARA WHITE in "HOLIDAY"

"MARCO MILLIONS" MARGALO GILLMORE, ALFRED LUNT (left)

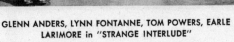

RITA VALE, GEORGE GAUL in "FAUST"

GLENN ANDERS, LYNN FONTANNE, TOM POWERS, EARLE LARIMORE in "STRANGE INTERLUDE"

PERCY WARAM, ELIOT CABOT, WINIFRED LENIHAN in "MAJOR BARBARA"

FLORENCE REED as
LADY MACBETH

HENRIETTA CROSMAN, OTIS SKINNER,
MRS. FISKE in
"THE MERRY WIVES OF WINDSOR"

LYN HARDING as
MACBETH

EVA LE GALLIENNE as
"PETER PAN"

ESTELLE TAYLOR, JACK DEMPSEY in
"THE BIG FIGHT"

JOHN HALLIDAY, FA
BAINTER in "JEALOUS

WILLIAM
COURTLEIGH

KATE
MAYHEW

LEE
TRACY

REGINA
WALLACE

OSGOOD
PERKINS

MAE WEST in
"DIAMOND LIL"

INA CLAIRE in
"OUR BETTERS"

ETHEL BARRYMORE in
"THE KINGDOM OF GOD"

and Ben Hecht, and played with great relish by Lee Tracy.

Mrs. Fiske, Otis Skinner and Henrietta Crosman appeared in "The Merry Wives of Windsor," George Arliss did "The Merchant of Venice" with Peggy Wood his Portia, and there were all-star revivals of "She Stoops to Conquer," "Diplomacy" and "The Beaux Stratagem." Eva Le Gallienne revived "Peter Pan" at her Civic Repertory Theatre where "The Cherry Orchard" was also given a production made unforgettable by the superb acting of Alla Nazimova. Lyn Harding appeared briefly in "The Patriot" which marked the American debut of John Gielgud in a minor role. Mr. Harding also played in "Macbeth" with Florence Reed. Sophie Treadwell's drama, "Machinal," brought Clark Gable and Zita Johann to the public's attention. "Holiday" by Philip Barry was well liked with Hope Williams and writer Donald Ogden Stewart in the cast. Helen Menken appeared in "Congai," Alice Brady was in "A Most Immoral Lady," Janet Beecher in "Courage," Bert Lytell played a dual role in "Brothers," Irene Bordoni was seen in "Paris," William Hodge in "Straight Thru the Door," Taylor Holmes in "The Great Necker," Dorothy Gish in "Young Love," Richard Bennett in "Jarnegan," Fay Bainter in "Jealousy," Walter Huston in "Elmer the Great,"

GLENN HUNTER, PAULINE LORD
in
"SHE STOOPS TO CONQUER"

ANTONY HOLLES, GEORGES RENAVENT, CHARLES COBURN, WILLIAM FAVERSHAM,
TYRONE POWER, ROLLO PETERS, GEORGETTE COHAN, (seated) HELEN
GAHAGAN, JACOB BEN-AMI, CECILIA LOFTUS, MARGARET ANGLIN,
FRANCES STARR in "DIPLOMACY"

FAY BAINTER, O. P. HEGGIE
in
"SHE STOOPS TO CONQUER"

ALTER HUSTON, KAY FRANCIS in
"ELMER THE GREAT"

CLARK GABLE, ZITA JOHANN in
"MACHINAL"

TOM HOWARD in
"RAIN OR SHINE"

C. AUBREY SMITH, JUNE WALKER in
"THE BACHELOR FATHER"

GRACE MENKEN, BERT LYTELL in
"BROTHERS"

OSEPHINE VICTOR | MAX FIGMAN | MARY YOUNG | ORVILLE CALDWELL | PATRICIA COLLINGE | ALEXANDER KIRKLAND | MAY VOKES | BERTON CHURCHILL | MRS. THOMAS WHIFFEN

Laurette Taylor in "The Furies," and Jack Dempsey, the world's heavyweight boxing champion, appeared with his wife Estelle Taylor in "The Big Fight." Other new plays were "The Bachelor Father," "The High Road," "Ringside," "Fast Life," "This Thing Called Love," "The Queen's Husband" and a modest comedy, "Skidding," which provided the germ for the Andy Hardy comedies, later so popular in the films.

In the musical field, Eddie Cantor was a solid success in "Whoopee," while other Ziegfeld hits were Marilyn Miller with Jack Donahue in "Rosalie" and Dennis King in "The Three Musketeers." "The New Moon" with Evelyn Herbert was a popular musical and so was "Hold Everything" with Victor Moore and Bert Lahr. Beatrice Lillie was delightful in "She's My Baby" and later with Noel Coward she captured her audiences in "This Year of Grace," a bright revue. The Marx Brothers were in "Animal Crackers," Joe Cook was in "Rain or Shine," Charles King and Flora LeBreton were in "Present Arms," Bill Robinson and Adelaide Hall were in "Blackbirds of 1928," Mitzi was in "The Madcap," Guy Robertson, Odette Myrtil and De Wolf Hopper were in "White Lilacs," W. C. Fields was in Earl Carroll's "Vanities," Will Rogers and Dorothy Stone were in "Three Cheers," Walter Woolf was in "The Red Robe."

EVA LE GALLIENNE, SAYRE CRAWLEY,
NAZIMOVA in "THE CHERRY ORCHARD"

ALEXANDER KIRKLAND, ERNEST LAWFORD in
"WINGS OVER EUROPE"

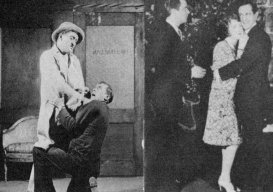

RICHARD BENNETT, JAMES BELL in "JARNEGAN"

HAL THOMPSON, IRENE PURCELL, TAYLOR HOLMES in "THE GREAT NECKER"

ANN ROTH, WILLIAM HODGE in "STRAIGHT THRU THE DOOR"

RICHARD TABER, HARRIET MacGIBBON in "RINGSIDE"

CHARLES EATON, MARGUERITE CHURCHILL, WALTER ABEL in "SKIDDING"

VIOLET HEMING, MI WATSON in "THIS THING CALLED

LAURA HOPE CREWS, FAY COMPTON, IAN HUNTER in "OLYMPIA"

REGINALD BARLOW, GYLES ISHAM, GLADYS HANSON, HELEN CROM DWIGHT FRYE, MARGUERITE TAYLOR, KATHERINE ALEXANDE WILLIAM BOREN, ROLAND YOUNG in "THE QUEEN'S HUSBAN

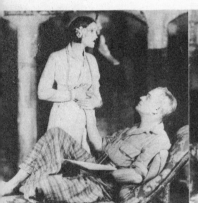

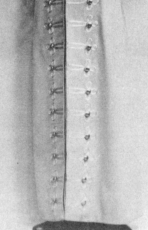

HELEN MENKEN, CHARLES TROWBRIDGE in "CONGAI"

EDNA BEST, HERBERT MARSHALL in "THE HIGH ROAD"

JOE COOK in "RAIN OR SHINE"

CHESTER MORRIS, CLAUDETTE COLBERT in "FAST LIFE"

SIDNEY BLACKMER, LENORE ULR "MIMA"

EVELYN HERBERT

STANLEY LUPINO

FAY COMPTON

HUGH SINCLAIR

GLADY GLAD

192 DUDLEY DIGGES

MARJORIE GATESON

ROBERT HALLIDAY, EVELYN HERBERT in "THE NEW MOON"

JULIUS TANNEN

VICTOR MOORE, HARRY T. SHANNON, BERT LAHR in "HOLD EVERYTHING"

ELLIS BAKER

BUSTER WEST

DENNIS KING in
"THREE MUSKETEERS"

FRANCHOT TONE in
"THE AGE OF INNOCENCE"

GEORGE ARLISS as
SHYLOCK

PEGGY WOOD as
PORTIA

CLARK GABLE in
"MACHINAL"

MARILYN MILLER in
"ROSALIE"

TREACHER, MITZI in
"THE MADCAP"

CARL RANDALL, JEANETTE
MacDONALD in "SUNNY DAYS"

MARX BROTHERS in
"ANIMAL CRACKERS"

ARTHUR MARGETSON, IRENE
BORDONI in "PARIS"

WILL ROGERS, DOROTHY
STONE in "THREE CHEERS"

JEANETTE
MacDONALD

ODETTE MYRTIL, GUY
ROBERTSON in "WHITE LILACS"

JOHN RUTHERFORD, EDDIE CANTOR in
"WHOOPEE"

FLORA LE BRETON, CHARLES
KING in "PRESENT ARMS"

WALTER WOOLF, HELEN
GILLILAND, JOSE RUBEN in
"THE RED ROBE"

MITZI in
"THE MADCAP"

KATHARINE CORNELL in
"THE AGE OF INNOCENCE"

ETHEL
SHUTTA

GEORGE
MacFARLANE

CLIFTON WEBB, BEATRICE LILLIE, JACK
WHITING in "SHE'S MY BABY"

LUELLA
GEAR

WARREN
HULL

193

JACOB BEN-AMI   EDITH BARRETT   EDWARD CRANDALL   JULIA HOYT

DOUGLAS MONTGOMERY   MARY ELLIS   ARTHUR BYRON   MIRIAM HOPKINS

1929

The first hit of 1929 was Elmer Rice's vivid drama "Street Scene" which had a long run and won the Pulitzer Prize. The cast included Erin O'Brien-Moore, Mary Servoss, Beulah Bondi and Horace Braham. In striking contrast to the realism of the above play was the sophistication of "Serena Blandish" with Ruth Gordon, Constance Collier, A. E. Matthews and Julia Hoyt.

Francine Larrimore was highly successful in "Let Us Be Gay," while "Strictly Dishonorable" by Preston Sturges was the most popular comedy of the year with Muriel Kirkland and Tullio Carminati. "June Moon," a satirical comedy about song writers, was also well patronized.

Claiborne Foster appeared in an interesting new play by Maxwell Anderson called "Gypsy." Leslie Howard and Margalo Gillmore were seen in "Berkeley Square," and Evelyn Laye was introduced to American audiences in "Bitter Sweet," which boasted a memorable score by Noel Coward.

Long runs were chalked up by "Michael and Mary" with Henry Hull and Edith Barrett, and by "Death Takes A Holiday" which featured Philip Merivale, Rose Hobart and James Dale. "The First Mrs. Fraser" with Grace George and A. E. Matthews was another hit.

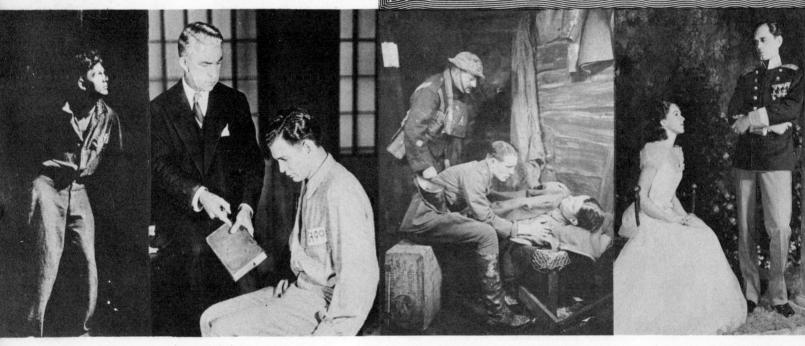

RUSSELL HARDIE   ARTHUR BYRON, RUSSELL HARDIE in "THE CRIMINAL CODE"   SYDNEY SEAWARD, COLIN KEITH-JOHNSTON, DEREK WILLIAMS in "JOURNEY'S END"   ROSE HOBART, PHILIP MERIVALE in "DEATH TAKES A HOLIDAY"

194   ERIN O'BRIEN-MOORE   "STREET SCENE"   BEULAH BONDI

"Journey's End" proved to be one of the most effective of war plays. It was given a fine production by a cast that included Leon Quartermaine, Derek Williams and Colin Keith-Johnston. "The Criminal Code" was also impressive. Arthur Byron played the lead, and in the cast was Russell Hardie who was making his first stage appearance.

David Belasco had a big hit in "It's A Wise Child." Another big hit was the delightful British comedy "Bird in Hand." Gertrude Lawrence and Leslie Howard were in "Candlelight." "Young Sinners," a comedy by Elmer Harris which featured Dorothy Appleby and Raymond Guion (Gene Raymond), also had a good run.

Laurence Olivier made his first American appearance in "Murder on the Second Floor," and Bette Davis and Donald Meek were seen in "Broken Dishes." Walter Huston was in "The Commodore Marries," but it was not successful, nor was "The Channel Road" which had been derived from de Maupassant by the team of Alexander Woollcott and George S. Kaufman, and which was acted by Anne Forrest and Siegfried Rumann.

Alfred Lunt and Lynn Fontanne appeared in S. M. Behrman's "Meteor;" Miriam Hopkins was seen in "The Camel Through the Needle's Eye;" George M. Cohan was in "Gambling;" and

JACK HAWKINS in "JOURNEY'S END"

DOROTHY PETERSON in "SUBWAY EXPRESS"

COLIN KEITH-JOHNSTON in "JOURNEY'S END"

JEAN DIXON in "JUNE MOON"

EDNA HIBBARD

PHILIP MERIVALE

ROSE HOBART

EARLE LARIMORE

...IEL KIRKLAND, LOUIS JEAN HEYDT, TULLIO ...ARMINATI in "STRICTLY DISHONORABLE"

FRANCINE LARRIMORE, WARREN WILLIAM, KENNETH HUNTER in "LET US BE GAY"

LESLIE HOWARD, MARGALO GILLMORE in "BERKELEY SQUARE"

GRACE GEORGE, A. E. MATTHEWS in "THE FIRST MRS. FRASER"

...DY HUGHES, CHARLES HICKMAN, HERBERT LOMAS, JILL ESMOND MOORE in "BIRD IN HAND"

LESLIE HOWARD, REGINALD OWEN, GERTRUDE LAWRENCE in "CANDLELIGHT"

HUGH SINCLAIR, RUTH GORDON in "SERENA BLANDISH"

RUTH GORDON

DOUGLAS MONTGOMERY, SHIRLEY O'HARA in "METEOR"

CLAUDETTE COLBERT, GLENN ANDERS in "DYNAMO"

FRANK CONROY, OTTO KRUGER, ALICE BRADY in "THE GAME OF LOVE AND DEATH"

BETTE DAVIS, DONALD MEEK in "BROKEN DISHES"

PHYLLIS KONSTAM, LAURENCE OLIVIER in "MURDER ON THE SECOND FLOOR"

GENE RAYMOND, DO APPLEBY in "YOUNG SI

JACOB BEN-AMI, JOSEPHINE HUTCHINSON, MERLE MADDERN in "THE SEA GULL"

EDITH BARRETT, HENRY HULL, HARRY BERESFORD in "MICHAEL AND MARY"

LEILA BENNETT, MINOR WATSON, MILDRED McCOY "IT'S A WISE CHILD"

"SUBWAY EXPRESS"

LEE PATRICK, JEAN DIXON, HARRY ROSENTHAL, FRANK OTTO, NORMAN FOSTER in "JUNE MOON"

LESTER VAIL, CLAIBORNE FOSTER, LOUIS CALHERN "GYPSY"

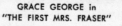

OTIS SKINNER in "A HUNDRED YEARS OLD"

ELSIE FERGUSON in "SCARLET PAGES"

EDWARD G. ROBINSON in "KIBITZER"

GRACE GEORGE in "THE FIRST MRS. FRASER"

WALTER HAMPDEN in "RICHELIEU"

MAURICE SCHWARTZ in
"JEW SUSS"

TOM PATRICOLA,
HARRY RICHMAN in
"GEORGE WHITE'S SCANDALS"

FRED ALLEN, PORTLAND
HOFFA in
"THE LITTLE SHOW"

LESTER ALLEN, IRENE DELROY,
PAUL FRAWLEY in
"TOP SPEED"

GUY ROBERTSON, QUEENIE
SMITH in
"THE STREET SINGER"

STANLEY RIDGES, JEANETTE
MacDONALD, FRANK McINTYRE in
"BOOM BOOM"

TILLY
LOSCH

CARY
GRANT

JESSIE
MATTHEWS

JACK
BUCHANAN

AILEEN
STANLEY

TAYLOR
HOLMES

Elsie Ferguson was in "Scarlet Pages." "Hot Chocolates," a Negro revue, was well received, as was "Harlem," another colored show which depicted a "rent party" on the stage. "Subway Express," a skillfully produced murder mystery, brought fame to Chester Erskin who had directed it; and from England came another thriller called "Rope's End." Basil Sydney and Mary Ellis were liked in "Meet the Prince," and Edward G. Robinson did brisk business with "Kibitzer."

Mrs. Fiske revived "Mrs. Bumpstead-Leigh," and also appeared in a new comedy called "Ladies of the Jury." Blanche Yurka played "Lady from the Sea," and Jane Cowl was seen in "Paolo and Francesca." Otis Skinner acted in "A Hundred Years Old" (also known as "Papa Juan"), and Nazimova was in "Katerina." Jacob Ben-Ami joined the Civic Repertory Company and appeared in "The Sea Gull" and "The Living Corpse." Alice Brady and Otto Kruger were seen together in both "Karl and Anna" and "The Game of Love and Death." The Players' Club revival of the year was "Becky Sharp" with Mary Ellis in the title role. Maurice Schwartz, noted Yiddish actor, had a hit with "Jew Suss" on the Lower East Side.

The outstanding musical shows of the year were "The Little Show" with Fred Allen, Clifton Webb, Romney Brent and Libby Holman, "Follow Thru" with Irene Delroy, Zelma O'Neal and Jack Barker, "Sweet Adeline" with Helen Morgan, Irene Franklin, Charles Butterworth and Violet Carlson, "Sons O' Guns" with Jack Donahue and Lily Damita, "Fifty Million Frenchmen" with William Gaxton, Genevieve Tobin and Helen Broderick, and "Wake Up and Dream" with Jack Buchanan, and Tilly Losch.

Fritzi Scheff appeared in a revival of "Mlle. Modiste." "Die Fledermaus" was done under the title of "A Wonderful Night," and among the players were Archie Leach (Cary Grant), Gladys Baxter and Solly Ward. Glenn Hunter became a song and dance man in "Spring Is Here." Other musicals of the year were "Boom Boom," "Lady Fingers," "Pleasure Bound," "Fioretta," "Grand Street Follies," "A Night in Venice," "Show Girl," "Sketch Book," "Murray Anderson's Almanack," "Street Singer," "Scandals."

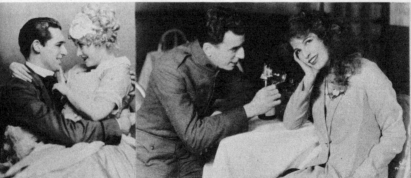

EDDIE FOY, JR., RUBY KEELER, JIMMY DURANTE,
KATHRYN HEREFORD in "SHOW GIRL"

LIBBY HOLMAN, CLIFTON WEBB in
"MOANIN' LOW" NUMBER in "THE LITTLE SHOW"

CARY GRANT, MARY McCOY in
"A WONDERFUL NIGHT"

JACK DONAHUE, LILY DAMITA in
"SONS O' GUNS"

ZELMA O'NEAL in
"FOLLOW THRU"

WILLIAM GAXTON, GENEVIEVE TOBIN in
"FIFTY MILLION FRENCHMEN"

EVELYN LAYE in
"BITTER SWEET"

IRENE FRANKLIN in
"SWEET ADELINE"

197

RUSSELL HARDIE   EUGENIE LEONTOVITCH   IVOR NOVELLO   KATHARINE HEPBURN

ALLA NAZIMOVA, ELIOT CABOT in
"A MONTH IN THE COUNTRY"

VERREE TEASDALE, DOROTHY HALL, MURIEL KIRKLAND in
"THE GREEKS HAD A WORD FOR IT"

NYDIA WESTMAN, ERNEST TRUEX in
"LYSISTRATA"

JEAN DIXON, HUGH O'CONNELL in
"ONCE IN A LIFETIME"

HARRY LAUDER

1930

The talking picture was coming into its own, and the result was a serious curtailment in the number of legitimate theatres in operation. Vaudeville was on the decline, permanent stock companies were unable to survive, and the number of touring companies was greatly reduced.

During the year 1930 there were two Pulitzer Prize awards: Marc Connelly's "The Green Pastures" for the 1929-30 season and Susan Glaspell's "Alison's House" for the 1930-31 season. The former, described as a fable play, was a simple re-telling of the Old Testament story by a colored preacher. The leading part was played by Richard B. Harrison. "Alison's House" was produced by Eva Le Gallienne's Civic Repertory Company, and could be called a literary play. It was based on incidents in the life of Emily Dickinson, the American poet.

Vicki Baum's "Grand Hotel," produced by Herman Shumlin and acted by a cast which included Eugenie Leóntovich, Siegfried Rumann, Hortense Alden, Henry Hull and Sam Jaffe, was a big hit. Mr. Shumlin also produced "The Last Mile," a prison play by John Wexley, with Spencer Tracy playing the lead. David Belasco presented "Dancing Partner" with Irene Purcell and Lynne Overman, and "Tonight or Never" with Helen Gahagan and Melvyn Douglas. The latter was Mr. Belasco's final

MARY BOLAND, WARREN WILLIAM in
"THE VINEGAR TREE"

"GRAND HOTEL"
Above (left and right): HENRY HULL, EUGENIE LEONTOVITCH
Center: HENRY HULL, HORTENSE ALDEN, SAM JAFFE, SIEGFRIED RUMANN

JAMES CAGNEY, JOAN BLONDEL
"PENNY ARCADE"

MAURICE
MOSCOVITCH

HELEN
GAHAGAN

ALBERT
HACKETT

ELSA
SHELLEY

JAMES BELL, SPENCER TRACY in
"THE LAST MILE"

FRANK MORGAN and Pupils in
"TOPAZE"

ALFRED LUNT, LYNN FONTANNE in
"ELIZABETH, THE QUEEN"

production as he died in New York City on May 15, 1931.

Alfred Lunt and Lynn Fontanne had a substantial success in Maxwell Anderson's "Elizabeth the Queen," and other Theatre Guild offerings were Shaw's "The Apple Cart," Philip Barry's "Hotel Universe" and Turgenev's "A Month in the Country" with Alla Nazimova.

Jed Harris produced a memorable revival of "Uncle Vanya" with Lillian Gish, Osgood Perkins, Walter Connelly and Eugene Powers. He also did the Gogol farce, "The Inspector General" with Romney Brent and Dorothy Gish.

Maurice Chevalier appeared in an evening of popular French songs and was assisted by Eleanor Powell and Duke Ellington's orchestra. The celebrated Scotch comedian, Harry Lauder, was seen on a coast-to-coast tour. From the Orient came Mei Lan-Fang, China's greatest actor, who appeared with remarkable success in a series of one-act plays selected from his extensive repertoire. Visitors from Greece did "Elektra" in the original with a company headed by Marika Cotopouli and Katina Paxinou.

Jane Cowl was successful in a revival of "Twelfth Night," and also was seen in a new comedy called "Art and Mrs. Bottle" in which she was supported by Katharine Hepburn. Katharine Cornell appeared in "Dishonored Lady," Leslie Banks and Helen

MAURICE
CHEVALIER

KATHARINE HEPBURN, JANE COWL in
"ART AND MRS. BOTTLE"

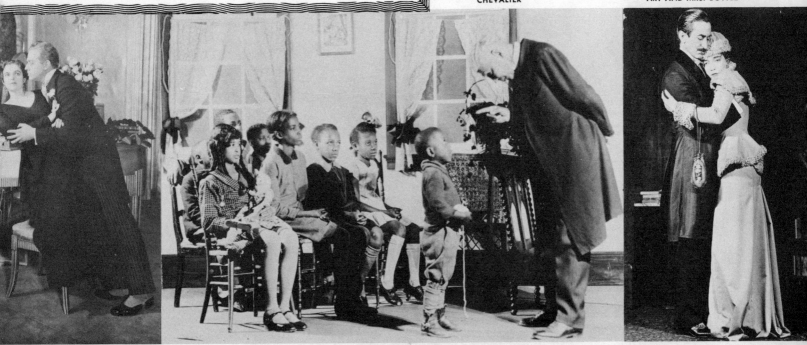

EN GAHAGAN, MELVYN DOUGLAS in
"TONIGHT OR NEVER"

"THE GREEN PASTURES"

OSGOOD PERKINS, LILLIAN GISH in
"UNCLE VANYA"

LESLIE BANKS, ISABEL
JEANS in
"THE MAN IN POSSESSION"

VIOLET KEMBLE COOPER,
TOM POWERS in
"THE APPLE CART"

GLENN HUNTER, JUNE
WALKER in
"WATERLOO BRIDGE"

LENORE ULRIC, RUSSELL
HARDIE in
"PAGAN LADY"

IVOR NOVELLO, PHOEBE
FOSTER in
"THE TRUTH GAME"

BASIL SYDNEY, MAR
ELLIS in
"CHILDREN OF DARKNE

HAIDEE
WRIGHT

BERT
LYTELL

BLANCHE
YURKA

IRENE
PURCELL

NORMAN
FOSTER

MARJORIE
WOOD

ALICE BRADY, GEORGE BRENT, GLENDA FARRELL
"LOVE, HONOR AND BETRAY"

GEORGE
JESSEL in
"JOSEPH"

GUY KIBBEE, MAYO METHOT, REED BROWN, JR. in
"TORCH SONG"

SALLY BATES, BRIAN DONLEVY, ROGER PRYOR, HENRY
HOWARD, MILDRED WALL, ALBERT HACKETT in
"UP POPS THE DEVIL"

PRESTON FOSTER, VIOLET HEMING, WALTER WOOLF,
GERMAINE GIROUX, MAY COLLINS in
"LADIES ALL"

Menken played in "The Infinite Shoe
black" and Glenn Hunter and June Walk
er were in "Waterloo Bridge." Elissa
Landi and Glenn Anders were in "A
Farewell to Arms," and Mary Ellis and
Basil Sydney acted in "Children of Dark
ness;" Fritz Leiber appeared in Shakes
pearean repertoire; and Maurice Mos
covitch played "The Merchant of Venice."
An outstanding hit was "Lysistrata" with
Violet Kemble Cooper, Miriam Hopkins,
Hope Emerson, Sydney Greenstreet and
Ernest Truex.

Hope Williams was seen in "Rebound,"
Frank Morgan in "Topaze," and Frank
Craven in "That's Gratitude." Alice
Brady played in "Love, Honor and Be
tray" supported by George Brent, Glenda
Farrell and Clark Gable; "Penny Arcade"
brought James Cagney and Joan Blondell
to the fore; and Mary Boland was seen
in "Ada Beats the Drum" and "The Vine
gar Tree." Leslie Banks and Isabel Jeans
were in "The Man in Possession," and
Ivor Novello and Benita Hume played
"Symphony in Two Flats." "Once in a
Lifetime" was a hit, and so were "The
Greeks Had a Word For It" and "Up Pops
the Devil."

Other interesting plays of the year were
"The Matriarch" with Constance Col
lier, "Torch Song" with Mayo Methot,

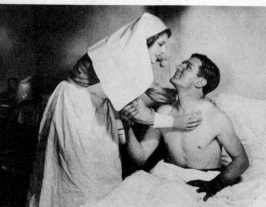

ELISSA LANDI, GLENN ANDERS in
"A FAREWELL TO ARMS"

CRANE WILBUR, ANNA MAY WONG in
"ON THE SPOT"

PAUL KELLY, SYLVIA
SIDNEY in
"BAD GIRL"

JANE COWL, LEON
QUARTERMAINE in
"TWELFTH NIGHT"

EDITH BARRETT, HAIDEE
WRIGHT in
"MRS. MOONLIGHT"

JOEY RAY, GLORIA
GRAFTON in
"THE SECOND LITTLE SHOW"

BERT LAHR, KATE
SMITH in
"FLYING HIGH"

LIBBY HOLMAN, FRED
MacMURRAY in
"THREE'S A CROWD"

CLAIRE
LUCE

GINGER
ROGERS

JACK
BENNY

HILDEGARDE
HALLIDAY

HARRY
RICHMAN

MARILYN
MILLER

DOROTHY STONE, ALLENE CRATER (MRS. STONE),
FRED STONE, PAULA STONE in "RIPPLES"

WILLIE HOWARD
in
"GIRL CRAZY"

DONALD FOSTER, GINGER ROGERS, ALLEN
KEARNS in "GIRL CRAZY"

"Ladies All" with Violet Heming and Walter Woolf, "Mrs. Moonlight" with Edith Barrett and Haidee Wright, "Mr. Gilhooley" with Helen Hayes and Arthur Sinclair, "Bad Girl" with Sylvia Sidney and Paul Kelly, "Pagan Lady" with Lenore Ulric, Russell Hardie and Franchot Tone, "On The Spot" with Crane Wilbur and Anna May Wong, "Five Star Final" with Berton Churchill, and "Scarlet Sister Mary" with Ethel Barrymore and Estelle Winwood appearing in black face. Elsa Shelley, who later became a playwright, was acting in "Courtesan," a one character play.

The most important musical shows were "Strike Up the Band" with Blanche Ring and Clark and McCullough, "Flying High" with Oscar Shaw, Bert Lahr and Kate Smith, "Fine and Dandy" with Joe Cook, "Girl Crazy" with Ethel Merman, Willie Howard and Ginger Rogers, and "Three's A Crowd" with Fred Allen, Clifton Webb and Libby Holman. Other musicals were "Smiles," "Ripples," "Simple Simon," "The International Review," "Garrick Gaieties," "Artists and Models," "Nina Rosa," "Earl Carroll's Vanities" and "The New Yorkers" with an all-star cast including Hope Williams, Richard Carle, Ann Pennington, Marie Cahill, Frances Williams, Charles King and Jimmy Durante.

ANN PENNINGTON, FRED WARING, FRANCES WILLIAMS, CHARLES KING, HOPE WILLIAMS, RICHARD CARLE,
MARIE CAHILL, LOU CLAYTON, JIMMY DURANTE, EDDIE JACKSON in "THE NEW YORKERS"

BLANCHE RING in
"STRIKE UP THE BAND"

CLIFTON WEBB, LIBBY HOLMAN, FRED ALLEN in
"THREE'S A CROWD"

ETHEL MERMAN in
"GIRL CRAZY"

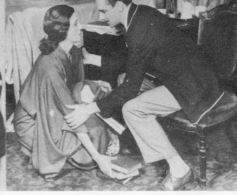

GLENN HUNTER, CHARLOTTE WYNTERS, LATHROP MITCHELL in "A REGULAR GUY"

RAYMOND MASSEY as HAMLET

KATHERINE ALEXANDER, CLEDGE ROBERTS in "THE LEFT BANK"

FLUSH in "THE BARRETTS OF WIMPOLE STREET"

RUSSELL HARDIE, CLAIRE L "SOCIETY GIRL"

HARRY ELLERBE

EDNA BEST

LATHROP MITCHELL

MADGE EVANS

JAMES T. POWERS

FLORA ZABELLE

CHARLES WALDRON

HOPE EMERSON

CHAR LAUGH

ALFRED LUNT, LYNN FONTANNE in "REUNION IN VIENNA"

1931 The economic depression continued to pall on theatrical activities, and with the talking motion pictures becoming firmly established, Hollywood gold had lured away from Broadway most of the better playwrights and promising young players.

In February Katharine Cornell became an actress-manager, producing as her first venture Rudolf Besier's "The Barretts of Wimpole Street." It proved to be one of the great successes of her career and she has since revived it several times. Directed by her husband, Guthrie McClintic, the original cast besides Miss Cornell included Brian Aherne, Charles Waldron, Joyce Carey, John Buckler, Brenda Forbes, John D. Seymour and Flush who became one of the most famous dogs in theatredom.

The Group Theatre was formed this year and under the auspices of the Theatre Guild produced Paul Green's "The House of Connelly" as their first offering. Among the players in the organization were Franchot Tone, Luther and Stella Adler, Robert Lewis, Clifford Odets, Russell Collins and Ruth Nelson. Another event of the year was the return to the stage of Maude Adams after an absence of thirteen years. With Otis Skinner she toured the country in "The Merchant of Venice," but she did not venture into New York.

The hits of the year were Gertrude Lawrence and Noel Coward in his own "Private Lives," Alfred Lunt and Lynn Fontanne in "Reunion in Vienna," Helen Hayes in "The Good Fairy," Leslie Banks in "Springtime for Henry," Francine Larrimore with Alexander Woollcott in "Brief Moment," Philip Merivale in "Cynara," the Theatre Guild production of Eugene O'Neill's

HELEN HAYES, WALTER CONNOLLY "THE GOOD FAIRY"

CORNELIA OTIS SKINNER in "THE LOVES OF CHARLES II"

LESTER LONERGAN, ALICE BRADY in "BRASS ANKLE"

PHILIP MERIVALE, ADRIANNE ALLEN in "CYNARA"

MADGE EVANS, HARRY ELLERBE in "PHILIP GOES FORTH"

DOROTHY GISH, ROLLO PETERS in "THE STREETS OF NEW YORK"

EDITH EVANS in "THE LADY WITH A L

KATHARINE CORNELL as ELIZABETH BARRETT
in
"THE BARRETTS OF WIMPOLE STREET"

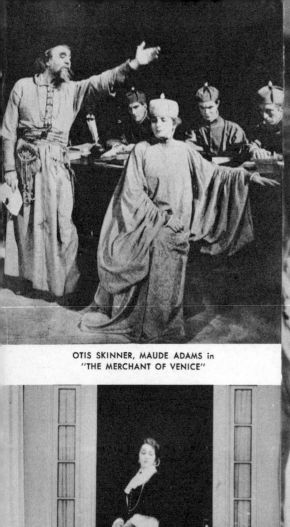

OTIS SKINNER, MAUDE ADAMS in
"THE MERCHANT OF VENICE"

BRIAN AHERNE, KATHARINE CORNELL in
"THE BARRETTS OF WIMPOLE STREET"

ALICE BRADY, ALLA NAZIMOVA in
"MOURNING BECOMES ELECTRA"

JENNIE MOSCOWITZ, PAUL MUNI in
"COUNSELLOR-AT-LAW"

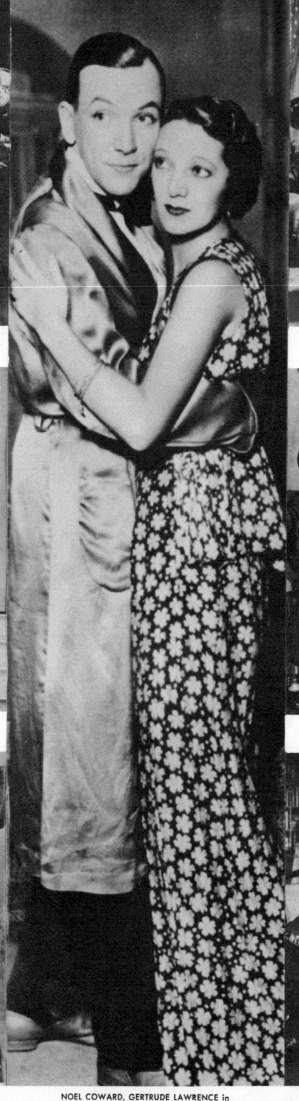

JOSEPH SCHILDKRAUT, PATRICIA COLLINGE in
"ANATOL"

NOEL COWARD, GERTRUDE LAWRENCE in
"PRIVATE LIVES"

ROBERT DOUGLAS, ALEXANDER WOOLLCOTT,
FRANCINE LARRIMORE in "BRIEF MOMENT"

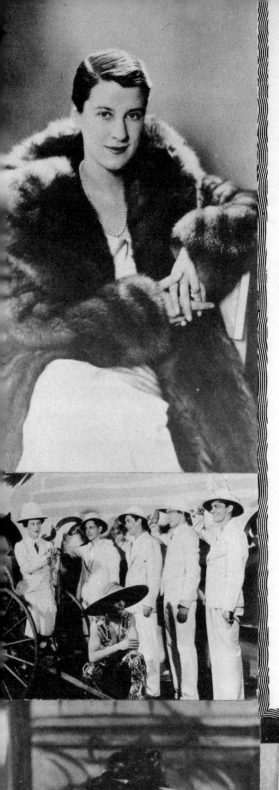

"Mourning Becomes Electra" with Nazimova and Alice Brady, Paul Muni in "Counsellor-at-Law," Ruth Gordon and Bert Lytell in "A Church Mouse," Elmer Rice's "The Left Bank" and Philip Barry's "Tomorrow and Tomorrow." Other new plays that received attention were "Green Grow the Lilacs" (which later blossomed into the musical "Oklahoma"), "The Bride the Sun Shines On," "The House Beautiful," "Philip Goes Forth" and "As Husbands Go."

Among the stars, Judith Anderson was in "As You Desire Me," Lionel Atwill appeared in "The Silent Witness," Mae West in "The Constant Sinner," Glenn Hunter in "A Regular Guy," Alice Brady was in "Brass Ankle," Lenore Ulric and Sidney Blackmer in "The Social Register," Mrs. Patrick Campbell in "The Sex Fable," Charles Laughton in "Payment Deferred," Edith Evans in "The Lady with a Lamp" and Cornelia Otis Skinner appeared in a series of character sketches of her own authorship.

Revivals of the year included "Hamlet" with Raymond Massey, Mary Servoss, Colin Keith-Johnston and Celia Johnson; Ethel Barrymore supported by McKay Morris, Anne Seymour and Walter Gilbert in "The School for Scandal," Robert Loraine in Strindberg's "The Father," Shaw's "Getting Married," "Anatol" with Joseph Schildkraut, Patricia Collinge, Miriam Hopkins and Anne Forrest, Eva Le Gallienne in "Camille," Walter Hampden and Fay Bainter in "The Admirable Crichton" and "The Streets of New York" with Dorothy Gish, Rollo Peters and Fania Marinoff.

"Of Thee I Sing" was the first musical comedy to win a Pulitzer Prize. George Gershwin wrote the music, Ira Gershwin the lyrics, George S. Kaufman and Morrie Myskind the book, and the cast included

WILLIAM GAXTON, LOIS MORAN, GEORGE MURPHY, VICTOR MOORE in "OF THEE I SING"
Top: VICTOR MOORE

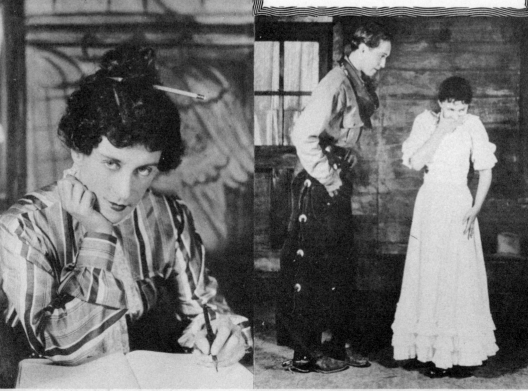

BEATRICE LILLIE in
"THE THIRD LITTLE SHOW"

FRANCHOT TONE, JUNE WALKER in
"GREEN GROW THE LILACS"

ED WYNN in
"THE LAUGH PARADE"

HELEN CHANDLER, LESLIE BANKS, FRIEDA INESCORT, NIGEL BRUCE in "SPRINGTIME FOR HENRY"

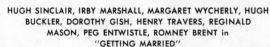

HUGH SINCLAIR, IRBY MARSHALL, MARGARET WYCHERLY, HUGH BUCKLER, DOROTHY GISH, HENRY TRAVERS, REGINALD MASON, PEG ENTWISTLE, ROMNEY BRENT in "GETTING MARRIED"

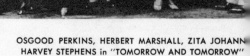

OSGOOD PERKINS, HERBERT MARSHALL, ZITA JOHANN, HARVEY STEPHENS in "TOMORROW AND TOMORROW"

CICELY OATES, CHARLES LAUGHTON, ELSA LANCHESTER in "PAYMENT DEFERRED"

HELEN CHANDLER

GENE RAYMOND

HARRIET LAKE (ANN SOTHERN)

RUDY VALLEE

BERT LYTELL, RUTH GORDON in "A CHURCH MOUSE"

ETHEL WATERS in "RHAPSODY IN BLACK"

Victor Moore, William Gaxton, Lois Moran and George Murphy.

Other major musicals were "The Band Wagon" with Fred and Adele Astaire, Frank Morgan and Helen Broderick, "The Cat and the Fiddle" with Bettina Hall and Georges Metaxa. "America's Sweetheart" with Jack Whiting and Harriet Lake (changed to Ann Sothern for films), "The Third Little Show" with Beatrice Lillie and Ernest Truex, "The Laugh Parade" with Ed Wynn, "You Said It" with Lou Holtz and Lyda Roberti, "The Wonder Bar" with Al Jolson, "Rhapsody in Black" with Ethel Waters, "Ziegfeld Follies" with Helen Morgan, Jack Pearl, Ruth Etting and Harry Richman, "George White's Scandals" with Willie Howard, Ethel Merman, Rudy Vallee and Ray Bolger, Earl Carroll's "Vanities" with Will Mahoney, "Billy Rose's Crazy Quilt" with Fannie Brice, Ted Healy and Phil Baker, and revivals of "The Geisha" with James T. Powers and "The Merry Widow" with Donald Brian.

HELEN BRODERICK

JACK PEARL

RUTH ETTING

PHIL BAKER

PATSY KELLY, AL JOLSON in "THE WONDER BAR"

JOSE RUBEN, JUDITH ANDERSON in "AS YOU DESIRE ME"

ANTHONY IRELAND, MRS. PATRICK CAMPBELL in "THE SEX FABLE"

DORIS CARSON, BETTINA HALL, EDDIE FOY, JR., GEORGES METAXA in "THE CAT AND THE FIDDLE"

ADELE and FRED ASTAIRE in "THE BAND WAGON"

JACK WHITING, HARRIET LAKE (ANN SOTHERN) "AMERICA'S SWEETHEART"

A. E. MATTHEWS, GRACE GEORGE, PEGGY CONKLIN,
ALICE BRADY in "MADEMOISELLE"

DIANA WYNYARD, CECILIA LOFTUS, MARY NASH, BASIL
RATHBONE, ARTHUR BYRON, ROBERT LORAINE,
ERNEST THESIGER in "THE DEVIL PASSES"

EMLYN WILLIAMS, ALEXANDRA CARLISLE, WILLIAM
HARRIGAN, WALTER KINGSFORD in
"CRIMINAL AT LARGE"

ZITA JOHANN

HERBERT MARSHALL

DIANA WYNYARD

CONWAY TEARLE

RBERT MARSHALL, MAY WHITTY, EDNA BEST in
"THERE'S ALWAYS JULIET"

LAURETTE TAYLOR, PEG ENTWISTLE, CHARLES
DALTON in "ALICE-SIT-BY-THE-FIRE"

1932

The theatre felt the economic depression in 1932. Many plays lowered their admission and members of the theatrical profession were severely affected. The year saw many low-budget plays of mediocre quality, but there were also several outstanding hits. Leslie Howard was immensely popular in "The Animal Kingdom," and Ina Claire had a great success in "Biography" by S. N. Behrman. "Dinner at Eight" by George S. Kaufman and Edna Ferber was a solid hit with Ann Andrews, Marguerite Churchill, Cesar Romero, Margaret Dale, Conway Tearle, Sam Levene, Olive Wyndham and Constance Collier. Also well patronized was Rachel Crothers' "When Ladies Meet" with Frieda Inescort, Walter Abel, Selena Royle, Spring Byington and Herbert Rawlinson.

The Group Theatre offered "Night Over Taos" by Maxwell Anderson and "Success Story" by John Howard Lawson. Laurette Taylor was seen in a revival of "Alice-Sit-By-The-Fire" with "The Old Lady Shows Her Medals" as a curtain-raiser. Pauline Lord who appeared in two artistic failures: "Distant Drums" and a revival of "The Truth About Blayds," was also seen in a successful play, "The Late Christopher Bean." Emlyn Williams and Alexandra Carlisle were in "Criminal at Large," and Francis Lederer and Patricia Collinge played "Autumn Crocus." Dorothy Gish later took over the feminine lead in this comedy. "The Devil Passes" was acted by Arthur Byron, Mary Nash, Ernest Thesiger, Basil Rathbone, Robert Loraine, Cecilia Loftus and Diana Wynyard. "Another Language" was capably acted by Mar-

PAULINE LORD, WALTER CONNOLLY in
"THE LATE CHRISTOPHER BEAN"

FRANCIS LEDERER, DOROTHY GISH in
"AUTUMN CROCUS"

SAM LEVENE, CONWAY TEARLE in "DINNER AT EIGHT"

CONSTANCE COLLIER, ANN ANDREWS

(Back row) WYRLEY BIRCH, WILLIAM PIKE, DOROTHY
STICKNEY, (Front row) GLENN ANDERS, MARGARET
WYCHERLY, HAL K. DAWSON in
"ANOTHER LANGUAGE"

COLIN KEITH-JOHNSTON,
JEAN DIXON, MARY SERVOSS
in
"DANGEROUS CORNER"

FRANCIS LEDERER

INA CLAIRE in "BIOGRAPHY"

LILLIAN GISH in "CAMILLE"

JOSEPH SCHILDKRAUT in "LILIOM"

MARY SERVOSS

RAYMOND HACKETT

ANNE SEYMOUR

HENR STEPHEN

garet Wycherly, Margaret Hamilton, Glenn Anders, John Beal and Dorothy Stickney.

Other new plays of the year were "Whistling in the Dark," "Riddle Me This," "Clear All Wires," "I Loved You Wednesday," "Dangerous Corner," "Carry Nation" and 'The Mad Hopes."

Roger Pryor appeared in "Blessed Event," Ruth Gordon in "Here Today," Jane Cowl in "A Thousand Summers," and Katharine Cornell in "Lucrece." Edna Best, Herbert Marshall and May Whitty played in 'There's Always Juliet;" Katharine Hepburn, Romney Brent and Colin Keith-Johnston were seen in "The Warrior's Husband;" Hope Williams, Beatrice Lillie and Leo G. Carroll were in "Too True to Be Good;" and Claude Rains and Nazimova were in "The Good Earth." Judith Anderson, Ian Keith and Nita Naldi acted in "Firebird;" Eugenie Leontovich and Moffat Johnston were in "Twentieth Century;" Osgood Perkins, Sally Bates and James Stewart were in "Goodbye Again;" Margaret Sullavan, June Walker and Humphrey Bogart were in "Chrysalis;" Alice Brady, Grace George and A. E. Matthews were in "Mademoiselle;" and Lillian Gish appeared in "Camille" with Raymond Hackett.

KATHARINE CORNELL, BRIAN AHERNE in "LUCRECE"

HERBERT RAWLINSON, FRIEDA INESCORT in "WHEN LADIES ME

FRANCHOT TONE, JANE COWL in "A THOUSAND SUMMERS"

HUMPHREY BOGART, MARGARET SULLAVAN in "CHRYSALIS"

RUTH GORDON, CHARLOTTE GRANVILLE in "HERE TODAY"

JOSEPHINE HUTCHINSON, LEONA ROBERTS in "ALICE IN WONDERLAND"

WILLIAM GARGAN, LESLIE HOWARD in "THE ANIMAL KINGDOM"

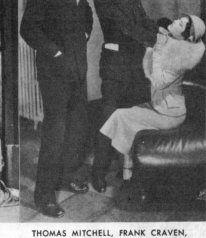

CLAUDE RAINS, ALLA NAZIMOVA in "THE GOOD EARTH"

THOMAS MITCHELL, FRANK CRAVEN, ERIN O'BRIEN-MOORE in "RIDDLE ME THIS"

MARGARET PERRY

GLENN ANDERS

DOROTHY GISH

HERBERT RAWLINSON

ROY ROBERTS, EUGENIE LEONTOVICH, MOFFAT JOHNSTON in "TWENTIETH CENTURY"

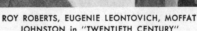

KATHARINE HEPBURN, COLIN KEITH-JOHNSTON in "THE WARRIOR'S HUSBAND"

BEATRICE LILLIE, HOPE WILLIAMS in "TOO TRUE TO BE GOOD"

OSGOOD PERKINS, SALLY BATES in "GOODBYE AGAIN"

Eva Le Gallienne revived "Liliom" with Joseph Schildkraut and produced "Alice in Wonderland." The Abbey Theatre Irish Players did "The Far-Off Hills," "The White-Headed Boy," "The New Gossoon," "The Rising of the Moon" and gave a single performance of "Oedipus Rex." In this company were Eileen Crowe, Ria Mooney, Barry Fitzgerald, Maureen Delany, Denis O'Dea, Arthur Shields and F. J. McCormick. Maurice Chevalier and Ruth Draper were seen in one-man shows.

The top musicals of the year were "Face the Music" with Mary Boland, J. Harold Murray and Hugh O'Connell, "Hot-Cha!" with Buddy Rogers, Lupe Velez and Bert Lahr, a revival of "Show Boat" with Dennis King and Paul Robeson new to the cast, "Flying Colors" with Charles Butterworth, Clifton Webb, Buddy Ebsen, Imogene Coca and Tamara Geva, "Music in the Air" with Al Shean, Walter Slezak, Reinald Werrenrath and Natalie Hall, "The Du Barry" with Grace Moore, "Take A Chance" with Ethel Merman and Jack Haley, "Walk a Little Faster" starring Beatrice Lillie and Clark and McCullough, Cole Porter's "Gay Divorcé" with Fred Astaire, Claire Luce and Luella Gear and Milton Aborn had a season of Gilbert and Sullivan operettas.

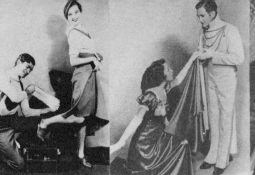

EMLYN
WILLIAMS

JOSEPHINE
HUTCHINSON

BUDDY and VILMA
EBSEN in
"FLYING COLORS"

IMOGENE COCA, CLIFTON
WEBB in
"FLYING COLORS"

DOROTHY STONE,
FRED STONE, in
"SMILING FACES"

NITA
NALDI

RUTH
DRAPER

BEATRICE LILLIE, PAUL McCULLOUGH, BOBBY
CLARK in "WALK A LITTLE FASTER"

BUDDY ROGERS, LUPE VELEZ, BERT LAHR in
"HOT-CHA!"

CHIC JOHNSON, OLE OLSEN, ETHEL MERM
"TAKE A CHANCE"

JACK
WHITING

DOROTHY
STONE

IMOGENE
COCA

STERLING
HOLLOWAY

VIVIAN
HART

ALLEN
WATEROUS

LIBBY
HOLMAN

QUEENIE SMITH, JOHN GARRICK in
"A LITTLE RACKETEER"

TESS
GARDELLA

LUPE
VELEZ

JACK
HALEY

CHARLES
BUTTERWORTH

CLAIRE LUCE,
FRED ASTAIRE in
"THE GAY DIVORCE"

KATHERINE CARRINGTON, AL SHEAN,
IVY SCOTT, WALTER SLEZAK in
"MUSIC IN THE AIR"

MARY BOLAND, HUGH O'CONNELL in
"FACE THE MUSIC"

GRACE
MOORE

WILLIAM
DANFORTH

BASIL
SYDNEY

LILLIAN
GISH

TONIO
SELWART

BASIL SYDNEY, MARGALO
GILLMORE in
"THE DARK TOWER"

NOEL
COWARD

MARY
BOLAND

OLGA
BACLANOVA

ORRIS, RICHARD KENDRICK, ALETA FREEL,
NNE REVERE in "DOUBLE DOOR"

1933

In 1933 two nostalgic comedies were major events of the theatre year. "One Sunday Afternoon," by James Hagen and acted by Francesca Bruning and Lloyd Nolan, enjoyed a long run. An even more potent evocation of the good old days was Eugene O'Neill's "Ah, Wilderness!" with George M. Cohan. Again two Pulitzer Prizes were given: the 1932-33 award going to Maxwell Anderson's "Both Your Houses," and the 1933-34 award going to "Men in White" by Sidney Kingsley and with Alexander Kirkland.

Lynn Fontanne, Alfred Lunt and Noel Coward appeared together in the latter's sophisticated comedy, "Design for Living." Edith Evans appeared briefly as an aging opera star in "Evensong," and Katharine Cornell played in "Alien Corn." Helen Hayes scored in the historical drama "Mary of Scotland." Produced by the Theatre Guild, the cast included Helen Menken and Philip Merivale. Tallulah Bankhead returned from her London triumph and was seen in "Forsaking All Others." "Uncle Tom's Cabin" was revived by the Players' Club with Otis Skinner as Uncle Tom and Fay Bainter as Topsy. George M. Cohan wrote and acted in "Pigeons and People," Bramwell Fletcher appeared in "Ten Minute Alibi," and Lillian Gish was seen in "Nine Pine Street" based on the Lizzie Borden case. Mrs. Patrick Campbell was seen in "A Party," Jean Arthur was in "The Curtain Rises," Basil Sydney did "The Dark Tower" and Florence Reed was in "Thoroughbred."

"Tobacco Road" began its long run and was first played by Henry Hull, Sam Byrd, Margaret Wycherly, Dean Jagger and Maude Odell. Katharine Hepburn played in "The Lake" sup-

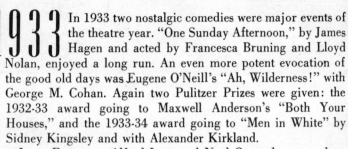

DONALD MACDONALD, FRED KEATING, TALLULAH
BANKHEAD, MILLICENT HANLEY, in
"FORSAKING ALL OTHERS"

ES FULLER, ROLAND YOUNG, ELIZABETH
ATTERSON, LAURA HOPE CREWS in
"HER MASTER'S VOICE"

FRANCESCA
BRUNING

JOSEPH
COTTEN

MARGARET
SULLAVAN

ROLAND
YOUNG

JAMES DALE, LAURENCE OLIVIER in
"THE GREEN BAY TREE"

LEY RIDGES,
ANDERSON in
E MASK AND
HE FACE"

EVA LE GALLIENNE,
RICHARD WARING in
"ROMEO AND JULIET"

GEORGE M. COHAN, EDA HEINEMANN, ELISHA COOK, JR., GENE LOCKHART,
MARJORIE MARQUIS, WALTER VONNEGUT, JR., ADELAIDE BEAN in
"AH, WILDERNESS!"

EDITH VAN CLEVE,
DOUGLAS MONTGOMERY
in
"AMERICAN DREAM"

FAY BAINTER
as
TOPSY

HENRY HULL as
JEETER LESTER

MARGARET WYCHERLY, SAM BYRD, RUTH HUNTER, DEAN JAGGER, HENRY HULL in
"TOBACCO ROAD"

MRS. PATRICK CAMPBELL in
"A PARTY"

LLOYD NOLAN, MARY HOLSMAN, FRANCESCA BRUNING,
RANKIN MANSFIELD in "ONE SUNDAY AFTERNOON"

ALFRED LUNT, NOEL COWARD, LYNN FONTANNE in
"DESIGN FOR LIVING"

KATHARINE CORNELL, LUTHER ADLER, JAMES RENNIE
"ALIEN CORN"

ELEANOR HICKS, CHARLES WALDRON, HUNTER GARDNER,
SETH ARNOLD, RAYMOND WALBURN, PEGGY CONKLIN,
TONIO SELWART in "THE PURSUIT OF HAPPINESS"

MIRIAM HOPKINS, GAGE CLARKE, JOSEPH COTTEN, HELEN
CLAIRE, REED BROWN, JR., FREDERIC WORLOCK,
CORA WITHERSPOON in "JEZEBEL"

ELISHA COOK, JR., CECILIA LOFTUS, BEN LACKLAN
RICHARD WHORF, RUTH GORDON in
"THREE-CORNERED MOON"

WALTER C. KELLY, SHEPPARD
STRUDWICK, MARY PHILIPS in
"BOTH YOUR HOUSES"

JOSEPH SPURIN-CALLEIA, BRAMWELL
FLETCHER, OSWALD YORKE in
"TEN MINUTE ALIBI"

MIRIAM HOPKINS in
"JEZEBEL"

ELEANOR PHELPS,
BLAINE CORDNER in
"WE, THE PEOPLE"

ELEANOR AUDLEY, PAUL McGRA
ALNEY ALBA, GEORGE M. COHA
"PIGEONS AND PEOPLE"

rted by Blanche Bates, Frances Starr,
offrey Wardell and Colin Clive. "She
ves Me Not," an engaging comedy,
atured Burgess Meredith, John Beal
d Polly Walters. Miriam Hopkins
ed in "Jezebel." "The Green Bay Tree"
Mordaunt Shairp was skillfully acted
James Dale and Laurence Olivier.
merican Dream," a dramatic trilogy
ich somehow missed the mark, was
ayed by Josephine Hull, Claude Rains,
ith Van Cleve and Douglas Mont-
mery. Elmer Rice was represented by
Ve, the People," W. Somerset Maugh-
n by "For Services Rendered," and
oliere's "The School for Husbands"
as revived. "Run, Little Chillun" was
successful negro folk drama by Hall
hnson.

Roland Young and Laura Hope Crews
re in "Her Master's Voice;" Audrey
ristie and Bruce Macfarlane were in
Sailor, Beware!;" Mary Morris and
nne Revere were in "Double Door;"
d Judith Anderson, Humphrey Bogart,
irley Booth and Leo G. Carroll were
"The Mask and the Face." "Three-
ornered Moon," a screwball comedy,
as acted by Ruth Gordon, Cecilia Loft-
, Brian Donlevy and Richard Whorf;
d the comedy about bundling, "The
ursuit of Happiness," featured Tonio
lwart and Peggy Conklin.

Jerome Kern's "Roberta" was the out-
anding musical comedy of the year. The
iginal cast included George Murphy,
ay Middleton, Bob Hope, Fay Temple-
n, Tamara, Sydney Greenstreet, Lyda
oberti and Fred MacMurray.

"Strike Me Pink" was a lively revue
ith Hope Williams, Jimmy Durante,
oy Atwell and Lupe Velez. Joe Cook
as seen in "Hold Your Horses," and
velyn Herbert sang in "Melody" sup-
orted by Walter Woolf, Everett Mar-
all, George Houston and Hal Skelly.
arilyn Miller, Helen Broderick, Clifton
ebb and Ethel Waters brightened the
ng-lasting "As Thousands Cheer." The
usic of Kurt Weill was heard in "Three
enny Opera," a revised version of John
ay's "Beggars' Opera." "Murder at the
anities" set a whodunit to music involv-
g James Rennie, Bela Lugosi and Olga
aclanova. William Gaxton and Victor
loore were co-starred in "Let 'Em Eat
ake." "Champagne Sec," none other
an "Die Fledermaus," was sung by
elen Ford, Peggy Wood, John E. Haz-
ard and Kitty Carlisle.

PHILIP MERIVALE   HELEN HAYES, HELEN MENKEN in   HELEN HAYES
"MARY OF SCOTLAND"

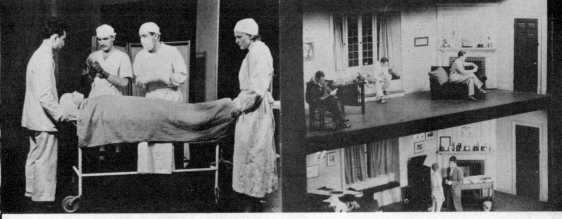

ELIA KAZAN, PHOEBE BRAND, SANFORD MEISNER,
ALEXANDER KIRKLAND, MARGARET BARKER in
"MEN IN WHITE"   "SHE LOVES ME NOT"

AUDREY CHRISTIE, BRUCE MACFARLANE, EDWARD   RUTH SHEPLEY, BRIAN DONLEVY in
CRAVEN in "SAILOR, BEWARE!"   "THREE AND ONE"

EDWARD CRAVEN,   LIONEL PAPE, FRANCES STARR, BLANCHE BATES,   KATHARINE HEPBURN,
BRUCE MACFARLANE in   KATHARINE HEPBURN in "THE LAKE"   COLIN CLIVE in
"SAILOR, BEWARE!"   "THE LAKE"

213

ETHEL WATERS
in
"AS THOUSANDS CHEER"

JUNE WALKER
in
"THE SCHOOL FOR HUSBANDS"

OSGOOD PERKINS

FAY TEMPLETON
in
"ROBERTA"

MOLLY
PICON

WALTER WOOLF
in
"MELODY"

JOSEPHINE HUS
ROBERT CHISHO
"THE 3-PENNY O

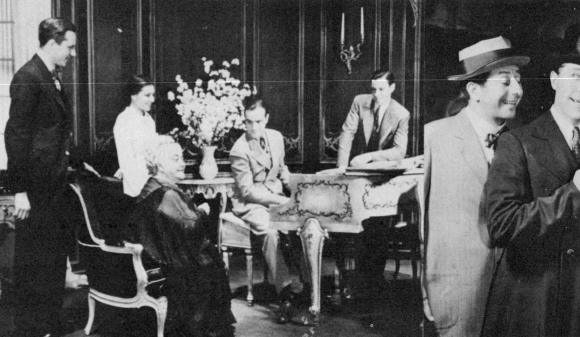

MARILYN MILLER, CLIFTON WEBB in
"AS THOUSANDS CHEER"

RAY MIDDLETON, TAMARA, FAY TEMPLETON, BOB HOPE,
GEORGE MURPHY in "ROBERTA"

DAVE CHASEN, JOE COOK in
"HOLD YOUR HORSES"

PEGGY
CONKLIN

GEORGE
HUSTON

LYDA
ROBERTI

GEORGE
MURPHY

PEGGY
WOOD

FRED
MacMURRAY

LAURA HOPE
CREWS

BLAINE
CORDNER

ROBERT
CHISHO

CLIFTON WEBB, HELEN BRODERICK in
"AS THOUSANDS CHEER"

WALTER WOOLF, EVELYN HERBERT,
HAL SKELLY in "MELODY"

WILLIAM GAXTON, LOIS MORAN, VICTOR
MOORE in "LET 'EM EAT CAKE"

HELEN FORD, KITTY CARLISLE in
"CHAMPAGNE SEC"

YVONNE
PRINTEMPS

LUCILE WATSON, ROMAINE CALLENDER in
"POST ROAD"

FRANCES STARR, HELEN
GAHAGAN, EDITH BARRETT in
"MOOR BORN"

SYBIL THORNDIKE, ESTELLE WINWOOD, VIOLA
KEATS in "THE DISTAFF SIDE"

JAMES STEWART,
JUDITH ANDERSON in
"DIVIDED BY THREE"

Y BAINTER, WALTER HUSTON in
"DODSWORTH"

1934 The biggest hits of 1934 were "The Children's Hour" by Lillian Hellman, "Dodsworth" with Walter Huston and Fay Bainter, and "Personal Appearance" with Gladys George. Moderate successes included "The Shining Hour" with Raymond Massey and Gladys Cooper, famous English star making her American debut, "No More Ladies" with Melvyn Douglas, Lucile Watson and Ruth Weston, "The Wind and the Rain" with Frank Lawton, Rose Hobart and Mildred Natwick, "The Milky Way" with Hugh O'Connell and Brian Donlevy, "The Distaff Side" with Sybil Thorndike and Estelle Winwood, "Merrily We Roll Along" with Walter Abel, Mary Philips, Kenneth MacKenna and Cecilia Loftus, "The First Legion" with Bert Lytell, Charles Coburn and Whitford Kane, "The Farmer Takes a Wife" with June Walker and Henry Fonda, "Post Road" with Lucile Watson, "Accent on Youth" with Constance Cummings, Nicholas Hannen and Irene Purcell. Artistic ventures were Clemence Dane's fantasy "Come of Age" with Judith Anderson, "Richard of Bordeaux" with Dennis King, "Yellow Jack" with Geoffrey Kerr, James Stewart and Myron McCormick, Sean O'Casey's "Within the Gates" with Lillian Gish and Bramwell Fletcher, a revival of "L'Aiglon" with Eva Le Gallienne and Ethel Barrymore, and an opera, "4 Saints in 3 Acts," with a libretto by Gertrude Stein and music by Virgil Thompson.

JOHN HALLIDAY, JANE COWL in
"RAIN FROM HEAVEN"

LLOYD
NOLAN

RUTH
WESTON

KENNETH
MacKENNA

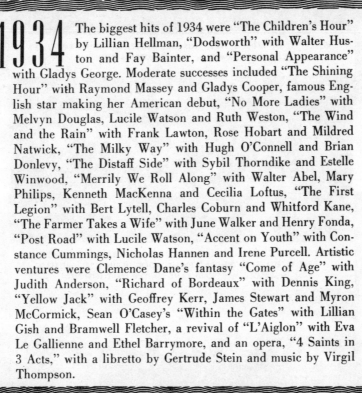
GLADYS
COOPER

FRANK
LAWTON

SYBIL
THORNDIKE

BRIAN
DONLEVY

SELENA
ROYLE

SPRING
BYINGTON

ARIA OUSPENSKAYA
in
"DODSWORTH"

EVA LE GALLIENNE
as
"L'AIGLON"

KATHARINE CORNELL
as JULIET

BASIL RATHBONE
as ROMEO

EDITH EVANS
as NURSE

BRIAN AHERNE
as MERCUTIO

in
"ROMEO AND JULIET"

215

ADRIENNE ALLEN, RAYMOND MASSEY, GLADYS COOPER in "THE SHINING HOUR"

ROBERT KEITH, ANNE REVERE, FLORENCE McGEE, KATHERINE EMERY, KATHERINE EMMETT in "THE CHILDREN'S HOUR"

PIERRE FRESNAY, YVONNE PRINTEMPS in "CONVERSATION PIECE"

HARLAN TUCKER, CHARLES COBURN, PEDRO DE CORDOBA, HAROLD MOULTON, BERT LYTELL, THOS. FINDLAY, PHILIP WOOD, JOHN LITEL, WILLIAM INGERSOLL, WHITFORD KANE in "THE FIRST LEGION"

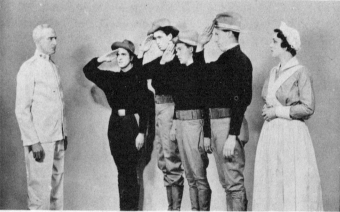

HENRY FONDA, KATE MAYHEW, JUNE WALKER in "THE FARMER TAKES A WIFE"

JOHN MILTERN, SAM LEVENE, JAMES STEWART, MYRON McCORMICK, EDWARD ACUFF, KATHERINE WILSON in "YELLOW JACK"

MELVYN DOUGLAS, LUCILE WATSON, REX O'MALLEY in "NO MORE LADIES"

DEAN JAGGER

IRENE BROWNE

GEORGE BLACKWOOD

ESTELLE WINWOOD

FRANCINE LARRIMORE, SAM LEVENE in "SPRING SONG"

FRANK LAWTON, ALEXANDER ARCHDALE, ROSE HOBART, LOWELL GILMORE in "THE WIND AND THE RAIN"

INA CLAIRE, WALTER SLEZAK in "ODE TO LIBERTY"

Among the stars, Francine Larrimore was in "Spring Song," Fred Stone appeared in "Jayhawker," Tallulah Bankhead was in "Dark Victory," Philip Merivale in "Valley Forge," Ina Claire in "Ode to Liberty," Jane Cowl in "Rain From Heaven," Jean Arthur in "The Bride of Torozko," Judith Anderson with James Stewart in "Divided By Three," Norma Terris with George Blackwood in "So Many Paths," and Katharine Cornell played in "Romeo and Juliet" with Basil Rathbone, Brian Aherne and Edith Evans.

Dramas of social protest were "Stevedore," "The Sailors of Cattaro" and "They Shall Not Die," suggested by the Scottsboro case, with Ruth Gordon and Claude Rains. Other plays on the boards were Eugene O'Neill's play "Days Without End," "Big Hearted Herbert" with J. C. Nugent, Elmer Rice's "Judgement Day," "Small Miracle," "Page Miss Glory," "Gold Eagle Guy," "Ladies Money" and "Moor Born," a play about the Bronte Sisters with Frances Starr, Helen Gahagan and Edith Barrett.

The D'Oyly Carte Opera Company from London made a visit to these shores and scored immediate success. Their first visit here was in 1879. The company, singing an extensive Gilbert and Sullivan repertoire during this visit, included Martyn Green, Darrell Fancourt, Muriel Dickson, Derek Oldham, Sydney Granville, Leslie Rands, Marjorie Eyre, Dorothy Gill and John Dean.

ETHEL BARRYMORE with Her Children SAMUEL and ETHEL COLT in "L'AIGLON"

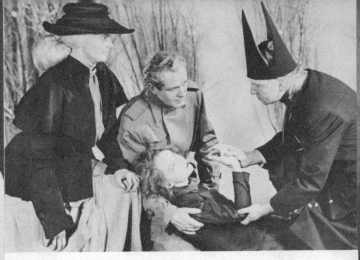

MARY MORRIS, LILLIAN GISH, BRAMWELL FLETCHER, MOFFAT JOHNSTON in "WITHIN THE GATES"

"STEVEDORE" with REX INGRAM (second from right)

GLADYS GEORGE, PHILIP OBER in "PERSONAL APPEARANCE"

HUGH O'CONNELL, LEO DONNELLY, WILLIAM FORAN BRIAN DONLEVY in "THE MILKY WAY"

DENNIS KING in "RICHARD OF BORDEAUX"

STEPHEN HAGGARD, JUDITH ANDERSON in "COME OF AGE"

MOLLY PICON   ROGER STEARNS   RAY DOOLEY   ALLAN JONES

Billie Burke, the widow of Flo Ziegfeld, gave the Messrs. Shubert permission to use the name, and so a "Ziegfeld Follies" opened at the Winter Garden with Fannie Brice and Willie Howard. "The Great Waltz" which glorified the music of the Strausses was given an elaborate production at the Center Theatre in Radio City with Guy Robertson, Marion Claire and Alexandra Danilova. "New Faces," an intimate revue, caught the public fancy with Leonard Sillman, Imogene Coca, Henry Fonda, Nancy Hamilton, Roger Stearns, Hildegarde Halliday and Charles Walter in the cast. Cole Porter's "Anything Goes" was a smash hit with Victor Moore, William Gaxton and Ethel Merman. Noel Coward's "Conversation Piece" brought Yvonne Printemps, Pierre Fresnay and Irene Browne to the New York stage; and Lucienne Boyer and Vincente Escudero were seen in "Continental Varieties." Other musicals of the year were "Life Begins at 8:40" with Bert Lahr, Ray Bolger, Luella Gear, Frances Williams and Brian Donlevy, "Saluta" with Milton Berle, "Calling All Stars" with Gertrude Niesen, "Say When" with Bob Hope, Harry Richman, and Taylor Holmes, "Revenge With Music" with Charles Winninger, Libby Holman and Georges Metaxa, and "Thumbs Up" with Clark and McCullough, Ray Dooley, Eddie Dowling, J. Harold Murray and Sheila Barrett.

ERIC LINDEN, MARGARET CALLAHAN in "LADIES' MONEY"

ROMAINE CALLENDER, FANIA MARINOFF in "JUDGMENT DAY"

JEAN ARTHUR, VAN HEFLIN in "THE BRIDE OF TOROZKO"

RAY BOLGER, LUELLA GEAR, FRANCES WILLIAMS, BERT LAHR in "LIFE BEGINS AT 8:40"

FANNIE BRICE as BABY SNOOKS in "ZIEGFELD FOLLIES"

VICTOR MOORE, BETTINA HALL, WILLIAM GAXTON in "ANYTHING GOES"

LILLIAN SAVIN, HAL CONKLIN, JUNE MEIER in "THE DRUNKARD"

IMOGENE COCA

CHARLES WALTER, IMOGENE COCA in "NEW FACES"

ROSE KING, RAY DOOLEY, BOBBY CLARK in "THUMBS UP"

LUCIENNE BOYER

"4 SAINTS IN 3 ACTS

WILLIE HOWARD in "ZIEGFELD FOLLIES"

PATRICIA BOWMAN, EVERETT MARSHALL, GERTRUDE NIESEN, JACK WHITING, MITZI MAYFAIR in "CALLING ALL STARS"

H. REEVES-SMITH, MARIE BURKE, GUY ROBERTSON, MARION CLAIRE in "THE GREAT WALTZ"

ALEXANDRA DANILOVA in "THE GREAT WALTZ

BOB HOPE, LINDA WATKINS, HARRY RICHMAN in "SAY WHEN"

MARTYN GREEN in "RUDDIGORE"

MARTYN GREEN, SYDNEY GRANVILLE in "THE YEOMEN OF THE GUARD"

ALLAN JONES, EVELYN HERBERT in "BITTER SWEET"

REX O'MALLEY, CHARLES WINNINGER in "REVENGE WITH MUSIC"

RALPH RICHARDSON
as
MERCUTIO

"DEAD END"

MAURICE EVANS
as
ROMEO

MARGO, BURGESS MEREDITH
in
"WINTERSET"

1935

The theatre was slowly recovering from the depression years and 1935 was the most satisfying since the crash of '29. The number of plays produced was less but the plays that did reach the boards were, as a whole, of a higher calibre. The Pulitzer Prize for the year went to Zoe Akins' "The Old Maid." The drama critics, who had been dissatisfied with the Pulitzer awards, formed an organization called the Drama Critics Circle to give out their own award for the best play. Their first selection went to Maxwell Anderson's "Winterset."

Helen Hayes was having one of her greatest successes with "Victoria Regina" and Leslie Howard was equally happy with "The Petrified Forest." Jane Cowl had a hit with "The First Lady" and Elisabeth Bergner, making her first American appearance, won acclaim in "Escape Me Never." Alfred Lunt and Lynn Fontanne played in Noel Coward's "Point Valaine," but it was a failure so they turned to Shakespeare's "The Taming of the Shrew" which was a hit. Katharine Cornell also returned to Shakespeare after the failure of "Flowers of the Forest." She revived "Romeo and Juliet" and this time her Romeo was Maurice Evans, a young English actor who was making his American debut. Her Mercutio was Ralph Richardson and the Nurse was played by Florence Reed and then by Blanche Yurka. Also in the cast was Tyrone Power, Jr. who won film fame later. Nazimova appeared in Shaw's "The Simpleton of the Unexpected Isles" but it failed so she turned to Ibsen's "Ghosts" and her portrayal of Mrs. Alving won the cheers of the critics and the public. Harry Ellerbe as Oswald also came in for his share of

JUDITH ANDERSON, HELEN MENKEN
in
"THE OLD MAID"

WILFRID LAWSON, JOAN MARION,
ERNEST LAWFORD, COLIN CLIVE in
"LIBEL"

IRENE RICH,
GEORGE M. COHAN in
"SEVEN KEYS TO BALDPATE"

COLIN KEITH-JOHNSTON
in
"PRIDE AND PREJUDICE"

MILLICENT GREEN,
ALAN BAXTER in
"BLACK PIT"

DORIS DALTON, DENNIS KING, LEO G. CARROLL
in
"PETTICOAT FEVER"

219

LESLIE HOWARD in
"THE PETRIFIED FOREST"

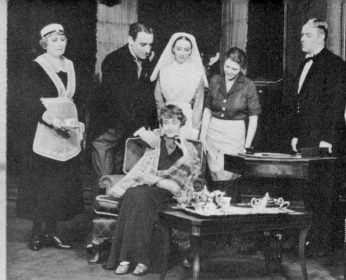

ELFRIDA DERWENT, HENRY DANIELL, GRACE GEORGE, JUSTINE CHASE,
BARBARA SHIELDS, THOMAS CHALMERS in
"KIND LADY"

GARSON KANIN
in
"BOY MEETS GIRL"

RUTH GORDON
in
"A SLEEPING
CLERGYMAN"

ELIA KAZAN
in
"WAITING FOR
LEFTY"

EDITH VAN C
in
"THREE MEN
A HORSE

TEDDY HART, WILLIAM LYNN, SHIRLEY BOOTH, MILLARD MITCHELL,
SAM LEVENE in
"THREE MEN ON A HORSE"

HUMPHREY BOGART
in
"THE PETRIFIED FOREST"

ONA MUNSON, HARRY ELLERBE, ALLA NAZIMOVA
in
"GHOSTS"

ALLA NAZIMOVA, ROMNEY BRENT in
"THE SIMPLETON OF THE
UNEXPECTED ISLES"

ROMAN BOHNEN, CLIFFORD ODE

JUDSON LAIRE, JANE COWL, THOMAS FINDLAY in
"FIRST LADY"

LILY CAHILL   MORGAN FARLEY   NANCE O'NEIL   PHILIP MERIVALE

CHARLES McCLELLAND, ALLYN JOSLYN, JOYCE ARLING, JEROME COWAN,
ROYAL BEAL in
"BOY MEETS GIRL"

HELEN HAYES in "VICTORIA REGINA"

TALLULAH BANKHEAD
in
"RAIN"

PIERRE FRESNAY
in
"NOAH"

praise. Grace George had a hit with "Kind Lady." Tallulah Bankhead revived "Rain" for 47 performances and then appeared in a light comedy, "Something Gay," supported by Hugh Sinclair and Walter Pidgeon.

Among the plays that were hits without any stars billed were "Dead End," "Blind Alley," "Three Men On A Horse," "Boy Meets Girl," "Awake and Sing," "The Night of January 16," "Pride and Prejudice," "Libel" and "Parnell." "Noah" with Pierre Fresnay was an artistic success. Moderate successes included "The Bishop Misbehaves" with Walter Connolly, "Petticoat Fever" with Dennis King, "Remember the Day" with Russell Hardie, Francesca Bruning and Frankie Thomas, "Fly Away Home" with Thomas Mitchell, "Moon Over Mulberry Street" with Gladys Shelley and Cornel Wilde, "Mulatto" with Rose McClendon, "Ceiling Zero" with Osgood Perkins and Margaret Perry, "Black Pit" with Alan Baxter, and "Till the Day I Die" and "Waiting for Lefty," two highly dramatic plays by Clifford Odets which were performed together. Nance O'Neil was in "Bitter Oleander" and "Night in the House," Eva Le Gallienne played "Rosmersholm," Ruth Gordon with Glenn Anders, Charlotte Walker and Ernest Thesiger played in "A Sleeping Clergyman," the Players' Club revived "Seven Keys to Baldpate" with

221

MARGARET RAWLINGS, JOHN EMERY,
EFFIE SHANNON in
"PARNELL"

BRENDA FORBES, ADRIANNE ALLEN, JOHN HALLORAN,
COLIN KEITH-JOHNSTON in
"PRIDE AND PREJUDICE"

ROY HARGRAVE, RUTH FELLOWS,
GEORGE COULOURIS in
"BLIND ALLEY"

OSGOOD PERKINS, LOUIS HAYWARD, LYNN FONTANNE,
ALFRED LUNT in
"POINT VALAINE"

LYNN FONTANNE, ALFRED LUNT in
"THE TAMING OF THE SHREW"

RICHARD
BENNETT

BLANCHE
SWEET

BERT LAHR, WILLIE AND EUGENE
HOWARD, CLIFF EDWARDS in
"GEORGE WHITE'S SCANDALS"

BEATRICE
DE NEERGAARD

ERIC
DRESSLER

TODD DUNCAN, ANNE BROWN in
"PORGY AND BESS"

"JUMBO"

JIMMY SAVO in
"PARADE"

JOHN GARFIELD, LUTHER ADLER, PHOEBE BRAND, ART SMITH in
"AWAKE AND SING"

RUSSELL HARDIE, FRANCESCA BRUNING,
FRANKIE THOMAS in
"REMEMBER THE DAY"

GRIFFITH JONES, ELISABETH BERGNER, HUGH SINCLAIR in
"ESCAPE ME NEVER"

ALAN MARSHAL, JANE WYATT,
WALTER CONNOLLY in
"THE BISHOP MISBEHAVES"

ARY
ILIPS

EDMUND
GWENN

WALTER WOOLF, NANCY McCORD in
MAY WINE"

WALTER
CONNOLLY

MARGO

MARY BOLAND
in
"JUBILEE"

LES WALTERS in
"JUBILEE"

JACKIE KELK, MONTGOMERY CLIFT in
"JUBILEE"

ELISABETH
BERGNER

George M. Cohan, Walter Hampden, James T. Powers, Josephine Hull, Irene Rich and Ernest Glendinning, and Philip Merivale with Gladys Cooper revived "Macbeth" and "Othello" with no success.

Mary Boland was a riotous hit in "Jubilee" supported by Melville Cooper, June Knight, Charles Walters and fifteen year old Montgomery Clift. The Theatre Guild produced "Porgy and Bess," a musical version of DuBose Heyward's "Porgy" with music by George Gershwin. Its original run was only 124 performances, but when Cheryl Crawford revived it in 1942 it was more successful and clocked up 286 performances.

Billy Rose's "Jumbo," a spectacular combination of circus and musical comedy was the last attraction to play the Hippodrome before it was torn down. "Jumbo" was a big hit but not a financial success. The cast included Jimmy Durante, Poodles Hanneford, Gloria Grafton and Donald Novis. Ken Murray was the principal comedian of "Earl Carroll's Sketch Book;" Beatrice Lillie, Ethel Waters, Eleanor Powell, Eddie Foy, Jr. and Paul Haakon were in "At Home Abroad;" Rudy Vallee, Bert Lahr and Eugene and Willie Howard were in "George White's Scandals" and a popular musical "May Wine" had Walter Woolf, Nancy McCord and Walter Slezak in the cast.

223

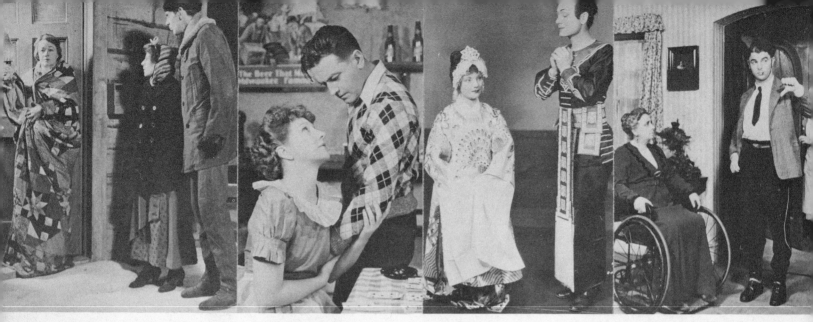

PAULINE LORD, RUTH GORDON, RAYMOND MASSEY
in
"ETHAN FROME"

MARY PHILIPS, RICHARD BARTHELMESS
in
"THE POSTMAN ALWAYS RINGS TWICE"

HELEN CHANDLER, BRAMWELL FLETCHER
in
"LADY PRECIOUS STREAM"

MAY WHITTY, EMLYN WILLIAMS, BETTY JARDI
in
"NIGHT MUST FALL"

JESSIE ROYCE
LANDIS

HENRY
TRAVERS

PAULINE
LORD

JOHN
BEAL

WENDY
HILLER

EMLYN
WILLIAMS

JUDITH
ANDERSON

RICHARD
BARTHELMESS

ILKA
CHASE

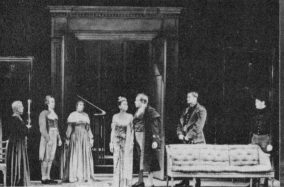    

EFFIE SHANNON, MYRON McCORMICK, RUTH MATTESON
KATHARINE CORNELL, WALTER ABEL, VICTOR
COLTON, FRANKLYN DAVIS in
"THE WINGLESS VICTORY"

KATHARINE CORNELL
as OPARRE

KATHARINE CORNELL
as SAINT JOAN

TYRONE POWER, JR., JOSEPH HOLLAND, KATHARINE CORN
in
"SAINT JOAN"

224   ALLA NAZIMOVA
in
"HEDDA GABLER"

RUTH GORDON
in
"THE COUNTRY WIFE"

1936 Two Pulitzer Prizes were awarded during the year 1936: Robert E. Sherwood's "Idiot's Delight" for the 1935-36 season and George S. Kaufman and Moss Hart's "You Can't Take It With You" for the 1936-37 season. The hit plays included "The Women" with Margalo Gillmore, Ilka Chase and Audrey Christie, "Brother Rat" with Eddie Albert, Frank Albertson and Jose Ferrer, "Tovarich" with John Halliday and Marta Abba, "Call It A Day" with Gladys Cooper and Philip Merivale, and "Stage Door" with Margaret Sullavan. Pauline Lord, Ruth Gordon and Raymond Massey won praise for their performances in "Ethan Frome." Miss Gordon also gave a rewarding performance in a spirited revival of "The Country Wife." Katharine Cornell revived "Saint Joan" with Maurice Evans playing The Dauphin. Later she appeared in Maxwell Anderson's "The Wingless Victory" while Maurice Evans was seen as Napoleon in "St. Helena." Ina Claire with Osgood Perkins appeared in "End of Summer;" Tallulah Bankhead was in George Kelly's "Reflected Glory;" Wendy Hiller was first seen on the New York stage in "Love on the Dole;" William Gillette, at the age of eighty, was appearing in a revival of "Three Wise Fools;" Nazimova revived "Hedda Gabler" with

JHN HALLIDAY, MARTA ABBA, JAMES TRUEX
in
"TOVARICH"

GERTRUDE LAWRENCE, NOEL COWARD
in
"TONIGHT AT 8:30"

FRANK CONLAN, FRANK WILCOX, JOSEPHINE HULL
in
"YOU CAN'T TAKE IT WITH YOU"

WALLACE FORD	HELEN FORD	VAN JOHNSON	MARY RYAN	CARL BRISSON	JANE PICKENS	JOHN GARFIELD	BETTY FIELD	PRESTON FOSTER

RY MASON, KATHLEEN FITZ, EDDIE ALBERT, JOSE FERRER, FRANK ALBERTSON in
BROTHER RAT"

JOHN BUCKMASTER, GLADYS COOPER, JEANNE DANTE, FLORENCE WILLIAMS, PHILIP MERIVALE in
"CALL IT A DAY"

ADRIENNE MARDEN, MARGALO GILLMORE, ILKA CHASE, AUDREY CHRISTIE, MARJORIE MAIN in
"THE WOMEN"

McKay Morris and Harry Ellerbe; Walter Hampden again played "Cyrano de Bergerac;" and the Players' Club revived "The County Chairman" with Charles Coburn, Alexander Kirkland, Mary Ryan, Dorothy Stickney and James Kirkwood.

John Gielgud scored a great success in "Hamlet" with Judith Anderson, Queen Gertrude and Lillian Gish, Ophelia. It ran for 132 performances while Leslie Howard who opened in "Hamlet" a month after Mr. Gielgud was not a success and played only 39 times. Emlyn Williams, appearing in his own play, "Night Must Fall," shared acting honors with May Whitty. Noel Coward and Gertrude Lawrence were seen in a series of short plays by Mr. Coward which were billed as "Tonight at 8:30." The first group consisted of "Hands Across the Sea," "The Astonished Heart" and "Red Peppers;" the second, of "We Were Dancing," "Fumed Oak" and "Shadow Play;" and the third, of "Ways and Means," "Still Life" and "Family Album."

Other new plays were Robert Turney's "Daughters of Atreus" with Eleonora Mendelssohn and Maria Ouspenskaya, "Russet Mantle" with Martha Sleeper and John Beal, "Lady Precious Stream" with Helen Chandler and Bramwell Fletcher, "Fresh Fields" starring Margaret Anglin, "Co-Respondent Unknown"

ALFRED LUNT   LYNN FONTANNE
in
"IDIOT'S DELIGHT"

JOHN GIELGUD, MALCOLM KEEN, JUDITH ANDERSON, ARTHUR BYRON, JOHN EMERY in
"HAMLET"

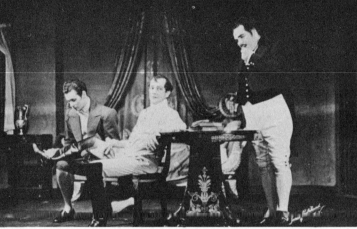

JOHN GIELGUD
as
HAMLET

JUDITH ANDERSON, LILLIAN GISH
in
"HAMLET"

BARRY SULLIVAN, MAURICE EVANS, JULES EPAILLY
in
"ST. HELENA"

MAURICE EVANS
in
"ST. HELENA"

OSGOOD PERKINS, INA CLAIRE,
DORIS DUDLEY in
"END OF SUMMER"

TALLULAH BANKHEAD, PHILLIP REED
in
"REFLECTED GLORY"

LESLIE HOWARD
as
HAMLET

| AUDREY CHRISTIE | HENRY HULL | CHRYSTAL HERNE | WILLIAM HARRIGAN | MARTA ABBA | ERNEST LAWFORD | MARGARET ANGLIN | WALTER ABEL | FLOREN EDNE |

226

MARGARET SULLAVAN, FRANCES FULLER
in
"STAGE DOOR"

EVELYN VARDEN, JAY FASSETT, MARTHA SLEEPER,
JAMES LARMORE, MARGARET DOUGLASS in
"RUSSET MANTLE"

FRANK VOSPER, JESSIE ROYCE LANDIS
in
"LOVE FROM A STRANGER"

"WHITE HORSE INN"
with KITTY CARLISLE (center)

SARGENT, PHILIP TONGE, MARGARET ANGLIN
in
"FRESH FIELDS"

LUELLA GEAR, RAY BOLGER, MONTY WOOLLEY
in
"ON YOUR TOES"

Reading the Play From "THE SHOW IS ON"
BEATRICE LILLIE (left of table), REGINALD GARDINER (right)

BERT LAHR'S 'SONG OF THE WOODMAN'
in
"THE SHOW IS ON"

ALEXANDER KIRKLAND, PHOEBE BRAND,
MARGARET BARKER in
"THE CASE OF CLYDE GRIFFITHS"

HOPE EMERSON, JOHN ALEXANDER
in
"SWING YOUR LADY"

CARL BRISSON, RUBY
MERCER in
"FORBIDDEN MELODY"

JOSEPHINE BAKER
in
"ZIEGFELD FOLLIES"

IMOGENE
COCA

WALTER C.
KELLY

DEREK
FAIRMAN

PAULA
TRUEMAN

BOB HOPE, ETHEL MERMAN
in
"RED, HOT AND BLUE"

MARIA OUSPENSKAYA,
ELEONORA MENDELSSOHN
in "DAUGHTERS OF ATREUS"

with James Rennie, Peggy Conklin and Ilka Chase, "The Post-man Always Rings Twice" with film star Richard Barthelmess, "Love From A Stranger" with Frank Vosper and Jessie Royce Landis, "Swing Your Lady" with Hope Emerson, John Alexander and Joe Laurie, Jr., and "Johnny Johnson" with John Garfield, Elia Kazan, Robert Lewis, Luther Adler and Russell Collins.

The Federal Theatre Project of the WPA began producing during the year and among the plays presented were "Chalk Dust," "The Living Newspaper," "Class of 1929" and T. S. Eliot's poetic drama, "Murder in the Cathedral."

Among the outstanding musicals were "On Your Toes" with Ray Bolger, "The Show Is On" with Beatrice Lillie and Bert Lahr, "The White Horse Inn" with William Gaxton and Kitty Carlisle, "New Faces of 1936" with Imogene Coca, Tom Ruther-furd and Van Johnson, "Red, Hot and Blue" with Ethel Merman, Jimmy Durante, Bob Hope and Paul and Grace Hartman, "Zieg-feld Follies" with Fannie Brice, Bobby Clark, Jane Pickens, Josephine Baker and Gypsy Rose Lee, and "Forbidden Melody" with Carl Brisson.

227

MAURICE EVANS as RICHARD II

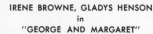

BRODERICK CRAWFORD, CLAIRE LUCE, WALLACE FORD in
"OF MICE AND MEN"

IRENE BROWNE, GLADYS HENSON
in
"GEORGE AND MARGARET"

CONWAY TEARLE, TALLULAH BANK
in
"ANTONY AND CLEOPATRA"

| LESLIE BANKS | SARA ALLGOOD | ROGER LIVESEY | KATHARINE HEPBURN | ROBERT LEWIS |

FRANCES FULLER, WHITFORD KANE, FLORA CAMPBELL in
"EXCURSION"

LEE BAKER, PHYLLIS WELCH, BURGESS MEREDITH in
"HIGH TOR"

1937

The most surprising event of the year was the sensational success Maurice Evans had with his revival of Shakespeare's "Richard II" which had not been presented in New York since 1878 when Edwin Booth played the young king. Opening in February it played 133 performances. Closing for the summer it resumed in September for 38 performances more before starting a coast-to-coast tour. Other successful revivals were "Candida" with Katharine Cornell, "A Doll's House" with Ruth Gordon and Dennis King and "Julius Caesar" presented in modern uniforms without scenery by the Mercury Theatre which had been organized by Orson Welles and John Houseman. Besides Mr. Welles, the cast included Joseph Cotten, Hiram Sherman, George Coulouris and Martin Gabel.

The Drama Critics' Circle award for the 1936-37 season went to Maxwell Anderson's "High Tor," and for the 1937-38 season to John Steinbeck's "Of Mice and Men." The Group Theatre had a success with Clifford Odets' "Golden Boy" and so did Alfred Lunt and Lynn Fontanne with "Amphitryon 38." "Antony and Cleopatra" as done by Tallulah Bankhead and Conway Tearle was a failure and so was "Othello" with Walter Huston in the title role and Brian Aherne as Iago.

The comedies popular in 1937 were "Room Service" with Eddie Albert and Betty Field, "Yes, My Darling Daughter" with

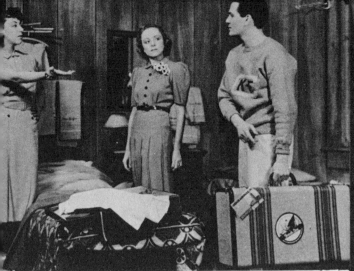

JANET FOX, KATHERINE LOCKE, JOHN GARFIELD
in
"HAVING WONDERFUL TIME"

URGESS MEREDITH, LILLIAN GISH
in
"THE STAR-WAGON"

ROGER LIVESEY, CLAUDIA MORGAN, SARA
ALLGOOD, IAN McLEAN in
"STORM OVER PATSY"

PAULINE FREDERICK, HENRY HULL, DUDLEY DIGGES, MARGO in
"THE MASQUE OF KINGS"

SAM LEVENE, ALEXANDER ARSO, EDDIE ALBERT, PHILIP LOEB in
"ROOM SERVICE"

KATHARINE CORNELL as CANDIDA

ORSON
WELLES

PAULINE
FREDERICK

EDDIE
ALBERT

MINNIE
DUPREE

CHARLES
RICHMAN

Lucile Watson and Violet Heming, "Susan and God" with Gertrude Lawrence, "Having Wonderful Time" with John Garfield, "Storm Over Patsy" with Sara Allgood and Roger Livesey, "Excursion" with Whitford Kane and Shirley Booth, "Father Malachy's Miracle" with Al Shean, "George and Margaret" with Irene Browne, "The Star-Wagon" with Lillian Gish and Burgess Meredith, and "French Without Tears" with Frank Lawton and Penelope Dudley Ward.

Max Reinhardt staged an impressive Biblical spectacle, "The Eternal Road," with a musical score by Kurt Weill. "The Masque of Kings" was played by Pauline Frederick, Henry Hull, Dudley Digges and Margo. George M. Cohan was in "Fulton of Oak Falls" and Ethel Barrymore in "The Ghost of Yankee Doodle." Orson Welles' revival of Marlowe's "Dr. Faustus" was the outstanding Federal Theatre production of the year, and the Abbey Theatre Players from Dublin returned in a repertory of Irish plays.

"Pins and Needles," an intimate revue presented by the International Ladies' Garment Workers' Union, was a big hit, and so was George M. Cohan in "I'd Rather Be Right." Other musicals that scored were "Babes in Arms," "Virginia," "Between the Devil," "Frederika" and "Hooray for What!" with Ed Wynn.

229

BENEDICT MacQUARRIE,
AL SHEAN in
"FATHER MALACHY'S MIRACLE"

MONA BARRIE, RONALD
GRAHAM in
"VIRGINIA"

GEORGE M. COHAN
in
"I'D RATHER BE RIGHT"

WYNN MURRAY, ALF
DRAKE in
"BABES IN ARMS"

DENNIS KING, RUTH GORDON, WALTER SLEZAK in
"A DOLL'S HOUSE"

ALFRED LUNT, LYNN FONTANNE in
"AMPHITRYON 38"

MAX REINHARDT'S
"THE ETERNAL ROAD"

JOY
HODGES

WALTER HUSTON
as
OTHELLO

EVELYN LAYE, JACK BUCHANAN,
ADELE DIXON in
"BETWEEN THE DEVIL"

ERNEST TRUEX, HELEN GLEASON, DENNIS KING, EDITH KING
in
"FREDERIKA"

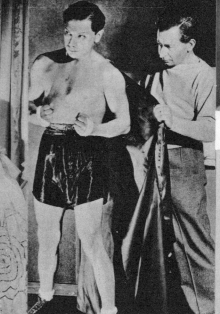

LUTHER ADLER, ART SMITH
in
"GOLDEN BOY"

RONALD
GRAHAM

BRIAN AHE
as
IAGO

NANCY KELLY,
GERTRUDE LAWRENCE, PAUL McGRATH in
"SUSAN AND GOD"

PEGGY CONKLIN, VIOLET HEMING, LUCILE WATSON,
CHARLES BRYANT in
"YES, MY DARLING DAUGHTER"

"JULIUS CAESAR"
with ORSON WELLES (left)

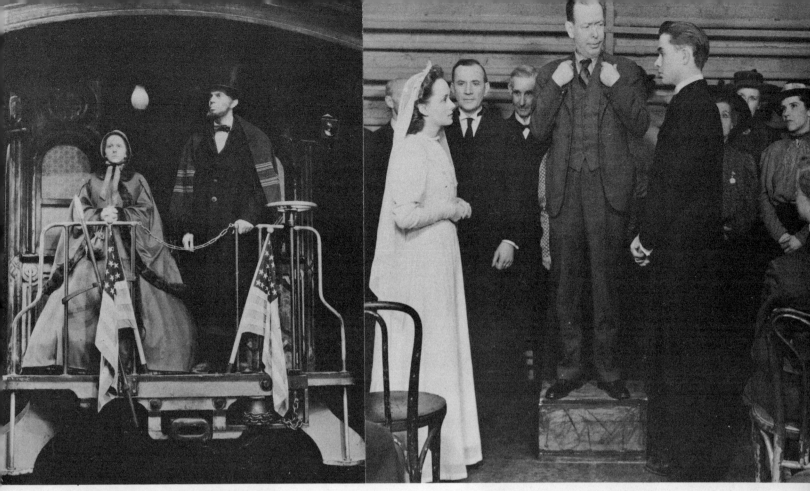

MURIEL KIRKLAND, RAYMOND MASSEY in
"ABE LINCOLN IN ILLINOIS"

MARTHA SCOTT, FRANK CRAVEN, JOHN CRAVEN in
"OUR TOWN"

MARGARET PERRY, FRANK
LOVEJOY in
"THE GREATEST SHOW
ON EARTH"

RICHARD GORDON, STEPHEN
COURTLEIGH, DORIS DALTON in
"THE FABULOUS INVALID"

LEIF ERICKSON, ELIZABETH
YOUNG in
"ALL THE LIVING"

WHITFORD KANE, MAURICE EVANS, DONALD RANDOLPH in
"HAMLET"

WHITFORD KANE
in
"HAMLET"

RAYMOND MASSEY
as
ABE LINCOLN

FRANK CRAVEN
in
"OUR TOWN"

1938 The Pulitzer Prize for the 1937-38 season went to Thornton Wilder's "Our Town" which was acted without scenery and employed a narrator. This role was acted by Frank Craven. The 1938-39 award was bestowed on Robert E. Sherwood's "Abe Lincoln in Illinois."

Other successes of the year included "On Borrowed Time" with Dudley Digges achieving stardom after forty years in the theatre; "What a Life," a comedy by Clifford Goldsmith about the Aldrich family which later became popular on the radio; "Oscar Wilde" with Robert Morley making his Broadway debut; and "Shadow and Substance" with Cedric Hardwicke, Julie Haydon and Sara Allgood.

"Hamlet" was produced for the first time on the New York stage in its full length version with Maurice Evans in the title role. The performance began at 6:30 with an intermission for dinner. Other revivals were "The Circle" with Grace George and Tallulah Bankhead, "Outward Bound" with Laurette Taylor, Florence Reed, Alexander Kirkland and Helen Chandler, "Lightnin'" with Fred Stone, "The Sea Gull" with Alfred Lunt and Lynn Fontanne, and the Mercury Theatre productions of "The Shoemaker's Holiday," "Heartbreak House" and "Danton's Death." Other plays of the year were "Whiteoaks" with Ethel Barrymore,

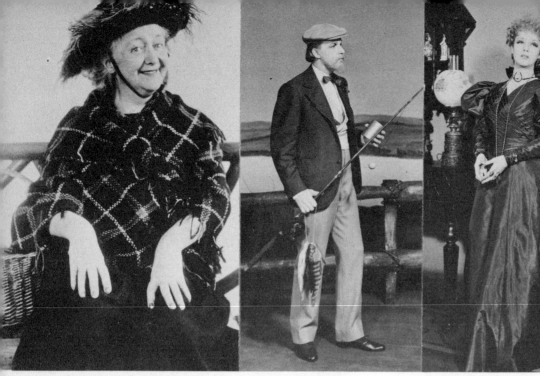
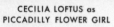

CECILIA LOFTUS as
PICCADILLY FLOWER GIRL

ALFRED LUNT in
"THE SEA GULL"

LYNN FONTANNE in
"THE SEA GULL"

ROBERT MORLEY as
OSCAR WILDE

FRANK CONROY, DUDLEY DIGGES, PETER HOLDEN
in
"ON BORROWED TIME"

CEDRIC HARDWICKE, JULIE HAYDON
in
"SHADOW AND SUBSTANCE"

HIRAM SHERMAN, WHITFORD KANE
in
"THE SHOEMAKER'S HOLIDAY"

JOHN CAROL, ROBERT MORLEY
in
"OSCAR WILDE"

MAIDEL TURNER, BETTY FIELD, EZRA STONE, JAMES CORNER
in
"WHAT A LIFE"

JOSEPH COTTEN, ALICE FROST, VINCENT PRICE
in
"THE SHOEMAKER'S HOLIDAY"

BRENDA FORBES, ERSKINE SANFORD, ORSON WELLES, M.
CHRISTIANS, JOHN HOYSRADT, PHYLLIS JOYCE, VINCE
PRICE, GERALDINE FITZGERALD, GEORGE COULOURIS in
"HEARTBREAK HOUSE"

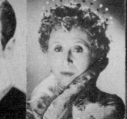

MAURICE EVANS   EVA LE GALLIENNE   CEDRIC HARDWICKE   GLADYS COOPER   ROBERT FLEMYNG   BLANCHE YURKA   GEORGE SIDNEY   CONSTANCE CUMMINGS   MARTIN GA

Spring Meeting" with Gladys Cooper and A. E. Matthews, "Once Is Enough" with Ina Claire, "Missouri Legend" with Dorothy Gish and Dean Jagger, "Merchant of Yonkers" with Jane Cowl, "Here Come the Clowns" with Eddie Dowling and Madge Evans, "Wine of Choice" with Alexander Woollcott and Claudia Morgan, "Madame Capet" with Eva Le Gallienne, "Bachelor Born," "Kiss the Boys Goodbye," "Rocket to the Moon," "The Fabulous Invalid," "Time and the Conways," "Dame Nature" and "All the Living." The Federal Theatre Project was very active and "Prologue to Glory," "Haiti" and "One-Third of a Nation" were its most interesting productions.

After playing for years in vaudeville, the team of Olsen and Johnson appeared on Broadway in a zany revue called "Hellzapoppin" which achieved a run of 1,404 performances. Victor Moore, William Gaxton and Sophie Tucker were the stars of "Leave It To Me," but a girl from Texas named Mary Martin won the most cheers singing "My Heart Belongs to Daddy," and Gene Kelly was in the chorus. Other musicals were "I Married An Angel" with Dennis King and Vera Zorina; "The Boys From Syracuse," a musical version of Shakespeare's "A Comedy of Errors," with Jimmy Savo and Eddie Albert; "Knickerbocker Holiday" with Walter Huston singing and dancing; "Sing Out the News" with Mary Jane Walsh and Hiram Sherman; "The Two Bouquets" with Alfred Drake and Patricia Morison; "Right This Way" with Blanche Ring, Joe E. Lewis and Guy Robertson; "You Never Know" with Lupe Velez, Clifton Webb and Libby Holman; "Great Lady" with Irene Bordoni, Tullio Carminati, Norma Terris and Andre Eglevsky; and Marc Blitzstein's "The Cradle Will Rock," a musical labor-drama which was played without scenery or costumes and with the composer playing the score and serving as an announcer at the piano.

ALEXANDER WOOLLCOTT in "WINE OF CHOICE"

LAURETTE TAYLOR in "OUTWARD BOUND"

ETHEL BARRYMORE in "WHITEOAKS"

GRACE GEORGE, TALLULAH BANKHEAD in "THE CIRCLE"

RICHARD BISHOP, DEAN JAGGER, JOSE FERRER, CLARE WOODBURY, DAN DURYEA, DOROTHY GISH (on floor) in "MISSOURI LEGEND"

PERCY WARAM, JANE COWL in "MERCHANT OF YONKERS"

[JES]SICA TANDY, MARY JONES, SYBIL THORNDIKE, HAZEL TERRY, [GO]DFREY KENTON, CHRISTOPHER QUEST, HELENA PICKARD in "TIME AND THE CONWAYS"

LENORE CHIPPENDALE, WYRLEY BIRCH, REYNOLDS DENNISTON, ETHEL COLT, STEPHEN HAGGARD, PETER FERNANDEZ, ETHEL BARRYMORE, RICHARD CARLSON, ROBERT SHAYNE in "WHITEOAKS"

SHELDON LEONARD, PHILIP OBER, HELEN CLAIRE, MILLARD MITCHELL, CARMEL WHITE, HUGH MARLOWE, BENAY VENUTA in "KISS THE BOYS GOODBYE"

[M]ARTHA SCOTT

ANDRE EGLEVSKY

GUS EDWARDS

ALICE FROST

JOE E. LEWIS

MARY MARTIN

LEIF ERICKSON

JANE COWL

PETER HOLDEN

DAISY BERNIER, HIRAM SHERMAN, MARY JANE
WALSH, MICHAEL LORING, in
"SING OUT THE NEWS"

SOPHIE TUCKER, WILLIAM GAXTON, VICTOR MOORE
in
"LEAVE IT TO ME"

OLE OLSEN, SHIRLEY WAYNE, CHIC JOHNSON
in
"HELLZAPOPPIN"

EDDIE ALBERT, JIMMY SAVO in
"THE BOYS FROM SYRACUSE"

MARY MARTIN singing "MY HEART BELONGS TO DADDY"
in "LEAVE IT TO ME", GENE KELLY is first left of Miss Martin

TEDDY HART, RONALD GRAHAM in
"THE BOYS FROM SYRACUSE"

CHARLES LASKY, VERA ZORINA WALTER SLEZAK, VIVIENNE SEGAL
in
"I MARRIED AN ANGEL"

WALTER
HUSTON

SOPHIE
TUCKER

PATRICIA MORISON, ALFRED
DRAKE in
"THE TWO BOUQUETS"

HIRAM SHERMAN
in
"SING OUT THE NEWS"

DOROTHY GISH
in
"MISSOURI LEGEND"

MILDRED NATWICK
in
"MISSOURI LEGEND"

WALTER HUSTON with JEANNE MADDEN and CHORUS
in
"KNICKERBOCKER HOLIDAY"

MARY JANE WALSH
in
"SING OUT THE NEWS"

RICHARD KOLLMA
in
"KNICKERBOCK
HOLIDAY"

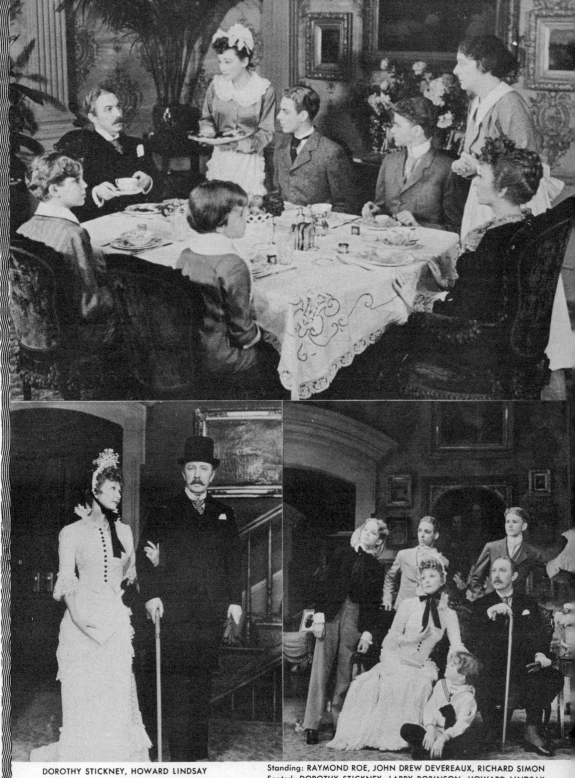

1939

Both the Pulitzer Prize and the Drama Critics' Circle Award for 1939 went to William Saroyan's "The Time of Your Life," but the greatest success of the year and the longest run in the history of the New York theatre was achieved by "Life With Father" with 3,224 performances. Howard Lindsay and Russel Crouse wrote it and Mr. Lindsay with his wife Dorothy Stickney played the leads in the original production. "Tobacco Road" which held the honor of the longest run on Broadway until now was still on the boards with James Barton in the lead. "The Man Who Came to Dinner" by Moss Hart and George S. Kaufman was another rousing hit with Monty Woolley creating the title role. Lillian Hellman's "The Little Foxes" provided Tallulah Bankhead with one of her finest roles with Patricia Collinge also outstanding in the cast. Katharine Hepburn was tremendously popular in Philip Barry's "The Philadelphia Story" and so was Gertrude Lawrence in "Skylark." Katharine Cornell with Laurence Olivier as her leading man also had a hit with "No Time For Comedy." Ethel Waters scored a personal triumph in "Mamba's Daughters" which was her first play without music. Maurice Evans' revival of "Henry IV, Part I" was a fine production skillfully staged by Margaret Webster.

Other plays and players of the year were "The American Way" with Fredric March and Florence Eldridge, "The Primrose Path" with Betty Field, Helen Westley, Russell Hardie and Betty Garde, "The Gentle People" with Franchot Tone and Sylvia Sidney, "The White Steed" with Barry Fitzgerald and Jessica Tandy, "Family Portrait" with Judith Anderson, "Ladies and Gentlemen" with Helen Hayes and Philip Merivale, "Key Largo" with Paul Muni, "Dear Octopus" with Lillian Gish, Lucile Watson and Jack Hawkins, "The Mother" with Nazimova and Montgomery Clift, "See My

DOROTHY STICKNEY, HOWARD LINDSAY

Standing: RAYMOND ROE, JOHN DREW DEVEREAUX, RICHARD SIMON
Seated: DOROTHY STICKNEY, LARRY ROBINSON, HOWARD LINDSAY

Top (Clockwise): HOWARD LINDSAY, KATHARINE BARD, JOHN DREW DEVEREAUX, RICHARD SIMON, DOROTHY BERNARD, DOROTHY STICKNEY, LARRY ROBINSON, RAYMOND ROE in
"LIFE WITH FATHER"

LILY CAHILL, WALLIS CLARK   NYDIA WESTMAN, ARTHUR MARGETSON   LILLIAN GISH, PERCY WARAM in "LIFE WITH FATHER"   DOROTHY GISH, STANLEY RIDGES   ELAINE IVANS, LOUIS CALHERN

JULIE HAYDON, EDDIE DOWLING in
"THE TIME OF YOUR LIFE"

MAURICE EVANS in
"HENRY IV, PART I"

PAUL MUNI in
"KEY LARGO"

MONTY WOOLLEY, DAVID BURNS in
"THE MAN WHO CAME TO DINNER"

EVELYN VARDEN, JAMES HARKER, JUDITH ANDERSON,
PHILIP COOLIDGE, TOM EWELL, LOIS AUSTIN, NORMAN
STUART, RONALD REISS, VIRGINIA CAMPBELL in
"FAMILY PORTRAIT"

LAURENCE OLIVIER, KATHARINE CORNELL
in
"NO TIME FOR COMEDY"

SAM LEVENE, ELSPETH ERIC, LEIF ERICKSON, PHILIP
COOLIDGE, BERT LYTELL, BRAMWELL FLETCHER in
"MARGIN FOR ERROR"

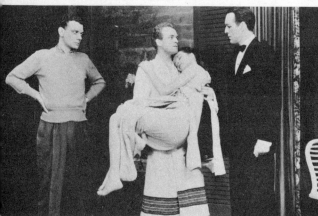

JOSEPH COTTEN, VAN HEFLIN, KATHARINE HEPBURN,
FRANK FENTON in
"THE PHILADELPHIA STORY"

ETHEL WATERS
in
"MAMBA'S DAUGHTERS"

BETTY GARDE, BETTY FIELD, HELEN WESTLEY,
MARILYN ERSKINE in
"PRIMROSE PATH"

FRANCES FARMER
LUTHER ADLER, in
"THUNDER ROCK"

CLIFTON WEBB, ESTELLE
WINWOOD in "THE IMPORTANCE
OF BEING EARNEST"

"THE AMERICAN WAY"

FLORENCE ELDRIDGE,
FREDRIC MARCH in
"THE AMERICAN WAY"

LILLIAN GISH,
JACK HAWKINS
"DEAR OCTOPUS"

KATHARINE HEPBURN in
"THE PHILADELPHIA STORY"

PATRICIA COLLINGE in
"THE LITTLE FOXES"

ENID MARKEY in
"MORNING'S AT SEVEN"

SHIRLEY BOOTH in
"THE PHILADELPHIA
STORY"

EDMOND O'BRIEN in
"HENRY IV, PART I"

LEE BAKER, TALLULAH BANKHEAD, CARL BENTON REID,
DAN DURYEA, CHARLES DINGLE in
"THE LITTLE FOXES"

NAZIMOVA,
MONTGOMERY CLIFT in
"THE MOTHER"

SYLVIA SIDNEY,
ELIA KAZAN in
"THE GENTLE
PEOPLE"

MILTON BERLE, EDDIE NUGENT,
TEDDY HART in
"SEE MY LAWYER"

TALLULAH BANKHEAD in
"THE LITTLE FOXES"

Lawyer" with Milton Berle, "Thunder Rock" with Luther Adler and Frances Farmer, "Morning's At Seven" with Dorothy Gish, Effie Shannon, John Alexander and Enid Markey, "The World We Make" with Margo, "Farm of Three Echoes" with Ethel Barrymore, "Margin For Error" with Bert Lytell, and "My Heart's in the Highlands."

The D'Oyly Carte Opera Company played a return engagement of Gilbert and Sullivan repertoire, and the year offered many new musicals. "DuBarry Was A Lady" with Ethel Merman, Bert Lahr and Betty Grable was a hit and so was "Too Many Girls" with Mary Jane Walsh, Marcy Westcott, Eddie Bracken, Desi Arnaz, Diosa Costello, Hal LeRoy and Van Johnson. Beatrice Lillie was in "Set to Music," Bill Robinson in "The Hot Mikado," Bobby Clark, Carmen Miranda, Bud Abbott and Lou Costello in "The Streets of Paris," and Donald Brian, Jack Whiting and Eve Arden were in "Very Warm For May." Among the revues were "George White's Scandals" with Willie and Eugene Howard, Ella Logan, Ben Blue and Ann Miller, "The Straw Hat Revue" with Imogene Coca, Danny Kaye, Alfred Drake and Jerome Robbins, and "One For the Money" with Nancy Hamilton, Brenda Forbes, Gene Kelly, Keenan Wynn, William Archibald and Alfred Drake.

237

CARMEN MIRANDA
in
"THE STREETS OF PARIS"

BILL ROBINSON, GWENDOLYN REYDE
in
"THE HOT MIKADO"

JAMES BARTON
in
"TOBACCO ROAD"

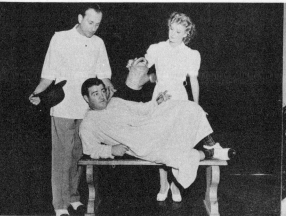

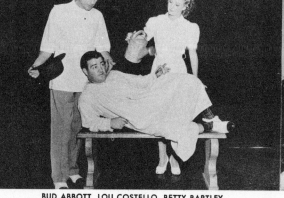

GERTRUDE LAWRENCE
in
"SKYLARK"

BUD ABBOTT, LOU COSTELLO, BETTY BARTLEY
in
"THE STREETS OF PARIS"

EVA LE GALLIENNE, FRANK FAY, ELSIE JANIS
in
"FRANK FAY VAUDEVILLE"

| BETTY GRABLE | CHARLES WALTERS | ETHEL MERMAN | ALFRED DRAKE | EVE ARDEN | MARTYN GREEN | HOPE WILLIAMS | GENE KELLY | NANCY HAMILTON |

238

RICHARD HAYDN, BEATRICE LILLIE
in
"SET TO MUSIC"

KEENAN WYNN, DON LOPER, BRENDA FORBES, ROBERT SMITH, GEORGE LLOYD,
PHILIP BOURNEUF, (Kneeling) WILLIAM ARCHIBALD, GENE KELLY in
"ONE FOR THE MONEY"

BETTY GRABLE, CHARLES WALTERS
in
"DuBARRY WAS A LADY"

ETHEL BARRYMORE in
"THE CORN IS GREEN"

LYNN FONTANNE, MONTGOMERY CLIFT, ALFRED LUNT
in
"THERE SHALL BE NO NIGHT"

RICHARD WARING, ETHEL BARRYMORE
in
"THE CORN IS GREEN"

BURGESS MEREDITH, INGRID BERGMAN
in
"LILIOM"

THOMAS SPEIDEL, MARY MASON, JOSE
FERRER, J. RICHARD JONES, PHYLLIS
AVERY in
"CHARLEY'S AUNT"

ALEXANDER KNOX, JESSICA TANDY
in
"JUPITER LAUGHS"

1940 One of the memorable events of 1940 was Emlyn Williams' "The Corn Is Green" which offered Ethel Barrymore one of the finest roles of her career. The Pulitzer Prize went to Robert E. Sherwood's "There Shall Be No Night" which had Alfred Lunt and Lynn Fontanne in the cast. Long runs were achieved by "My Sister Eileen," "Johnny Belinda," "The Male Animal," "George Washington Slept Here" and "Separate Rooms." Flora Robson made her American debut in "Ladies in Retirement;" Jane Cowl and Peggy Wood were in "Old Acquaintance;" Walter Huston with Jessie Royce Landis was in "Love's Old Sweet Song;" Pauline Lord appeared in "Suspect;" George M. Cohan's last appearance on the stage was in "The Return of the Vagabond;" Franchot Tone and Lenore Ulric were in "The Fifth Column;" Molly Picon was playing in English in "Morning Star;" Gladys George starred in "Lady in Waiting;" and Florence Reed was in "The Flying Gerardos." John Barrymore returned to Broadway in "My Dear Children," while his daughter Diana Barrymore made her New York debut in "Romantic Mr. Dickens." Other new plays were "Two On An Island," Shaw's "Geneva," "Jupiter Laughs" and "Flight to the West."

WALTER HUSTON, JESSIE ROYCE LANDIS
in
"LOVE'S OLD SWEET SONG"

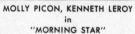

MOLLY PICON, KENNETH LEROY
in
"MORNING STAR"

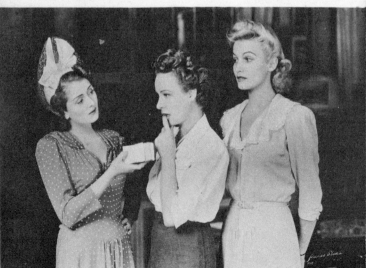

SHEILA TRENT, SHIRLEY BOOTH, JO ANN SAYERS
in
"MY SISTER EILEEN"

HELEN CRAIG, WILLARD PARKER
in
"JOHNNY BELINDA"

LENORE ULRIC, FRANCHOT TONE
in
"THE FIFTH COLUMN"

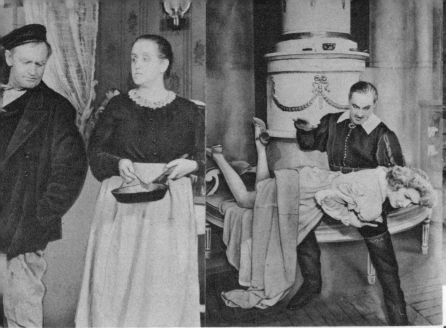

BARRY FITZGERALD, SARA ALLGOOD
in
"JUNO AND THE PAYCOCK"

JOHN BARRYMORE, DORIS DUDLEY
in
"MY DEAR CHILDREN"

PEGGY FRENCH, KENDALL CLARK, JEAN DIXON, ERNEST TRUEX,
PERCY KILBRIDE in
"GEORGE WASHINGTON SLEPT HERE"

There were many impressive revivals this year. Jose Ferrer was most successful with "Charley's Aunt." Laurence Olivier and Vivien Leigh appeared in "Romeo and Juliet;" Helen Hayes and Maurice Evans were in "Twelfth Night;" "Liliom" was played by Ingrid Bergman and Burgess Meredith; Sara Allgood and Barry Fitzgerald did "Juno and the Paycock;" and the Players' Club revived "Love for Love" with an all-star cast.

The musical hits included "Louisiana Purchase" with Victor Moore, William Gaxton, Vera Zorina and Irene Bordoni, "Panama Hattie" with Ethel Merman and James Dunn, "Cabin in the Sky" with Ethel Waters, Todd Duncan and Katherine Dunham, "Hold On To Your Hats" with Al Jolson and Martha Raye, "Boys and Girls Together" with Ed Wynn, "Higher and Higher" with Jack Haley and Marta Eggerth, "Keep Off the Grass" with Ray Bolger, Jimmy Durante and Ilka Chase, "Two For the Show" with Eve Arden, Betty Hutton, Alfred Drake, Keenan Wynn, William Archibald, Brenda Forbes and Tommy Wonder, and "Meet the People."

The first of the ice shows which became so popular opened at the Center Theatre in Radio City. It was called "It Happens On Ice" and it featured Joe Cook.

JANE COWL, KENT SMITH
in
"OLD ACQUAINTANCE"

JOHN CRAVEN, BETTY FIELD
in
"TWO ON AN ISLAND"

ALAN DINEHART, LYLE TALBOT,
GLENDA FARRELL in
"SEPARATE ROOMS"

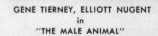

GENE TIERNEY, ELLIOTT NUGENT
in
"THE MALE ANIMAL"

HELEN HAYES, MAURICE EVANS
in
"TWELFTH NIGHT"

LAURENCE OLIVIER, VIVIEN LEIGH
in
"ROMEO AND JULIET"

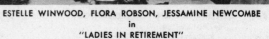

ESTELLE WINWOOD, FLORA ROBSON, JESSAMINE NEWCOMBE
in
"LADIES IN RETIREMENT"

241

VIVIENNE SEGAL, GENE KELLY
in
"PAL JOEY"

VAN JOHNSON, JUNE HAVOC
in
"PAL JOEY"

VICTOR MOORE, WILLIAM GAXTON, VERA ZORINA
in
"LOUISIANA PURCHASE"

KATHERINE DUNHAM, REX INGRAM in "CABIN IN THE SKY"

SARA ALLGOOD in 'JUNO AND THE PAYCOCK"

JOHN BARRYMORE in "MY DEAR CHILDREN"

FLORA ROBSON in "LADIES IN RETIREMENT"

SOPHIE STEWART in "TWELFTH NIGHT"

JACK HALEY, MARTA EG in "HIGHER AND HIGH

IRENE BORDONI
in
"LOUISIANA PURCHASE"

ETHEL MERMAN, RAGS RAGLAND, FRANK
HYERS, PAT HARRINGTON in
"PANAMA HATTIE"

ETHEL WATERS, DOOLEY WILSON
in
"CABIN IN THE SKY"

DIANA BARRYMORE
in
"ROMANTIC MR. DICKENS"

GLADYS GEORGE
in
"LADY IN WAITING"

GLENN LANGAN
in "GLAMOUR
PREFERRED"

PEGGY WOOD

DUDLEY DIGGES

CORNELIA OTIS SKINNER
in
PLAYERS CLUB revival of "LOVE FOR LOVE"

BOBBY CLARK

DOROTHY GISH

AL JOLSON
in
"HOLD ON TO YOUR HATS"

MARTHA

NTON SUNDBURG, JOSEPHINE HULL, JEAN ADAIR, HENRY HERBERT
in
"ARSENIC AND OLD LACE"

BETSY BLAIR, EUGENE LORING
in
"THE BEAUTIFUL PEOPLE"

LEO G. CARROLL, JUDITH EVELYN, VINCENT PRICE
in
"ANGEL STREET"

C. AUBREY SMITH
in
"SPRING AGAIN"

GRACE GEORGE
in
"SPRING AGAIN"

FRANCES STARR
in
"CLAUDIA"

CONRAD JANIS, PATRICIA
PEARDON in
"JUNIOR MISS"

VINCENT PRICE
in
"ANGEL STREET"

JUDITH EVELYN
in
"ANGEL STREET"

LOUIS BORELL, HELEN HAYES
in
"CANDLE IN THE WIND"

1941

The Drama Critics' Circle Award for 1941 went to Lillian Hellman's "Watch on the Rhine" which had Lucile Watson, Paul Lukas, Mady Christians and John Lodge in the cast. Two plays which had extremely long runs were "Arsenic and Old Lace" and "Angel Street." Josephine Hull, Boris Karloff, John Alexander and Jean Adair were in the former, while Judith Evelyn scored a personal triumph in the latter. "Claudia" with Dorothy McGuire. Donald Cook. Frances Starr and Olga Baclanova was an extremely popular comedy, and so were "Junior Miss" with Francesca Bruning. Alexander Kirkland and Patricia Peardon, and Noel Coward's "Blithe Spirit" with Peggy Wood, Clifton Webb, Leonora Corbett and Mildred Natwick.

"Spring Again" was acted by Grace George and C. Aubrey Smith, "The Talley Method" by Ina Claire and Philip Merivale, "Candle in the Wind" by Helen Hayes, Tonio Selwart and Evelyn Varden, "Clash By Night" by Tallulah Bankhead, Joseph Schildkraut and Robert Ryan, "Native Son" by Canada Lee, "The Wookey" by Edmund Gwenn, "Theatre" by Cornelia Otis Skinner, "Anne of England" by Barbara Everest and Flora Robson, and "Hope For A Harvest" by Fredric March and Florence

DIANA BARRYMORE, JAMES LA CURTO
in
"THE LAND IS BRIGHT"

BARBARA ROBBINS, ALEXANDER KIRKLAND, FRANCESCA
BRUNING, PHILIP OBER in
"JUNIOR MISS"

DOROTHY McGUIRE, DONALD COOK, FRANCES STARR
in
"CLAUDIA"

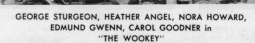

GEORGE STURGEON, HEATHER ANGEL, NORA HOWARD,
EDMUND GWENN, CAROL GOODNER in
"THE WOOKEY"

ETHEL
LEVEY

BORIS
KARLOFF

LUCILE WATSON, MADY CHRISTIANS, PAUL LUKAS
in
"WATCH ON THE RHINE"

CECIL HUMPHREYS, RALPH FORBES, WHITFORD KANE, KATHARINE
CORNELL, RAYMOND MASSEY in
"THE DOCTOR'S DILEMMA"

ALICE BELMORE CLIFFE, KATHA-
CORNELL in
"THE DOCTOR'S DILEMMA"

EDITH
MEISER

PAULA
LAURENCE

GERTRUDE LAWRENCE

LEONORA CORBETT, CLIFTON WEBB, PEGGY WOOD
in
"BLITHE SPIRIT"

MILDRED NATWICK
in
"BLITHE SPIRIT"

MARGARET DALE, DANNY KAYE, GERTRUDE LAWRENCE
in
"LADY IN THE DARK"

ENID MARKEY, HARRY CAREY
in
"AH, WILDERNESS!"

ROBERT
RYAN

CANADA
LEE

DOROTHY
McGUIRE

MAURICE EVANS, JUDITH ANDERSON
in
"MACBETH"

VICTOR MATURE   BERT LYTELL   WILLARD PARKER
in
"LADY IN THE DARK"

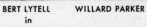

BERG NELSON, JO ANN DEAN
in
"IT HAPPENS ON ICE"

HANS VON TWARDOWSKI, BARBARA EVEREST, FLORA ROBSON
in
"ANNE OF ENGLAND"

SOPHIE TUCKER in the Strip Tease Number in
"HIGH KICKERS"

BARBARA
EVEREST

DANNY
KAYE

ANADA LEE, RENA MITCHELL
in
"NATIVE SON"

CHIC JOHNSON, CARMEN MIRANDA, OLE OLSEN
in
"SONS O' FUN"

Top: DANNY KAYE, (seated) EVE ARDEN, EDITH MEISER, VIVIAN
VANCE, (on floor) BENNY BAKER, JACK WILLIAMS in
"LET'S FACE IT"

CAROL
GOODNER

RALPH
FORBES

A CLAIRE, PHILIP MERIVALE
in
"THE TALLEY METHOD"

KENNETH BOWERS, ROSEMARY LANE, GIL STRATTON, JR.,
JACK JORDON, JR., MARTY MAY in
"BEST FOOT FORWARD"

CORNELIA OTIS
SKINNER

JOHN
LODGE

Eldridge. Other new plays of the year were "Mr. and Mrs. North," "The Beautiful People," "The Land Is Bright," "In Time to Come," "Out of the Frying Pan" and "Letters to Lucerne."

"Macbeth" was well received with Maurice Evans and Judith Anderson, and other Shakespearean productions were "As You Like It" with Helen Craig, Alfred Drake and Carol Stone and "Twelfth Night" with Beatrice Straight and Hurd Hatfield. Katharine Cornell revived "The Doctor's Dilemma" with a fine cast, and "Ah, Wilderness!" was revived with Harry Carey.

Gertrude Lawrence was a big hit in "Lady in the Dark" with Danny Kaye, Bert Lytell, Victor Mature and Macdonald Carey in her original support. Later Mr. Kaye played in "Let's Face It," a musical version of "The Cradle Snatchers." Olsen and Johnson hit the jackpot again with their rowdy revue "Sons O' Fun." "It Happens On Ice" was a popular ice show; Sophie Tucker and George Jessel were in "High Kickers;" Eddie Cantor returned to the stage in "Banjo Eyes;" Willie Howard was in "Crazy With the Heat" and Rosemary Lane, Nancy Walker and June Allyson were in "B   Foot Forward."

JUNE CLYDE, EDDIE CANTOR, AUDREY CHRISTIE
in
"BANJO EYES"

LEO G.
CARROLL

TALLULAH BANKHEAD, FLORENCE ELDRIDGE, FREDRIC MARCH, FRANCES HEFLIN, MONTGOMERY CLIFT in "THE SKIN OF OUR TEETH"

MONTGOMERY CLIFT

TALLULAH BANKHEAD

LARRY HUGO, VIOLA FRAYNE, FRANCES HEFLIN, CONRAD NAGEL, MIRIAM HOPKINS in "THE SKIN OF OUR TEETH"

FLORA ROBSON in "THE DAMASK CHEEK"

KATHARINE CORNELL, GERTRUDE MUSGROVE, TOM POWERS, JUDITH ANDERSON in "THE THREE SISTERS"

ESTELLE WINWOOD in "THE PIRATE"

| GLENN LANGAN | DORIS NOLAN | WILLIAM PRINCE | WENDY BARRIE |

246 LUISE RAINER

FLORENCE REED in "THE SKIN OF OUR TEETH"

RALPH MORGAN

1942 The Pulitzer Prize for 1942 was given to Thornton Wilder's controversial comedy "The Skin of Our Teeth" which was originally played by Tallulah Bankhead, Fredric March, Florence Eldridge, Florence Reed and Montgomery Clift.

"The Doughgirls," Joseph Fields' comedy about wartime Washington, was a substantial hit. Another highly successful comedy with a wartime background was "Janie" acted by Gwen Anderson, Linda Watkins and Herbert Evers. Joseph Schildkraut and Eva Le Gallienne appeared in Thomas Job's murder play, "Uncle Harry;" and Maxwell Anderson's "The Eve of St. Mark" was acted by William Prince and Aline MacMahon. Paul Muni appeared in "Yesterday's Magic" supported by Jessica Tandy and Alfred Drake. Katharine Hepburn and Elliott Nugent were in "Without Love;" Alfred Lunt, Lynn Fontanne and Estelle Winwood in "The Pirate;" and Mary Anderson scored as the neurotic young heroine of "Guest in the House."

"The Three Sisters" was revived by Katharine Cornell, Judith Anderson, Ruth Gordon, Dennis King, Edmund Gwenn, Tom Powers, Kirk Douglas, McKay Morris, Alexander Knox; and Miss Cornell also revived "Candida" with the support of Burgess Meredith, Raymond Massey and Mildred Natwick. Mary Boland,

CELESTE HOLM, JESSIE ROYCE LANDIS, EMMETT ROGERS in "PAPA IS ALL"

GREGORY PECK, GLADYS COOPER in "THE MORNING STAR"

RALPH FORBES, LUISE RAINER in "A KISS FOR CINDERELLA"

JOAN SPENCER, LEON AMES, MARY ANDERSON in "GUEST IN THE HOUSE"

ALFRED LUNT, LYNN FONTANNE in "THE PIRATE"

HELEN WALKER, ALEXANDER KNOX in "JASON"

EDDIE DOWLING, JULIE HAYDON in "HELLO, OUT THERE"

ELLIOTT NUGENT, KATHARINE HEPBURN in "WITHOUT LOVE"

Walter Hampden, Bobby Clark and Helen Ford were in "The Rivals;" Katina Paxinou played in "Hedda Gabler;" and Luise Rainer, Ralph Forbes and Glenn Langan were in "A Kiss for Cinderella."

"Jason" was played by Alexander Knox, Nicholas Conte and Helen Walker; "Papa Is All" by Jessie Royce Landis, Carl Benton Reid and Celeste Holm; "Cafe Crown" by Sam Jaffe, Morris Carnovsky and Sam Wanamaker; and "The Moon Is Down" by Ralph Morgan, Otto Kruger, William Eythe and Whitford Kane.

Flora Robson, Margaret Douglass, Myron McCormick, Celeste Holm and Zachary Scott were in "The Damask Cheek;" Gladys Cooper, Gregory Peck and Wendy Barrie in "The Morning Star;" Eddie Dowling and Julie Haydon in a double bill of "Magic" and "Hello, Out There;" and Dorothy Gish and Louis Calhern in "The Great Big Doorstep." Alec Guinness and Nancy Kelly were in "Flare Path;" Rhys Williams, Dudley Digges, Colin Keith-Johnston and Whitford Kane in "Lifeline;" and Lillian Gish, Stuart Erwin and Enid Markey in "Mr. Sycamore." "Heart of a City" was played by Gertrude Musgrove, Margot Grahame and Richard Ainley, and "The Strings, My Lord, Are False" by Walter Hampden and Ruth Gordon.

DOROTHY SARNOFF

HAL LeROY

BERTHA BELMORE

MYRON McCORMICK

"JANIE"

247

JOSEPH SCHILDKRAUT, EVA LE GALLIENNE
in
"UNCLE HARRY"

DICKIE MONAHAN, LOUIS CALHERN,
GERALD MATTHEWS, DOROTHY GISH in
"THE GREAT BIG DOORSTEP"

MARGOT GRAHAME, DENNIS HOEY,
GERTRUDE MUSGROVE, BEVERLY ROBERTS in
"HEART OF A CITY"

WILLIAM PRINCE, ALINE MacMAHON
in
"THE EVE OF ST. MARK"

MARIA PALMER, WHITFORD KANE, GEORGE KEANE,
LYLE BETTGER, RALPH MORGAN, JANE SEYMOUR in
"THE MOON IS DOWN"

DORIS NOLAN, VIRGINIA FIELD, ARLENE FRANCIS,
ARLEEN WHELAN in
"THE DOUGHGIRLS"

RUTH VIVIAN, FLORA ROBSON, MARGARET DOUGLASS
in
"THE DAMASK CHEEK"

BURGESS MEREDITH   MILDRED NATWICK   ALEXANDER KNOX   JULIE HAYDON   GREGORY PECK   GLADYS GEORGE   NICHOLAS CONTE

KATINA PAXINOU, KAREN MORLEY
in
"HEDDA GABLER"

TOP: MARY BOLAND, (centre) BOBBY CLARK, MARY BOLAND, WALTER HAMPDEN, (right) HELEN FORD
in
"THE RIVALS"

JESSICA TANDY, PAUL MUNI
in
"YESTERDAY'S MAGIC"

GEORGE JESSEL, KITTY CARLISLE, JACK
LEY, SALLY and TONY DeMARCO, ELLA
LOGAN in "SHOW TIME"

SKIPPY BAXTER, CAROL LYNNE
in
"STARS ON ICE"

GYPSY ROSE LEE, BOBBY CLARK
in
"STAR AND GARTER"

CONSTANCE MOORE, BENAY VENUTA,
RAY BOLGER in
"BY JUPITER"

"THIS IS THE ARMY"

"PORGY AND BESS"

ROBERT and LEWIS HIGHTOWER with FLOWER HUYER in
"BY JUPITER"

GIE HART, JIMMY SAVO
in
NE, WOMEN AND SONG"

AVON LONG
in
"PORGY AND BESS"

KATINA
PAXINOU

GRACIE
FIELDS

TOMMY
WONDER

JOHN LUND, ALICE
PEARCE in
"NEW FACES OF 1942"

GOWER & JEANNE
in
"COUNT ME IN"

BERT WHEELER

GYPSY ROSE LEE

HILDEGARDE

"By Jupiter" was the most popular musical comedy of the
year, and the leading roles were played by Ray Bolger, Constance Moore, Ronald Graham and Bertha Belmore. "Rosalinda,"
a new version of "Die Fledermaus," was produced by the New
Opera Company and acted by Dorothy Sarnoff, Virginia Mac-
Watters and Oscar Karlweis. "Porgy and Bess" was revived with
great success.

A series of vaudeville shows were presented this year. Lou
Holtz, Willie Howard, Phil Baker, Paul Draper and Hazel Scott
were in "Priorities of 1942;" Victor Moore, William Gaxton and
Hildegarde in "Keep 'Em Laughing;" Gracie Fields, Paul and
Grace Hartman and Argentinita in "Top-Notchers;" Ed Wynn,
Smith and Dale, Jane Froman and Carmen Amaya in "Laugh,
Town, Laugh!"; and George Jessel, Jack Haley and Ella Logan
were in "Show Time."

Bobby Clark and Gypsy Rose Lee were very popular in "Star
and Garter;" Jimmy Savo and Margie Hart in "Wine, Women
and Song;" Charles Butterworth, Luella Gear, Hal LeRoy and
Mary Healy in "Count Me In;" and Leonard Sillman, John Lund,
Marie Lund and Alice Pearce were in "New Faces of 1943."

ALFRED DRAKE
as CURLY

ALFRED DRAKE and
JOAN ROBERTS
in "OKLAHOMA"

JOAN ROBERTS
as LAUREY

"OKLAHOMA"

CELESTE HOLM
as
ADO ANNIE

JOSEPH BULOFF
as
ALI HAKIM

BETTY GARDE
as
AUNT ELLER

1943 The outstanding theatrical event of 1943 was the Theatre Guild's musical, "Oklahoma," which had the phenomenal run of 2,248 performances in New York, and which was also immensely popular on the road and in England. Leading roles in the original company were played by Alfred Drake, Joan Roberts, Betty Garde, Celeste Holm, Joseph Buloff and Howard da Silva.

The Drama Critics' Circle Award went to Sidney Kingsley's "The Patriots" which was acted by Raymond Edward Johnson, Cecil Humphreys, House Jameson and Madge Evans. There was no Pulitzer Prize awarded during the year. John Van Druten's "The Voice of the Turtle" was the most important comedy of the year, and its three characters were created by Margaret Sullavan, Elliott Nugent and Audrey Christie. Helen Hayes appeared in "Harriet," Elisabeth Bergner in "The Two Mrs. Carrolls," Katharine Cornell in "Lovers and Friends," Billie Burke in "This Rock," and Elsie Ferguson returned to the stage in "Outrageous Fortune." "Kiss and Tell" was played by Jessie Royce Landis, Joan Caulfield, Richard Widmark and Robert Keith; "Tomorrow the World" by Ralph Bellamy, Shirley Booth and Skippy Homeier; and "Three's A Family" by Doro Merande, Katharine Bard, Ruth Weston and William Wadsworth. Paul Robeson, Jose Ferrer, Uta Hagen and Margaret Webster appeared in an extremely successful revival of "Othello," and George Coulouris played in "Richard III."

Moss Hart's drama of the Air Force, "Winged Victory," had a long and successful run, and among the servicemen who appeared in the cast were Mark Daniels, Don Taylor, Barry Nelson, Alan Baxter, Michael Harvey, Donald Hanmer, George Reeves, Walter Reed, Peter Lind Hayes, Richard Travis, Ray Middleton and John Tyers. Eugenie Leontovich, Elena Miramova, Ludmilla Toretzka, Minnie Dupree, Charles Korvin and Carl Gose were in "Dark Eyes;" Sam Wanamaker, John Ireland, Barbara O'Neil and Morris Carnovsky in "Counterattack;" Geraldine Fitzgerald, Gregory Peck and Stella Adler in "Sons and Soldiers;" and Blanche Sweet, Virginia Gilmore, Dean Harens and Zachary Scott in "Those Endearing Young Charms." Betty Field, Ann Thomas and George Lambert appeared in "A New Life;" Oscar Homolka in "The Innocent Voyage;" Joan Blondell in "The Naked Genius," and Richard Widmark, Glenn Anders and Beatrice Pearson in "Get Away Old Man."

Mary Martin made a great hit in "One Touch of Venus" with John Boles, Kenny Baker and Paula Laurence; Ethel Merman had a hit in "Something For the Boys;" and also popular was the "Ziegfeld Follies" which had a cast that included Milton Berle, Arthur Treacher, Ilona Massey and Dean Murphy. "Carmen Jones" proved a sensation of the

HARRY STOCKWELL,
EVELYN WYCKOFF

MARY HATCHER,
WILTON CLARY

JOSE FERRER as
IAGO

MARGARET WEBSTER, JOSE FERRER
in
"OTHELLO"

PAUL ROBESON as
OTHELLO

JAMES ALEXANDER,
PEGGY ENGEL

HOWARD KEEL,
MARY HATCHER

MARGARET SULLAVAN, ELLIOTT NUGENT, AUDREY CHRISTIE in
"THE VOICE OF THE TURTLE"

KATHERINE DUNHAM
in
"TROPICAL REVUE"

JOHN RAITT, BETTY JANE WATSON
CURLYS and LAUREYS of "OKLAHOMA"

BOB KENNEDY, EVELYN WYCKOFF

BILLIE BURKE
in
"THIS ROCK"

DEAN NORTON, ELSIE FERGUSON
in
"OUTRAGEOUS FORTUNE"

ELSIE FERGUSON

251

SHIRLEY BOOTH, SKIPPY HOMEIER, RALPH BELLAMY in "TOMORROW THE WORLD"

JACK MANNING, EDNA THOMAS, HELEN HAYES, SYDNEY SMITH in "HARRIET"

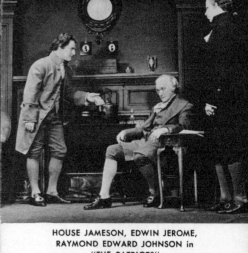

HOUSE JAMESON, EDWIN JEROME, RAYMOND EDWARD JOHNSON in "THE PATRIOTS"

BETTY FIELD, GEORGE LAMBERT in "A NEW LIFE"

VICTOR JORY, ELISABETH BERGNER in "THE TWO MRS. CARROLLS"

GREGORY PECK, GERALDINE FITZGERALD in "SONS AND SOLDIERS"

EUGENIE LEONTOVICH, ELENA MIRAMOVA, LUDMILLA TORETZKA in "DARK EYES"

BLANCHE SWEET, DEAN HARENS, VIRGINIA GILMORE, ZACHARY SCOTT in "THOSE ENDEARING YOUNG CHARMS"

| RICHARD TRAVIS | CHARLES KORVIN | JOAN BLONDELL | MICHAEL HARVEY | BEATRICE PEARSON | WALTER REED | ILONA MASSEY | JOHN BOLES | JAMES MONKS |

252 RICHARD WIDMARK, FRANCES BAVIER, ROBERT KEITH, JOAN CAULFIELD, JESSIE ROYCE LANDIS, TOMMY LEWIS in "KISS AND TELL"

SAM WANAMAKER, MORRIS CARNOVSKY in "COUNTERATTACK"

GEORGE COULOURIS as RICHARD III

EDMOND O'BRIEN, KEVIN McCARTHY, DON TAYLOR, KEITH ANDES, MARK DANIELS, DICK HOGAN in "WINGED VICTORY"

MARTA EGGERTH, JAN KIEPURA in
"THE MERRY WIDOW"

MURIEL SMITH, JACK CARR in
"CARMEN JONES"

MARY MARTIN, KENNY BAKER in
"ONE TOUCH OF VENUS"

BILL JOHNSON, ETHEL MERMAN in
"SOMETHING FOR THE BOYS"

MILTON BERLE, ILONA MASSEY, ARTHUR TREACHER,
SUE RYAN, DEAN MURPHY in
"ZIEGFELD FOLLIES"

ROBERT CHISHOLM,
VIVIENNE SEGAL in
"A CONNECTICUT YANKEE"

HARRY K. MORTON,
ANN PENNINGTON in
"THE STUDENT PRINCE"

ERA-ELLEN

MILTON
BERLE

MURIEL
SMITH

LUTHER
SAXON

LAWRENCE
FLETCHER

VIVIENNE
SEGAL

RICHARD
WIDMARK

VIRGINIA
GILMORE

RAY
MIDDLETON

"EARLY TO BED"
JOHN LUND left

year, and was given a lusty performance by an all-colored cast headed by Muriel Smith and Luther Saxon. The Bizet operatic score was used in a special arrangement, and the Carmen story was re-told in a modern war-plant background by Oscar Hammerstein 2nd. Other new musicals of the year were "Early to Bed" with Richard Kollmar, John Lund, Muriel Angelus, Jane Kean and George Zoritch; "Laugh Time" with Ethel Waters, Frank Fay, Bert Wheeler and Buck and Bubbles; "What's Up" with Jimmy Savo; and "My Dear Public" with Willie Howard and Nanette Fabray. Marta Eggerth and Jan Kiepura revived "The Merry Widow" with great success, and "A Connecticut Yankee" played by Robert Chisholm, Vivienne Segal, Dick Foran and Vera-Ellen was also revived.

253

BARTLETT ROBINSON, KAY COULTER, HOWARD SMITH, PHYLLIS POVAH,
JOHN DALL, VIRGINIA GILMORE in
"DEAR RUTH"

MONTGOMERY CLIFT, CORNELIA OTIS SKINNER,
DENNIS KING in
"THE SEARCHING WIND"

LEO G. CARROLL, MARGARET PHILLIPS,
JANET BEECHER in
"THE LATE GEORGE APLEY"

"ANNA LUCASTA"

1944

"Harvey," Mary Chase's fantastic comedy about an invisible rabbit, won the Pulitzer Prize, chalked up 1,517 performances on Broadway, and was a great success throughout the country. Its role of Elwood Dowd offered Frank Fay the best acting part of his career and Josephine Hull was also happily cast. "Anna Lucasta," a drama of Negro family life in a small industrial town, was another big hit with Hilda Simms playing the title role. Other plays that had notably long runs include "I Remember Mama" with Mady Christians and Oscar Homolka; "Ten Little Indians" with Estelle Winwood, Halliwell Hobbes, Claudia Morgan and Michael Whalen; "Jacobowsky and the Colonel" with Louis Calhern, Oscar Karlweis and Annabella; "The Late George Apley" with Leo G. Carroll, Janet Beecher, Margaret Dale and Margaret Phillips; "Over 21," a comedy by and with Ruth Gordon; and "Wallflower," a comedy by Reginald Denham and actress Mary Orr who also appeared in it.

Ethel Barrymore played in "Embezzled Heaven," Billie Burke and Frank Craven in "Mrs. January and Mr. X," Pauline Lord appeared in "Sleep, My Pretty One," Mae West was in "Catherine Was Great," and Eva Le Gallienne with Joseph Schildkraut revived "The Cherry Orchard." Cornelia Otis Skinner, Dennis

FRIEDA INESCORT, MYRON McCORMICK,
MARTHA SCOTT in
"SOLDIER'S WIFE"

ELSPETH ERIC, ENID MARKEY,
RUSSELL HARDIE in
"SNAFU"

ANTHONY KEMBLE COOPER, HARRY WORTH, HALLIWELL HOBBES, MICHAEL WHALEN,
ESTELLE WINWOOD, J. PAT O'MALLEY, BEVERLY ROBERTS, NICHOLAS JOY,
NEIL FITZGERALD in "TEN LITTLE INDIANS"

MARTHA SCOTT, JOHN BEAL, VICKI CUMMINGS
in
"THE VOICE OF THE TURTLE"

BETTY FIELD, ELLIOTT NUGENT, AUDREY CHRIST
in
"THE VOICE OF THE TURTLE"

MARGO, FREDRIC MARCH in
"A BELL FOR ADANO"

EVA LE GALLIENNE, JOSEPH SCHILDKRAUT
in
"THE CHERRY ORCHARD"

KAY ALDRIDGE, PHILIP LOEB, RUTH GORDON
in
"OVER 21"

King and Montgomery Clift appeared in "The Searching Wind;" Fredric March and Margo in "A Bell For Adano;" Zasu Pitts in "Ramshackle Inn;" Martha Scott, Glenn Anders and Lili Darvas in "Soldier's Wife;" and Ilka Chase in "In Bed We Cry." "School for Brides" was a popular farce and Elsa Shelley's "Pick-Up Girl" was an interesting play about juvenile delinquency. Other plays that had substantial runs were "Chicken Every Sunday," "Decision" and "Snafu."

There were many popular musicals on the boards this year. Gertrude Niesen supported by Jackie Gleason, Buster West, Val Valentinoff and Irina Baranova had a big hit with "Follow the Girls." "Song of Norway" with a score and book based on the melodies and life of Edvard Grieg was highly successful, and so was "Bloomer Girl" with Celeste Holm, Mabel Taliaferro, Joan McCracken, David Brooks and Margaret Douglass. Other hits were "Mexican Hayride" with Bobby Clark, June Havoc, Wilbur Evans and Paul Haakon; "Laffing Room Only" with Olsen and Johnson; and "On the Town" with Betty Comden, Adolph Green, Nancy Walker, Cris Alexander, Sono Osato and John Battles. Beatrice Lillie, Bert Lahr, and Alicia Markova were in "Seven Lively Arts;" Allan Jones and Nanette Fabray in "Jack-

MAE WEST with JOEL ASHLEY, PHILIP HUSTON and COMPANY in
"CATHERINE WAS GREAT"

DONALD BUKA, KATINA PAXINOU
in
"SOPHIE"

ALBERT BASSERMAN, ETHEL BARRYMORE
in
"EMBEZZLED HEAVEN"

ABELLA, J. EDWARD BROMBERG, OSCAR KARLWEIS,
LOUIS CALHERN in
"JACOBOWSKY AND THE COLONEL"

SIDNEY BLACKMER, MARY PHILIPS in
"CHICKEN EVERY SUNDAY"

MADY CHRISTIANS, MARLON BRANDO, JOAN TETZEL, NANCY MARQUAND,
CAROLYN HUMMEL, RICHARD BISHOP in
"I REMEMBER MAMA"

FRANK FAY

JESSE WHITE, FRANK FAY, TOM SEIDEL, JANET TYLER
in
"HARVEY"

FRANK FAY, JOSEPHINE HULL

     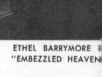

BURL IVES in
"SING OUT, SWEET LAND!"

MAE WEST in
"CATHERINE WAS GREAT"

LEO G. CARROLL in
"THE LATE GEORGE APLEY"

HILDA SIMMS in
"ANNA LUCASTA"

LOUIS CALHERN in
"JACOBOWSKY AND THE
COLONEL"

ETHEL BARRYMORE
"EMBEZZLED HEAVEN"

PAULINE
LORD

BENNY
FIELDS

ILKA
CHASE

LOIS WHEELER,
RICHARD WIDMARK in
"TRIO"

GERTRUDE
NIESEN

MICHAEL
WHALEN

MARY
ORR

FREDRIC MARCH
in
"A BELL FOR ADANO"

IRRA PETINA
in
"SONG OF NORWAY"

JAMES McMAHON, SUNNIE O'DEA, JOEL MARSTON,
MICHAEL KING in
"WALLFLOWER"

MADY CHRISTIANS
in
"I REMEMBER MAMA"

RAY JACQUEMOT
in
"SING OUT, SWEET LAND"

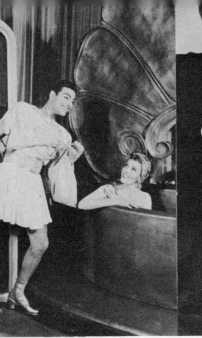

ONALD BUKA, JARMILA NOVOTNA
in
"HELEN GOES TO TROY"

ALMA KAYE, ALFRED DRAKE
in
"SING OUT, SWEET LAND!"

CHARLES HOWARD, MARGARET DOUGLASS
in
"BLOOMER GIRL"

CELESTE HOLM, DAVID BROOKS
in
"BLOOMER GIRL"

OLSEN, BRUCE EVANS, CHIC JOHNSON
in
"LAFFING ROOM ONLY"

ALICE PEARCE, CRIS ALEXANDER, NANCY WALKER
in
"ON THE TOWN"

ANTON DOLAN, ALICIA MARKOVA
in
"SEVEN LIVELY ARTS"

BERT LAHR, BEATRICE LILLIE
in
"SEVEN LIVELY ARTS"

BERT
LAHR

HELENA
BLISS

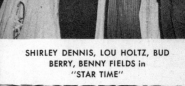

SHIRLEY DENNIS, LOU HOLTZ, BUD
BERRY, BENNY FIELDS in
"STAR TIME"

pot;" Alfred Drake and Burl Ives
in "Sing Out, Sweet Land!;" Lou
Holtz and Benny Fields in "Star
Time;" Jarmila Novotna, Ernest
Truex, William Horne and Donald
Buka in "Helen Goes to Troy," and
June Havoc was in "Sadie Thomp-
son," a musical version of "Rain."
"Hats Off to Ice" was the ice show
of the year with Freddie Trenkler
featured.

RUTH WESTON
in
"OKLAHOMA"

FREDDIE TRENKLER
in
"HATS OFF TO ICE"

SHELLEY WINTERS
in
"OKLAHOMA"

CHARLES CONWAY, GERTRUDE NIESEN,
VAL VALENTINOFF in
"FOLLOW THE GIRLS"

257

RAYMOND MASSEY, GERTRUDE LAWRENCE
in
"PYGMALION"

MAURICE EVANS, LILI DARVAS
in
"HAMLET"

ANNE BURR, RICHARD BASEHART, JOHN LUND
in
"THE HASTY HEART"

SAM LEVENE, BURT LANCASTER
in
"A SOUND OF HUNTING"

BURT
LANCASTER

JANE
WYATT

RICHARD
HART

MABEL
TALIAFERRO

CHARLES
LANG

MAY
WHITTY

NOAH
BEERY

KAY
JOHNSON

ALAN
BAXTER

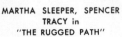

MARTHA SLEEPER, SPENCER
TRACY in
"THE RUGGED PATH"

MONTGOMERY CLIFT, EDMUND GWENN,
CATHERINE WILLARD in
"YOU TOUCHED ME!"

JUDITH EVELYN, VIRG
WEIDLER in
"THE RICH FULL

BETTY FIELD in
"DREAM GIRL"

1945 The Drama Critics' Circle Award went to Tennessee Williams' "The Glass Menagerie" with Laurette Taylor triumphant in the leading role. The rest of the cast included Eddie Dowling, Julie Haydon and Anthony Ross. The Pulitzer Prize was given to Howard Lindsay and Russel Crouse's "State of The Union" which was played by Ralph Bellamy, Ruth Hussey and Kay Johnson. Other outstanding plays were "The Hasty Heart" with John Lund and Richard Basehart, "Deep Are the Roots" with Barbara Bel Geddes, Charles Waldron, Carol Goodner and Gordon Heath, "Dark of the Moon" with Carol Stone and Richard Hart, "Home of the Brave" with Alan Baxter and Russell Hardie, and "A Sound of Hunting" with Sam Levene and Burt Lancaster. These last two were war plays which were artistic, but not commercial successes. Other plays seen include "Rebecca," "The Overtons," "You Touched Me!," "The Mermaids Singing," "Kiss Them For Me," "The Wind Is Ninety," "Strange Fruit," "Common Ground," "Therese," "The Deep Mrs. Sykes," "The Rich Full Life" and "Foxhole in the Parlor."

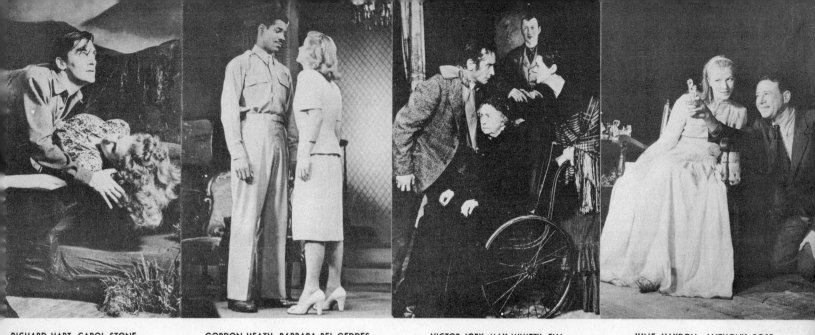

RICHARD HART, CAROL STONE
in
"DARK OF THE MOON"

GORDON HEATH, BARBARA BEL GEDDES
in
"DEEP ARE THE ROOTS"

VICTOR JORY, MAY WHITTY, EVA
LE GALLIENNE in
"THERESE"

JULIE HAYDON, ANTHONY ROSS
in
"THE GLASS MENAGERIE"

KIRK DOUGLAS | LILI DARVAS | WILBUR EVANS | ZASU PITTS | JOHN LUND | CAROLE LANDIS | JOHN ARCHER | BARBARA BEL GEDDES | DONALD MURPHY

RICHARD ARLEN
in
"HOT FOR MANEUVERS"

WENDELL COREY, FRANCES REID,
KIRK DOUGLAS in
"THE WIND IS NINETY"

CANADA LEE as
CALIBAN in
"THE TEMPEST"

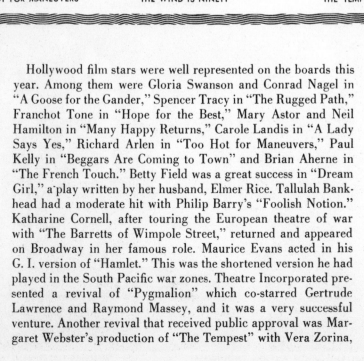

Hollywood film stars were well represented on the boards this year. Among them were Gloria Swanson and Conrad Nagel in "A Goose for the Gander," Spencer Tracy in "The Rugged Path," Franchot Tone in "Hope for the Best," Mary Astor and Neil Hamilton in "Many Happy Returns," Carole Landis in "A Lady Says Yes," Richard Arlen in "Too Hot for Maneuvers," Paul Kelly in "Beggars Are Coming to Town" and Brian Aherne in "The French Touch." Betty Field was a great success in "Dream Girl," a play written by her husband, Elmer Rice. Tallulah Bankhead had a moderate hit with Philip Barry's "Foolish Notion." Katharine Cornell, after touring the European theatre of war with "The Barretts of Wimpole Street," returned and appeared on Broadway in her famous role. Maurice Evans acted in his G. I. version of "Hamlet." This was the shortened version he had played in the South Pacific war zones. Theatre Incorporated presented a revival of "Pygmalion" which co-starred Gertrude Lawrence and Raymond Massey, and it was a very successful venture. Another revival that received public approval was Margaret Webster's production of "The Tempest" with Vera Zorina,

LAURETTE TAYLOR in
"THE GLASS MENAGERIE"

259

CLAIRE CARLETON, JOHN HUBBARD, RUSS BROWN,
WYNNE GIBSON in
"GOOD NIGHT, LADIES"

ALAN BAXTER, RUSSSELL HARDIE, JOSEPH PEVNEY, HENRY
BARNARD, KENDALL CLARK, EDUARD FRANZ in
"HOME OF THE BRAVE"

CATHERINE WILLARD, RICHARD MARTIN, JEAN DIXO
NEIL HAMILTON in
"THE DEEP MRS. SYKES"

HENRY HULL, TALLULAH BANKHEAD,
DONALD COOK in
"FOOLISH NOTION"

(Upper Level) CANADA LEE, ARNOLD MOSS, VERA ZORINA (On Steps) GEORGE VOSKOVEC,
JAN WERICH, PHILIP HUSTON, FRANCES HEFLIN, VITO CHRISTI in
"THE TEMPEST"

GLORIA SWANSON, CONRAD NAGEL, JOHN C
in
"A GOOSE FOR THE GANDER"

DONALD MURPHY, MARY
HEALY in
"COMMON GROUND"

BEATRICE PEARSON, WALTER ABEL
in
"THE MERMAIDS SINGING"

JUDY HOLLIDAY, DENNIS KING, JR., JAYNE COTTER,
RICHARD DAVIS, RICHARD WIDMARK in
"KISS THEM FOR ME"

NEIL HAMILTON, MARY ASTOR
in
"MANY HAPPY RETURNS"

BRAMWELL FLETCHER,
BARRYMORE
"REBECCA"

KATHERINE DUNHAM,
AVON LONG in
"CARIB SONG"

MYRON McCORMICK, KAY JOHNSON, RALPH BELLAMY, MINOR WATSON, RUTH HUSSEY
in
"STATE OF THE UNION"

MELCHOR FERRER, JANE WHIT
in
"STRANGE FRUIT"

JOMO VINCENT, LUBA MALINA, TAYLOR HOLMES
in
"MARINKA"

WILLIAM ARCHIBALD, IMOGENE COCA
in
"CONCERT VARIETIES"

EDDIE FOY, JR., ODETTE MYRTIL, MICHAEL O'SHEA
in
"THE RED MILL"

RES GRAY, LEW PARKER, JOAN ROBERTS,
JOHNNY DOWNS IN
"ARE YOU WITH IT?"

MAUREEN CANNON, WILBUR EVANS
in
"UP IN CENTRAL PARK"

JAN KIEPURA, MARTA EGGERTH
in
"POLONAISE"

JOAN McCRACKEN, WILLIAM TABBERT, MITZI GREEN,
DAVID BURNS, DON DE LEO in
"BILLION DOLLAR BABY"

BETTY FIELD, KEVIN O'SHEA WENDELL COREY,
JAMES GREGORY in
"DREAM GIRL"

JOHN ARCHER, IRENE MANNING
in
"THE DAY BEFORE SPRING"

WILLIAM GAXTON, SHIRLEY BOOTH,
VICTOR MOORE in
"HOLLYWOOD PINAFORE"

CHARLES LANG, DONALD KOHLER, JACK WHITING,
ARLENE FRANCIS, GLENDA FARRELL in
"THE OVERTONS"

AURVYN VYE, JEAN DARLING,
in
"CAROUSEL"

JAN CLAYTON, JOHN RAITT

Canada Lee and Arnold Moss. "Good Night, Ladies," which proved to be a modern version of the old Al Woods farce "Ladies' Night," ran over a year in Chicago but it lasted only 78 performances in New York.

In the musical field, "Oklahoma" was still running on Broadway and on the road, and the Theatre Guild had another big hit with "Carousel," the musical version of "Liliom" by Richard Rodgers and Oscar Hammerstein 2nd. Michael Todd had a hit too with "Up In Central Park" featuring Wilbur Evans, Maureen Cannon and Noah Berry, Sr., while the revival of "The Red Mill" with Eddie Foy, Jr., Michael O'Shea, Dorothy Stone and Odette Myrtil ran for over a year. Mitzi Green, William Tabbert and Joan McCracken were in "Billion Dollar Baby"; Joan Roberts, Harry Stockwell, Ethel Levey and Taylor Holmes played in "Marinka"; John Archer, Irene Manning, Bill Johnson, Patricia Marshall and Tom Helmore appeared in "The Day Before Spring"; Jan Kiepura and Marta Eggerth were singing in "Polonaise," and Victor Moore and William Gaxton were starring in "Hollywood Pinafore."

1946

An important event of 1946 was the visit of the Old Vic Theatre Company from London. The leading players of this organization were Laurence Olivier, Ralph Richardson, Margaret Leighton, Joyce Redman, Michael Warre, Ena Burrill, Miles Malleson and Nicholas Hannen. Their repertory consisted of "Oedipus," "Henry IV, Parts I and II," "Uncle Vanya" and "The Critic." Garson Kanin's bright comedy, "Born Yesterday," was the biggest hit among the straight plays, and "Annie Get Your Gun" starring Ethel Merman was the smash hit of the musicals. Among the long-run comedies were "O Mistress Mine" with Alfred Lunt and Lynn Fontanne, "Happy Birthday" with Helen Hayes, "Present Laughter" with Clifton Webb, and a revival of "Burlesque" with Bert Lahr and Jean Parker.

Ingrid Bergman appeared in Maxwell Anderson's "Joan of Lorraine"; Ina Claire was in "The Fatal Weakness"; Walter Huston was in "Apple of His Eye"; Katharine Cornell appeared in "Antigone" and also revived "Candida" with Marlon Brando playing Marchbanks; Fredric March and Florence Eldridge were in Ruth Gordon's play "Years Ago"; Lillian Hellman's "Another Part of the Forest," which dealt with the same Hubbard family depicted in "The Little Foxes," was played by Patricia Neal, Mildred Dunnock, Margaret Phillips, Leo Genn and Percy Waram; and Louis Calhern and Dorothy Gish were in "The Magnificent Yankee." The Theatre Guild produced "The Iceman Cometh," Eugene O'Neill's first play since 1934. In the cast were Dudley Digges and James Barton. Also the Guild revived "The Winter's Tale" with Jessie Royce Landis, Florence Reed and Henry Daniell and "He Who Gets Slapped" with Dennis King, Stella Adler, John Abbott and Susan Douglas.

ETHEL MERMAN in "ANNIE GET YOUR GUN"

MILDRED NATWICK, BURGESS MEREDITH, EITHNE DUNNE in "THE PLAYBOY OF THE WESTERN WORLD"

DENNIS KING, SUSAN DOUGLAS in "HE WHO GETS SLAPPED"

PAUL DOUGLAS, JUDY HOLLIDAY in
"BORN YESTERDAY"

ther revivals were "Lady Windermere's Fan" with Cornelia
Otis Skinner, Estelle Winwood and Cecil Beaton who also de-
signed the costumes; "The Playboy of the Western World" with
Burgess Meredith; "Cyrano de Bergerac" with Jose Ferrer;
"The Would-Be Gentleman" with Bobby Clark; and "The
Duchess of Malfi" with Elisabeth Bergner and Canada Lee, well-
known colored actor, playing in white face. Among the new
plays were "Second Best Bed" starring Ruth Chatterton; "Truck-
line Cafe" with Virginia Gilmore, Marlon Brando and David
Manners, "I Like It Here" with Bert Lytell, Beverly Bayne and
Oscar Karlweis, "No Exit" with Claude Dauphin and Annabella,
"Wonderful Journey" with Donald Murphy and Sidney Black-
mer, and "A Flag Is Born" with Paul Muni.

This year saw the foundation of the American Repertory
Theatre by Cheryl Crawford, Eva Le Gallienne and Margaret
Webster. They produced "Henry VIII," "What Every Woman
Knows," "John Gabriel Borkman," "Pound On Demand" and
"Androcles and the Lion." The featured players included Walter
Hampden, Ernest Truex, Richard Waring, Victor Jory, June
Duprez in addition to Miss Le Gallienne and Miss Webster.

"Call Me Mister" with Jules Munshin, Betty Garrett and Bill
Callahan was a long-run favorite among the musicals, and so was
"Three To Make Ready" with Ray Bolger, Brenda Forbes, Gor-
on MacRae and Arthur Godfrey. Mary Martin was seen in
"Lute Song"; Victor Moore and William Gaxton were in "Nellie
Bly"; Orson Welles produced and appeared in "Around the
World in Eighty Days"; Richard Tauber was in "Yours Is My
Heart"; and "Show Boat" was revived with Carol Bruce, Charles
Fredericks and Jan Clayton.

RALPH RICHARDSON, JOYCE REDMAN
in
"HENRY IV, PART II"

LAURENCE OLIVIER, MARGARET
LEIGHTON in
"HENRY IV, PART I"

LAURENCE OLIVIER
in
"OEDIPUS"

KATHARINE CORNELL in
"ANTIGONE"

JOSE FERRER in
"CYRANO DE BERGERAC"

INGRID BERGMAN in
"JOAN OF LORRAINE"

RALPH RICHARDSON in
"HENRY IV"

CAROL
STONE

ROMNEY
BRENT

STELLA
ADLER

CEDRIC
HARDWICKE

BEVERLY
BAYNE

PHILIP
HUSTON

JOYCE
REDMAN

BILL
CALLAHAN

BETTY
GARRET

HELEN HAYES, GRACE VALENTINE, ENID MARKEY
in
"HAPPY BIRTHDAY"

FREDRIC MARCH, FLORENCE ELDRIDGE
in
"YEARS AGO"

DOROTHY GISH, LOUIS CALHERN
in
"THE MAGNIFICENT YANKEE"

ALFRED LUNT, LYNN FONTANNE, DICK VAN PAT
in
"O MISTRESS MINE"

PATRICIA NEAL, PERCY WARAM, MILDRED DUNNOCK
in
"ANOTHER PART OF THE FOREST"

MARLON BRANDO, CELIA ADLER, PAUL MUNI
in
"A FLAG IS BORN"

RUTH FORD, CLAUDE DAUPHIN, ANNABELLA
in
"NO EXIT"

MARY MARTIN in "LUTE SONG"

JESSIE ROYCE LANDIS in "THE WINTER'S TALE"

JUDY HOLLIDAY in "BORN YESTERDAY"

INA CLAIRE in "THE FATAL WEAKNESS"

DOROTHY GISH in "THE MAGNIFICENT YANKEE"

ESTELLE WINWOOD in "LADY WINDERMERE'S FAN"

JOHN BUCKMASTER

EVELYN VARDEN

PAUL DOUGLAS

RUTH CHATTERTON

CHARLES FREDERICKS

JEAN PARKER

MARLON BRANDO

PATRICIA NEAL

DAVID MANNERS

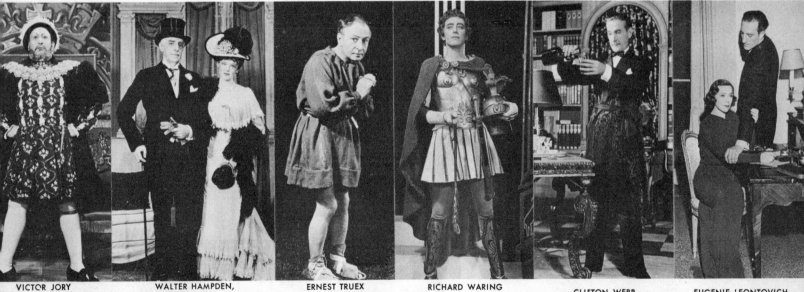

VICTOR JORY in "HENRY VIII"

WALTER HAMPDEN, EVA LE GALLIENNE in "WHAT EVERY WOMAN KNOWS" AMERICAN REPERTORY THEATRE PRODUCTIONS

ERNEST TRUEX in "ANDROCLES AND THE LION"

RICHARD WARING

CLIFTON WEBB in "PRESENT LAUGHTER"

EUGENIE LEONTOVICH, BASIL RATHBONE in "OBSESSION"

CANADA LEE (in white face), ELISABETH BERGNER in "THE DUCHESS OF MALFI"

LEONORE HARRIS, JAN STERLING, MARTA LINDEN, CLIFTON WEBB, DORIS DALTON, EVELYN VARDEN in "PRESENT LAUGHTER"

CORNELIA OTIS SKINNER, HENRY DANIELL in "LADY WINDERMERE'S FAN"

KATHARINE CORNELL, ALBERT BIONDO, CEDRIC HARDWICKE, HORACE BRAHAM, MERLE MADDERN, BERTHA BELMORE, RUTH MATTESON, JAMES MONKS in "ANTIGONE"

DONALD MURPHY in
"WONDERFUL JOURNEY"

BEATRICE PEARSON in
"THE VOICE OF THE TURTLE"

RAY BOLGER in
"THREE TO MAKE READY"

BOBBY CLARK in
"THE WOULD-BE GENTLEMAN"

FLORENCE REED in
"THE WINTER'S TALE"

HENRY DANIELL in
"THE WINTER'S TALE"

JEAN PARKER, BERT LAHR
in
"BURLESQUE"

JIMSEY SOMERS, WALTER HUSTON
in
"APPLE OF HIS EYE"

MARLON BRANDO, KATHARINE CORNELL
in
"CANDIDA"

STELLA ANDREVA, RICHARD
TAUBER in
"YOURS IS MY HEART"

CHARLES FREDERICK
JAN CLAYTON in
"SHOW BOAT"

MARY WICKES, MARTHE ERROLLE, ROBERT CHISHOLM, LEONORA
CORBETT, ARTHUR MARGETSON, RUTH MATTESON,
CHARLES PURCELL in
"PARK AVENUE"

BIBI OSTERWALD, GORDON MacRAE, ROSE INGHRAM, RAY BOLGER,
BRENDA FORBES, ARTHUR GODFREY in
"THREE TO MAKE READY"

BUDDY EBSEN, COLETTE LYONS, RALPH DUMKE,
CAROL BRUCE, ROBERT ALLEN in
"SHOW BOAT"

VICTOR MOORE, WILLIAM GAXTON
in
"NELLIE BLY"

RAY MIDDLETON, ETHEL MERMAN
in
"ANNIE GET YOUR GUN"

ALAN MANSON, CHANDLER COWLES, BETTY
GARRETT, GEORGE HALL, HARRY CLARK in
"CALL ME MISTER"

ORSON WELLES, STEFAN SCHNABEL
in
"AROUND THE WORLD IN EIGHTY DAYS"

1947

The most important play of 1947 was Tennessee Williams' "A Streetcar Named Desire" which won both the Pulitzer Prize and the Drama Critic's Circle Award for 1947-48. The leading roles were originally played by Jessica Tandy, Marlon Brando, Kim Hunter and Karl Malden. Later Judith Evelyn and Ralph Meeker headed one road company and Uta Hagen and Anthony Quinn another. Arthur Miller's "All My Sons" won the Drama Critics' Award for the 1946-47 season. Other outstanding plays were "The Heiress" with Wendy Hiller, Basil Rathbone, Patricia Collinge and Peter Cookson, "Command Decision" with Paul Kelly, and "The Winslow Boy" with Frank Allenby, Valerie White and Michael Newell.

Judith Anderson received the greatest acclaim of her career for her acting in Robinson Jeffers' adaptation of "Medea." In her supporting company were Florence Reed and John Gielgud who was replaced later by Dennis King. Mr. Gielgud was also seen in "Crime and Punishment" with Lillian Gish and Dolly Haas and revivals of "The Importance of Being Earnest" and "Love For Love." Other successful revivals were "Man and Superman" with Maurice Evans, and "Antony and Cleopatra" with Katharine Cornell, Godfrey Tearle, Lenore Ulric and Kent Smith. Also, Jane Cowl revived "The First Mrs. Fraser" and Judith Evelyn "Craig's Wife." Donald Wolfit and his company of English players appeared in "King Lear," "As You Like It," "The Merchant of Venice," "Hamlet" and "Volpone." The American Repertory Theatre revived "Yellow Jack" with Alfred Ryder and "Alice In Wonderland" with Bambi Linn. Financial difficulties beset the organization this year and they disbanded.

Among the comedy hits were "John Loves Mary" with William Prince, Nina Foch and Tom Ewell, "For Love or Money" with John Loder, June Lockhart, Vicki Cummings and Mark Daniels, and "A Young Man's Fancy" with Lenore Lonergan and Bill Talman. "The Story of Mary Surratt" was an artistic success with Dorothy Gish magnificent in the title role. Tallulah Bankhead had a failure with "The Eagle Has Two Heads," and James Mason, film star, fared no better with "Bathsheba."

The Experimental Theatre was organized this year by the Dramatist Guild and Actors Equity to contribute new ideas to the theatre. It was sponsored by the American National Theatre and Academy, and the plays produced were "The Wanhope Building," "O'Daniel," "As We Forgive Our Debtors," "The Great Campaign" and "Galileo."

The three outstanding musicals of the year were "High Button Shoes," "Finian's Rainbow" and "Brigadoon."

RICHARD HYLTON, LEONE WILSON, GRACE MILLS, KATHRYN GRILL, JOHN GIELGUD, FLORENCE REED, JUDITH ANDERSON above: JUDITH ANDERSON in "MEDEA"

KIM HUNTER, NICK DENNIS, MARLON BRANDO, RUDY BOND, JESSICA TANDY, KARL MALDEN in
"A STREETCAR NAMED DESIRE"

MARLON BRANDO, JESSICA TANDY
in
"A STREETCAR NAMED DESIRE"

| THORLEY WALTERS | CLAIRE LUCE | ALFRED RYDER | VICKI CUMMINGS | CICELY COURTNEIDGE | DOROTHY GISH | KENT SMITH | LILLIAN GISH | RALPH CLANTON |

ALAN WEBB, FRANK ALLENBY, MICHAEL KINGSLEY,
VALERIE WHITE, MICHAEL NEWELL in
"THE WINSLOW BOY"

DONALD WOLFIT, ROSALIND IDEN
in
"VOLPONE"

PAMELA KELLINO, JAMES MASON
in
"BATHSHEBA"

ANN MASON, NINA FOCH, WILLIAM PRINCE,
LORING SMITH, TOM EWELL in
"JOHN LOVES MARY"

JAMES WHITMORE, PAUL KELLY in
"COMMAND DECISION"

DOLLY HAAS, JOHN GIELGUD in
"CRIME AND PUNISHMENT"

DOROTHY GISH, KENT SMITH in
"THE STORY OF MARY SURRATT"

HELMUT DANTINE, TALLULAH BANKHEAD
"THE EAGLE HAS TWO HEADS"

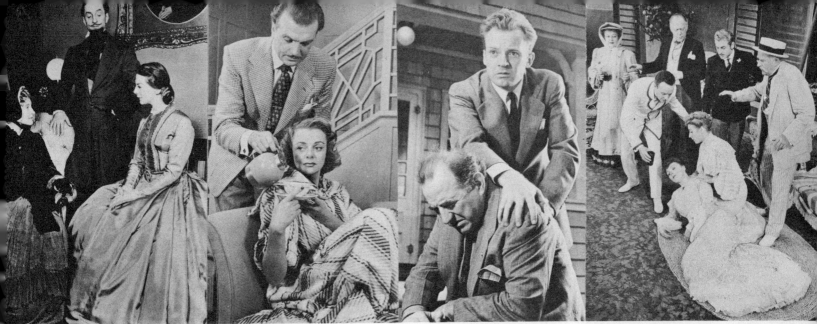

TY LINLEY, BASIL RATHBONE, WENDY HILLER
in
"THE HEIRESS"

JOHN LODER, JUNE LOCKHART
in
"FOR LOVE OR MONEY"

ED BEGLEY, ARTHUR KENNEDY
in
"ALL MY SONS"

MAURICE EVANS, FRANCES ROWE, CARMEN MATHEWS,
(Back Row) JOSEPHINE BROWN, VICTOR SUTHERLAND,
CHESTER STRATTON, MALCOLM KEEN in
"MAN AND SUPERMAN"

MARGARET
WYCHERLY

THOMAS
MITCHELL

PATRICIA
COLLINGE

MARK
DANIELS

FLORENCE
REED

BARRY
NELSON

BETH
MERRILL

JAMES
MASON

BAMBI
LINN

JN GIELGUD
in
E FOR LOVE"

BEATRICE STRAIGHT
in
"EASTWARD IN EDEN"

PAUL KELLY
in "COMMAND
DECISION"

WENDY HILLER
in
"THE HEIRESS"

DENNIS KING
in
"MEDEA"

JANE COWL in
"THE FIRST MRS.
FRASER"

MAURICE EVANS
in "MAN
AND SUPERMAN"

KATHARINE CORNELL
in "ANTONY
AND CLEOPATRA"

GODFREY TEARLE in
"ANTONY AND
CLEOPATRA"

"Street Scene," a Kurt Weill musical version of Elmer Rice's drama of the same name, was sung by Brian Sullivan, Anne Jeffreys, Polyna Stoska and Norman Cordon. Paul and Grace Hartman were a hit in their intimate revue "Angel in the Wings." Other musicals include revivals of "The Cradle Will Rock," "Sweethearts" with Bobby Clark, and "The Chocolate Soldier" with Keith Andes and Frances McCann, also Cicely Courtneidge with Thorley Walters in "Under the Counter," "Allegro" produced by the Theatre Guild, "Music In My Heart" with Vivienne Segal and Charles Fredericks, and "The Medium" and "The Telephone," two short operas by Gian-Carlo Menotti produced commercially on Broadway as a double bill.

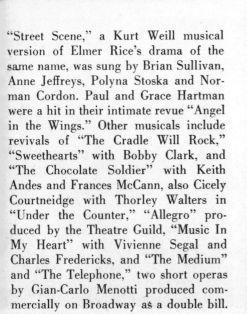

ROBERT FLEMYNG, JANE BAXTER, MARGARET
RUTHERFORD, PAMELA BROWN, JOHN GIELGUD in
"THE IMPORTANCE OF BEING EARNEST"

JUDITH EVELYN
in
"CRAIG'S WIFE"

DOUGLAS WATSON, GODFREY TEARLE,
KATHARINE CORNELL in
"ANTONY AND CLEOPATRA"

PHIL SILVERS, NANETTE FABRAY in
"HIGH BUTTON SHOES"

MACK SENNETT BALLET in
"HIGH BUTTON SHOES"

LOIS LEE, MARK DAWSON in
"HIGH BUTTON SHOES"

JAMES MITCHELL in
"BRIGADOON"

MARION BELL in
"BRIGADOON"

BOBBY CLARK in
"SWEETHEARTS"

DAVID WAYNE in
"FINIAN'S RAINBOW"

MARK DAWSON in
"HIGH BUTTON SHOES"

NANETTE FABRAY in
"HIGH BUTTON SHOES"

KEITH ANDES in
"THE CHOCOLATE SOLDIER"

"BRIGADOON"

BRIAN SULLIVAN, ANNE JEFFREYS
in
"STREET SCENE"

THORLEY WALTERS, CICELY
COURTNEIDGE in
"UNDER THE COUNTER"

ANNAMARY DICKEY, LISA KIRK, JOHN BATTLES, ROBERTA JONAY,
WILLIAM CHING (Back Row) JOHN CONTE, MURIEL O'MALLEY,
PAUL PARKS, LILY PAGET in
"ALLEGRO"

GRACE AND PAUL HARTMAN
in
"ANGEL IN THE WINGS"

DONALD RICHARDS, ELLA LOGAN, ALBERT SHARPE
in
"FINIAN'S RAINBOW"

LEO COLEMAN, MARIE POWERS
in
"THE MEDIUM"

BILLIE LOU WATT, BILLY REDFIELD, NANCY
WALKER, ELLEN HANLEY in
"BAREFOOT BOY WITH CHEEK"

ROBERT MORLEY, LEUEEN MacGRATH
in
"EDWARD, MY SON"

ESTELLE WINWOOD, MARTITA HUNT, NYDIA WESTMAN
in
"THE MADWOMAN OF CHAILLOT"

MICHEAL MacLIAMMOIR, HILTON EDWARDS
in
"JOHN BULL'S OTHER ISLAND"

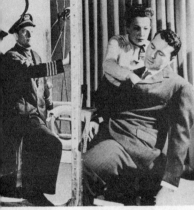

JOHN GARFIELD   NAN McFARLAND, RALPH
in   ROBERTS in
"SKIPPER NEXT TO GOD"   "LONG VOYAGE HOME"

1948 "Mister Roberts," by Thomas Heggen and Joshua Logan, was the outstanding hit of 1948 with Henry Fonda, William Harrigan, Robert Keith and David Wayne in the original cast. Other big successes were Maxwell Anderson's "Anne of the Thousand Days," "Edward, My Son" and "The Madwoman of Chaillot." Moderate hits include "Strange Bedfellows," "Light Up the Sky," "Summer and Smoke," "The Silver Whistle," "Me and Molly," "Joy to the World" and "The Respectful Prostitute" in which Meg Mundy scored a big hit. "Life With Mother" continued the chronicles of the Day family with Howard Lindsay and Dorothy Stickney in the leads. It was well received by the critics but ran only 262 performances in New York and its long planned road tour was halted after one week. Madeleine Carroll of films made her debut on Broadway in "Goodbye, My Fancy" and so did Charles Boyer in "Red Gloves." "Harvey" was still popular and among the actors who played Elwood P. Dowd were Joe E. Brown, James Dunn, James Stewart, Bert Wheeler, Jack Buchanan and Brock Pemberton who produced it.

After a long road tour, Tallulah Bankhead settled down to a long run on Broadway with her revival of "Private Lives" with Donald Cook. Other revivals were "The Play's the Thing" with Louis Calhern, Faye Emerson and Arthur Margetson. "You Never Can Tell" with Leo G. Carroll, Tom Helmore, Ralph Forbes and Frieda Inescort, Gertrude Lawrence with Graham Payn in "Tonight at 8:30" and "Ghosts" and "Hedda Gabler" with Eva Le Gallienne. Michael Redgrave and Flora Robson revived "Macbeth" and in their company were Geoffrey Toone,

FLORA ROBSON   MICHAEL REDGRAVE
in
"MACBETH"

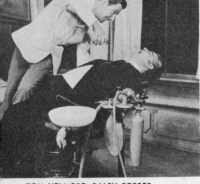

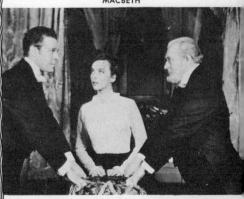

JOHN ARCHER, JOAN TETZEL, CARL BENTON REID
in
"STRANGE BEDFELLOWS"

TOM HELMORE, RALPH FORBES
in
"YOU NEVER CAN TELL"

JOHN DALL, CHARLES BOYER
in
"RED GLOVES"

SAM WANAMAKER   CONRAD NAGEL, MADELEINE CARROLL   MADELEINE CARROLL
in
"GOODBYE, MY FANCY"

JOYCE REDMAN, REX HARRISON
in
"ANNE OF THE THOUSAND DAYS"

JOCELYN BRANDO, DAVID WAYNE, HENRY FONDA
in
"MISTER ROBERTS"

MARGARET PHILLIPS, TOD ANDREWS
in
"SUMMER AND SMOKE"

WILLIAM HARRIGAN, HENRY FONDA
in
"MISTER ROBERTS"

LOUIS CALHERN in
"THE PLAY'S THE
THING"

ROBERT WADE, DOROTHY STICKNEY, HOWARD LINDSAY,
RUTH HAMMOND, ROBERT EMHARDT in
"LIFE WITH MOTHER"

FAYE EMERSO
"THE PLAY'S
THING"

BARRY NELSON, BARTLETT ROBINSON, VIRGINIA
FIELD, GLENN ANDERS, SAM LEVENE in
"LIGHT UP THE SKY"

FRITZI SCHEFF
in
"BRAVO"

ALFRED DRAKE, MARSHA HUNT
in
"JOY TO THE WORLD"

MICHEAL MacLIAMMOIR
in
"THE OLD LADY SAYS 'NO!'"

TALLULAH BANKHEAD
in
"PRIVATE LIVES"

KARL WEBER, MEG MUNDY
in
"THE RESPECTFUL PROSTITUTE"

JOSE FERRER, ELEANOR WILSON, DORO MERANDE
in
"THE SILVER WHISTLE"

GERTRUDE BERG, JOAN LAZER, LESTER CARR,
PHILIP LOEB in
"ME AND MOLLY"

GRAHAM PAYN, GERTRUDE LAWREN
in
"TONIGHT AT 8:30"

"THE GLADIOLA GIRL" NUMBER in "LEND AN EAR" CAROL CHANNING (extreme right)
p: BOB SCHEERER, CAROL CHANNING, WILLIAM EYTHE, ANNE RENEE ANDERSON, GENE NELSON

RAITT, DOROTHY SARNOFF
in
"MAGDALENA"

SID CAESAR, DAVID BURNS
in
"MAKE MINE MANHATTAN"

BAMBI LINN, WILLIE HOWARD
in
"SALLY"

RAY BOLGER
in
"WHERE'S CHARLEY?"

HARLES BOYER   MARGARET WEBSTER   TOD ANDREWS   GEORGE TOZZI, KITTY CARLISLE   NYDIA WESTMAN   PETER LIND HAYES   MARGARET PHILLIPS
in
"THE RAPE OF LUCRETIA"

BEATRICE LILLIE, JACK HALEY
in
"INSIDE U.S.A."

BOBBY CLARK, IRENE RICH
in
"AS THE GIRLS GO"

Whitfield Connor and Beatrice Straight. The Dublin Gate Theatre headed by Micheal MacLiammoir, Hilton Edwards and Meriel Moore visited New York with repertory including "John Bull's Other Island," "The Old Lady Says 'No!'" and "Where Stars Walk"—the latter two written by Mr. MacLiammoir.

The Experimental Theatre continued productions and the following plays later reached Broadway: "Skipper Next to God," "Ballet Ballads," "Hope's the Thing" and "Seeds in the Wind."

"Kiss Me, Kate" with Alfred Drake and Patricia Morison, and Ray Bolger in "Where's Charley?," a musical version of "Charley's Aunt," were the outstanding musicals. "Lend An Ear," a bright intimate revue, was also popular. The D'Oyly Carte Opera Company returned for a successful season of Gilbert and Sullivan repertoire. Benjamin Britten's "Rape of Lucretia" was done with Kitty Carlisle. Other musicals were "As the Girls Go," "Inside U.S.A.," Villa-Lobos' "Magdalena," "Love Life," "My Romance," "Small Wonder," a revival of "Sally," "Make Mine Manhattan," "Look, Ma, I'm Dancin'," and the ice show "Howdy, Mr. Ice."

IRRA
PETINA

MARK
DAWSON

HARRISON THOMSON, JINX CLARK

THE BRUISES
in
"HOWDY, MR. ICE"

CISSY TRENHOLM, RUDY RICHARDS

NANETTE FABRAY, LYLE BETTGER
RAY MIDDLETON in
"LOVE LIFE"

UTA
HAGEN

NANCY WALKER
in "LOOK, MA,
I'M DANCIN'"

PATRICIA MORISON, ALFRED DRAKE, LISA KIRK, HAROLD LANG
in
"KISS ME, KATE"

ANNE JEFFREYS, KEITH ANDES
in
"KISS ME, KATE"

SONO OSATO, PAUL GODKIN
in
"BALLET BALLADS"

JOHN
TYERS

ALLYN
McLERIE

JACK BUCHANAN

JAMES STEWART
JOSEPHINE HULL

JOE E. BROWN

JAMES DUNN

in
"HARVEY"

BYRON
PALMER

274

MARY McCARTY
in
"SMALL WONDER"

MARTYN GREEN
in "THE YEOMEN
OF THE GUARD"

CHARLES DORNING, MARGARET
MITCHELL, JOAN GILLINGHAM in
"PATIENCE"
D'OYLY CARTE OPERA COMPANY

ELLA HALMAN
in
"IOLANTHE"

ALFRED DRAKE
in
"KISS ME, KATE"

J. COBB, MILDRED DUNNOCK   DON KEEFER, HOWARD SMITH, CAMERON MITCHELL, MILDRED DUNNOCK, ARTHUR KENNEDY
in
"DEATH OF A SALESMAN"
    THOMAS MITCHELL, JUNE WALKER   MEG MUNDY

CHARLTON HESTON

TODD DUNCAN, LESLIE BANKS
in
"LOST IN THE STARS"
    JOAN COPELAND, LEE GRANT, RALPH BELLAMY,
WARREN STEVENS, ROBERT STRAUSS in
"DETECTIVE STORY"
    CEDRIC HARDWICKE, JOHN BUCKMASTER, LILLI PALMER,
ARTHUR TREACHER, RALPH FORBES in
"CAESAR AND CLEOPATRA"
    ALLYN McLERIE
MARY McCARTY in
"MISS LIBERTY"

KEN MURRAY

LYNN FONTANNE, ALFRED LUNT
in
"I KNOW MY LOVE"

1949 On April 7, 1949, "South Pacific" opened and broke all kinds of records while making theatrical history. It opened to the largest advance sale on record and in its second year it was playing to standing room. Never within memory has the demand for seats been as great as for this attraction which also won the Pulitzer Prize. In the original cast were Mary Martin, Ezio Pinza, Juanita Hall, Myron McCormick, William Tabbert and Betta St. John. The music was by Richard Rodgers, the lyrics by Oscar Hammerstein 2nd, and the book based on James A. Michener's "Tales of the South Pacific" was by Mr. Hammerstein and Joshua Logan.

The Drama Critics' Circle Award went to Arthur Miller's "Death of A Salesman." Lee J. Cobb and Mildred Dunnock played in the original cast while Thomas Mitchell and June Walker trouped with the National Company. Sidney Kingsley's "Detective Story" was another big hit. "The Traitor" with Walter Hampden, Lee Tracy, Louise Platt and Richard Derr received critical acclaim but failed at the box office. "Clutterbuck," which brought stardom to Arthur Margetson, was liked and so was "I Know My Love" which starred Alfred Lunt and Lynn Fontanne. The moderate successes were "The Velvet Glove" with Grace George and Walter Hampden, "Two Blind Mice" with Melvyn Douglas and "Yes, M'Lord" with A. E. Matthews. Mae West revived "Diamond Lil" successfully and "Caesar and Cleopatra" with Cedric Hardwicke and Lilli Palmer had a good run. "They Knew What They Wanted" with Paul Muni and Carol Stone, "The Father" with Raymond Massey, "Richard III" with Richard Whorf, and "Twelfth

MAE WEST
in
"DIAMOND LIL"

PETER COOKSON

JEAN CARSON

WHITFIELD CONNOR

MARY MARTIN
in
"SOUTH PACIFIC"

HENRY SLATE, MYRON McCORMICK, MARY MARTIN, Top: EZIO PINZA, MARY MARTIN,
Center Left: JUANITA HALL, BETTA ST. JOHN, WILLIAM TABBERT
Center Right: EZIO PINZA in
"SOUTH PACIFIC"

BILL CALLAHAN

PETER HOBBS, TOM McDERMOTT, CHARLES NOLTE in "UNIFORM OF FLESH"

LAURA PIERPONT, MELVYN DOUGLAS, MABEL PAIGE, HOWARD ST. JOHN in "TWO BLIND MICE"

RICHARD DERR, LEE TRACY, LOUISE PLATT in "THE TRAITOR"

CAMERON MITCHELL

JACKIE COOPER

NANCY ANDREWS

HAROLD LANG

HAZEL DAWN, JR.

RICHARD DERR

LILLI PALMER

JACK COLE

CAROL CHANNING in "GENTLEMEN PREFER BLONDES"

JANE PICKENS, PRISCILLA GILLETTE in "REGINA"

GRACE GEORGE in "THE VELVET GLOVE"

TOM HELMORE, ARTHUR MARGETSON in "CLUTTERBUCK"

Night" were revived but aroused no interest. Emlyn Williams appeared in "Montserrat," Katharine Cornell in "That Lady," Betty Field with Barry Nelson in "The Rat Race," Maurice Evans in "The Browning Version," John Garfield in "The Big Knife" and Ruth Gordon in "The Smile of the World." Jean Pierre Aumont, film star, appeared in his own play, "My Name is Aquilon," while Jackie Cooper, also of films, appeared with Jessie Royce Landis in "Magnolia Alley." None of these plays made the grade. The plays produced by the Experimental Theatre this year were "Uniform of Flesh," "Cock-A-Doodle-Doo," "The Nineteenth Hole of Europe" and "Sister Oakes."

"Ken Murray's Blackouts" which ran for over seven years in Hollywood lasted only 51 performances on Broadway. "Lost in the Stars" with a Maxwell Anderson book and Kurt Weill music was well received. "Regina," Marc Blitzstein's musical version of "The Little Foxes," with Jane Pickens was an artistic success while "Gentlemen Prefer Blondes' was a big hit and skyrocketed Carol Channing into the spotlight. Other musicals include "Miss Liberty," "Texas, Li'l Darlin'," "Touch and Go," "Along Fifth Avenue" and "All For Love."

JEAN PIERRE AUMONT, LILLI PALMER in 'MY NAME IS AQUILON"

RICHARD WHORF as RICHARD III

GRACE AND PAUL HARTMAN in "ALL FOR LOVE"

KATHARINE HEPBURN
in
"AS YOU LIKE IT"

1950 The year 1950 saw several interesting productions on the boards. Among them was the Drama Critics' Circle Award winner, "The Member of the Wedding," which Carson McCullers adapted from her own book. Ethel Waters received much praise for her performance and so did Julie Harris and an eight year old boy named Brandon De Wilde. Other successes included T. S. Eliot's "The Cocktail Party" with Alec Guinness, Cathleen Nesbitt and Robert Flemyng; Clifford Odets' "The Country Girl" starring Paul Kelly and Uta Hagen; "Come Back, Little Sheba" by William Inge and with Shirley Booth and Sidney Blackmer both receiving great acclaim for their fine performances; "The Happy Time," a comedy with Claude Dauphin, Richard Hart and Eva Gabor; "Affairs of State" with Celeste Holm, Reginald Owen and Shepperd Strudwick; "Bell, Book and Candle" with Lilli Palmer and Rex Harrison; "Season in the Sun" with Richard Whorf, Nancy Kelly, Grace Valentine and Paula Laurence; "The Innocents," William Archibald's dramatization of Henry James' "The Turn of the Screw," with Beatrice Straight; and Christopher Fry's "The Lady's Not For Burning" starring John Gielgud and Pamela Brown. "A Phoenix Too Frequent," another of Mr. Fry's plays and his first to be produced in America, was done earlier in the year but failed.

JEAN ARTHUR
in
"PETER PAN"

HELEN HAYES
in
"THE WISTERIA TREES"

MARIE POWERS, LEON LISHNER, PATRICIA NEWAY
in
"THE CONSUL"

LEORA DANA, CLAUDE DAUPHIN, JOHNNY STEWART
in
"THE HAPPY TIME"

ISOBEL ELSOM, BEATRICE STRAIGHT, IRIS MANN,
DAVID COLE in
"THE INNOCENTS"

WILLIAM PRINCE
in
"AS YOU LIKE IT"

Center: MARSHA HUNT, MAURICE EVANS, VICTOR JORY, DENNIS KING, GAVIN GORDON
in
"THE DEVIL'S DISCIPLE"

BORIS KARLOFF
in
"PETER PAN"

KATHARINE HEPBURN, WILLIAM PRINCE
in
"AS YOU LIKE IT"

MILDRED HUGHES, GRACE and PAUL HARTMAN
in
"TICKETS, PLEASE!"

MARCIA HENDERSON, JEAN ARTHUR
in
"PETER PAN"

279

SIDNEY BLACKMER

LONNY CHAPMAN, SIDNEY BLACKMER,
JOAN LORRING in
"COME BACK, LITTLE SHEBA"

PAUL KRAUSS, SIDNEY BLACKMER,
WILSON BROOKS, SHIRLEY BOOTH in
"COME BACK, LITTLE SHEBA"

SHIRLEY BOOTH

ETHEL WATERS

BRANDON DE WILDE, JULIE HARRIS, ETHEL WATERS
in
"THE MEMBER OF THE WEDDING"

JULIE HARRIS

Among the revivals that scored include "As You Like It" with Katharine Hepburn as Rosalind breaking the long-run record of that play; "Peter Pan" with Jean Arthur in the title role breaking Maude Adams' record run; "The Devil's Disciple" with Maurice Evans and Dennis King; and "The Relapse," Sir John Vanbrugh's Restoration comedy which had never been performed before professionally in this country. Louis Calhern revived "King Lear" which ran 48 performances, a long-run record of consecutive performances of that play in New York.

Two British hits which starred two distinguished English actresses were only moderately successful in this country, namely, Flora Robson in "Black Chiffon," and Edith Evans in "Daphne Laureola."

Helen Hayes acted in "The Wisteria Trees;" Fredric March and Florence Eldridge were in "Now I Lay Me Down To Sleep" and later in the year in Arthur Miller's version of Ibsen's "An Enemy of the People;" Dorothy Gish was in "The Man;" Basil Rathbone and Valerie Taylor were in "The Gioconda Smile;" Lillian Gish was in "The Curious Savage;" Barbara Bel Geddes and Kent Smith were seen briefly in "Burning Bright." a play by John Steinbeck; Martha Scott supported by Charlton Heston, Carroll McComas and Charles Nolte appeared briefly in "Design For A Stained Glass Window;" Jessica Tandy starred in "Hilda Crane;" and "Ring Round The Moon" featured Lucile Watson.

During the summer, Sam Wanamaker formed what he called the Festival Theatre and gave three revivals without much public support. These were "Parisienne" with Francis Lederer, Faye Emerson and Romney Brent; "The Lady From the Sea" with Luise Rainer, and "Borned in Texas" with Anthony Quinn and Marsha Hunt.

JESSICA TANDY
in
"HILDA CRANE"

LUCILE WATSON
in
"RING ROUND THE MOON"

BETHEL LESLIE, HELEN HAYES, PEGGY CONKLIN, KENT SMITH, DOUGLAS WATSON,
WALTER ABEL in
"THE WISTERIA TREES"

ALEC GUINNESS, CATHLEEN NESBITT, ERNEST CLARK, EILEEN PEEL,
ROBERT FLEMYNG GREY BLAKE in
"THE COCKTAIL PARTY"

 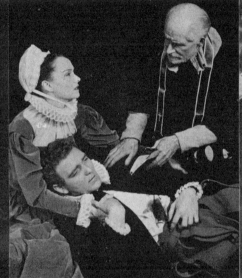  

BARBARA BEL GEDDES, KENT SMITH
in
"BURNING BRIGHT"

MARTHA SCOTT, CHARLES NOLTE, JOHN McKEE
in
"DESIGN FOR A STAINED GLASS WINDOW"

ANTHONY IRELAND, FLORA ROBSON
in
"BLACK CHIFFON"

FRANCIS LEDERER, LEE GRANT
in
"ARMS AND THE MAN"

EDITH EVANS

ALEC GUINNESS

FLORA ROBSON

281

DON HANMER, DOROTHY GISH
in
"THE MAN"

LOUIS CALHERN
in
"KING LEAR"

REGINALD OWEN, CELESTE HOLM
in
"AFFAIRS OF STATE"

PAMELA BROWN, JOHN GIELGUD
in
"THE LADY'S NOT FOR BURNING"

LILLI PALMER, REX HARRISON
in
"BELL, BOOK AND CANDLE"

CELESTE HOLM
in
"AFFAIRS OF STATE"

MADGE ELLIOTT, CYRIL RITCHARD, JOHN EMERY, RUTH MATTESON
in
"THE RELAPSE"
Above: SCENE FROM "THE RELAPSE"

New Yorkers also had their first taste of the theatre-in-the-round when ballroom in the Hotel Edison was dubbed the Arena Theatre and revivals o "The Show-Off" with Lee Tracy, "Julius Caesar" with Basil Rathbone an Alfred Ryder, and "Arms and the Man" with Francis Lederer and Sam Wan maker were presented.

The American National Theatre and Academy purchased the Guild Theatr renamed it the ANTA Playhouse, and late in the year presented a series o plays such as "The Tower Beyond Tragedy" starring Judith Anderson, "Th Cellar and The Well" and a revival of "Twentieth Century" starring Glori Swanson and José Ferrer.

Among the musicals, the greatest hits were "Guys and Dolls" based o Damon Runyon stories, and "Call Me Madam" starring Ethel Merman. Othe musicals seen included Gian-Carlo Menotti's musical drama, "The Consul;" Charlotte Greenwood in "Out Of This World;" "Arms and the Girl" wit Nanette Fabray; "Pardon Our French" with Olsen and Johnson; "Bless You All," a revue with Mary McCarty, Jules Munshin, Pearl Bailey and Valeri Bettis; and Lawrence Tibbett, opera star, made his Broadway debut in "Th Barrier," a musical drama.

UTA HAGEN, PAUL KELLY
in
"THE COUNTRY GIRL"

ETHEL MERMAN, RUSSELL NYPE
in
"CALL ME MADAM"

WILLIAM REDFIELD
in
"OUT OF THIS WORLD"

LAWRENCE TIBBETT
in
"THE BARRIER"

VALERIE BETTIS
in
"GREAT TO BE ALIVE"

ALFRED RYDER
in
"JULIUS CAESAR"

BARBARA ASHLEY

TORIN THATCHER

PEARL BAILEY

REX HARRISON

JANET COLLINS

JULES MUNSHIN

PRISCILLA GILLETTE

RICHARD WHORF, NANCY KELLY
in
"SEASON IN THE SUN"

JOHN ARCHER, EDNA BEST
in
"CAPTAIN BRASSBOUND'S CONVERSION"

DENISE DARCEL, CHIC JOHNSON
in
"PARDON OUR FRENCH"

NINA FOCH, RICHARD DERR
in
"A PHOENIX TOO FREQUENT"

283

ROMNEY BRENT, FRANCIS LEDERER, FAYE EMERSON, HELMUT DANTINE
in
"PARISIENNE"

PEARL BAILEY   JOHN CONTE   NANETTE FABRAY   GEORGES GUETARY.
in
"ARMS AND THE GIRL"

CHARLOTTE GREENWOOD
in
"OUT OF THIS WORLD"

CECIL PARKER
in
"DAPHNE LAUREOLA"   VIVIENNE SEGAL, STUART ERWIN
in
"GREAT TO BE ALIVE"   DENHOLM ELLIOTT
in
"RING ROUND THE MOON"   CHARLOTTE GREENWOOD and ENSEMBLE
in
"OUT OF THIS WORLD"

ANNA MINOT, RALPH ROBERTSON, FREDRIC MARCH, FLORENCE ELDRIDGE,
RICHARD TRASK in
"AN ENEMY OF THE PEOPLE"

VIVIAN BLAINE, SAM LEVENE
in
"GUYS AND DOLLS"

ROBERT ALDA, ISABEL BIGLEY
in
"GUYS AND DOLLS"

SHIRLEY BOOTH, JOHNNY JOHNSTON,
MARCIA VAN DYKE in
"A TREE GROWS IN BROOKLYN"

BILLIE WORTH, JOE E. BROWN
in
"COURTIN' TIME"

KIM HUNTER, CLAUDE RAINS
in
"DARKNESS AT NOON"

DENNIS KING, CHARLES NOLTE
in
"BILLY BUDD"

SHIRLEY BOOTH
in
"A TREE GROWS IN BROOKLYN"

CLAUDE RAINS
in
"DARKNESS AT NOON"

1951

Sidney Kingsley's "Darkness At Noon," starring Claude Rains, won the Drama Critics' Circle Award while no Pulitzer Prize was awarded for a play. The biggest hits were F. Hugh Herbert's "The Moon Is Blue" starring Barbara Bel Geddes, Donald Cook and Barry Nelson; "The Fourposter," a two character play, starring Jessica Tandy and Hume Cronyn, and "Gigi" which brought stardom to Audrey Hepburn. Other plays that met with success were "Stalag 17," "Point Of No Return" with Henry Fonda, "The Rose Tattoo" featuring Maureen Stapleton and Eli Wallach, and revivals of "Twentieth Century" starring Gloria Swanson and José Ferrer, and "The Constant Wife" starring Katharine Cornell, Grace George and Brian Aherne. "Billy Budd," an adaptation of Herman Melville's novel of the same name, was an artistic success. Dennis King was starred but Charles Nolte in the title role received most of the critical acclaim. The First Drama Quartette, consisting of Charles Boyer, Charles Laughton, Cedric Hardwicke and Agnes Moorehead, gave readings of Shaw's "Don Juan In Hell" and played to S. R. O. for 104 performances. Other plays on the boards included Philip Barry's last play, "Second Threshold," with Clive Brook and Margaret Phillips, Lillian Hellman's "The Autumn Garden" with Fredric March and Florence Eldridge, "Remains To Be Seen" with Howard Lindsay and Jackie Cooper, "Glad Tidings" starring Melvyn Douglas, "Gramercy Ghost" with Sara Chur-

CHARLES NOLTE
in
"BILLY BUDD"

285

BARBARA BEL GEDDES, BARRY NELSON
in
"THE MOON IS BLUE"

CLIVE BROOK, MARGARET PHILLIPS
in
"SECOND THRESHOLD"

BARBARA BEL GEDDES
in
"THE MOON IS BLUE"

DON MURRAY PHYLLIS LOVE
in
"THE ROSE TATTOO"

ELI WALLACH, MAUREEN STAPLETON
in
"THE ROSE TATTOO"

YUL BRYNNER
in
"THE KING AND I"

GERTRUDE LAWRENCE, YUL BRYNNER
in
"THE KING AND I"

GERTRUDE LAWRENCE
in
"THE KING AND I"

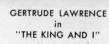

KATHARINE BLAKE, VIVIEN LEIGH, MAIRHI RUSSELL, EDMUND PURDON, LAURENCE OLIVIER in "ANTHONY AND CLEOPATRA"

JOSEPHINE BROWN, AUDREY HEPBURN, MICHAEL EVANS, DORIS PATSTON, BERTHA BELMORE in "GIGI"

LAURENCE OLIVIER, VIVIEN LEIGH in "CAESAR AND CLEOPATRA"

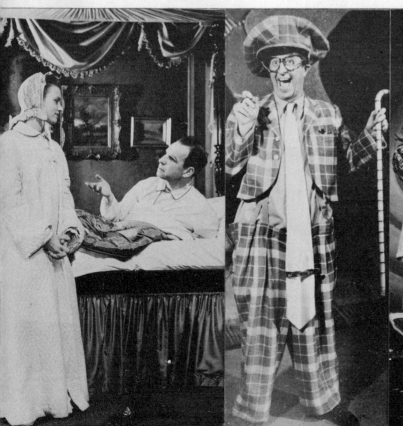

JESSICA TANDY, HUME CRONYN in "THE FOURPOSTER"

PHIL SILVERS in "TOP BANANA"

BERT LAHR in "TWO ON THE AISLE"

KATHARINE CORNELL, BRIAN AHERNE, GRACE GEORGE in "THE CONSTANT WIFE"

HERBERT EVERS, JOAN McCRACKEN, EDDIE DOWLING
in
"ANGEL IN THE PAWNSHOP"

HAILA STODDARD, EDWARD EVERETT
HORTON in
"SPRINGTIME FOR HENRY"

ROBERT STRAUSS, HARVEY LEMBECK, ALLAN MELVIN, ROBERT SHA
in
"STALAG 17"

WILLIAM MARSHALL, JAMES FULLER
in
"THE GREEN PASTURES"

JOSE FERRER, ROBERT STRAUSS, GLORIA SWANSON, DONALD FOSTER,
WILLIAM LYNN in
"TWENTIETH CENTURY"

ROBERT F. SMITH, ROBERT STERLING,
SARAH CHURCHILL in
"GRAMERCY GHOST"

JUDY HOLLIDAY
in
"DREAM GIRL"

MARTYN GREEN
in
"THE GONDOLIERS"

GLORIA SWANSON
in
"TWENTIETH CENTURY"

FRIDOLIN (GRATIEN GELINAS)
in
"TI-COQ"

ETHEL GRIFFIES
in
"THE AUTUMN GARDEN"

JOHN ERICSON
in
"STALAG 17"

ERNEST TRUEX
in
"FLAHOOLEY"

PIERRE RENOIR, LOUIS JOUVET, DOMINIQUE BLANCHAR
in
"L'ECOLE DES FEMMES"

KATINA PAXINOU in
"THE HOUSE OF
BERNARDA ALBA"

RICHARD WARING
in
"GRAMERCY GHOST"

OBERT CUMMINGS,
NN SOTHERN in
AITHFULLY YOURS"

JACKIE COOPER,
JANIS PAIGE in
"REMAINS TO BE SEEN"

TONY BAVAAR,
OLGA SAN JUAN,
JAMES BARTON in
"PAINT YOUR WAGON"

ANN CROWLEY,
KENNETH NELSON,
in "SEVENTEEN"

GLORIA SWANSON,
ALAN WEBB,
DAVID NIVEN in
"NINA"

FLORENCE ELDRIDGE,
FREDRIC MARCH in
"THE AUTUMN GARDEN"

PATRICIA SMITH,
HENRY FONDA, COLIN
KEITH-JOHNSTON in
"POINT OF NO RETURN"

TOM HELMORE,
GINGER ROGERS in
"LOVE AND LET LOVE"

JAMES DALY,
JOHN BUCKMASTER,
UTA HAGEN in
"SAINT JOAN"

DOUGLAS
WATSON

DOLORES GRAY
in
"TWO ON THE AISLE"

CHARLES
NOLTE

CEDRIC HARDWICKE, CHARLES BOYER,
AGNES MOOREHEAD, CHARLES LAUGHTON in
"DON JUAN IN HELL"

WARD LINDSAY
"REMAINS TO BE
SEEN"

AUDREY HEPBURN
in
"GIGI"

OLIVIA DE
HAVILLAND in
"ROMEO AND JULIET"

MELVILLE COOPER
in
"MAKE A WISH"

chill and Robert Sterling, "Angel In The Pawnshop" co-starring Eddie Dowling and Joan McCracken. Fridolin, a great Canadian favorite, made his Broadway debut in "Ti-Coq," a success in his own country which was not duplicated here. Louis Jouvet fared better with his French troupe in Molière's "L'Ecole Des Femmes" which played a limited engagement.

Among the revivals were "Romeo and Juliet" with Olivia De Havilland, Douglas Watson and Jack Hawkins, "Saint Joan" with Uta Hagen, "The Green Pastures" with William Marshall playing De Lawd, "The Green Bay Tree" with Joseph Schildkraut, "Springtime For Henry" with Edward Everett Horton, and "Peer Gynt" with John Garfield.

In the musical field, Rodgers and Hammerstein's "The King And I" with Gertrude Lawrence and Yul Brynner in the title roles was the greatest success. Other musicals that were liked were "A Tree Grows In Brooklyn" with Shirley Booth, "Two On The Aisle" with Bert Lahr and Dolores Gray, "Top Banana" with Phil Silvers, "Paint Your Wagon" with James Barton, "Courtin' Time" with Joe E. Brown and Billie Worth, "Make A Wish" with Nanette Fabray and Melville Cooper, "Flahooley" with Ernest Truex, "Seventeen," "Bagels and Yox," and Gilbert and Sullivan operettas sung by the D'Oyly Carte Company.

The year closed with Laurence Olivier and Vivien Leigh in revivals of "Antony and Cleopatra" and "Caesar and Cleopatra."

HELEN HAYES, MILDRED CHANDLER,
MARGA ANN DEIGHTON, ENID MARKEY in
"MRS. McTHING"

BASIL RATHBONE, ADRIENNE CORRI,
WILLIAM WHITMAN in "JANE"

WILLIAM PRINCE, MARTIN BROOKS,
MARIAN WINTERS, JULIE HARRIS
in "I AM A CAMERA"

ANN
CROWLEY

JAMES
DALY

DIANA
HERBERT

JOHN
CROMWELL

MAUREEN
STAPLETON

DONALD
MURPHY

ENID
MARKEY

KARL
MALDEN

GRACE
VALENTIN

HELEN HAYES in
"MRS. McTHING"

ROBERT PRESTON, MARTHA SCOTT,
ELLIOTT NUGENT in
"THE MALE ANIMAL"

JULIE HARRIS in
"I AM A CAMERA"

KEVIN McCARTHY,
CELESTE HOLM in
"ANNA CHRISTIE"

JOHN GARFIELD
in "GOLDEN BOY"

MAURICE EVANS, DIANA
LYNN in "THE WILD
DUCK"

ANNE JEFFREYS,
BILLY CHAPIN,
JOHN RAITT in
"THREE WISHES FOR JAMIE"

PAUL HARTMAN,
JACK CARSON
in "OF THEE
I SING"

MARTHA WRIGHT,
GEORGE BRITTON
in "SOUTH PACIFIC"

Z MILLER, HELEN WOOD, ORGE MARTIN, ROBERT FORTIER   HAROLD LANG   VIVIENNE SEGAL, HAROLD LANG in "PAL JOEY"   VIVIENNE SEGAL   LIONEL STANDER, HELEN GALLAGHER, HAROLD LANG

DICK ALLMAN   GERALDINE BROOKS   ERIC SINCLAIR   GRACE KELLY   JOHN WILLIAMS   CLORIS LEACHMAN   RICHARD BURTON   DIANA LYNN   ELI WALLACH

BEATRICE LILLIE in "AN EVENING WITH BEATRICE LILLIE"

EMLYN WILLIAMS in "READINGS FROM CHARLES DICKENS"

1952

"I Am A Camera" by John Van Druten won the Critics' Circle Award and also brought stardom to Julie Harris. Joseph Kramm's "The Shrike," which starred José Ferrer and Judith Evelyn, won the Pulitzer Prize.

Helen Hayes in Mary Chase's "Mrs. McThing," Katharine Hepburn in Shaw's "The Millionairess," Elliott Nugent in a revival of "The Male Animal," Maurice Evans in a mystery play "Dial 'M' For Murder," Shirley Booth in "The Time Of The Cuckoo," Margaret Sullavan in "The Deep Blue Sea," and "The Seven Year Itch" with Tom Ewell were very successful. Other attractions were Mary Chase's "Bernardine," S. N. Behrman's "Jane" starring Edna Best and Basil Rathbone, Christopher Fry's "Venus Observed" with Rex Harrison and Lilli Palmer, Van Druten's "I've Got Sixpence" with Edmond O'Brien, Viveca Lindfors and Patricia Collinge, "Time Out For Ginger" with Melvyn Douglas, "See The Jaguar" with Arthur Kennedy, and a revival of "The Children's Hour."

Of the musicals a revival of "Pal Joey" had greater success and ran longer than the original production; "Wish You Were Here" was a hit in spite of bad critical notices; Bette Davis returned to the stage in a revue "Two's Company"; "My Darlin' Aida" was a Broadway version of Verdi's opera; and "New Faces" was an intimate revue of Leonard Sillman's series.

Among revivals that failed were "Candida" with Olivia De Havilland, "Much Ado About Nothing" with Claire Luce, "Anna Christie" with Celeste Holm, "Golden Boy" with John Garfield, "Desire Under The Elms" with Karl Malden, Carol Stone and Douglas Watson, and the musical revivals of "Four Saints In Three Acts," "Of Thee I Sing" and "Shuffle Along."

"South Pacific," "Guys and Dolls," "The King And I," "The Moon Is Blue" and "The Fourposter" now starring Betty Field and Burgess Meredith were holdovers and still flourishing.

Beatrice Lillie had great success with "An Evening With Beatrice Lillie," and among the one-man shows Emlyn Williams impersonated and gave brilliant readings of Charles Dickens, Cornelia Otis Skinner acted in "Paris '90" of her own authorship, and Maurice Schwartz performed briefly in "Conscience."

Jean-Louis Barrault and Madeleine Renaud and their French company from Paris had great success with their repertoire of plays, and so did the Greek National Theatre, headed by Katina Paxinou and Alexis Minotis, with "Electra" and "Oedipus Tyrannus."

ALEXIS MINOTIS, KATINA PAXINOU in "OEDIPUS TYRANNUS"

CORNELIA OTIS SKINNER in "PARIS '90"

As the Lion Tamer   As Yvette Guilbert

GERALDINE BROOKS, DINO DiLUCA,
DONALD MURPHY, SHIRLEY BOOTH
in "THE TIME OF THE CUCKOO"

JOHN WILLIAMS, LILLI PALMER, JOHN MERIVALE,
EILEEN PEEL, HURD HATFIELD, CLAUDIA MORGAN,
REX HARRISON in "VENUS OBSERVED"

ROBERT HELPMANN, KATHARINE HEPBURN,
CYRIL RITCHARD, CAMPBELL COTTS in
"THE MILLIONAIRESS"

SHIRLEY BOOTH in "THE
TIME OF THE CUCKOO"

BILL MULLIKIN, MICHAEL DOMINICO, ROBERT CLARY, JIMMY RUSSELL, ALLEN CONROY,
2nd Row: CAROL NELSON, VIRGINIA BOSLER, LEONARD SILLMAN (producer), CAROL LAWRENCE.
3rd Row: VIRGINIA de LUCE, JUNE CARROLL, RONNY GRAHAM, EARTHA KITT, ROSEMARY O'REILLY.
Top Row: JOSEPH LAUTNER, ALICE GHOSTLEY, PAUL LYNDE in "NEW FACES OF 1952"

KATHARINE HEPBURN in
"THE MILLIONAIRESS"

DOROTHY SARNOFF, ELAINE
MALBIN in "MY DARLIN'
AIDA"

Scene from "MY DARLIN' AIDA"

IRIS MANN, PATRICIA
NEAL, KIM HUNTER in
"THE CHILDREN'S HOUR"

GLYNIS JOHNS in
"GERTIE"

VIVECA LINDFORS, EDMUND
O'BRIEN in "I'VE GOT
SIXPENCE"

OLIVIA DE HAVILLAND
in
"CANDIDA"

JOHN KERR, CAMILLA DEWITT,
JOHNNY STEWART in
"BERNARDINE"

ARTHUR KENNEDY
in "SEE THE
JAGUAR"

DOUGLAS WATSON,
CAROL STONE in
"DESIRE UNDER THE ELMS"

BASKETBALL COURT SCENE

PATRICIA MARAND, HARRY CLARK, SHEILA BOND,
JACK CASSIDY, PAUL VALENTINE
in "WISH YOU WERE HERE"

SWIMMING POOL SCENE

GUSTI HUBER, RICHARD DERR,
MAURICE EVANS in "DIAL 'M'
FOR MURDER"

MADELEINE RENAUD in
"LES FAUSSES CONFIDENCES"

JEAN-LOUIS BARRAULT
as HAMLET

TOM EWELL, VANESSA BROWN in
"THE SEVEN YEAR ITCH"

GUSTI HUBER

BETTE DAVIS AND COMPANY   BETTE DAVIS AND DANCERS
in "TWO'S COMPANY"

MELVYN DOUGLAS

JUDITH EVELYN, JOSE
FERRER in "THE SHRIKE"

ROBERT BROWN,
JUDITH ANDERSON in
"COME OF AGE"

ANTONY EUSTREL, CLAIRE LUCE,
MELVILLE COOPER
in "MUCH ADO ABOUT NOTHING"

JANET BLAIR
in
"SOUTH PACIFIC"

JAMES HANLEY,
MARGARET SULLAVAN in
"THE DEEP BLUE SEA"

WALTER SLEZAK, JEROME COWAN,
DARREN McGAVIN in
"MY THREE ANGELS"

ROSALIND RUSSELL
in
"WONDERFUL TOWN"

EDITH ADAMS, ROSALIND RUSSELL
in
"WONDERFUL TOWN"

FRANCHOT TONE, BETSY VON FURSTENBERG
in
"OH, MEN! OH, WOMEN!"

1953 Two plays were recipients of both the Pulitzer Prize and the Drama Critics' Circle Award: William Inge's "Picnic" for the 1952-53 season, and John Patrick's "The Teahouse Of The August Moon" for the 1953-54 season. Both had great success. "Picnic" had a National company touring the country, and the John Patrick prize winner had two companies on the road.

Among other plays that reached hit proportions were "Tea and Sympathy," "The Solid Gold Cadillac," "My Three Angels," "Sabrina Fair" and "The Fifth Season," which introduced Yiddish star, Menasha Skulnik, to the English-speaking stage. Moderate successes included "Oh, Men! Oh, Women!," "The Love Of Four Colonels," "The Crucible" and "Mid-Summer" which introduced to the Broadway stage, Geraldine Page who had made a big hit in an Off-Broadway production of "Summer and Smoke." Katharine Cornell, playing in "The Prescott Proposals" for producer Leland Hayward, was appearing for the first time in many years under any management other than her own. Jose Ferrer had a season of revivals at the City Center in "Charley's Aunt," "Cyrano de Bergerac," "The Shrike" and "Richard III." The latter was not met with critical approval. The City Center also revived "Love's Labour's Lost," "The Merchant Of Venice" and Shaw's "Misalliance." The G. B. Shaw opus was so well received that it was moved to Broadway's Music Box for a regular run.

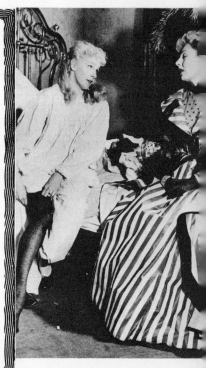

GERALDINE PAGE, VICKI CUMMINGS
in
"MID-SUMMER"

ELI WALLACH, JO VAN FLEET
in
"CAMINO REAL"

RUTH McDEVITT, RETA SHAW, ARTHUR O'CONNELL, EILEEN HECKART,
KIM STANLEY, ELIZABETH WILSON in
"PICNIC"

JANICE RULE, RALPH MEEKER
in
"PICNIC"

JOAN DIENER
in
"KISMET"

ALFRED DRAKE
in
"KISMET"

YUKI SHIMODA, MARY ANN REEVE, WILLIAM HANSEN, MARIKO NIKI, HAIM WINANT, DAVID WAYNE, JOHN FORSYTHE, PAUL FORD, HARRY JACKSON, LARRY GATES in
"THE TEAHOUSE OF THE AUGUST MOON"

JOHN FORSYTHE, DAVID WAYNE, MARIKO NIKI
in
"THE TEAHOUSE OF THE AUGUST MOON"

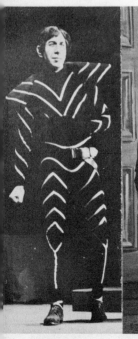

JOSE FERRER
as
RICHARD III

LUTHER ADLER
as
SHYLOCK

MARGARET PHILLIPS
as
PORTIA

DAVID WAYNE
in "THE TEAHOUSE
OF THE AUGUST MOON"

BEN GAZZARA
in
"END AS A MAN"

MENASHA SKULNIK
in
"THE FIFTH SEASON"

VICTOR
BORGE

ALEJANDRO ULLOA
as
DON JUAN TENORIO

BARRY JONES, JEROME KILTY, JAN FARRAND,
RICHARD KILEY, RODDY McDOWALL, DOROTHY SANDS
in "MISALLIANCE"

WALTER HAMPDEN
in
"THE CRUCIBLE"

RUTH
DRAPER

JOHN
KERR

JOSEPHINE
HULL

SCOTT
MERRILL

GERALDINE
PAGE

HARRY
BELAFONTE

LEORA
DANA

RICHARD
KILEY

BETSY
VON FURSTENBERG

MURRAY
MATHESON

ANNE VERNON, JOHN GRANGER
in
"THE LITTLE HUT"

DEBORAH KERR, JOHN KERR
in
"TEA AND SYMPATHY"

WILLIAM THORNTON, EARLE HYMAN
in
"OTHELLO"

ANNE JACKSON, ELI WALLACH,
DOUGLAS WATSON in
"THE SCARECROW"

HERMIONE GINGOLD
in
"JOHN MURRAY ANDERSON'S ALMANAC"

LILLIAN GISH
in
"THE TRIP TO BOUNTIFUL"

SUSAN STRASBERG, HELEN CRAIG
in
"MAYA"

FELIX AYLMER, MINOO DAVER, KATHARINE
CORNELL, ROGER DANN, BEN ASTAR in
"THE PRESCOTT PROPOSALS"

RAYMOND MASSEY, TYRONE POWER,
JUDITH ANDERSON in
"JOHN BROWN'S BODY"

LILLI PALMER, REX HARRISON, LEUEEN
MacGRATH, STEFAN SCHNABEL in
"THE LOVE OF FOUR COLONELS"

| WILL GEER | EDITH KING | PETER KELLEY | EVA MARIE SAINT | ARTHUR O'CONNELL | MILDRED DUNNOCK | ORSON BEAN | VIVIAN BLAINE | BEN GAZZARA |

BILL HAYES, ISABEL BIGLEY
in
"ME AND JULIET"

Among the musicals that enhanced the theatrical scene
were "Kismet," a musical version of Otis Skinner's famous
success of the same title; "Wonderful Town," a musical
version of "My Sister Eileen;" "Can-Can" and "Me and
Juliet," two originals; and a revue, "John Murray Anderson's Almanac."

Solo performers included Ruth Draper, who met with her
usual acclaim, and Victor Borge, who broke all sorts of
records with his one-man show called "Comedy In Music."

The most controversial play was Tennessee Williams'
"Camino Real" which was a box office failure.

Off-Broadway productions were becoming an important
factor. "End As A Man" which brought Ben Gazzara into
the limelight, revivals of "The Scarecrow," "Maya," "The
Little Clay Cart" and "Othello" with Earle Hyman praised
in the title role, were all well received. Most important of the
Off-Broadway theatre was the Phoenix which opened December 1, 1953.

On Saturday night, May 30, 1953, Shirley Booth in "The
Time Of The Cuckoo" was the last to trod the stage of the
Empire Theatre. The famous old playhouse, which opened
January 25, 1893, closed its doors forever, and was turned
over to a wrecking crew. The end had come for the historic
theatre which the great Charles Frohman had built.

GWEN VERDON, ERIK RHODES
in
"CAN-CAN"

REYNOLDS EVANS, WENDELL PHILLIPS, JOSEPHINE HULL,
HENRY JONES, GEOFFREY LUMB, in
"THE SOLID GOLD CADILLAC"

LUELLA GEAR, CATHLEEN NESBITT, JOHN CROMWELL, JOSEPH
COTTEN, MARGARET SULLAVAN, RUSSELL COLLINS in
"SABRINA FAIR"

LLOYD NOLAN, HENRY FONDA, JOHN HODIAK

ROBERT GIST, JAMES BUMGARNER, CHARLES NOLTE,
HENRY FONDA, JOHN HODIAK

"THE CAINE MUTINY COURT MARTIAL"

AINSLIE PRYOR, CHARLES NOLTE

BRIAN AHERNE, EDNA BEST, LYNN FONTANNE, ALFRED LUNT
in
"QUADRILLE"

GERALDINE PAGE, LOUIS JOURDAN
in
"THE IMMORALIST"

WARREN BERLINGER, MARY LEE DEARRING, MACDONALD CAREY,
KITTY CARLISLE in
"ANNIVERSARY WALTZ"

EZIO PINZA, WALTER SLEZAK
in
"FANNY"

JAMES DEAN
in
"THE IMMORALIST"

PATRICIA JESSEL
in "WITNESS
FOR THE PROSECUTION"

HORACE BRAHAM, PATRICIA JESSEL, ERNEST CLARK,
FRANCIS L. SULLIVAN, ROBIN CRAVEN, GENE LYONS
RALPH ROBERTS in "WITNESS FOR THE PROSECUTION"

EDDIE FOY, JR., RETA SHAW
in
"THE PAJAMA GAME"

CAROL HANEY; TOP: JOHN RAITT, JANIS PAIGE, MARION COLBY,
THELMA PELLISH, BUZZ MILLER in
"THE PAJAMA GAME"

NANCY KELLY, PATTY McCORMACK
in
"THE BAD SEED"

SHIRLEY BOOTH, WILBUR EVANS
in
"BY THE BEAUTIFUL SEA"

1954 Outstanding money-makers of the year included a distinguished production of Herman Wouk's popular novel, "The Caine Mutiny Court Martial," "The Bad Seed," "Witness For The Prosecution," "Ondine," "Anastasia," "Anniversary Waltz," "Lunatics and Lovers," and a revival by the Old Vic Company of "A Midsummer Night's Dream." The moderate successes were Noel Coward's "Quadrille" which starred the Lunts, "The Flowering Peach," "The Rainmaker," "Wedding Breakfast," "King Of Hearts," "The Tender Trap," "The Remarkable Mr. Pennypacker" and "The Immoralist."

Among the stars, Ina Claire returned to the stage in "The Confidential Clerk;" Tallulah Bankhead appeared in "Dear Charles;" Julie Harris had no luck with "Mlle. Colombe," and Mary Boland faired no better with "Lullaby;" Helen Hayes revived "What Every Woman Knows" at the City Center, and Mary Martin caused a favorable stir with a musical version of "Peter Pan."

"The Pajama Game," the outstanding musical success, was produced by three newcomers, Harold S. Prince, Robert E. Griffith and Frederick Brisson. Other musicals worth mention were "The Boy Friend," "Fanny," "By The Beautiful Sea" starring Shirley Booth, and Gian-Carlo Menotti's opera, "The Saint Of Bleecker Street," which despite favorable reviews, failed to win cash adherents.

From Japan came the famous Azuma Kabuki Dancers and Musicians to add novelty and interest to a not too distinguished theatrical year.

Off-Broadway continued to flourish. "The Threepenny Opera" with music by Kurt Weill, "The Golden Apple," "The Cretan Woman," "The Sea Gull" and "The Boy With A Cart" were some of the well patronized attractions away from the main stem.

LARRY ROBINSON, TOM RAYNOR, TALLULAH
BANKHEAD, GRACE RAYNOR in
"DEAR CHARLES"

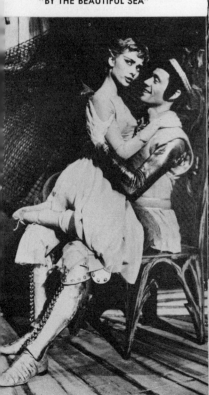

AUDREY HEPBURN, MEL FERRER
in
"ONDINE"

MENASHA
SKULNIK

HERMIONE
GINGOLD

DEBORAH
KERR

LLOYD
NOLAN

RICHARD NEWTON, INA CLAIRE, JOAN
GREENWOOD, CLAUDE RAINS in
"THE CONFIDENTIAL CLERK"

DONALD COOK, JACKIE COOPER, PATCHWORK, REX THOMPSON, DAVID LEWIS, CLORIS LEACHMAN, HILDA HAYNES in "KING OF HEARTS"

BURGESS MEREDITH in "THE REMARKABLE MR. PENNYPACKER"

CAROL CHANNING in "WONDERFUL TOWN"

JANET RILEY, JACK MANNING, ROBERT PRESTO in "THE TENDER TRAP"

VIVECA LINDFORS, EUGENIE LEONTOVICH in "ANASTASIA"

JOHN HEWER, JULIE ANDREWS in "THE BOY FRIEND"

SHEILA BOND, NAT CANTOR, BUDDY HACKETT, DENNIS KING in "LUNATICS AND LOVERS"

JONATHAN LUCAS, KAYE BALLARD, PRISCILLA GILLETTE, STEPHEN DOUGLASS in "THE GOLDEN APPLE"

HELEN HAYES, KENT SMITH in "WHAT EVERY WOMAN KNOWS"

MARIA DI GERLANDO, DAVID AIKEN, GABRIELLE RUGGIERO, DAVID POLERI in "THE SAINT OF BLEECKER STREET"

MARY MARTIN, CYRIL RITCHARD in "PETER PAN"

WININ WANKYO, KIKUNOJO ONOE
OF
THE AZUMA KABUKI DANCERS

MARY BOLAND
in
"LULLABY"

MENASHA SKULNIK
in "THE
FLOWERING PEACH"

MIRA ROSTOVA, MONTGOMERY CLIFT, SAM JAFFE, KEVIN McCARTHY,
JUDITH EVELYN, GEORGE VOSKOVEC, JOHN FIEDLER, MAUREEN
STAPLETON, WILL GEER, JUNE WALKER in "THE SEA GULL"

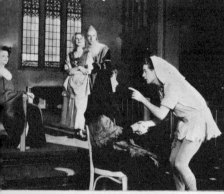

FLORIDA FRIEBUS, HELEN ALEXANDER,
ROBINSON STONE, CYNTHIA LATHAM, BILL PENN
in "THE BOY WITH A CART"

ELI WALLACH, JULIE HARRIS
in
"MADAMOISELLE COLOMBE"

WILLIAM ANDREWS, JACQUELINE BROOKES
in
"THE CRETAN WOMAN"

DARREN McGAVIN, GERALDINE PAGE
in
"THE RAINMAKER"

ROBERT HELPMANN, STANLEY HOLLOWAY, MOIRA SHEARER, PHILIP GUARD
in
"A MIDSUMMER NIGHT'S DREAM"

ANTHONY FRANCIOSA, HARVEY
LEMBECK, VIRGINIA VINCENT, LEE
GRANT in "WEDDING BREAKFAST"

SCOTT MERRILL, LOTTE LENYA
in "THE THREEPENNY OPERA"

RICHARD
DAVALOS

JOAN
GREENWOOD

PAUL
NEWMAN

EILEEN
HECKART

DON
MURRAY

DOROTHY GREENER, PETER CONLOW, MEL
LARNED, DODY GOODMAN in
"SHOESTRING REVUE"

KATHARINE CORNELL, TYRONE
POWER in
"THE DARK IS LIGHT ENOUGH"

DAVID LEVIN, DENNIE MOORE, LOU JACOBI, GUSTI HUBER, JOSEPH SCHILDKRAUT,
EVA RUBINSTEIN, JACK GILFORD, SUSAN STRASBERG in
"THE DIARY OF ANNE FRANK"

ED BEGLEY, TONY RANDALL, PAUL MUNI (also above), LOUIS HECTOR
in
"INHERIT THE WIND"

GLORIA MARLOWE, DAVID DANIELS
in
"PLAIN AND FANCY"

HELEN HAYES, DON MURRAY, HELLER
HALLIDAY, GEORGE ABBOTT in
"THE SKIN OF OUR TEETH"

DARREN
McGAVIN

KIM
STANLEY

DAVID
DANIELS

KAY
MEDFORD

JACK
LORD

ORSON BEAN, LEW GALLO,
JAYNE MANSFIELD in "WILL
SUCCESS SPOIL ROCK HUNTER?"

CAROL CHANNING, DAVID KASHNER, STEVE REEVES
in
"THE VAMP"

1955 For the fourth consecutive season, the Pulitzer Prize Play Committee and the Drama Critics' Circle were in accord. Both awards were given "Cat On A Hot Tin Roof" for the 1954-55 season, and "The Diary Of Anne Frank" for the 1955-56 season.

Of the other serious plays "Inherit The Wind," "The Lark" and "Tiger At The Gates" were in the hit class, while "The Desperate Hours" and "A View From The Bridge" had moderate success. On the lighter side, plays to win favor included "Bus Stop," "The Matchmaker," "The Chalk Garden," "Janus," "The Desk Set" and "Will Success Spoil Rock Hunter?"

Thornton Wilder's "The Skin Of Our Teeth," which was revived as a Salute To France, played a limited engagement in New York and on tour. The cast was headed by Helen Hayes, Mary Martin, Florence Reed and George Abbott. Notable among the musicals were "Damn Yankees" and "Plain and Fancy," and in a lesser degree, "Silk Stockings" and "Pipe Dream." Off-Broadway, the intimate "Shoestring Revue" was well liked. "The Vamp," starring Carol Channing, was the outstanding musical flop.

Katharine Cornell and Tyrone Power scored with "The Dark Is Light Enough" on tour, but failed to win audiences in New York.

From France, the National Comedie Francaise, in repertoire and making their first appearance in the United States, were well received, while Marcel Marceau, famous pantomimest, had a sensational success both critically and financially.

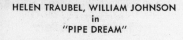
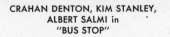

HELEN TRAUBEL, WILLIAM JOHNSON
in
"PIPE DREAM"

CRAHAN DENTON, KIM STANLEY,
ALBERT SALMI in
"BUS STOP"

ROBERT MORSE, EILEEN HERLIE, ARTHUR HILL, ROSAMUND GREENWOOD,
PHIL LEEDS   Top: RUTH GORDON
in "THE MATCHMAKER"

"JOYCE GRENFELL (above) REQUESTS THE PLEASURE"

PAUL NEWMAN, GEORGE GRIZZARD, KARL MALDEN, NANCY COLEMAN, MALCOLM BRODERICK, PATRICIA PEARDON in "THE DESPERATE HOURS"

BARBARA BEL GEDDES and BEN GAZZARA (also top), MILDRED DUNNOCK, MADELEINE SHERWOOD, PAT HINGLE, FRED STEWART, R. G. ARMSTRONG in "CAT ON A HOT TIN ROOF"

"ARLEQUIN POLI PAR L'AMOUR" and above "LE BOURGEOISE GENTILHOMME" WITH THE FRENCH NATIONAL COMEDIE FRANCAISE COMPANY

HILDEGARDE NEFF, DON AMECHE in "SILK STOCKINGS"

MARCEL MARCEAU

MARGARET SULLAVAN, ROBERT PRESTON, CLAUDE DAUPHIN in "JANUS"

ANDY GRIFFITH, MYRON McCORMICK, RODD McDOWALL in "NO TIME FOR SERGEANTS"

ANTHONY FRANCIOSA, BEN GAZZARA, SHELLEY WINTERS
in
"A HATFUL OF RAIN"

FRANK MILAN, SHIRLEY BOOTH
in
"THE DESK SET"

STEPHEN DOUGLASS, GWEN VERDON
in
"DAMN YANKEES"

BORIS KARLOFF, RALPH ROBERTS, ROGER
DE KOVEN, JULIE HARRIS in
"THE LARK"

LEO CICERI, LEUEEN MacGRATH, MICHAEL REDGRAVE
TOP: MICHAEL REDGRAVE
in "TIGER AT THE GATES"

VAN HEFLIN, GLORIA MARLOWE, RICHARD
DAVALOS, JACK WARDEN, EILEEN HECKART
in "A VIEW FROM THE BRIDGE"

PERCY WARAM, MARIAN SELDES, GLADYS COOPER,
BETSY VON FURSTENBERG, SIOBHAN McKENNA
in "THE CHALK GARDEN"

CHRISTOPHER PLUMMER
in
"THE LARK"

LAURENCE HARVEY
in
"ISLAND OF GOATS"

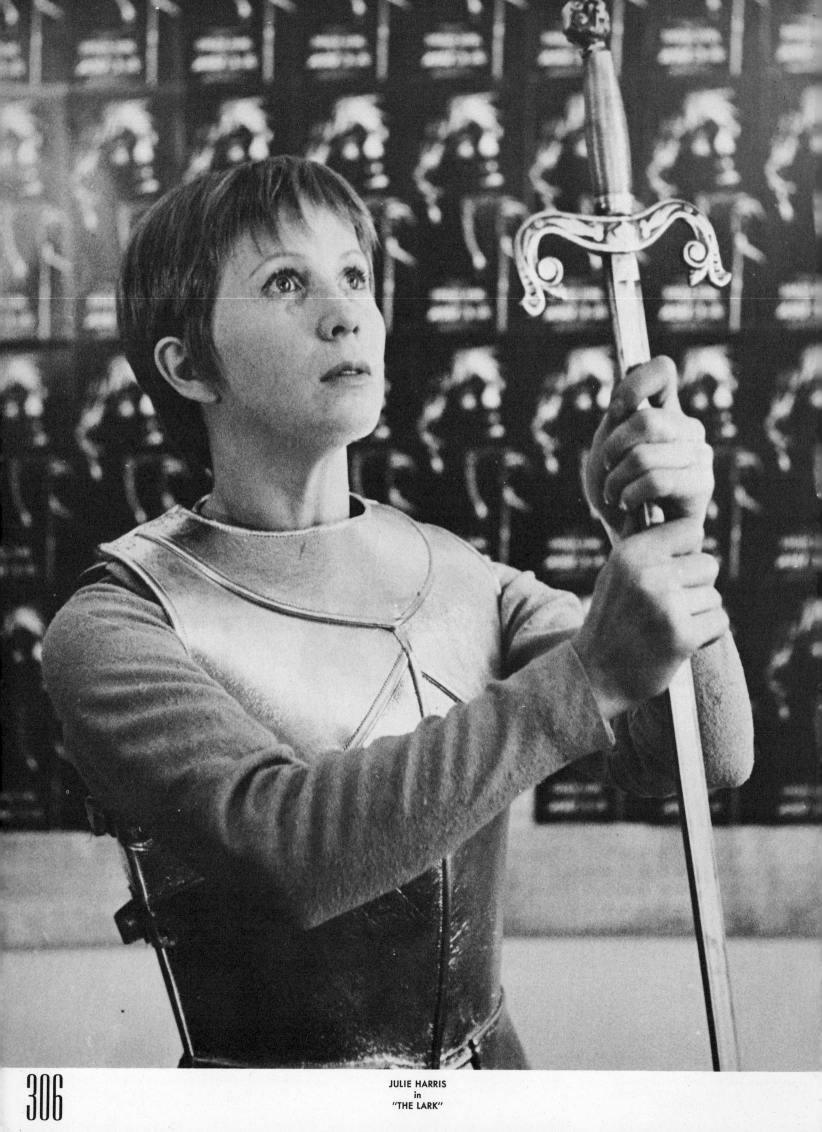

JULIE HARRIS
in
"THE LARK"

SAMMY DAVIS, JR., OLGA JAMES
in
"MR. WONDERFUL"

FRONT ROW: BOB SHAVER, ROD STRONG, JOHNNY LAVERTY, BILL McCUTCHEON, JIMMY SISCO; 2nd ROW: BILLIE HAYES, SUZANNE BERNARD, LEONARD SILLMAN, DANA SOSA, FRANCA BALDWIN; 3rd ROW: T. C. JONES, MAGGIE SMITH, JANE CONNELL, VIRGINIA MARTIN, ANN HENRY; TOP ROW: TIGER HAYNES, JOHNNY HAYMER, AMRU-SANI, JOHN REARDON, INGA SWENSON in "NEW FACES OF '56"

DAVID WAYNE, SARAH MARSHALL
DON HANMER
in "THE PONDER HEART"

BERT LAHR
in
"WAITING FOR GODOT"

1956 The first half of the year brought one of the great musicals of theatrical history, "My Fair Lady," adapted from G. B. Shaw's "Pygmalion" with book and lyrics by Alan Jay Lerner and music by Frederick Loewe. Julie Andrews and Rex Harrison were the stars, and featured roles were played by Stanley Holloway, Cathleen Nesbitt, Robert Coote, Viola Roache, John Michael King and Philippa Bevans. Another outstanding musical, "The Most Happy Fella" by Frank Loesser, was based on Sidney Howard's "They Knew What They Wanted." Other musicals presented on Broadway before July first were "Shangri-La," "New Faces of '56" and "Mr. Wonderful."

"Middle Of The Night," Paddy Chayefsky's first produced play, and "Time Limit!" were outstanding among the straight plays.

Notable among the productions that were financial failures were an exciting production of Christopher Marlowe's "Tamburlaine, The Great" with Anthony Quayle and the Festival Company of Stratford, Canada; Sean O'Casey's "Red Roses For Me"; "Mister Johnson," a play by Norman Rosten based on the novel by Joyce Cary; and Samuel Beckett's controversial "Waiting For Godot" in which Bert Lahr played his first straight role to critical acclaim.

Alfred Lunt and Lynn Fontanne had a moderate success with the Howard Lindsay and Russel Crouse play, "The Great Sebastians," and David Wayne scored mildly in "The Ponder Heart." A revival of Noel Coward's "Fallen Angels" attracted attention because of its stars, Nancy Walker and Margaret Phillips.

ANTHONY QUAYLE
in
"TAMBURLAINE THE GREAT"

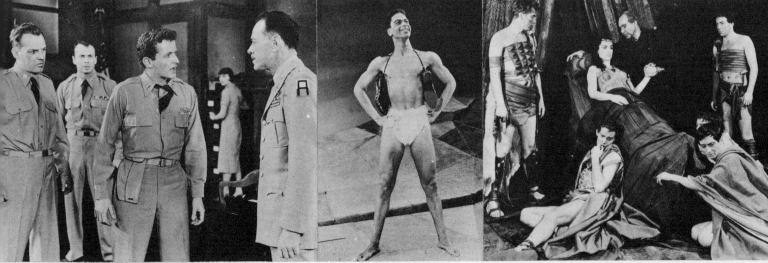

ARTHUR KENNEDY, RICHARD KILEY, THOMAS CARLIN, ALLYN McLERIE, HARVEY STEPHENS in "TIME LIMIT!"

EARLE HYMAN
in
"MISTER JOHNSON"

WILLIAM HUTT, NEIL VIPOND, BARBARA CHILCOTT, ANTHONY QUAYLE, LOUIS NEGIN, TED FOLLOWS, WILLIAM SHATNER in "TAMBURLAINE THE GREAT"

SUSAN JOHNSON, ROBERT WEEDE, JO SULLIVAN
in
"THE MOST HAPPY FELLA"

ALFRED LUNT, LYNN FONTANNE
in
"THE GREAT SEBASTIANS"

EDWARD G. ROBINSON, JUNE WALKER, JOAN CHAMBERS, EFFIE AFTON
in
"MIDDLE OF THE NIGHT"

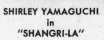

EDWARD G. ROBINSON
in "MIDDLE OF THE NIGHT"

NANCY WALKER, MARGARET PHILLIPS
in
"FALLEN ANGELS"

SAM LEVENE
in
"THE HOT CORNER"

DENNIS KING, JOAN HOLLOWAY,
HAROLD LANG, JACK CASSIDY
in "SHANGRI-LA"

SHIRLEY YAMAGUCHI
in
"SHANGRI-LA"

ROBERT COOTE, JULIE ANDREWS, REX HARRISON
TOP: VIOLA ROACHE, GORDON DILWORTH, JOHN MICHAEL KING, JULIE
ANDREWS, OLIVE REEVES-SMITH, CATHLEEN NESBITT

JULIE ANDREWS

STANLEY HOLLOWAY   JULIE ANDREWS, REX HARRISON   CATHLEEN NESBITT   JULIE ANDREWS, REX HARRISON   REX HARRISON

INDEX

313

315

317

Supplementary Index for the Years 1953 - 1956